CONTEMPORARY HISTORY SERIES

General Editor: James F. McMillan
Professor of History, University of Strathclyde

THE COLD WAR

Titles in the Contemporary History series

THE COLD WAR
An International History, 1947–1991
S. J. Ball

AFRICAN DECOLONIZATION
H. S. Wilson

FRANCO'S SPAIN
Jean Grugel and Tim Rees

The Cold War
An International History, 1947–1991

S. J. BALL
Lecturer in Modern History,
University of Glasgow

A member of the Hodder Headline Group
LONDON • NEW YORK • SYDNEY • AUCKLAND

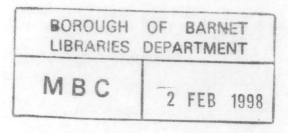
First published in Great Britain in 1998 by
Arnold, a member of the Hodder Headline Group
338 Euston Road, London NW1 3BH
175 Fifth Avenue, New York, NY 10010
http://www.arnoldpublishers.com

Distributed exclusively in the USA by St Martin's Press, Inc.
175 Fifth Avenue, New York, NY 10010

British Library Cataloguing in Publication Data
A catalogue entry for this book is available from the British Library

Library of Congress Cataloging-in-Publication Data
Ball, S. J. (Simon J.)
  The Cold War: an international history, 1947–1991 / S. J. Ball.
    p.   cm. — (Contemporary history series)
  Includes bibliographical references (p.) and index.
  ISBN 0–340–64546–6 – ISBN 0–340–59168–4 (pbk.)
    1. World politics—1945– 2. Cold War 3. United States—
  Foreign relations—Soviet Union. 4. Soviet Union—Foreign
relations—United States. I. Title II. Series: Contemporary history
series
(London, England)
D843, B253 1997
327 73047—dc21

ISBN 0 340 59168 4 (pb)
ISBN 0 340 64546 6 (hb)

Production Editor: Liz Gooster
Production Controller: Sarah Kett
Cover design: Juan Heyward

Composition by York House Typographic Ltd
Printed and bound in Great Britain by J. W. Arrowsmith Ltd, Bristol

For my parents

Contents

Preface

I would have found it impossible to undertake this work without help from a number of people. Christopher Wheeler asked me to write a book on the Cold War. He, and his anonymous readers, encouraged my hubristic attempt to do the 'whole thing'. My colleague Evan Mawdsley was of inestimable assistance. The documentary Special Subject he and I teach at Glasgow was the basis for this book. He has tried to steer me around the complexities of Soviet politics and allowed me to pillage his well-stocked bookshelves. Evan read and commented upon a draft of the manuscript with exemplary care. He has attempted, with only partial success, to save me from my own infelicities. I am deeply grateful for his efforts. Richard Aldous of University College, Dublin, with whom I collaborated on a study of the division of Europe in the 1940s, was indispensable. I benefited greatly from Richard's brilliant study of British diplomacy. I benefited even more from his magnificent hospitality in Dublin. My friends in the Departments of Modern and Medieval History at the University of Glasgow have created the happy environment in which I teach and write. The university itself encouraged this project by the award of study leave in Martinmas Term, 1994. It has been my pleasure to test my ideas concerning the history of the Cold War on some extremely talented students. I received particular help from members of my Cold War Origins class of 1995. I hope this book serves as an enjoyable reminder of their Senior Honours year.

S. J. Ball
Glasgow, 1997

Abbreviations

ABM	anti-ballistic missile
AEC	Atomic Energy Commission
ALCM	air-launched cruise missile
ARVN	Army of the Republic of Vietnam
BMD	ballistic missile defence
CCP	Chinese Communist Party
CDU	Christian Democratic Union
CFM	Council of Foreign Ministers
CGT	Trade Union Confederation
CIA	Central Intelligence Agency
COMECON (CMEA)	Council for Mutual Economic Aid
COSVN	Central Office for South Vietnam
CPSU	Communist Party of the Soviet Union
CPV	Chinese People's Volunteers
CSCE	Conference on Security and Cooperation in Europe
CWIHP	Cold War International History Project
CWIHPB	*Cold War International History Project Bulletin*
DIA	Defence Intelligence Agency
DPRK	Democratic People's Republic of Korea
DRA	Democratic Republic of Afghanistan
DRV	Democratic Republic of Vietnam
ECSC	European Coal and Steel Community
EEC	European Economic Community
ERP	European Recovery Programme
FBS	forward-based systems
FDP	Free Democratic Party
FLN	National Liberation Front
FRG (BRD)	Federal Republic of Germany
FRUS	*Foreign Relations of the United States*
GDR (DDR)	German Democratic Republic
GLCM	ground-launched cruise missile
GLF	Great Leap Forward
GSFG	Group of Soviet Forces in Germany

GVN	Government of Vietnam
ICBM	inter-continental ballistic missile
ICP	Indochinese Communist Party
IISS	International Institute for Strategic Studies
IMEMO	Institute of World Economy and International Relations
INF	intermediate nuclear forces
IRBM	intermediate-range ballistic missile
JCS	Joint Chiefs of Staff
KMT	Kuomintang
KPD (DKP, KDP)	German Communist Party
LRINF	long-range intermediate nuclear forces
MIRV	multiple independently-targetable re-entry vehicle
MPD	Main Political Directorate
MRV	multiple re-entry vehicle
NATO	North Atlantic Treaty Organisation
NIE	National Intelligence Estimate
NLF	National Liberation Front
NSC	National Security Council
NVN	North Vietnam
OSD	Office of the Secretary of Defense
OSS	Office of Strategic Services
PAVN	People's Army of Vietnam
PCF	French Communist Party
PDPA	People's Democratic Party of Afghanistan
PKI	Indonesian Communist Party
PLA	People's Liberation Army
PLAF	People's Liberation Armed Forces
PLAAF	People's Liberation Army Air Force
PPS	Policy Planning Staff
PRC	People's Republic of China
PSP	Popular Socialist Party
PTB	partial test ban
ROK	Republic of Korea
SACEUR	Supreme Allied Commander Europe
SALT	Strategic Arms Limitation Talks
SAM	surface-to-air missile
SEATO	South East Asia Treaty Organisation
SED	Socialist Unity Party
SKWP	South Korean Workers' Party
SLBM	submarine-launched ballistic missile
SLCM	sea-launched cruise missile
SPD	Social Democratic Party

SRINF	short-range intermediate nuclear forces
SSBN	nuclear-powered ballistic missile submarine
START	Strategic Arms Reduction Talks
SVN	South Vietnam
SWNCC	State–War–Navy Co-ordinating Committee
TVD	theatre of operations
USAF	United States Air Force
VNQDD	Vietnamese Nationalist Party
VWP (VNWP, WPV)	Vietnam Workers' Party

Many of the names mentioned in this book are transliterated. I have tried to use the most familiar form; thus, Mao Zedong but Chiang Kai-shek. I have anglicised spelling in quotations drawn from American sources.

1

Introduction

'Cold War' was a term which the governing élites of the major world powers believed accurately described the international system between 1947 and 1991. It signified an irreconcilable conflict between, and sometimes within, states. On the one hand were those who believed that the world economic system was unavoidably capitalist and, to a lesser extent, that the preferred political system was liberal democratic. On the other side were those who had imbibed the lessons of the Bolshevik revolution of 1917: that states would be ruled by a small self-selecting revolutionary élite which could abandon capitalistic economic organisation. Military victory in the Second World War ensured that the United States would lead those states which took the former position, the Soviet Union the latter. At no time was the Cold War regarded as the sole component of the international system. In each state there were leaders who favoured other views, championing, amongst others things, internal reform, national renewal, imperial consolidation or intra-capitalist competition. As the British intellectual historian Isaiah Berlin wrote in 1953:

> There is a line among the fragments of the Greek poet Archilocus which says: 'The fox knows many things, but the hedgehog knows one big thing' ... taken figuratively the words can be made to yield a sense in which they mark one of the deepest differences which divide writers and thinkers, and, it may be, human beings in general. For there exists a great chasm between those, on one side, who relate everything to a single central vision, one system, less or more coherent or articulate, in terms of which they understand, think and feel ... and, on the other side, those who pursue many ends, often unrelated and even contradictory, connected, if at all, only in some *de facto* way.[1]

In each of the major powers the Cold War paradigm dominated its competitors for the entire post-war period. Hedgehogs struggled against foxes and usually won.

There already exist some quite clearly defined, mainly American, schools of thought about the origins of the Cold War (and thus implicitly about its course). Between the 1950s and 1980s historians in the United States and Europe developed four main approaches. Orthodox historians (it should be noted that these terms were used as forms of both opprobrium and of self-congratulation) tended to argue that a mixture of Marxist-Leninist ideology, military victory, unjustified Stalinist paranoia about Western encirclement and traditional Russian expansionism made the Soviet Union an inherently aggressive power after 1945. It had ambitions to subjugate Eastern Europe, subvert Western Europe and dominate emerging post-colonial nations through ideology and aid. The United States was unable to save Eastern Europe but prudently shored up the military, economic and political resistance of many other countries, often through alliances and direct intervention. The main lineaments of this approach were laid down in a number of memoirs by American leaders. The *locus classicus* of this school was the recollections of Harry S. Truman published in book form as early as 1955 and 1956. The two volumes were written by a team of journalists for serialisation in an American news magazine but there is no doubt that they reflected Truman's views shortly after the end of his presidency. Truman also relied a great deal on the memories and interpretations of his former Secretary of State, Dean Acheson. Acheson later published his own memoir, entitled *Present at the Creation*, which strengthened the orthodox canon.[2] In later work the prudence of those 'present at the creation' of a Western alliance is admired since it ensured the final collapse of a Soviet system which proved unworkable without the political and economic exploitation of new countries.

In the 1960s, with America involved in a damaging war in Vietnam, this prudential view of American leaders seemed less convincing to some young American historians. Revisionists argued that the origins of the Cold War could be found in the beliefs and actions of the American politico-economic governing élite. Shaken by the threat to its own position presented by the collapse of first the economic and then the political international order in the 1930s, this élite was convinced that it could only survive and prosper in an international capitalist economic system dominated by the United States and protected by American military might. The Soviet Union was irrelevant to this order economically and a military threat to it. The USSR had, therefore, to be isolated and undermined. Revisionist historians tended to stress the aggressive intentions of the USA towards the USSR, the Soviet Union's economic, and even military, weakness and American exploitation of and intervention in non-European countries.

Another strand to the critique of American foreign policy was provided by Gar Alperovitz, an American who had done his postgraduate work in England. Alperovitz published a book based on his doctorate entitled *Atomic Diplomacy: Hiroshima and Potsdam* in 1965. It argued that the Truman administration did not take the decision to use atomic weapons against Japan in order to avoid the massive casualties of a sea-borne invasion, as Truman had claimed. According to Alperovitz, key American leaders were aware that the Japanese were preparing to surrender. Instead the decision to drop the A-bomb was taken to demonstrate American power to the Soviet Union.[3]

Both 'economic' and 'atomic' revisionists questioned the key tenets of American foreign policy at a time when that foreign policy was in crisis because of the shock of defeat in Vietnam. Since their claims were based on a strained reading of the available evidence and impugned the reputation of men known and revered by many still in positions of power, revisionist views were the subject of much hostile comment. The most widely read counter-blast was John Lewis Gaddis's *The United States and the Origins of the Cold War* published in 1972. Two decades later, Melvyn Leffler argued, in a massively researched book (*A Preponderance of Power*, 1992), that America did indeed seek a 'preponderance of power' in the post-war world. Leffler, however, rejected economic factors as the primary motivation for American expansion-ism and instead settled upon the 'national security paradigm' as an explanation. This 'paradigm' suggests that the Truman administration and its successors acted on the basis of a reasonable set of ideas, based on recent history, about the dangerous instability of the international system. Leffler avoided a detailed consideration of Soviet actions on the grounds that it was only possible to produce a book based on proper archival research for the United States.

Most post-revisionist historians acknowledge that the archives demonstrate that American governments did not always act for the altruistic motives cited in their rhetoric, but argue that US administrations were practitioners of a prudent *realpolitik*. Such *realpolitik* was, at the very least, based on a reasonable analysis of Soviet statements and actions and was probably the best response to a Soviet Union which was, in fact, aggressively expansionist. To some extent, however, revisionism was sustained by another group: senior officials who repented of their actions in office. The best-known of these critics were George Kennan, the State Department's key expert on the Soviet Union in 1946–7, and, ironically, Robert McNamara, US Secretary of Defense from 1961 to 1968. Both came to believe that American policy had increased rather than lessened the risk of nuclear war and that any search for victory over the Soviet Union should be subordinated to attempts to reduce the danger of catastro-phe.[4]

Latter-day revisionists have no clear view about the end of the Cold War. The logical position – that it was terminated by purposeful and ruthless American action – does not tend to appeal to individuals who hold the American political establishment in contempt. They argue that the Cold War distorted the international order, keeping millions of non-Europeans in unnecessary poverty and victims of cruel political repression. Revisionist historians also tend to believe that American foreign policy corrupted the American body politic.[5]

This typology of Cold War historiography is necessarily simplified, but it does accurately portray two features of much of this work. First, it assumes that the Cold War was merely a name for a Soviet–American conflict played out on a global scale. Second, even within this bilateral context, the emphasis is on

American motivations and policy. Although these tendencies have been criticised, there are, actually, good reasons why they arose. No-one would deny that the Soviet–American relationship was of key importance; and historians have a well-justified reluctance to concentrate on areas where there is a dearth of evidence to support their conclusions. Since the collapse of the Soviet Union in 1991 it has been possible to check previous assumptions to some extent by archival work in Russia and former Warsaw Pact countries. Yet the history of the Cold War continues to suffer from an imbalance. The properly documented study of Soviet policy is in its infancy when compared to that carried out in the United States over the past 40 years.

Nevertheless, a critique of the 'America-first' approach has been developed since the late 1970s. This critique was most famously articulated by the British historian Donald Cameron Watt in 1978. Watt and those he encouraged to follow his lead have shown that in the immediate post-war period the Attlee government in Britain conceived of the Cold War in a different fashion from the Truman administration in the United States and for different reasons. Furthermore Britain had considerable powers of independent action. It was not the passive victim of a Soviet–American conflict but played a vital role in shaping the definition and conduct of the Cold War. The British and American archives remain those most accessible to historians, but the trend of questioning the passivity and powerlessness of other Cold War participants has continued. It first spread to Western Europe but more recently has been apparent in countries such as China. The evidence from each country has tended to suggest that the ideas of powerful allies were not unquestioningly adopted. Rather, on a range of issues, states and movements had their own foreign-policy priorities, often based upon long-standing concerns which were melded with the Soviet–American conflict.

The aim of the present book is to explain why the Cold War remained central to international relations for so long. It addresses four main questions. First, how are we to regard the 'polarity' of the Cold War? To interpret the Cold War as bipolar is to stress the centrality of the direct interaction between the Soviet Union and the United States and the impact they had on other states. A multipolar view, by contrast, not only suggests that other states helped shape the individual actions of the two main protagonists, but that interactions between states other than the USSR and the USA actually shaped the Cold War system itself. There is a difference between a multipolar Cold War and a multipolar world. It has been argued, for instance, that after about 1970 the Cold War became 'tripolar' with the emergence of China as a political, if not an economic or military, superpower. It has also been argued that about the same time the world capitalist system started to become 'tripolar' with the emergence of roughly balanced zones of advanced industrial prosperity in North America, Western Europe and East Asia. It is important to ask whether the Cold War not only passed through bipolar and multipolar stages but whether polarity also related to issue. For instance, whereas the signature of strategic arms limitation treaties in 1972 was a bipolar issue, the signature of the 1975 Helsinki accords, which attempted to define the territorial settlement in Europe, was evidently multipolar.

Second, the problem of polarity alerts us to another line of investigation. How integrated was the Cold War? How far did actions in the Formosa Strait really affect those in Berlin? Did Cold War policy-makers see themselves dealing with an interlinked global system or a series of regional systems? To return to Archilocus's fable, how erinacine were the hedgehogs, how vulpine were the foxes? (Berlin's essay actually turned on his characterisation of Leo Tolstoy as a fox who wanted to be a hedgehog.) Some American leaders were explicitly globalists. Dean Acheson, John Foster Dulles and Henry Kissinger all openly discussed the global linkages in their foreign policy. Yet even under their respective tenures as Secretary of State, distinct differences in their conduct of the Cold War in different regions were apparent. In particular, it seems possible to speak of an Asian Cold War and a European Cold War. If the Cold War was, in practice, fractured along geographical lines for American hedgehogs, how much more so was it for participants lacking America's economic and military global reach?

Third, do the best interpretations emerge from an examination of interstate relations or the political process in each country under consideration? If foreign-policy-making is regarded as the nexus between domestic and international politics, which side of the link shapes it most strongly? In most states involved in the Cold War at least part of the state apparatus charged with formulating foreign policy and the individuals within it made genuine attempts to understand and respond to the actions of other states but, at the same time, organisations within the state, whether governments or ruling movements, sought legitimacy for themselves or even the state itself through foreign policy. Some states, such as North Vietnam between 1954 and 1975, were actually involved in a struggle for survival which only a successful foreign policy could guarantee. But foreign policy could threaten the legitimacy of even a stable political system, as the conduct of the Vietnam War did in America. Foreign policy could legitimise a regime which other factors tended to undermine – the situation in the Soviet Union for most of its history. If we identify the scope of those threatened by foreign-policy failure – the nation, the political system, the government, an organisation, an individual – and the severity of the challenge which would arise from failure, fundamental, serious or minor, we can note that the wider the scope and the more severe the challenge the more important management of the domestic political process became, except in those cases where the threat derived from crude direct intervention by a foreign power. Even in those cases defeating the enemy could be less important than keeping control of the internal political process – a contention borne out by the histories of the Korean and Indochinese wars.

Fourth, in asking which political processes shaped choice, how much choice do we ascribe to national leaders? In any analysis of decision-making one has to ask four questions. Which decisions were taken and why? Which options were considered but rejected and why? Which were the options known to decision-makers but rejected without serious consideration and why? Which options, in hindsight, did policy-makers display no awareness of and why? The dichotomy between ideology and *realpolitik* is sometimes seen as the main interpretative challenge in analysing these four aspects of decision-making. The ideological prism of leaders often determined the decisions they were able to take. States which stressed the importance of the sources of national power rather than the structure of the international system could be regarded as less ideological. Yet *realpolitik* – the assumption that all states will do the utmost to increase their power whilst guaranteeing their own survival – is itself an ideology, its adherents claiming access to objective truth in much the same way as Marxist-Leninists did. *Realpolitik* would suggest that the Soviet Union was a huge continental power looking to Europe in the west, Central Asia in the south and North East Asia in the east. The United States was bound to have foreign-policy concerns across both the Atlantic and the Pacific, oceans upon which it had recently fought a global conflict. Britain and France were relatively small West European powers dealing with unravelling colonial empires. They would all behave accordingly. Decision-making was often a battleground between ideologues (the hedgehogs) and those who saw the specificity of various situations (the foxes). One would expect that in states possessing an officially promulgated state ideology there would be more ideologues and that they would have more influence, but this should not blind one to the existence of ideologues in states without a self-proclaimed ideology.

The leaderships of Cold War states all had some conception about the sources of national power. Potentially power could be drawn from the military capabilities and organisation of the state, its economic, financial and techno-logical capabilities and its possession of allies and clients. How did state leaderships see the balance between these sources of power, what means did they see of strengthening any or all of them, and what were the threats they saw to maintaining or increasing them? How were these national sources of power viewed in relation to the international system? How was that system conceived both as a reality and as an ideal? What were the opportunities for achieving an ideal system and what were the threats to that achievement? What place did national leaderships see for war in this system? What were the risks and opportunities involved in the use of armed force?

This book concentrates on those states which were vital in shaping the Cold War rather than those which were most affected by it. It also concentrates on states at the points of their greatest influence. It is based on a threefold typology of states. In this typology, the superpowers are obviously central. When William Fox coined the term 'superpower' in 1944 he meant the United States, the Soviet Union and Great Britain. The term would rarely be used subsequently of Britain, even in the late 1940s. Some observers have even doubted whether the Soviet Union was ever a superpower: Paul Dibb coined the phrase 'the incomplete superpower' to describe it. The defining nature of the superpower, even if solely defined in terms of military capability, was of overwhelming plenitude which no other states could even consider matching. For instance, Britain's defence spending, which took up a relatively high proportion of its national income, amounted to only 31 per cent of the United States' and 26 per cent of the Soviet Union's in 1948 and these figures had fallen to 9.5 per cent and 12 per cent by 1959.[6] If we take this narrow military measure, the Soviet Union remained a superpower until its demise in 1991. From the early 1970s it became fashionable to talk of the People's Republic of China as a potential superpower. It is probably best, however, to classify the PRC with Britain and France as a major power. As Winston Churchill, rather testily, pointed out in 1954: 'Many people ... exaggerate the power and importance of China as a military factor, and talk about six hundred million Chinese ... When I was young I used to hear much talk about the "Yellow Peril".'[7] A major power in Cold War terms was one with a global reach and the capacity for significant independent diplomatic and military action. British and French potential for such action was diminished after the mid-1950s but was far from extinguished. In passing, this book argues that France's role in the Cold War has been underrated in English-language historiography whilst Britain's has been overrated. Although the British had different interests from the Americans and often argued with them, they usually conformed to US positions. If Britain had not cleaved so closely to the United States, possibly pursuing the 'third force' ideas floated in the 1940s, it would have had a much greater impact on the Cold War.

The final category of Cold War state was the 'battleground' power: those countries which through chance, position or calculation became the nodal points of Cold War conflict. Three main countries are included under this heading: Germany, Korea and Vietnam. None of these 'countries' was a state. Each was divided by and during the Cold War: Germany from 1949 to 1989, Korea from 1946 to the present and Vietnam between 1954 and 1975. It can be demonstrated that political leaders in both Korea and Vietnam vigorously sought to internationalise their struggles to seize and hold power. The irruption of these national struggles into the Cold War changed its course. Yet because of its geographical position, economic potential and historical role, Germany was the essential 'battleground' for the whole Cold War.

The book is organised into five chronological chapters. Chapter 1 begins *in media res* at the start of 1947. The origins of the Cold War can be traced to 1943 when it became clear that the temporary coalition created by German aggression would emerge victorious. Its ideological roots stretch further back to the Bolshevik revolution in 1917. Yet the term 'Cold War' only came into use in

1947 as a widely accepted description of a new international system. Since the purpose of this work is to describe the system in action over its entire existence, I have resisted the temptation to delve too deeply into the early origins of the conflict, a subject on which much more has been written than on later periods, not least because of the pattern of archival releases in the United States and Great Britain. Chapters 1 and 5, which deal with the opening and end of the Cold War, cover periods of approximately five years each. In the interests of balance the intervening three chapters each cover roughly a decade. I have tried to avoid selecting neat turning points. In dealing with multilateral relations, whilst taking a close interest in the internal workings of states, these often become somewhat frayed. For instance, the death of Mao in 1976 was considerably more important to China than the December 1972 mutual recognition treaty between West and East Germany with which Chapter 3 ends. There is a narrative as well as an analytical thread in this book, but the reader will notice that material has sometimes been shifted out of its strict chronological order in the interests of clarity.

NOTES

1 Isaiah Berlin, *The Hedgehog and the Fox: An Essay on Tolstoy's View of History* (London, Phoenix, 1992), p. 3.
2 David McCullough, *Truman* (New York, Simon and Schuster, 1992), pp. 936–49; Dean Acheson, *Present at the Creation* (New York, Norton, 1969).
3 Gar Alperovitz, *The Decision to Use the Atom Bomb and the Architecture of an American Myth* (London, HarperCollins, 1995), pp. 3–14.
4 Fred Halliday, *From Potsdam to Perestroika: Conversations with Cold Warriors* (London, BBC, 1995), pp. 8–33.
5 Fred Inglis, 'Killed by the Cold', *The Times Higher Education Supplement* (30 October 1992), pp. 17–19.
6 Percentages derived from Paul Kennedy, *The Rise and Fall of the Great Powers* (London, Fontana, 1989), p. 495.
7 Churchill to Eisenhower, 7 December 1954, in Peter G. Boyle, ed., *The Churchill–Eisenhower Correspondence, 1953–1955* (Chapel Hill, University of North Carolina Press, 1990), pp. 179–80.

2

The Search for Preponderance, 1947–1952

THE AMERICAN WORLD VIEW

In April 1947 the Democratic Party grandee Bernard Baruch gave a speech before the legislature of the state of South Carolina. 'Let us not be deceived', he warned. '[W]e are today in the midst of a cold war.'[1] American foreign policy in the first six months of 1947 was in the process of reification, coalescing around the concept to which Baruch gave a name. The great rhetorical pillars of this change were two speeches: one an address to Congress by the President, Harry Truman, the other delivered by the Secretary of State, George Marshall, at Harvard University. Both concerned aid to Europe. Truman's words in March persuaded the legislature to release funds to Greece and Turkey to assist their governments in resisting leftist subversion. In June, Marshall adumbrated an ambitious plan to extend economic aid to all European countries.

In 1947 the US government presented a dual face. If the President had ever been tentative and unsure in the strange field of foreign affairs he was becoming less so. At the beginning of 1947 he dismissed his first Secretary of State, the Baruch and Roosevelt protégé, James F. Byrnes, for daring to arrogate too much independence to himself, and replaced him with the great soldier, Marshall. Yet with Byrnes went Rooseveltian confidence in a better world order based upon superpower cooperation. In both domestic and foreign affairs Roosevelt had always made it his policy to exude confidence in the future, asserting his 'firm belief that the only thing we have to fear is fear itself'. Truman, Marshall and their advisers, on the other hand, chose to exude pessimism, not about the United States, but about Europe. Truman told Congress:

> It would be an unspeakable tragedy if these countries [Greece and Turkey, but by implication all European nations], which have struggled so long against overwhelming odds, should lose that victory for which they sacrificed so much. Collapse of free institutions and loss of independence would be disastrous not only for them but for the world. Discouragement and possibly failure would quickly be the lot of neighbouring peoples striving to maintain their freedom and independence . . . the effect will be far-reaching to the West as well as to the East.[2]

More tersely, Marshall commented to his audience, 'I need not tell you, gentlemen, that the world situation is very serious. That must be apparent to all

Map 1 The Soviet Union in Eastern Europe

Territory annexed by USSR 1939–1940, and re-incorporated in USSR in 1945

Former German and Czechoslovak territory annexed by USSR in 1945

States in which Communist regimes came to power between 1945 and 1948

Occupied by the USSR, 1945–55

The 'Iron Curtain' in 1955

FINLAND

Vyborg

Tallinn • Leningrad

SWEDEN

ESTONIA • Pskov

LATVIA

SOVIET UNION

LITHUANIA

Kaunas • Vilnius

• Minsk

Königsberg

GDR since 1949

Stettin

annexed by Poland from Germany

Białystok

Bremen

Berlin

SILESIA

Poznan

Pinsk

• Bonn

Dresden

Breslau

Warsaw

FRG

Erfurt

Prague

Cracow

POLAND

Przemysl

Lwów

FRANCE

Nuremberg

CZECHOSLOVAKIA

GALICIA

Munich •

Vienna •

Uzhgorod

Chernivtsy

BESSARABIA

Kishinyov

SWITZ.

AUSTRIA

• Budapest

Jassy

Trieste

HUNGARY

ROMANIA

Belgrade •

Bucharest •

ITALY

YUGOSLAVIA

BULGARIA

Sofia •

Tirana •

ALBANIA

TURKEY

GREECE

0   200 miles

0   300 km

intelligent people. . . . the rehabilitation of the economic structure of Europe quite evidently will require a much longer time and greater effort than had been foreseen.'[3] It is true that both Truman and Marshall were preparing and cajoling the US political and economic élite to take 'immediate and resolute action', but their pessimism is nevertheless notable, since the basic assumptions of that élite about the international system were optimistic. The war and its outcome were regarded as a triumph for the United States, not least because it had expunged the weakness and political disengagement of the post-First World War era. It seemed self-evident that American engagement, political, military and economic, was the linchpin of a functioning and healthy world system and that the spectacular success of the American economy during the war had made such engagement painlessly possible.

There was a straightforward explanation for the growth of pessimism: fear of an expansionist Soviet Union, using indirect, and thus hard to resist, tactics to bring the countries of Europe under its sway. Yet this pessimism also had another source: an attitude, verging on disdain, towards the nations of Western Europe; a belief that they could succeed neither politically nor economically except under American tutelage. This mixture of optimism and pessimism combined powerfully at the beginning of 1947, after nearly two years' gestation, to produce purposeful American action for the reconstruction of the world order. Between 1947 and 1950 this action was concentrated in Europe. Initially, it had the twin aims of rebuilding Western Europe and Germany whilst keeping the political situation on the continent fluid. The commitment to fluidity rapidly disappeared. At first, economic instruments were stressed over military but this stress was also rapidly reversed.

STALIN'S WORLD VIEW

Many years after Stalin's death certain aspects of his approach to international affairs remained clear in the minds of his associates. 'Well, what does the "Cold War" mean?' Vyacheslav Molotov asked rhetorically. 'Aggravated relations', he said, in answer to his own question. 'We had to secure what had been conquered . . . we had to introduce order everywhere. That's the Cold War. Of course you have to know the limits. I think that in that respect Stalin kept very sharply within the limits.'[4] Molotov was probably Stalin's closest collaborator in the field of foreign policy. He had worked closely with him since 1921 and was Foreign Minister between 1939 and 1949. Yet even Molotov had to guess at the nature of his leader's conduct. Andrey Gromyko, who was successively ambassador to Washington, the United Nations and London under Stalin, qualified his recollection of Soviet motives in precipitating the 1948 Berlin crisis with the remark that 'of course nobody ever asked him [Stalin] directly' what those motives were.[5] Nikita Khrushchev, who had been a member of the

Politburo since 1939, recalled that 'Stalin behaved like Almighty God with a host of angels and archangels. He might listen to us, but the main thing was he spoke and we listened. He did not explain his reasoning, but passed down the word to lesser mortals.'[6]

Stalin took decisive action in the immediate post-war period to re-exert his control over any areas of Soviet foreign and defence policy on which the exigencies of war had loosened his grip. Stalin's personality thus had a peculiarly influential role in shaping the Cold War. Yet very little direct evidence exists to show what motivated him. What does exist, however, is a considerable amount of circumstantial evidence. Both the public and private statements of Soviet leaders are of use since they are reflections. Men did not give Stalin advice, they told him what they believed he wished to hear. Stalin often did not make clear his own views, thus provoking 'debates' in which senior figures attempted to perform exegeses of the dictator's remarks. The political position of the figure who performed this task most pleasingly would improve; the penalties for misguessing were severe.

The conduct of this macabre dance suggests three broad conclusions about Stalin's general attitude to international relations. First, he perceived a very high level of threat. If the capitalist nations were not joining together to strangle the Soviet Union, their own internal contradictions threatened to produce a war which might engulf it. This theoretical position, which was shared by others, was sharpened by intense paranoia. A junior member of the Central Committee recorded one of Stalin's last pronouncements on international affairs in which he told his would-be successors that 'a difficult struggle with the capitalist world lay ahead and that the most dangerous thing in this struggle [which he criticised senior members of the Politburo for doing] was to flinch, to take fright, to retreat, to capitulate'.[7] Notwithstanding this, and second, Stalin believed in his own 'personal genius'. The belief was genuine, although it also strengthened his own political position – if only Stalin could ensure the survival of the Soviet Union he was irreplaceable. Third, Stalin had a firm grasp of the limits of power. Despite his paranoia Stalin was not, at least until the last months of his life, a nihilist in the sense Hitler had been. Triumph and self-destruction were not opposite sides of the same coin. Disaster should be avoided, not welcomed. Stalin had reached his position in the Soviet Union in the face of intense opposition by dint of clever and ruthless political tactics. If he was to achieve the same mastery over international politics, similar tactics would be required.

At least one Stalinist foreign-policy cohort, Foreign Minister Molotov, saw the international situation as fluid at the beginning of 1947. In the foreign-policy assessment prepared at his order in the autumn of 1946 the Soviet Union was portrayed as having both the opportunity and need to pursue an activist foreign policy. Opportunity lay in the failure of a Western bloc to cohere. The Soviet Union could exacerbate tensions between capitalist countries, thus ensuring that they would not ally against the Soviet Union. Risks existed, since the Soviet Union had not yet constructed its own bloc. The potential 'new democracies' in Eastern Europe were still vulnerable to capitalist infiltration. According to the Molotov line, the war had caused severe economic and political dislocation to the British empire and continental Europe. There was little chance of the dislocation being overcome in the short term: a 'situation [which] provides American monopolistic capital with prospects for enormous shipments of goods and the importation of capital into these countries ... to infiltrate their national economies'. The Soviet Union was immune to such penetration because of the autarkic nature of its economy. Its political position was strong because of the 'Soviet armed forces ... located on the territory of Germany and other formerly hostile countries'. Yet the advantage of such a sphere of influence 'cannot help but be regarded by the American imperialists as an obstacle in the path of the expansionist policy of the United States'.

Molotov and his ambassador in Washington, Nikolay Novikov, saw American domestic politics as an important factor shaping US–Soviet relations. They portrayed Truman as abandoning Roosevelt's policy of striving 'to strengthen the cooperation of the three great powers' in favour of a bipartisan anti-Soviet foreign-policy coalition with the Republicans. There were three outward signs of this new policy. The 'colossal' rise in the budget for the army and navy. The strengthening of American armed forces was twinned with an 'attempt to create an atmosphere of war psychosis ... thus making it easier for the US government to carry out measures for the maintenance of high military potential'. The second outward sign was the establishment of a global system of American military bases and the third an 'understanding with England concerning the partial division of the world on the basis of mutual concessions'. The structure of American foreign policies, however, provided the Soviet Union with key opportunities. The possibility of pushing it back into Rooseveltian cooperation existed as did the possibility of driving a wedge between Britain and America. The two great capitalist powers were possible allies, but by expanding into areas such as the Near East 'American capital has English capital as its greatest and most stubborn competitor'. Such competition prevented a stable Anglo-American alliance from emerging. American leaders might 'have a sympathetic attitude toward the idea of a military alliance with England' and, indeed, 'in practice ... maintain very close contact on military questions' but 'the current relations between England and the United States, despite the temporary attainment of agreements ... are plagued with internal contradictions and cannot be lasting'.

If the relationship between Britain and the United States was global, America also had an activist policy in Europe. Its main aim was to limit or dislodge Soviet influence from the Soviet Union's neighbours, first by creating political obstacles to the consolidation of regimes friendly to the USSR, and then political opportunities 'for the penetration of American capital into their

economies'. The key country for this policy was Germany, where allied
occupation was to be terminated and the 'prerequisites' for a 'revival of an
imperialist Germany' established. On balance, Molotov did not see the main
risk as an immediate American–Soviet war but the exertion of political pressure
on the Soviet Union to force it out of its 'security zone and into passivity'.[8] Of
course Molotov was self-serving. In a fluid international situation diplomacy
was at the core of Soviet actions rather than a form of propaganda. Since
diplomacy was under Molotov's remit its importance was reflected in his own
power. Nevertheless, Stalin agreed with his Foreign Minister that the international situation was still fluid. In January he criticised the communists in the
western zones of Germany for being 'too influenced by the old revolutionary
programme of the KPD' and instructed them to campaign as nationalists
demanding German unity.[9]

Whatever the tactics adopted by the Soviet leadership, the Molotov line
indicates the nature of its strategic concerns. At the beginning of 1947 the
Soviet Union was not hovering between aggressive diplomacy and defensive
retrenchment: the choice was between defensive aggression or expansive
aggression. The West might threaten in Europe, in which case active measures
would have to be taken to avert such a threat. If the Soviet Union was left
relatively unmolested, however, this would be because the capitalist states had
fallen on each other. It was a classic Stalinist theme that the Soviet Union
would have to take an active part in such a conflict. From mid-1947 onwards
Soviet policy was based on tight control of client states and a determined
probing of Western resolve. Behind this shield Soviet military power was to be
built up for a putative conflict with capitalism one or two decades hence.
Military power was central to Stalin's conduct of international relations. Indeed
the Soviet Union owed its international influence to the role of the Red Army
in the defeat of Nazi Germany.

At the beginning of 1946 Stalin had announced his thoughts on the nature of
the Second World War. The war, he said, had been 'an inevitable result of the
development of world economic and political forces on the basis of modern
monopoly capitalism'. Some nations were denied raw materials and markets
and attempted to seize them by force. Yet Stalin did not confine his thoughts to
the recently ended conflict. His theory was universal. Although the Second
World War had been different from the First and the exact circumstances of a
future conflict would be different again, Stalin's view had not changed much
during the war.[10] As early as 1939 he had identified the 'distinguishing feature
of the new imperialist war' as 'being waged by aggressor states ... [on the]
interests of the non-aggressive states ... while the latter draw back and retreat,
making concession after concession to the aggressors'. The way forward for the
Soviet Union was clear: strengthened armed forces and alliances of convenience
with capitalist countries.[11] Stalinist practice as enacted by Molotov made it clear
that such alliances could be made with 'aggressor' states as much as with 'non-

aggressive' states. In his last programmatic statement, the *Economic Problems of Socialism in the USSR* of 1952, Stalin returned to exactly the same theme. Those who believed that 'owing to the development of new international conditions since the Second World War, wars between capitalist countries had ceased to be inevitable' were wrong. It was mistaken to see the United States as so dominant that it could 'prevent [capitalist countries] from going to war among themselves and weakening one another'. Germany, Britain, France, Italy and Japan would simply not 'tolerate the domination and oppression endlessly'. As in the past the Soviet Union would have a key role to play in these conflicts. As in the past America and Britain had resurrected Germany to use against the Soviet Union, only to find it turning on them, thus necessitating an alliance with Russia, so similar patterns would occur in the future.[12]

As in foreign affairs, to quote Khrushchev once more, Stalin 'completely monopolised all decisions about our defence including – I'd even say especially – those involving nuclear weapons and delivery systems'. Again, as in foreign affairs, Stalin pursued a two-line policy. In the short term Soviet military power was concentrated on dominating and exploiting the conquered territories. In the long term, however, Stalin had much more ambitious plans for military–economic development centring round nuclear weapons. He strained every nerve of the Soviet scientific, design, industrial and espionage communities to find a means of threatening the United States with nuclear weapons.

In 1945–46 partisan warfare was endemic in the western half of the Soviet Union. In April 1946 Interior Minister Kruglov reported to Stalin that 8360 partisans and the leaders of the Ukrainian nationalist movement had been killed or captured in the western Ukraine. Despite this and similar successes in Belorussia, Latvia and Estonia, Stalin was far from satisfied with internal security operations and continued to give them attention and priority.[13] Two Ukrainian guerrilla organisations continued to operate until about 1954. Although a new stage in the demobilisation of the Red Army was instituted between June and September 1946, it was still a huge force. The Soviets claimed that the armed forces were reduced from 11.4 million men in 1945 to 2.9 million in 1948, although Western analysts continue to believe that the true figure was near 4 million in the late 1940s. Large numbers of these troops were deployed in reconstruction tasks, such as construction, factory and agricultural labour, disaster relief and mine clearance operations (the latter was a huge task) within the Soviet Union itself.[14] In September 1946 Stalin and Andrey Zhdanov led a campaign for agricultural reform, launched as a response to agricultural disaster in the Ukraine, where the grain harvest was one-sixth lower than it had been in 1945, which involved a forcible reorganisation of collective farms.[15] Outside the Soviet Union the Red Army was involved in internal security and stripping the conquered territories of usable goods. Between 60 000 and 70 000 dismantlers entered Germany with the Red Army. In October 1946 the German-staffed military research and development centres which had been operating in the Soviet zone were shipped back to the Soviet Union with up to 40 000 German scientists.[16] Zhdanov used the incompetence with which the dismantling of German industry was carried out as a stick to beat his political rival Georgiy Malenkov, but the policy was still in place at the beginning of 1947.[17]

In these circumstances the Soviet occupation forces in Germany were instructed, in November 1946, to deploy at least 50 kilometres away from the borders of the western zones. The 'plan for the active defence of the territory of the Soviet Union' produced by the general staff early in 1947 had as one of its primary missions 'to ensure the reliable repulse of aggression and the integrity of the frontiers established by international agreements after World War Two'. Stalin did not intend to launch an invasion of Western Europe in the short term. His attention was focused on the nuclear issue. It was only after the Soviet Union had exploded its first atomic bomb in August 1949 that Stalin shifted his forces in Europe into a high-readiness offensive posture. According to Khrushchev's figures the size of the armed force was increased from 2.9 million men in 1948 to 4.6 million in 1952. The published defence budget for 1950–51 showed a 21 per cent rise. GSFG (Group of Soviet Forces in Germany) was reorganised as a striking force and expanded by 80 000 men between the summer of 1949 and the spring of 1950. In October the Soviet Marshal Roskossovsky was appointed as Polish Minister of Defence, and conscription, intended to produce armed forces of 400 000 men, was introduced. At the end of his life Stalin became even more concentrated on preparing an offensive.[18]

Stalin understood the central importance of nuclear weapons. The Soviet Union had had an atomic weapons programme since 1943. This was greatly accelerated in 1945. Lavrentiy Beria, who was in overall charge of the programme, reported to Stalin on its progress every week thereafter. In public Stalin claimed that the bomb changed little. Declaratory military strategy was unchanged from Stalin's wartime pronouncement on the 'permanently operating factors', which explicitly rejected surprise attack, such as that so calamitously misjudged by Stalin in June 1941, as a cause of victory. In September 1946 Stalin publicly stated that atomic weapons 'cannot decide the outcome of a war'. Indeed some of the advice Stalin received pointed to the non-decisive nature of atomic weapons. Soviet experts tended to believe that, although the United States would soon possess hundreds of nuclear weapons, the scarcity of uranium and the vast expense involved in production would place a ceiling on its stockpile. One commentator estimated that the explosive yield of all the bombs dropped on Germany was equal to 330 A-bombs. He argued that the strategic bombing offensive had not brought Germany to its knees and an attack of the same magnitude would not crush the Soviet Union.

Despite these calculations Stalin was far from sanguine about the risk of nuclear attack. His main fear was of nuclear blackmail. Malenkov told the

Italian communist Nenni in November 1947 that the 'United States is not in a position to start a war but was conducting a cold war, a war of nerves'. Soviet defence efforts were actually concentrated on ensuring that a significant amount of doubt could be introduced into American nuclear planning. As analysed in 1950, this planning consisted of three major aspects: an atomic air attack on Soviet military–economic and administrative–political centres to demoralise the population as a whole and the armed forces in particular; a naval and land blockade of the Soviet Union to create a war of attrition; and only much later a land invasion of Russia. This strategy would be rendered ineffective by Soviet air defences and the deployment of Soviet land forces. The Soviets would then respond by using nuclear weapons against NATO forces and would invade and conquer Western Europe before American reinforcements could cross the Atlantic. In order to fulfil these goals, high priority was given to air defence and the long-range air force. In 1947 new jet fighters flew and a massive new system of anti-aircraft guns and radar was built. In the next year the Soviet air defence forces were established as a separate branch of the armed forces.

Such defensive responses were highly unsatisfactory as far as Stalin was concerned. As soon as Molotov informed him that the Soviet Union was in a position to make an atomic bomb in November 1947 the Soviet leadership began to stress deterrence. In November 1947 Molotov announced that 'this secret [of the A-bomb] has long ceased to be a secret', an announcement which it was hoped would leave 'the majority of reactionary politicians and journalists realising that . . . the imperialist camp has lost thereby one of its most powerful means of blackmailing people'. Following the actual explosion of the Soviet A-bomb Malenkov declared that 'if the imperialists start a third world war, it will mean the end not of individual capitalist states but of all the capitalist world . . . the American people are beginning to realise that if the warmongers start a new slaughter . . . [it] will visit the American continent too . . . the warmongers will inevitably be suffocated and drowned in it.' Stalin did not, however, actually believe in deterrence since, in the words of his chief propagandist, Mikhail Suslov, the Soviet atomic bomb 'drives the imperialist and warmongering camp into fresh outbursts of frenzied fury'. Stalin wanted Soviet preponderance in nuclear weapons.[19] The Soviet H-bomb programme had been initiated as early as 1946 and was given priority in 1949 once it became clear that technical difficulties could be overcome. According to Andrey Sakharov, Stalin and Beria 'already understood the potential of the new weapon, and nothing could have dissuaded them from going forward with its development. Any US move towards abandoning or suspending work on a nuclear weapon would have been perceived either as a cunning, deceitful manoeuvre, or as evidence of stupidity or weakness.'[20] In April 1947, months before the first test flight of the Soviet Union's B-29 copy, the Tu-4, Stalin demanded the design and production of ICBMs. 'Do you realise the tremendous strategic importance of machines of this sort?', he asked rhetorically in April 1947. 'They could be an effective straitjacket for that noisy shopkeeper Harry Truman. We must go ahead with it, comrades. The problem of the creation of transatlantic rockets is of extreme importance to us.' Stalin personally badgered the aircraft designer Tupolev to build an intercontinental jet bomber against the latter's technical doubts (which later proved well founded).[21]

A vast industrial effort was made to meet Stalin's demands. The Kyshtym complex, for instance, was built east of the Urals between 1945 and 1948 by about 70 000 forced labourers to produce plutonium. The military research and development budget more than quintupled between 1945 and 1953 and the number of researchers tripled between 1940 and 1950.[22] Significant use was made of foreign expertise: for instance, German scientists made some of the major advances which allowed the Soviets to explode their first nuclear device using enriched uranium in October 1951. Yet as Stalin consolidated the Soviet sphere after July 1947 he also attempted to create an enclosed military–industrial system. Molotov demanded 'merciless criticism' of 'grovelling and servility' to Western culture. In August 1948 Yuriy Zhdanov, Zhdanov's son and Stalin's future son-in-law, was forced to make a public apology to Stalin for criticising T. D. Lysenko, a crackpot agrobiologist who rejected the 'Western' science of genetics.[23] The period from the summer of 1947 was one of technological triumphalism for Stalin and his cohorts. The crash nuclear programme, and particularly the hydrogen bomb programme, seemed to show the Soviet system in its best light: high-level political decisions, rapid concentration of resources, indigenous technical advance and highly visible results on international politics. Between 1945 and 1953 there was remarkably little change in Stalinist strategy. It consisted of economic recuperation, military modernisation, especially the development of nuclear weapons, the construction of an inviolable security zone in both Europe and the Far East, extreme distrust of the Western powers in the short term and certainty of inevitable conflict with them in the long term. The bases of this strategy were firmly rooted within Stalinist political culture. They were not the product of external stimuli.

THE FUTURE OF EUROPE

Franklin Roosevelt, Joseph Stalin and Winston Churchill had first seriously discussed the fate of Europe in November 1943 when they met at Teheran. The most important issue then was a strategy to defeat Germany. They agreed on war plans for 1944: the British and Americans would open a 'second front' in northern France, the Soviets would launch a new offensive on the Eastern front through Belorussia. The 'Big Three' sketched out ideas for a new map of Europe. At their final meeting they agreed that Germany would have to be broken up in some fashion. Roosevelt also put forward plans for a new United

Nations organisation, to be dominated by the 'four policemen': the three plus China. When Roosevelt met Stalin alone, the President said that he was prepared to move the Polish border to satisfy Soviet security needs.

On 6 June 1944 forces of the United States and the British empire landed in Normandy. They established a secure bridgehead but continued to meet determined German opposition. It was not until mid-August that the invading armies broke out and moved to liberate France and the Low Countries. The Red Army also launched a massive offensive in June, capturing Minsk in early July and pushing on into Poland. With victory against Germany seemingly a matter of time, Roosevelt discussed its future with Churchill at Quebec in September 1944. Henry Morgenthau, the US Treasury Secretary, tabled radical proposals: the war-making industries in the Ruhr and the Saar would be liquidated and Germany would be converted into an agricultural and pastoral nation. The next month Churchill visited Moscow for talks with Stalin. He summoned the leaders of the Polish government-in-exile from London and attempted to broker an agreement with the Polish regime established by the advancing Soviets at Lublin. At a late-night meeting in the Kremlin on 9 October, Churchill also produced a proposal for Anglo-Soviet zones of influence in the Balkans. Both leaders initialled the proposal and wrote a joint letter to Roosevelt, reporting an 'extraordinary atmosphere of goodwill' at their meeting. By the time Churchill and Stalin came to negotiate the future of the Balkans, however, the Red Army had already occupied Rumania and Bulgaria. On 20 October, Soviet troops captured Belgrade. In Greece the Germans had evacuated Athens. British troops arrived a few days later and a coalition government with both rightists and leftists was established. In December 1945, the left-wingers left the coalition: five days later they initiated an insurrection in Athens. A truce was signed in January 1945 but, following a plebiscite in September 1946, which endorsed the retention of the monarchy, the communists relaunched the civil war.

In northern Europe the Red Army continued its advance, capturing Warsaw in January 1945 and pushing on to the Oder, less than 40 miles from Berlin. Almost all pre-war Soviet territory was back in Soviet hands. In February 1945 Roosevelt, Stalin and Churchill met once more at Yalta in the Crimea. Stalin agreed to the formation of the United Nations and promised to enter the war against Japan within months of Germany's surrender. In return, Roosevelt offered him territorial concessions at the expense of Japan and China. They discussed the fate of Germany, including the possibility of dismemberment, but not in any great detail. Instead the proposal to divide Germany into four temporary occupation zones was finalised. The great powers decided that $20 billion would be the base figure for German reparations, half going to the Soviet Union. The most detailed discussions held in Yalta concerned Poland. The three finally agreed that a 'broadly based' Polish Provisional Government of National Unity should be established. The communist Lublin government would form the basis of the new administration. It would, however, also include their rivals, the London Poles. 'Free and unfettered' elections would follow 'on the basis of universal suffrage and the secret ballot'. Poland's eastern frontier would follow the Curzon line, proposed in the 1920s before Polish successes in their war with the Soviet Union.

On 8 May 1945 Germany surrendered. In July 1945 the powers met once more at Potsdam. The Soviets were granted parts of east Prussia. The western Neisse was accepted as the Polish frontier with Germany, thus giving Poland the coalfields of Silesia. A Council of Foreign Ministers was charged with drawing up peace treaties with Italy, Romania, Bulgaria, Hungary and Finland, whilst preparing a peace with a newly constituted Germany. At the insistence of the new President, Harry Truman, each power agreed to raise reparations from its own zone of occupation, with the Soviets receiving 25 per cent of reparations from the western zones. The country was to be governed by a four-power Allied Control Council but the Soviets soon cut off their zone from the others and started to introduce Soviet-style organisation in agriculture and industry. In April 1946 the Social Democrats in the Soviet zone were forced to merge with the Communists to form the Socialist Unity Party (SED), which was given political control of the zone. The Soviets also demanded enhanced reparations from Germany to reconstruct their war-ravaged economy. The United States and Britain refused to countenance such exactions, fearing they would destroy hopes of reviving the German economy. In May 1946, General Lucius Clay, commanding the US zone, suspended reparations payments altogether.

Yet American planners did not see this post-war settlement as necessarily unhealthy. The basic assumption of America's European policy was stated by George Kennan's Policy Planning Staff (PPS) in May 1947:

> The PPS does not see communist activities as the root of the difficulties of Western Europe. It believes that the present crisis results in large part from the disruptive effect of the war on the economic, political and social structure of Europe and from a profound exhaustion of physical plant and spiritual vigour. . . . American aid to Europe should be directed not to the combating of communism as such but the restoration of the economic health and vigour of European society.[24]

There was thus some doubt whether the offer of substantial aid to Europe made by Marshall in June was primarily offensive or defensive. The offer was made to all European countries: not only those dominated by the Soviet Union but the USSR itself. A more widely spread aid package had the advantage of keeping pan-European politics fluid. Even if the Soviet Union was militarily dominant in Eastern Europe it could be balanced by American economic penetration of the area.

In response Stalin downgraded the attempt to seek arrangements with capitalist countries. Molotov's Foreign Ministry suggested that the 'reactionary forces' behind the policy were opposed by other substantial groups in American political and economic life. An analysis published on 21 March claimed that 'farsighted and circumspect elements' viewed the 'new course' in American policy with alarm. 'They are alive', it noted, 'to the lessons of the recent past, which show how dangerous reckless pretensions to world dominion are to the peoples of the countries from which they emanate.' Again, the implication was that American policy was malleable.[25] This was not the view, however, taken by the circle around another contender for Stalin's favour, indeed the man viewed as his most likely successor, Andrey Zhdanov. Zhdanov was already active on the domestic front, leading a large-scale cultural crack-down known as the *Zhdanovschina*. The Zhdanovites emerged on to the foreign-policy stage in May 1947. They rejected any attempt to portray the United States as malleable and dismissed the utility of diplomatic manoeuvres with capitalist countries. It was misguided to seek accommodations with a country which had, in the words of Zhdanov's ally Nikolay Voznesensky, 'waxed fat on the people's blood during the Second World War' and now stood 'at the head of the imperialist and anti-democratic camp and has become the instigator of imperialist expansion everywhere in the world'.[26] The United States' internal dynamic could not be mitigated by diplomacy. The United States was moving towards a war with socialism in order to secure its own world domination, to prevent an economic crisis of capitalism and to crush any hope of working-class revolution in America itself. All that mattered was the strength of the Soviet Union and the cohesion of a communist bloc under its leadership. Molotov continued to reject the Zhdanovite approach. His journal *New Times* claimed on 16 May that: 'the working out of agreed decisions on the [German] problem requires time, patience, goodwill, and serious effort ... the position of the powers on the disputed issues has become more clearly defined ... this clears the way to the necessary, if exacting, work of reconciling the different points of view and arriving at agreed decisions.' The Soviet political élite was using foreign policy as a means of competing for Stalin's favour. The short-term outcome of that competition was decided in the summer of 1947 as the Soviets had to develop a rapid response to the offer of American economic aid to Europe.

Molotov and Novikov had identified the danger that the United States might attempt to penetrate the recently conquered states of eastern and central Europe by economic means. It seemed that this threat had manifested itself even more rapidly than had been expected when George Marshall floated the plan which was to take his name on 5 June 1947. Molotov highlighted the parts of the speech in which Marshall emphasised the serious economic situation in Europe, the risks this posed to the United States itself and his commitment that the United States would do 'everything within its power so as to assist in the return of normal economic conditions in the world'. He was also exercised by the proposed plan's structure: agreement between European countries on their economic needs, European initiative and the economic role of the United States. In other words Marshall was moving to block off both the Soviet's 'expansive aggression' option in the case of intra-capitalist conflict and their 'defensive aggression' option: the consolidation of a Soviet bloc in Eastern Europe.

The reaction of the Molotov coterie, in line with their previous positions, was that the Americans were hostile, that they were acting because of their own internal economic imperatives, but that the impact of American policies could be blunted by skilful diplomacy. In the recollection of a veteran of Molotov's secretariat, 'the best plan was to accept that proposal and make an attempt, if not to eliminate, at least to minimise its negative aspects and ensure that they should not impose any conditions on us. In a word it should be something like Lend-Lease. Comrade Molotov was, in fact, a supporter of just this kind of approach.' Such a rebuff would weaken the United States and be to the long-term benefit of the Soviet Union.

Although there had been initial surprise at Marshall's speech, the British and French governments decided to organise a conference to respond to the American offer. On 18 June their foreign ministers, Ernest Bevin and Georges Bidault, invited the Soviet Union to Paris to discuss the plan. The Politburo decided to accept the invitation. On 22 June Molotov cabled the Soviet embassies in Poland, Czechoslovakia and Yugoslavia to instruct them to encourage their host governments to 'take the initiative in arranging their participation in the drawing up of such an economic programme, and announce their desire to participate'. Molotov then turned to Novikov and Yevgeniy Varga to produce an analysis supporting his policies. Both argued that the plan had grown out of an incipient economic crisis in the United States. Both pointed to the need for American 'monopoly capitalists' to rebuild their overseas markets. Varga and Novikov also suggested that the American government was involved in a high-risk policy, endangering its own economy to stave off an even graver crisis. On this economic structure the United States had placed a superstructure of political goals. The Americans intended to hinder the 'democratisation' of Europe by 'putting forward the demand of removing the "iron curtain" as a precondition for the ostensible economic reconstruction of Europe'. Their aim was to create an anti-Soviet bloc by extruding Russia from participation in the plan whilst forcing all other European states to cooperate in seeking American aid. For Molotov's followers the United States was ambitious but vulnerable to Soviet counter-measures. 'Our relationship to the Marshall Plan', Novikov argued, 'should be expressed in an attempt to gain a decisive role in the formation of a programme of reconstruction and development of the national economies of the European countries.' The Soviet Union would try and channel aid on a piecemeal basis to countries under its own control and by such 'participation in the design of the programme ... hinder the realisation of the American plans for the subordination of Europe'.

Stalin was not convinced. He could see no evidence of a split between the capitalist powers which the Soviet Union could exploit. In the short term Britain and France were effectively bankrupt; they could not finance a European recovery plan without American aid. They would, therefore, submerge any differences with the United States in order to get funds to finance their own recovery. Only after that recovery was complete would they baulk at American leadership. At the end of June Soviet intelligence sources in London sent a full account of Anglo-American negotiations on the plan which suggested that the two countries were allied on this issue. They had agreed to reconstruct Europe as a world industrial centre rather than simply giving subsistence aid, to set up a central organisation to coordinate activity in the fields of coal, steel, transport, agriculture and food, and to use Germany as a centrepiece for their programme. 'Using the pretext of credits the Great Powers are attempting to form a Western bloc and isolate the Soviet Union', Stalin concluded.[27] Molotov walked out of the Paris conference on 2 July. Britain and France subsequently invited all European nations, except the USSR and Spain, to participate in further talks.

The Soviet government briefly flirted with the idea of sending its Eastern European ally governments to the next conference on the plan in order to wreck it. This was also too much for Stalin. He told the Czechs that if they went to Paris to discuss aid it 'would show that you want to cooperate in an action aimed at isolating the Soviet Union', thus creating 'a break in the front' and 'a success for the Western Great Powers'.[28] Molotov had never pursued an independent foreign-policy line. As Khrushchev later noted, 'Molotov was just a shadow of Stalin when it came to military affairs and international politics.' Molotov had merely attempted to interpret and embellish his leader's wishes. At the beginning of July 1947 Stalin changed his mind and simply handed the initiative to the existing advocate of a hard-line 'no diplomacy' policy, Zhdanov. Molotov then adapted to the new line. Czechoslovakia, Poland, Hungary, Yugoslavia, Romania, Bulgaria and Albania accepted their invitations but were forced to withdraw by the Soviets. The prospect of a fluid European future was thus blocked. American leaders were, however, neither surprised nor particularly disappointed when the Soviet Union rejected the offer and forced its clients to follow suit: a defensive programme was complex enough but much more manageable.[29] The European Recovery Programme as it emerged through 1947 was a cooperative venture between the US government, specially organised in the form of the European Cooperation Administration, and the Western European countries grouped into the Organisation for European Economic Cooperation. Between 1948 and 1951 it financed the shipment of over $10 billion of food, fuel, raw materials and machinery to Europe.[30] As initially conceived, this aid and other programmes should have been enough to ensure that Western Europe survived and flourished. Marshall aid was to be in lieu of a major military commitment. It proved, however, to be the first step to such a commitment, rendering the American policy-making élite more suggest-ible to further requests for aid.[31]

The most pressing call for such aid came from France. France epitomised the link between the old European and global order and the new Cold War system. The nascent Fourth Republic possessed both a purposeful foreign policy and the desire for the status of a great power, but was so economically and militarily weak it had to seek a superpower patron. The American government was extremely receptive to such pleas. As one analysis had it, 'if the Communists won [power in France], Soviet penetration of Western Europe, Africa, the Mediterranean and the Middle East would be greatly facilitated, and our position in our zone of occupation [in Germany] rendered precarious if not untenable'.[32] The American ambassador in Paris, Jefferson Caffery, urged that every effort should be made to aid France since there was a real chance of it becoming the linchpin of a Western alliance. He wrote at the end of March 1947, 'A year ago I was discouraged about the possibility of preventing the Communists from eventually taking over this country; now I have come to believe that they will not take it over; but the process of organising the genuine democratic forces into an effective machine will be long and tedious; and without a doubt the Communists if they don't take it over will struggle hard to keep it weak and divided.'[33] If America took vigorous action to prop up France, bringing it into a functioning security and economic system, as well as intervening directly in French politics by supporting certain groups and movements with anti-communist credentials, it could guarantee the safety of Western Europe. Thus present French weakness and its future potential strength exercised a strong influence over American thinking about the future of Europe.

In early May 1947 French Communist Party (PCF) ministers were expelled from the government over their support for a series of major strikes in the Renault car factories.[34] The concern about security in France was particularly acute since there was a genuine fear of communist action within the country. Even before the PCF was expelled from the government the Prime Minister, Paul Ramadier, warned President Auriol that there was a clandestine paramili-tary organisation in operation south of the Loire.[35] Intelligence reports routed through the Ministry of the Interior suggested that the Soviet embassy was directly involved in preparing the PCF and the communist trade union federation, the CGT, to disrupt Marshall aid. Reports from local prefects indicated widespread public sympathy with the ousted PCF. In August 1947 French intelligence reports passed to the Americans suggested that Soviet officials had told the PCF leadership that the Marshall Plan was 'too little too late' to save France, that the PCF must 'prepare for the sharpening of conflict between the working classes and the bourgeoisie' by reinforcing the 'illegal apparatus' with 'trusted militants' and to pursue a 'parallel' policy of building up both the legal and illegal organisations.[36]

The Soviets had, indeed, launched a new policy. The venue was Szklarska Poreba in western Poland. Delegates from European communist parties were gathered there for a week in late September 1947 to take part in the initiation of the new line. Stalin's chief representatives at the meeting were Zhdanov and Georgiy Malenkov. The delegates they met were specifically chosen from within the national communist parties on the basis of their loyalty to the Soviet Union. Zhdanov ran the meeting but sought instructions from Stalin at each turn.[37] The policy which emerged from Szklarska Poreba had two main components: first, the institution of a 'no diplomacy' policy towards the West backed up by disruptive activities by Western European communist parties. Diplomacy now became an arm of agitprop. It was no longer expected to yield benefits in its own right. The second component of the programme was the creation of a bloc in Eastern Europe completely under Soviet domination. An important part of this second component was that the Eastern European communists should will their own subjugation. The institutional innovation which was to tie the two components together was the Communist Information Bureau or Cominform.

Zhdanov presented an analysis of the international situation to the meeting which was merely an articulation of the policy shift upon which Stalin had decided in July. This in itself was, with one very important exception, the same as the view Molotov and his subordinates had embroidered for Stalin at the beginning of the year. The new development in the view of the international system presented by Zhdanov was the denial of any immediate conflict between the United States and the other, weakened, capitalist powers. In Zhdanov's formulation:

> the Attlee government in Britain and the Ramadier Socialist government in France clutched at the 'Marshall Plan' as an anchor of salvation. Britain . . . has already used up the American loan of 3 750 000 million dollars granted to her in 1946 . . . the terms were so onerous as to bind Britain hand and foot. Even when caught in the noose of financial dependence on the USA, the British Labour government could conceive of no other alternative than the receipt of new loans.

In the long term there would be a 'further aggravation of the general crisis of capitalism' but in the all-important medium term the United States would endeavour to build 'a "Western Bloc"', centred around Germany, 'as an American protectorate'.[38]

The Soviet response was to turn on the Western communists and to force the Eastern communists to plead for help. Even before the meeting the SED in the Soviet zone of Germany was genuinely pleading for Soviet intervention. The SED leadership had come to the conclusion that not only would the party be smashed in any competitive elections but that the grass roots of the party itself were becoming increasingly anti-Soviet.[39] At Szklarska Poreba the Hungarian

and Czech delegates expressed similar worries. Meanwhile, Zhdanov merci-
lessly criticised the French and Italian communists. He sneered at their
parliamentary tactics and 'the mistakes of the leadership of the French and
Italian parties in response to the new "crusade" against the working class by
world imperialism'. They had not 'unmasked the Truman–Marshall plan, the
American plan of enslavement of Europe'.[40] Jacques Duclos, the PCF representative, was pilloried. Zhdanov denounced PCF tactics as naive and told the
meeting that 'the departure of the Communists from the Ramadier government
was regarded by the French communist party as an internal French matter,
when the real reason for the exclusion of the Communists from the government
was American demands. Now it has become completely clear that the removal
of the Communists from the government was a prior condition for receipt of
American credits.'[41] In fact the Americans were rather more impressed with
PCF tactics than the Soviets. In July 1947 the State Department worriedly
reported that the

> US would have great difficulty in taking any vigorous action since the re-entry of the
> Communists into the government would be substantially a French internal matter and
> any positive action on the part of this country at that time would no doubt serve to raise
> the cry of direct interference in French internal affairs and turn large sections of French
> public opinion against the US ... In short the situation created in France, as serious as
> it would be for US interests, would not be susceptible of treatment by open official US
> government action [covert action was another matter]. It is a very good illustration of
> the difficulties we face in dealing with the tactics of invisible penetration and eventual
> capture of a modern democratic state by a resolute and well-organised minority.[42]

Although the announcement of the founding of the Cominform was delayed in
order not to undermine communist support in the French municipal elections,
Zhdanov instructed the French (and Italian) communists to stop being the
'victims of imperialists' intimidation and blackmail' and underestimating 'the
will of the people to defend the basic national rights and interests of their
country' by engaging in direct action to disrupt the Marshall Plan.[43]

The chosen weapon for this disruption was a series of strikes developing into
a virtual general strike in November 1947. In October 1947 the American
embassy reported that

> the Communists are now convinced that because of the hardening of anti-Communist
> sentiment resulting from the recent reactivation of the Comintern [i.e. the Cominform]
> and their all-out efforts to sabotage French economic recovery the other political parties
> will not in the near future permit them to re-enter a coalition government. Therefore to
> carry out Moscow's orders to sabotage at all costs French recovery the Communists are
> necessarily to adopt more 'open and revolutionary' tactics than they previously
> employed regardless of whether or not such action may harm their standing throughout
> the country at large.

In fact the French government was able to contain the political impact of the strikes and the CGT proved unable to prolong its action much beyond November 1947. This did not necessarily reduce the sense of threat. The CGT broke up in the aftermath of the strikes, when some leaders left to found their own socialist trades union, a development upon which Caffery commented: 'the *scission* . . . in the CGT is the most important event that has occurred since the Liberation'.[44] Unsurprisingly, the new union attracted substantial American funding.

The Western communist parties became more disruptive, launching violent strikes and reorganising to be more effective oppositionists with a greater element of Soviet control. Yet Stalin expected little from these actions since he held the Western communists in the utmost contempt.[45] He placed more faith in the purge of all non-communists from the governments of Czechoslovakia, Bulgaria, Romania and Hungary between September 1947 and February 1948. The communist parties also began to purge themselves of any who were believed not to be wholly committed to the Stalinist line. Of course these actions had been open to Moscow since 1945, simply because of the occupying presence of the Red Army. In 1947 Stalin no longer believed that there was any point in keeping the European situation, outside Germany, fluid. The key conclusion reached at Szklarska Poreba was that the 'chief danger at this present juncture' lay in underrating the strength of communism and overrating the strength of the enemy. 'Just as in the past the Munich policy untied the hands of the Nazi aggressors', Zhdanov declared, 'so today concessions to the new course of the United States and the imperialist camp may encourage its inspirers to be even more insolent and aggressive.'[46] The phrase chosen, at a late juncture, to encapsulate this policy was 'two camps'; it rapidly became and endured as one of the key images of the Cold War.[47]

Once Stalin had decided to consolidate 'his already-won positions' he was relentless.[48] He turned upon Tito and the Yugoslav Communist Party, the staunchest supporters of the two-camps thesis, at the beginning of 1948, because they were not under his control. In November and December 1947 Yugoslavia had signed treaties of alliance with Bulgaria, Romania and Hungary. In January 1948 the Bulgarian communist leader Georgi Dimitrov announced that a customs union would be formed between Bulgaria and Yugoslavia as a prelude to a federation of Balkan states. He was summoned to Moscow and informed that such an action was not permissible. The Yugoslav leader, Tito, sent representatives to the Soviet Union but did not go himself. On 19 March Stalin announced that Soviet economic and military advisers would be withdrawn from Yugoslavia. Soviet representatives incited friendly members of the Yugoslav CP's Central Committee to overthrow Tito. On 12 April 1948, however, the Central Committee decided to resist these demands. On 28 June 1948 Yugoslavia was expelled from the Cominform. One side-effect of this reorientation in the Balkans was that both Yugoslavia and Bulgaria began to

withdraw support from the communist guerrilla movement in Greece, which
had done so much to convince Americans that the fate of Europe was in the
balance. Militarily defeated, the Greek Communist Party announced it had
discontinued the armed struggle on 16 October 1949. Zhdanov, who had
cooperated with the Yugoslavs, was consigned to political eclipse and died,
probably of natural causes, in August 1948.

<h2 style="text-align:center">THE GERMAN QUESTION</h2>

The European Recovery Programme (ERP) was intimately linked to the
eventual political and economic fate of Germany which was, unavoidably, a
point of direct contact between the United States and the Soviet Union. In
March 1947 a report by former President Herbert Hoover caused considerable
debate by suggesting that the United States should stop dismantling German
industry and start planning to reintegrate the industrial powerhouse of the
Ruhr back into the German economy. The US government had already
acknowledged the need for economic integration when it agreed to merge its
zone with that of Britain to form an entity known as the Bizone. In March 1947
the Moscow Council of Foreign Ministers (CFM) broke up without agreeing
the terms for a final peace treaty with Germany. On 29 May a major
reorganisation of the Bizone, which gave Germans greatly increased responsibility for economic life, was announced. In September this trend was
accentuated when direct responsibility for coal production in the Bizone was
transferred into German hands. American leaders in Germany, most notably
the head of the military government, General Lucius Clay, were at the forefront
of this pragmatic reorganisation of a nascent West German state. Clay,
however, saw the development of such a state as a springboard from which the
United States could contest for dominance in the Soviet zone and, subsequently, in Eastern Europe. Policy-makers in Washington were much more
defensive: they viewed with alarm the perpetual instability which would be
created in Europe by a divided Germany. As Colonel Charles Bonesteel, the
War Department's key expert on Germany, observed: 'the fundamental problem is to achieve a free and independent Germany under adequate safeguards
... [a divided Germany could have] catastrophic consequences and would
create an ever present threat to peace. However, a unified Germany wholly
dominated by or genuinely aligned with the Soviets could ... be an even greater
threat.'[49] At a declaratory level, however, the US government was still committed to German unification by four-power agreement. The logic of the ERP
militated, however, against an attempt to keep options open for too long. The
complete failure of the London CFM in November–December 1947 made
further delay pointless. As the CFM was breaking up, the USA, Britain and
France agreed to include their occupation zones in Germany in the ERP. In

response the Soviets withdrew from the Allied Control Commission for Germany and attempted to restrict rail traffic to Berlin.

Berlin presented a difficult problem for the Truman administration. It too was under four-power control and divided into occupation zones but the city was deep within the Soviet zone of Germany. It was both extremely vulnerable and of great symbolic importance. A decision had to be made whether to face military realities or to defend the indefensible: a policy which could rest on little more than bluff and perceived Soviet fear of escalation. Although no clear decisions were taken on Berlin in March 1948 the problem was not allowed to interfere with economic developments in the wider German sphere. As Lucius Clay commented: 'Anything we do to strengthen the Bizonal administration will create a hazard with respect to the USSR in Berlin. On the other hand, appeasement of USSR will continue the present unsatisfactory administration of Bizonal Germany and make economic reconstruction difficult if not impossible.'[50] On 7 June the Western powers' London conference concluded that Germany should have a formal constitution. German provincial leaders were to convene a constituent assembly. In addition, an international authority would allocate Ruhr coal, coke and steel production between Germany and other European countries. The region would, however, remain politically part of Germany. The State Department view was that, 'the London agreements mark the first broad, constructive step toward the resolution of the German problem since Potsdam'. In June 1948 France, the Western nation which had most virulently opposed the reconstruction of Germany, was finally faced with Anglo-American insistence that a West German state should be created. René Massigli, the French ambassador in London, argued that France could not refuse these demands, since if it did America and Britain would set up a state in their existing fused 'Bizone'; France would then be excluded from any international authority in the Ruhr, would be unable to finance its own zone of occupation, would be excluded from any future dialogue with the Soviet Union on the future of Germany and would undermine existing cooperation with the Anglo-Saxons within the Marshall Plan. The Quai d'Orsay (the French foreign ministry) agreed that 'to refuse to ratify this accord would be equivalent to France renouncing its role on the continent' and added: 'no Franco-German political cooperation will be possible if American and Soviet propaganda pose simultaneously as defenders of the German people against the "maximalism" of a France obsessed. In 1948 it was clear to the professional makers of foreign policy that France's German policy had finally ended in failure; a new policy was obviously needed.'[51] The Quai argued that French political and public opinion had to be educated to accept both German revival and Franco-German *rapprochement*. France could 'offer to a future German government a third solution between American economic expansionism and Soviet political expansionism' in the form of 'a Franco-German economic and political association'. Yet Germany remained a divisive issue in French politics: the London accords were only approved 'with reservations' by a vote of 297 to 289 in the French National Assembly.[52]

In Germany, Soviet policy had to be based on direct interaction with the United States, Britain and France. Stalin had little direct control of the German situation. The withdrawal of the Soviet representative from the Allied Control Commission in March was a futile gesture. The Western powers' only vulnerable area was West Berlin. On 16 June the Soviet Union withdrew from the Control Commission for Berlin. On 18 June the USA, Britain and France announced that a new German currency would be introduced into their zones. On 22 June the Soviet military governor ordered that only a new Soviet zone currency should be used in Berlin. The next day, however, the three Western powers extended their currency reforms into their zones of the city. On 24 June the Soviets started to blockade the city. Although the potential for a crisis had been apparent since March there was confusion in the US administration about the correct response to the blockade. Three options were canvassed: to withdraw; 'to retain our position in Berlin by all possible means' (Clay favoured fighting through with a land convoy, 'accepting the possibility of war as a consequence if necessary'); or 'to maintain our unprovocative but firm stand in Berlin, utilising first every local means, and subsequently every diplomatic means'.[53] Unsurprisingly, Truman selected the third non-policy. The Americans stumbled on to the solution of an airlift somewhat by chance. Clay initiated the flying of supplies as a limited operation which 'will substantially increase the morale of the German people and will unquestionably seriously disturb the Soviet blockade'.[54] That the airlift succeeded beyond all reasonable expectations and was able to feed and supply the Berlin population into 1949 saved policy-makers in Washington from their own lack of foresight.

Stalin regarded Berlin merely as a lever. He called it 'insignificant' and offered to call off the blockade in August if the Western powers would delay the formation of a German state.[55] The Soviets had, however, already accepted that such an outcome was unlikely. The possibility of forming an East German state was floated within the Socialist Unity Party (SED) in March 1948. The representative of the Soviet military government, Colonel Tyulpanov, issued new orders to the party in May 1948. He told them that a new situation had arisen: 'a division of Germany into two parts which develop according to different laws has come about'. In this new situation 'the changes in the . . . state situation of the Soviet Zone dictate a drastic improvement of the organisational and ideological work of the party'. On the other hand Stalin did not want his 'Teutons' to go too far but to 'instead zigzag – [following] opportunistic politics towards socialism'. In other words, the SED had to follow 'national front' policies for the 'unity of Germany and a just peace treaty'.

The success of the airlift enabled existing trends towards the creation of a German state to continue. Initially, the prime ministers of the German *Länder* rejected the formation of a western German state but on 1 September 1948 a majority of prime ministers voted to form a constituent assembly. By the summer of 1948 the secular trend in American policy was towards the creation of a western German state. There was, however, determined opposition to such a move, most notably from George Kennan who was rapidly moving away from the mainstream of policy-making on a number of issues. Kennan argued that: 'it is in our national interest to press at this time for a sweeping settlement of the German problem which would involve the withdrawal of Allied forces from at least the major portion of Germany, the termination of military government and the establishment of a German government with real power and independence.' The recreation of a united, independent German state would avoid the 'congealment of Europe along the present lines'. Kennan used the economic logic of German–European integration to argue against West Germany, for he claimed it would be economically unviable:

> there is no prospect of German viability. ERP will certainly not eliminate the dependence upon ourselves of the western zones of a divided Germany. ... we must find some way to broaden the background of German recovery and to relieve ourselves of the excessive responsibility we now bear for German economy. ... In carrying on with an effort to bring recovery to the western portions alone of a divided Germany, we are really working for the unattainable.[56]

Most policy-makers read the situation in a different way: there was little to be gained from a reunified Germany. Politically, it could either associate with the Soviet Union or, just as bad, manoeuvre between the superpowers regaining independent strength. Economically, it would be so dominant in Europe that the remodelling of the Western economy in the US image would be threatened. It seemed better to nurture a western German economy as part of the ERP but free of any Soviet influence. The route to such a solution seemed open because of the success of the Berlin airlift: the blockade was lifted on 12 May in return for an agreement to reconvene the CFM. This body met in May and June 1949, for the last time, to no purpose. In early April the USA, Britain and France agreed their constitutional position *vis-à-vis* a new German state: a new occupation statute and trizonal agreement which merged their zones into a single identity. The Basic Law produced by the constituent assembly in the west was approved by the truncated Allied Control Comission (ACC). It paved the way for national elections in August, in which the Communist Party (KPD) was humiliated. On 17 September the Christian Democrat Konrad Adenauer was elected as the first Chancellor of the new state; the Federal Republic of Germany was proclaimed formally three days later. The People's Provisional Chamber of the German Democratic Republic (GDR) was created in response on 7 October 1949. Stalin continued to use his zigzag policy, pushing for German unification in 1950 and 1952. His policy was 'unity, peace treaty – carry on agitating' to disrupt West Germany and the Western alliance whilst consolidating the communist hold in the East. He actually saw 'no chances of compromise' but instead a 'dangerous border' guarded by an East German army, which 'would have to learn to shoot', backed by Soviet troops.[57] These events prompted the re-emergence of the optimistic strand in American thinking. Dean Acheson declared that the Soviets were 'back on the defensive. ... They are visibly afraid of the fact that they have lost Germany.' Omar Bradley, the Joint Chiefs of Staff (JCS) chairman, also noted with satisfaction that 'the tide of communism is being stemmed in Europe. We are not impelled by crisis, or desperation, or fear of impending war.'[58]

Although the rebirth of a West German state had its origins in the ERP, by the time it came into being the entire strategic situation in Europe had been transformed by a developing military alliance. 'Thus the main objective is not the unification of Germany as an end in itself. The end in view is to support the Western European strength which has already been achieved and expand it.'[59] Yet in 1949 an important gap between ends and means had opened up. Economic diplomacy, and the place of Germany in it, left the United States ill-prepared to meet demands for military security emanating from the Western European states. The US was able to respond to these demands on a political level relatively quickly but security policy proved much harder to recast.

In January 1948 the British Foreign Secretary, Ernest Bevin, engaged Marshall in a debate about the desirability of a Western European security alliance.[60] On 17 March 1948 Britain, France, the Netherlands, Belgium and Luxembourg signed the Treaty of Brussels. The treaty established a 50-year military alliance with a permanent organisation in London. Within five days of the treaty the USA, Britain and Canada were holding exploratory talks about a military alliance between North America and Western Europe. Truman was able to get Republican support for the 'progressive development of regional and other collective arrangements for individual and collective self-defence'.[61] In July 1948 the original three participants were joined by the other Brussels powers. A draft treaty was in existence by September and further negotiations led to the signature of the North Atlantic treaty in April 1949, to which Italy, Norway, Denmark, Iceland and Portugal also adhered. The treaty committed the USA to 'such action as it deems necessary, including the use of armed force, to restore and maintain the security of the North Atlantic area'.[62]

American national security and military planning, however, remained confused and did not address these new commitments. The first attempt by the National Security Council (NSC) to define an overall national security policy in March 1948 rejected a 'defensive policy [of] attempting to be strong everywhere [which] runs the risk of being weak everywhere'. Instead it called for the 'organisation of a world-wide counter-offensive ... strengthening the military potential of the United States, and secondly, mobilising and strengthening the potential of the non-Soviet world ... [giving] first priority to Western Europe'.[63] The matching military plan, a short-term plan for a non-policy, 'contemplated that the initial withdrawal of Allied forces will be to the Rhine. ... US forces will withdraw through France either to French coastal ports or to the Pyrenees.' The main military effort would be to 'initiate as early as practicable an air offensive against vital elements of the Soviet war-making capacity'. Strategic Air Command would be deployed 'to bases in England (alternatively to Iceland), and to the Khartoum–Cairo–Suez area and conduct operations from these bases and Okinawa utilising available atomic bombs'.[64]

Truman was unhappy with this war plan and called for another option to 'resist a Russian attack without using atomic bombs for the reason we might not have them available either because they might at that time be outlawed or because the people of the United States might not at the time permit their use for aggressive purposes'.[65] Secretary of Defense James Forrestal obstructed the President's request for an alternative plan on the grounds that, since Truman insisted on a rigorous budget ceiling, atomic deterrence was the only affordable option for the USA. By the time the draft North Atlantic treaty emerged, the USA was effectively committed to the strategic air offensive as the primary means of waging war. The first definitive statement of national security policy, the product of a project initiated by Forrestal in the summer of 1948, saw a world in which 'the capabilities of the USSR to threaten US security by the use of armed forces are dangerous and immediate': it foresaw a situation in which 'no later than 1955 the USSR will probably be capable of serious air attacks against the United States with atomic, biological and chemical weapons'.[66]

Although the war plan based on this paper and the North Atlantic treaty took a more sanguine view of Soviet military capabilities than its predecessors, the military asked for substantial increases to the atomic programme, causing the chairman of the Atomic Energy Commission (AEC), David Lilienthal, to ask: 'Why? What assumptions have changed? More formidable rival?'[67] At the end of 1947 the JCS had formulated a military requirement for 400 A-bombs in the US arsenal by the end of 1953. In 1949 they asked for the production of thousands. As General Eisenhower told Louis Johnson, Forrestal's successor at Defense: 'Since we have always stressed the value of military preparation as a deterrent to war it seems to me obvious ... that we cannot and must not fail to provide a respectable long-range strategic bombing force. ... I am quite sure that if we are erring in any direction it is in failure to allocate a sufficiently high percentage of our reduced appropriations to the certainty that we can launch and sustain a vigorous bombing offensive on a moment's notice.'[68]

These pressures were immeasurably increased by the explosion of the first Soviet A-bomb in August 1949. Lilienthal noted 'the shock and impact, the recriminations, the whole box of trouble it portended'. Although the emergence of an operational Russian nuclear force was already factored into planning, it is hard to overstate the psychological impact of the Soviet bomb, not least in Congress. The harried Lilienthal, a continual butt of Congressional criticism, reported: '[the] proposed expansion programme: a whopping big one. More and better bombs. Where this will lead ... is difficult to see. We keep saying, "We have no other course"; what we should say is "We are not bright enough to see any other course". The day has been filled, too, with talk of supers, single weapons capable of desolating a vast area.'[69] Truman, indeed, approved the development of the H-bomb in January 1950. Lilienthal commented: 'there has been so much talk in Congress and everywhere and people are so excited he hasn't any alternative but to go ahead and that was what he was going to do'.[70] As Lilienthal realised, however, nuclear developments did not really address the reality of the United States' new alliance commitments: 'the full import of the Russians' success, and their prospect of a substantial stockpile ... hasn't yet sunk in, so far as the Natl Military Establishment is concerned, too busy with the inter-service row, or just not able to grasp it. ... Would we launch an atomic attack on R. if she moved into Europe, if we knew this meant Russian bombs on London, say? A close question, they said – meaning, I guessed, that we wouldn't.'[71]

George Kennan too had seen the danger. He argued against the signature of the North Atlantic treaty because it was not, 'the main answer to the Soviet effort to dominate the European continent, and will not appreciably modify the nature or danger of Soviet policies [in which] ... military force plays a major role only as a means of intimidation'. The attempt to meet the remote risk of war created the 'danger of a general preoccupation with military affairs, to the detriment of economic recovery and of the necessity for seeking a peaceful solution to Europe's difficulties'. Although Kennan pointed to the 'solemn warning recently given by the Joint Chiefs of Staff concerning the increasing discrepancy between our commitments and our military resources',[72] he was actually worried less by the short-term gap between rhetoric and performance and more by the long-term tendency for resources to grow in order to meet commitments.

A lobby for just such a solution, led ably by Kennan's successor at the PPS, Paul Nitze, emerged from the H-bomb decision. A working party from the State and Defense departments and the military drew up a case for meeting new commitments. Eventually christened NSC 68, it was delivered to Truman, with support from both Acheson and Johnson, in April 1950.[73] The authors of NSC 68 argued that: 'Without superior aggregate military strength, in being and readily mobilisable, a policy of "containment" – which is in effect a policy of calculated and gradual coercion – is no more than a policy of bluff.' They went on: 'the United States and its allies, apart from a powerful atomic blow, will be compelled to conduct delaying actions, while building up their strength for a general offensive. A frank evaluation of the requirements, to defend the United States and its vital interests and to support a vigorous initiative in the cold war, on the one hand, and of present capabilities, on the other, indicates that there is a sharp and growing disparity between them.' The clear implication of the document was that the United States should meet its alliance commitments on the ground, since 'the capabilities of our allies are in an important sense, a function of our own', as well as continuing the nuclear build-up.[74] Although the paper included no costings it obviously had important cost implications. The State Department planners thought the defence budget might be pushed up from $13.5 billion to $35 billion, or even as high as $50 billion. The military planners were much more conservative and envisaged an increase to about $18 billion.[75] It seems likely that Truman would have allowed some increase in defence expenditure; but the recasting of strategy envisaged by some of the drafters would only be possible in the crisis atmosphere which engulfed American policy-makers after the outbreak of a shooting war in Korea. In fiscal year 1951 expenditure on the armed forces reached $48 billion and in fiscal year 1952 nearly $61 billion.[76]

THE CHINESE ROAD TO THE COLD WAR

Chinese political development, in many ways, ran at a tangent to developments in world politics. At the beginning of 1947 the country was wracked by a civil war which had proceeded in fits and starts since the 1920s. China was recognised as a great power and was one of the five permanent members of the UN security council but it was the Nationalist government of the Kuomintang (KMT) led by Chiang Kai-shek rather than the increasingly victorious Chinese Communist Party (CCP) which was recognised by both the United States and the Soviet Union. China's civil war was thus discrete from the European 'civil war' of 1939–45 which had ruptured the existing international order. Whereas the Second World War is usually regarded as coeval with this European war, beginning with the German invasion of Poland, China's Second World War had, arguably, begun in 1937 with the invasion of China by Japan and only finished with the Japanese defeat of August 1945.

The CCP was dominated by a faction, led by Mao Zedong, which had emerged victorious from intra-party power struggles in the 1930s. Most of the senior communist leaders directly linked to the Soviet Union had been ousted in those struggles. In 1947 the communist leadership could be described, if the romantic connotations of the phrase are jettisoned, as a 'band of brothers': each of the senior leaders had functioned in both military and political roles during the civil war. Mao was the outstanding *primus inter pares* but there was, in the late 1940s, a collegial aspect in both decision-making and the implementation of decisions. There was also real political struggle between individuals and ideas rather than the in-fighting of courtiers around Stalin. China's emerging communist leadership was to play a central role in shaping the Cold War, largely because they possessed a certain latitude in deciding their own foreign-policy orientation. Mao may have needed Stalin but he was never his client.

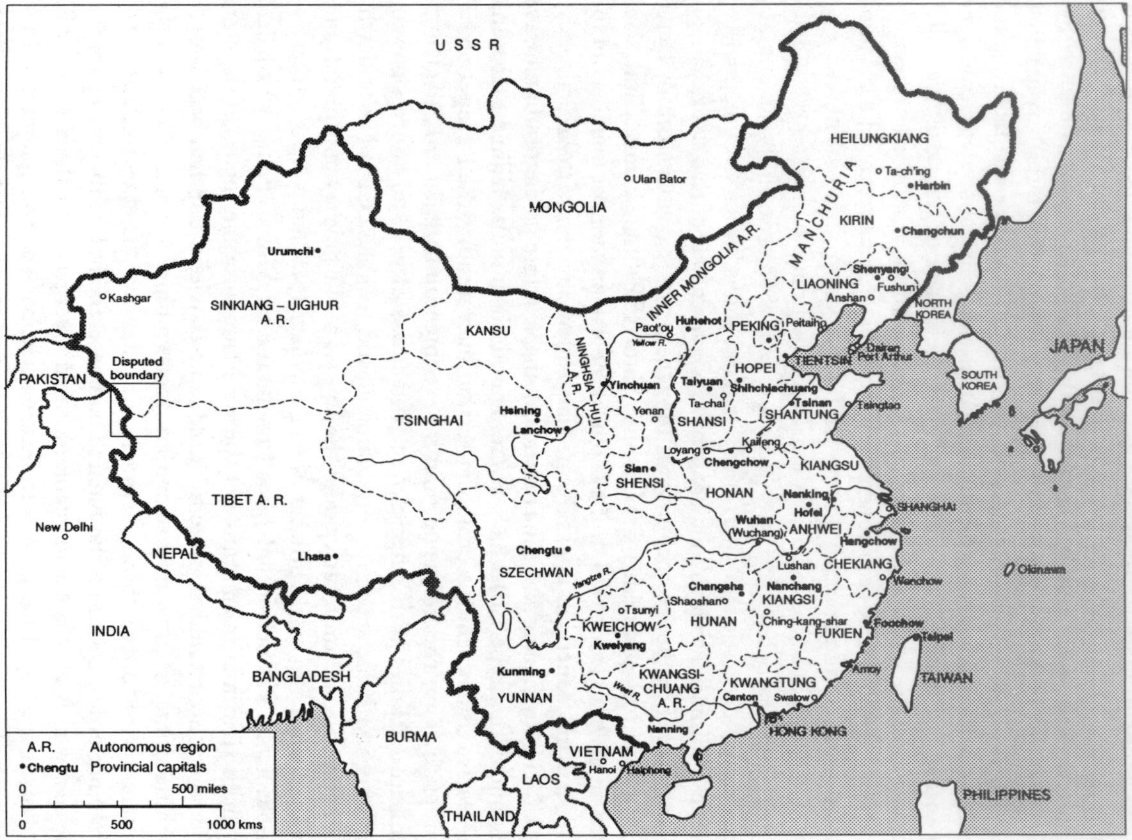
USSR
MONGOLIA
Ulan Bator
HEILUNGKIANG
Ta-ch'ing
Harbin
MANCHURIA
KIRIN
Changchun
Shenyang
Fushun
LIAONING
Anshan
NORTH KOREA
SOUTH KOREA
JAPAN
INNER MONGOLIA A.R.
Urumchi
Kashgar
SINKIANG – UIGHUR A.R.
KANSU
Disputed boundary
PAKISTAN
TSINGHAI
Hsining
Lanchow
NINGHSIA - HUI A.R.
Yinchuan
Paot'ou
Yellow R.
Huhehot
PEKING
Peitaiho
Dairen
Port Arthur
TIENTSIN
HOPEI
Shihchiachuang
Taiyuan
Ta-chai
Yenan
SHANSI
Tsinan
Tsingtao
SHANTUNG
Loyang
Kaifeng
Chengchow
Sian
SHENSI
KIANGSU
HONAN
Nanking
Hofei
SHANGHAI
Wuhan
(Wuchang)
ANHWEI
Hangchow
TIBET A. R.
New Delhi
NEPAL
Lhasa
Chengtu
SZECHWAN
Yangtze R.
Lushan
CHEKIANG
Okinawa
Wenchow
Changsha
Shaoshan
Nanchang
KIANGSI
Tsunyi
HUNAN
Ching-kang-shan
KWEICHOW
Kweiyang
FUKIEN
Foochow
Taipei
INDIA
TAIWAN
Amoy
BANGLADESH
Kunming
YUNNAN
KWANGSI-CHUANG A.R.
West R.
KWANGTUNG
Canton
Swatow
Nanning
HONG KONG
BURMA
VIETNAM
Hanoi
Haiphong
LAOS
THAILAND
PHILIPPINES
A.R. Autonomous region
Chengtu Provincial capitals
0 500 miles
0 500 1000 kms

Map 2 China

Mao had made his distance from Stalin clear in August 1946 when he posited the existence of a 'vast intermediate zone', of which China was a key part, owing allegiance to neither the United States nor the Soviet Union. Within this zone the A-bomb was irrelevant to the conduct of international politics; in Mao's famous phrase it was a 'paper tiger'. The concept of the 'intermediate' zone was implicitly anti-Stalinist. The 'anti-imperialist camp' was not simply an extension of Soviet power. In the same way indigenous revolutions were not simply a gambit the Soviet leadership could use in the conduct of its foreign policy but one of the key factors in international politics.[77] If Mao was implicitly anti-Soviet, his rhetoric was explicitly anti-American. He contended that 'US imperialists ... draw up a plan for enslaving the world, to run amok like wild beasts in Europe, Asia and other parts of the world'. In other words the Americans would attempt to subvert the intermediate zone because of their own internal crisis. 'The economic power of US imperialism', Mao maintained, 'is confronted with unstable and daily shrinking domestic and foreign markets. The further shrinking of these markets will cause economic crises to break out ... Irreconcilable domestic and international contradictions, like a volcano, menace US imperialism every day'.[78] China, for Mao, was a nexus of this struggle.

Mao's belief in the internal crisis of capitalism may have been drawn from the same sources as Stalin's similar belief, but CCP foreign policy was also based on the conviction that China had been a peculiarly unfortunate victim of European and American imperialism. The underlying theme of CCP policy was a form of nationalism: China must be cleansed of foreign domination. Mao concluded: 'the imperialists have always looked down on the Chinese people. We need to teach them a good lesson, so that their minds will no longer be so muddled.'[79] Thus the 'cleansing' was to have three concrete aims: to overturn all unequal treaties with other powers; to end privileges and concessions to foreigners in China; and to reunify China to include Manchuria in the north and Taiwan in the south fully under the control of the government in Peking. Mao explained this well-spring of Chinese policy to Stalin's envoy, Anastas Mikoyan, who was berated for three days at the beginning of February 1949.[80] In April 1949 Zhou Enlai, soon to be the prime and foreign minister of the new Chinese state, declared that 'no country can any longer interfere in China's domestic affairs. To this end we have struggled for more than a hundred years!' His statement had something of sting in the tail, however, since he added 'we should not even depend on the Soviet Union and the new democracies'.

As early as 1946 Zhou had reportedly told George Marshall that 'we will certainly lean to one side; however, the extent depends on your policy towards us'. In other words the new China would be linked to the Soviet Union in some way but whether that link would be exclusive rested on a Chinese judgement of how best they could secure their independence. In 1949 Mao still maintained that 'the Chinese Communist Party should have an ally. If Chiang Kai-shek and the reactionaries form an alliance with the United States, the CCP must align itself with the Soviet Union. It is a fond dream of the United States to split China from the Soviet Union. However, the CCP cannot afford to make enemies of both sides; no force can prevent it from having two friends or even more.'[81]

At an early stage the CCP leadership were convinced that their international future lay with the Soviet Union. At one level this was seen as an alliance of two countries with comparable revolutionary experience. Yet this shared experience merely created the general preconditions for amity. The CCP actually wanted two things from the Soviet Union: investment in economic reconstruction and protection from outside intervention. For the Chinese this would be an alliance of convenience. They could not turn to the United States or Britain for economic aid since such aid might challenge the CCP's developing grip on political power. The CCP leadership urgently needed economic aid for two reasons. In the short term the ravages of the civil war needed to be ameliorated.[82] Yet this sought-after amelioration was simply part of larger plans for the reshaping of China's political economy. In September 1948 Mao told the CCP Politburo: 'the Soviet Union will assist us in preparing for the transition from the completion of new democracy to socialism, and first of all it will help us develop the economy'. The CCP needed to build a regime which would guarantee its own permanent hold on power. If a huge population was to be successfully controlled, the CCP had to 'solve the problem of clothing and food for the people and how to arrange production and reconstruction'. Further than this, however, the aim was 'not only to restore production but [to] strive to construct a new, modernised, and powerful national economy'. By the autumn of 1948, at the very latest, Mao had decided that the best way forward was to copy 'the Soviet experiences of the two economic recovery and reconstruction periods, that is, the periods after the success of the October revolution and after the end of the Second World War'. The most pressing necessity of this politico-economic programme was to secure the most direct route to political power through a 'reorganised and transformed' People's Liberation Army (PLA).[83]

In the immediate post-war period Stalin had not cared about the political complexion of China's government as long as it was weak. Stalin had two basic ambitions in his relations with China. First, he wanted to use China as a means of containing whichever Western power threatened to dominate East Asia. Second, he had every intention of preserving Russia's privileges and economic concessions in China. In 1945 he concluded a treaty with the KMT government. Ostensibly, this treaty was aimed at Japan. Stalin told T. V. Soong, the KMT negotiator, that, 'Japan will not be ruined even if she accepts unconditional surrender, like Germany . . . One should keep Japan vulnerable from all sides . . . then she will keep quiet . . . Japan will restore her might in 20, 30 years. [The] whole plan of our relations with China is based on this. Now our preparation in the Far East in case Japan restores her might is inadequate.' His views were not changed by the use of atomic power against Japan. Stalin couched the retention of Russian privileges in terms of the Japanese threat. It is worth noting that the 1950 Sino-Soviet treaty which replaced the 1945 version was still couched in terms of the Japanese threat. In 1945 it seemed likely, and in 1950 it was the case, however, that the United States would be the dominant power in Japan.

Stalin's approach to Asia began to change at exactly the same time as his approach to Eastern Europe. As one front closed down another was opened. Yet the opportunities for Soviet action in China were actually the product of internal Chinese developments: by the autumn of 1947 it had become clear to observers, whatever their political persuasion, that the CCP would defeat the KMT in the civil war. According to the recollection of the senior Soviet official Mikhail Kapista, 'proceeding from strategic consideration, Stalin advocated assistance to the Chinese communists but also understood the limitations of Soviet capabilities to shape the situation in China and to influence its policy. He often said that the Russian and Chinese revolutions were two different matters.' By May 1948, when Mao appealed directly to the Soviet leader for assistance in the reconstruction of China, Stalin had begun to see the Chinese revolution as worth dealing with in order to create a bulwark to Soviet power. He told the representative he sent to Mao, I. V. Kovalev, that, 'we will definitely render all possible assistance to the new China. If socialism is victorious in China and other countries follow the same road, we can consider the victory of socialism throughout the world to be guaranteed. No unexpected events can threaten us. Because of that, we must not spare any effort or resources in assisting the Chinese communists.' Thus in Stalin's schema China had an offensive and defensive role. He wanted the CCP to take on the oxymoronical role of gradualist revolutionaries, firmly under Soviet guidance. As he explained to Liu Shaoqi, a Moscow educated Chinese leader, 'the centre of revolution ... has shifted to China and East Asia'. At the same time he warned the CCP against overconfidence. In particular he vetoed a CCP assault on Taiwan in July 1949 since it would lead to clashes with American air and naval forces and could provide the pretext for an American assault on both China and the Soviet Union. He made clear that he had much more important priorities than Chinese national reunification, and suggested that Mao should have too. At the same time Stalin seems to have believed that a Sino-Soviet coalition, with the Soviets in the leading role, had a long-term likelihood of victory.[84]

At the beginning of 1949 Soviet protection against foreign intervention was far from being an entirely defensive measure. The Chinese leadership had a fairly astute grasp of likely American policy. As CCP forces prepared to move against the Nationalists in southern China the leadership certainly took into account 'the possibility that the US government may send troops to occupy some of the coastal cities and fight'. Even after the successful campaign south of the Yangtze the possibility that 'those imperialist countries, which were unwilling to see their failure in China' might 'make military intervention in China's affairs, just as the imperialist countries did to the Soviet Union after the Russian Bolshevik revolution' was actively considered.[85] On the whole, however, the CCP leadership was sanguine about these risks. 'According to our experience', Mao told Mikoyan, 'the military forces of the United States do not want to be involved in China's civil war.' They had intervened indirectly by supplying the KMT but since 'those wretches failed to satisfy the desires of their American bosses' the USA would be much more concerned with Europe than Asia. Thus it was unlikely that the CCP's 'ability to wage the War of Liberation to a successful conclusion' would be impaired. What really exercised Mao was the likelihood that 'the KMT forces are going to retreat to Taiwan and then they will confront us across the strait and refuse to engage in negotiations with us'. In this situation the CCP would face a major problem for 'what is involved here is the United States. Taiwan is actually under the protection of American imperialism.'[86] Mao had every intention of invading Taiwan as soon as it was militarily feasible. If this was to happen then an alliance with the Soviet Union was of fundamental importance. Only the Soviets could both supply the PLA with the necessary *matériel* for such an operation and play the pivotal role of preventing or deflecting American intervention.

A tie with the Soviet Union might make China an unappealing target for Western intervention but it was essentially an inoculation; the Soviets themselves were the potential interventionists in the north-east, in Manchuria, and in the north-west in Sinkiang. In June 1949 the CCP publicly declared its allegiance to the Soviet Union in a statement issued by Mao: 'Externally, unite in a common struggle with those nations of the world which treat us as equal and unite with the peoples of all countries. That is, ally ourselves with the Soviet Union, with the People's Democratic countries, and with the proletariat and the broad masses of the people in other countries, and form an international united front ... We must lean to one side.'[87] Yet this statement was not as unambiguously pro-Soviet as it seemed at first. The statement had been the subject of fierce debate within the Chinese leadership. Zhou Enlai had found it necessary to criticise those who 'still had illusions of US imperialism'. Significantly, Mao had rejected the attempt to retain friendly relations with both the United States and the Soviet Union, on the grounds that such an attempt would weaken the drive to seize and keep power. Some of those who had 'illusions' were anti-KMT non-communists, still a significant political factor in 1949–50, but there were disagreements even within the CCP Politburo.[88] It was argued that the Soviet Union was actually 'pursuing an aggressive policy' towards China. Outer Mongolia, which the Chinese believed should be integrated into the new China, was under effective Soviet control; Manchuria was a Soviet sphere of influence; the Soviet Union still adhered to the unequal treaty it had made with the Nationalists in 1945; the Soviets still held the port cities of Dairen and Port Arthur. All of these problems could be exacerbated if China became reliant on the Soviet Union politically and economically: such aid would never be unconditional.[89]

Even in August 1949 the CCP's envoy to Moscow, Liu Shaoqi, commented that 'if the imperialists choose a policy of recognition of the new government of China [the People's Republic of China (PRC) was declared on 1 October 1949], then we shall be prepared to establish diplomatic relations with them', although he went on to reiterate Mao's suggestion to Mikoyan that the Soviet Union should establish relations before any other power.[90] Perhaps the most revealing account of Chinese thinking was provided by an exegetical letter on Mao's statement written by Deng Xiaoping in July 1949. Deng twinned the 'lean to one side' policy with the Taiwan problem: 'we should quickly ... take the offshore islands and Taiwan ... at the same time we propose a foreign policy of "leaning to one side"'. According to Deng 'Chairman Mao says that this leaning is on our initiative, and it is better than being forced to lean to one side in the future [Deng's overt suggestion was that the 'forcing' would be done by imperialists, but the statement is obviously double-edged] ... lean to one side and *rely on ourselves*' (emphasis added: Deng was here talking about domestic policy but his words are, once again, double-edged).[91]

In 1949–50 Mao believed that the CCP had little choice but to ally with the USSR if the revolution was to survive and prosper. The party had to have funds for reconstruction. In January and February Mao went to Moscow to personally negotiate a formal Sino-Soviet treaty with Stalin. In order to do so Mao had to abase himself before the Soviet leader. Stalin drove a hard bargain. The protocols he attached to the treaty guaranteeing Soviet rights in China were regarded as 'two bitter pills' by the Chinese, which 'only imperialists would consider imposing'.[92] Despite the potential of the Sino-Soviet alliance Stalin remained extremely suspicious of Mao. When Kovalev visited Moscow in December 1948 to report on his mission, he noticed Stalin was 'keenly interested whose side the Chinese communists took on the then acute Yugoslav problem ... [from] February 1949 he repeatedly asked me in his radio messages about the genuine attitude of the Chinese communists'. Primed by Stalin's existing suspicions, Kovalev looked for and found evidence that the CCP still wanted to maintain a relationship with the USA and reported this to Stalin. Not only did the Soviet leader insist on keeping Soviet concessions in China, such as the Changchun railroad, but he insisted that a secret protocol was attached to the Sino-Soviet alliance which banned all third-party nationals from Sinkiang and Manchuria.[93] According to Kapista, even though Mao was 'extremely dissatisfied with the document ... Stalin wanted to totally exclude the American presence in Manchuria and Sinkiang'. Stalin was worried that the CCP either wanted to reach an accommodation with the Americans or to manoeuvre the Soviet Union into a war with the USA on its behalf.[94]

THE KOREAN CONTRIBUTION

Korea was formally annexed by Japan in 1910 after the latter's victory in the Russo-Japanese War of 1904–5. It was only taken from Japanese control after

Japan's total defeat in 1945. At the Potsdam conference in August, Korea was divided into two zones of occupation: a Soviet zone north of the 38th parallel and an American zone south of it.[95] At first sight, therefore, Korea seemed a virgin battleground for superpower struggle. Like Germany, a nation which had previously been regarded as a whole was divided; unlike Germany that nation had already been subjugated for 35 years. Also unlike Germany the potential resources of Korea were not regarded as a threat by either the Soviet Union or the United States. Korea was, however, to have fundamental influence on American approaches to the Cold War. Despite this, until June 1950, the United States was essentially reactive to events on the Korean peninsula. It played a key role in the reconstruction of the Korean state in the south, which was formalised in August 1948 by the setting up of the Republic of Korea, but this construction was mainly seen as an attempt to preserve the status quo at the end of the war. The Soviet Union played a much more active role in determining northern Korea's relations with its external environment, but it has recently become clear that the origins of the Korean War lay in the interaction of the three poles of the Soviet Union–Korea–China triangle rather than simply being a product of either a Soviet–Korean or indeed a Sino-Korean patron–client relationship.

In reorganising Korea into two separate states both the United States and the Soviet Union seized the idea of installing charismatic leaders whom they believed they could control. In the American case it was Syngman Rhee, a propagandist for Korean nationalism with patrons in the War Department and the Office of Strategic Services (OSS) who admired his virulently anti-communist rhetoric. Rhee was born in 1875 and had left Korea in 1905 to study in the United States, returning only briefly in 1910–11, before going into exile until 1945.[96] The Soviets chose Kim Il Sung, a guerrilla leader born in 1912, who had fought the Japanese in Manchuria and Korea and who had then fled to the Soviet Union in about 1940. In 1942 he was made a captain in a Korean battalion organised by the Soviets as a nucleus for a future Korean People's Army.[97] He too returned to Korea in 1945 with the Soviet occupying forces. Although Kim and Rhee were both initially dependent on their patrons, their propagandist skills, which had first recommended them, yielded domestic support in their respective zones. They had certain characteristics in common: they were both personally self-aggrandising, they were both ruthless, they were both adept at exploiting the geo-political sensitivities of the superpowers and they both had a vision of Korean national unity under their own unchallenged leadership.

Neither the Americans nor the Soviets were particularly at home in dealing with Korean affairs. Both were more concerned with its symbolism and its potential economic role in their own systems. For neither was the peninsula of above mid-level concern: it was not a country of overriding strategic importance. In consequence Korean client leaders, although lacking military or

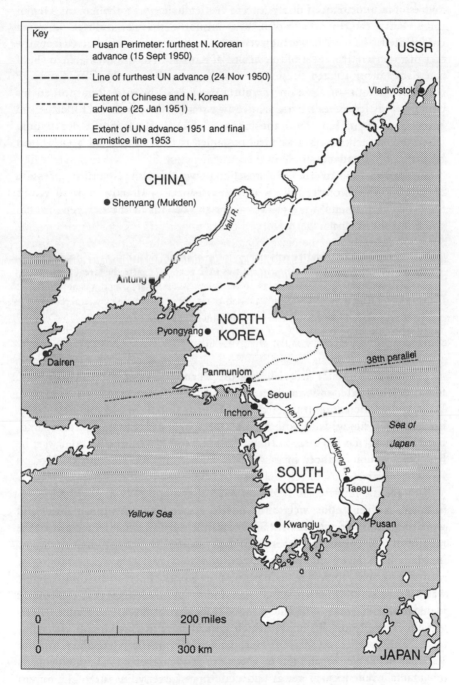

Pusan Perimeter: furthest N. Korean
advance (15 Sept 1950)

------ Line of furthest UN advance (24 Nov 1950)

-------- Extent of Chinese and N. Korean
advance (25 Jan 1951)

.... Extent of UN advance 1951 and final
armistice line 1953

USSR

Vladivostok

CHINA

● Shenyang (Mukden)

Yalu R.

Antung

NORTH
KOREA

Pyongyang ●

Dairen

Panmunjom

36th parallel

Seoul

Inchon

Han R.

Sea of
Japan

Naktong R.

SOUTH
KOREA

Taegu

Yellow Sea

● Kwangju

Pusan

0   200 miles

0   300 km

JAPAN

Map 3 The Korean War

paramilitary power in 1945, were soon able to create for themselves a wide degree of latitude. Rhee initially entered into alliance with the Korean Democratic Party (KDP) which was, as a senior American military observer commented, 'the most powerful force in Korea . . . their power derives from the fact that they control most of the wealth of Korea'.[98] He was then able to slight them after being elected President in 1948. According to the CIA, the KDP could not overthrow Rhee in the autumn of 1948 because they needed his personal prestige. Rhee's personal prestige stemmed from the fact that he had been absent from Korea for the entire course of the Japanese occupation, whereas any man of wealth who had remained in the country had been, almost by definition, a collaborator.[99]

Kim was also able to establish himself in power through physical suppression of enemies and the creation of a personality cult. Already in 1946 Kim's 'guerrilla companions' were claiming, for the benefit of the northern propaganda apparatus, that:

> this sort of person has an extremely strong power of attraction to others . . . the sublime
> good fortune of our guerrilla detachment was to have at our centre the Great Sun. Our
> general commander; great leader; sagacious teacher; and intimate friend was none other
> than general Kim Il Sung. Our unit was an unshakeable one following General Kim and
> having General Kim as the nucleus. The General's embrace and love are like the Sun's
> and when our fighters look up and receive the General, their trust, self-sacrifice and
> devotion are such that they will gladly die for him.[100]

Thus, from an early stage, Kim's propaganda stressed Korean suffering, fortitude, national identity and their ultimate manifestation in his own person. Propaganda is here important evidence of intent since it had so much to create: unlike Mao Zedong, with whom Kim's personality cult might be compared, Kim had not led a huge revolutionary movement in a successful civil war; he had been a junior officer in a struggle whose outcome was not decided in Korea.

Kim and Rhee were far from unaware of the wider Cold War. Kim, for instance, saw the importance of the Soviet atomic bomb in world politics and worried about the dynamics of the capitalist system as it was expressed in the relationship between the United States and Japan. Their interest in the international system was, however, almost wholly based on the possibility of maintaining and expanding their position in Korea. Their overriding interest was peninsular: specifically, unification under their own aegis. Each produced ideological constructs to mobilise support for and propagate this aim. Rhee's was the 'One-People Principle' which he launched in April 1949. He maintained that 'our race has been one race, our territory has been one unity, and our *Volkgeist* has been one, and one has been our economic class'. The rhetoric was of organic wholeness, of racial and class homogeneity. A 1948 CIA report explained the principle in more practical terms: 'Rhee has devoted his whole life to the cause of an independent Korea with the ultimate objective of personally controlling that country. In pursuing this end he has shown few scruples about the elements which he has been willing to utilise for his personal advancement, with the important exception that he has always refused to deal with Communists.'[101] On the other side of the new border Kim 'never believed in peaceful unification; he never had such an idea. He only stuck to the idea of armed unification.' According to one of his comrades in Russian exile, although Kim 'did not speak explicitly about armed unification . . . he was telling us we were future generals and would fight together'.[102] Kim too stressed the racial and class homogeneity of Korea. Although he did not publicly articulate the concept of *Juche* – putting Korea and things Korean first in all spheres of life – until 1955, it was implicit in all his statements and actions in the late 1940s. In 1947 he called for the creation of 'a unified, self-reliant, independent state free of foreign interference' which would develop 'an independent economy, an economic foundation to make our Motherland a wealthy and powerful and independent country'. Although Kim had to be circumspect, it is clear that 'free of foreign interference' meant free of Soviet as well as American interference. Mention of an independent economy was important. In March 1949 the Democratic People's Republic of Korea (DPRK), established in September 1948, signed economic agreements with the Soviet Union. The primary agreement dealt with Soviet exploitation of Korean mineral resources and Kim bargained long and hard over it. North Korean propaganda noted the unreliability of Soviet aid.[103] The 'absence of armed aid from international sources' during the anti-Japanese struggle before 1941 was noted. So too was the fact that only when Japan was 'fighting the whole world' did the Soviet Union see fit to declare war on it. The Soviets may have played a role in the final liberation but 'the Korean people at home and abroad overthrew Japanese imperialism . . . it's a fact that the Korean people fought Japan for a half-century'.[104]

The Soviet Union's relationship with the Korean Communist Party was indulgent.[105] It was a measure of their trust in Kim and their belief in his reliance on them that the Soviets withdrew their troops from North Korea at the end of 1948, some months before the Americans withdrew theirs from the south, when the original intention had been to keep 'Soviet troops in the zone north of the 38th parallel . . . for the same period of time as the American occupation of the remaining part of Korea'.[106] In early 1949, when Kim complained of repeated forays across the border by Republic of Korea (ROK) troops, Stalin told him: 'What are you talking about? Are you short of arms? We shall give them to you. You must strike them in the teeth. Strike them, strike them.'[107] There seems to have been a basic assumption in favour of aiding Kim. The telegram Stalin sent to Kim agreeing to establish diplomatic relations with the newly founded DPRK bears striking similarities to Khrushchev's later recollections. Stalin wrote: 'The Soviet government, invariably defending the right of the Korean people to create their united independent state, salutes the formation of the Korean government and wishes it success in its activity toward national rebirth and democratic development.'[108] Khrushchev recalled: 'You may ask why [the Soviet leadership supported Kim]. We sympathised with the North Koreans ... We wanted to see the people of South Korea overthrow capitalism and establish the power of the people just as it had been established in North Korea.'[109]

Both sides were ready to use military force to overcome the other. As soon as the two states were established, large-scale guerrilla activity was launched in an attempt to destabilise the south and to destroy its regime. The CIA estimated that in 1948 the South Korean Workers' Party (SKWP), the partner of Kim's ruling party in the north, had about 10 000 cadre members active in the ROK supported by 600 000 active supporters and two million members of front organisations, about 10 per cent of the south's population. The Rhee regime earned the respect of American observers through its ability to mobilise military, police and paramilitary forces to stamp out such guerrilla activity. A report written at the end of 1949 noted that:

> the suppression of Communism appeared to be increasingly successful. The government had mobilised its forces in many ways. Security forces were ruthlessly stamping out the Communist party organisation and guerrilla resistance, using whatever methods were considered necessary ... the Great Korean Youth Corps and Student's National Defence Corps were instilling patriotism and teaching military drill. Agents were everywhere watching actions and conversations; every organisation has its watchers for communist behaviour.[110]

The southern regime was also bellicose. In the autumn of 1949 Rhee stated: 'I am sure that we could take Pyongyang ... in three days. And an all-Korean border with Manchuria would be easier to defend than the 38th parallel.' He was immediately backed up; first by his Defence Minister who claimed that ROK troops 'were ready to drive into North Korea. If we had our own way we would have started already ... we are strong enough to march up and take Pyongyang within a few days'; and then by the ROK army's chief of staff who commented: 'we cannot help using force if [the DPRK] has an aggressive intention. We are training the Army for that purpose.'[111] In January 1950 the US envoy Philip Jessup reported talks with Rhee in which the latter 'explained that they would have a much better strategic defence line if their forces moved into North Korea and expressed confidence that they could defeat northern opposition'. Jessup drew the conclusion that '[Rhee's] statements lend credence to the belief that he has not objected when South Korean forces along the 38th parallel have from time to time taken the initiative'.[112] Rhee wished to secure two things: an American security guarantee against attack from the north and American military aid and help for the ROK army to enable an armed unification of Korea to take place. In the autumn of 1949, with the southern regime enjoying notable successes against communist guerrillas, the latter objective seems to have been uppermost. In early 1950 the former seemed more important. In June 1950 when John Foster Dulles, the leading Republican spokesman on international affairs and Truman's negotiator for the Japanese peace treaty, visited Korea it was the security guarantee which Rhee pressed upon him. 'Throughout the evening', recalled a UN observer, who was present, 'Rhee pursued the twin topics of a North Korean attack and how the US would respond.' Dulles brushed him off with vague talk about the international balance of power. 'Rhee kept asking, "But what if there is an attack?" '[113]

Kim Il Sung pursued a similar strategy to Rhee from the spring of 1949 onwards, seeking aid from both Russia and China for a campaign of armed unification, but with much more success. Kim pursued a two-pronged strategy. From his own resources he believed he could seriously damage the southern regime but he also lobbied Stalin intensively to give him Soviet military aid to conquer the south. Even though the guerrilla campaign of 1949 had proved to be a failure it remained an important part of the June 1950 invasion plan. Kim, who held talks with Stalin in Moscow in March and April 1949 and March 1950, continued sedulously to push the line that the south was an easy target. According to Khrushchev, Kim told Stalin he 'wanted to touch the South with the point of a bayonet . . . after the first impulse from North Korea, there would be an internal explosion and the people's power would be established, which means the same power as exists in North Korea.' M. S. Kapista recalled that 'after October [1949] the Koreans were impressed by the Chinese military victory and the fact the Americans had fled from mainland Korea completely; they were sure that the same could be accomplished in Korea quite quickly. They came with such a proposal to Moscow in November–December 1949.' Kim certainly managed to convince Soviet observers in Korea, most notably the Soviet ambassador Terentiy Shytkov, that this analysis was correct. In March 1950 Kim 'made four points to persuade Stalin that the United States would not participate in the war. (1) it would be a decisive surprise attack and the war would be won in three days; (2) there would be an uprising of 200 000 Party members in South Korea; (3) there were guerrillas in the southern provinces of South Korea; and (4) the United States would not have time to participate.' Pak Hon Yong, the leader of the SKWP, also attended this vital meeting. He argued with even more force than Kim that a '200 000 strong detachment of Communists in South Korea were ready to rebel at the first signal from the North, and that the population of the South were waiting for land reform such as those already conducted in the North' (these claims were falsified in June 1950 and Kim had Pak executed after the war).[114]

Kim also sought help from the CCP. He had been in contact with it during the civil war. In late 1946 refugees had fled from the Nationalists into Korea and had been cared for by their fellow communists. Some of Kim's lieutenants were drawn from organisations set up for Koreans in China by the CCP in 1942.[115]. Yet at the beginning of 1950 the CCP's sights were still firmly set on the final defeat of the KMT and the conquest of Taiwan. In the autumn of 1949 Mao had decided that 'Taiwan ought to be settled during the summer of 1950.' The CCP Central Committee's official policy was summed up in the statement: 'the liberation of Taiwan [is] . . . the most important task for the whole party'. The CCP was not overly concerned with Korea. In fact the CCP decided to go ahead with the demobilisation, reorganisation and rectification of the PLA as Mao had stated it would in January 1949.[116] The invasion of Taiwan was postponed until 1951 in order to ensure that the force used would be guaranteed of success.[117] Korea remained a side-show. Kim does not seem to have had an any more exalted view of the Chinese than he had of the Soviets. He remarked in 1946: 'we will help them, but we don't have to give them full support . . . these Chinese are too sluggish. If I had one division I would destroy the [Nationalist] army right now.' He was, however, perfectly willing to use the CCP for his own ends. Indeed Stalin insisted that he seek Mao's help and Kim visited the Chinese leader in May 1950. There seems little doubt that Kim played both ends off against the middle, emphasising his Chinese connections to Stalin and Stalin's support to Mao. It was, however, Stalin who was Kim's main backer until September 1950, although he was to let Kim down in June 1950 in the same fashion as he betrayed Mao in October 1950; by refusing, at the last minute, to allow key Soviet specialists to go into combat. In Moscow the Soviet leader ordered military aid to Korea to be stepped up. The value of such aid more than tripled between 1949 and 1950 and its effects were obvious to observers in Korea: 'as soon as Kim Il Sung returned home, the weapons began to arrive in huge numbers . . . the quantities were obviously bigger than before. This was the final stage in the preparations for war. On arrival, the weapons were immediately distributed among the troops deployed along the 38th parallel.' By 25 June 1950 the Korean army had been supplied with 258 T-34 tanks, 178 warplanes and 1600 artillery pieces. In addition the Soviet Union sent military advisers who formed a working command group. In May 1950 the Koreans presented their war plans to the Soviets. Although the Soviet military rejected some aspects of the Korean plans and wrote their own they accepted the optimistic Korean view of the war's course: the Soviet war plan envisaged the capture of Seoul three to four days after the invasion and complete victory within a month.[118]

Although Korean leaders were working within a system imposed on them by European powers at the end of the Second World War, the Korean War was created by those Korean leaders in order to achieve goals specific to Korea. North Korea's invasion of South Korea had a number of extra-peninsular reverberations. In the short term it redounded to the benefit of the Soviet Union. The Soviets were able to embroil the United States in a costly conflict whereas they risked only *matériel* and enjoyed the luxury of a laboratory for their equipment and combat techniques in a conflict which they did not see as strategically vital on its own terms. Khrushchev reports: 'What was Stalin's reaction [to the defeat of North Korea after MacArthur's Inchon landings]? Here I was a witness. Stalin said, "So what? If Kim Il Sung fails, we are not going to participate with our troops. Let it be. Let the Americans now be our neighbours in the Far East." [119] The subsequent involvement of China in the war made that country an anathema in American political life for two decades; it completed the alienation of American governments from the CCP. In the longer term the war provoked the United States and other Western countries to institute a massive build-up of military power. Korea also came to symbolise how close the Cold War came to 'hot war': in Syngman Rhee's July 1950 phrase: 'if we should lose the Cold War by default we will regain our free world in the end by a hot war regardless of cost'. Despite the war's Korean origins its outbreak virtually ended Korea's international political influence. North Korea was so far beyond the pale that it ceased to have any significant leverage on the future course of the Cold War: a pariah role which Kim Il Sung's regime embraced with some relish for the rest of the conflict. South Korea too became of marginal importance aside from its symbolic role. The Americans had no interest in Korea *per se*: the Truman administration pursued a policy of masterly inaction, even after Rhee made himself a virtual dictator in fixed presidential elections in August 1952, because they saw no-one to replace him and had no wish to disrupt their war effort on the peninsula. [120]

CHINA AND KOREA

Even after the North Koreans launched their invasion of the south on 25 June 1950 the Chinese leadership believed that they could continue to cultivate their own affairs. On 30 June Zhou commented that 'the change in the situation adds difficulties to our plan to attack Taiwan ... the present plan for our armed forces is to continue demobilising the ground forces, strengthen the navy and air force, and postpone the schedule for attacking Taiwan.' What actually brought Korea to the centre of Chinese attention was the link that the Americans made between war in Korea and the security of Taiwan. Before 25 June 1950 the Truman administration had been reluctant to give Chiang's regime any security guarantees. This had led to hopes in the CCP that it still might be able to invade Taiwan. In April 1950 Mao had instructed Liu Shaoqi to start producing foreign-policy statements 'in a more tactical way' with less emphasis on China's global role in the struggle between socialism and imperialism in order to avoid irritating American foreign-policy-makers. [121] Truman's decision to interpose the US Seventh Fleet between the PRC and Taiwan by taking naval control of the Formosa Strait struck at the heart of CCP policy. The PRC was already committed to supporting communist revolutions in Asia as a general principle. The Korean situation made such support a practical necessity. Mao made the changed situation explicit in a statement he issued on 28 June 1950: 'The US invasion of Asia can only touch off the broad and resolute opposition of Asian people. On January 5, Truman said in an announcement that the United States would not intervene in Taiwan. Now his conduct proves what he said was false ... The United States thus reveals its imperialist nature in its true colours ... the United States is unable to justify in any way its intervention in the internal affairs of Korea, the Philippines, and Vietnam.'[122]

It is doubtful that Chinese support for the North Koreans alone would have affected the course of the Cold War in the fundamental way the Korean War eventually did. It was the direct intervention of the PLA (under the cover of 'Chinese People's Volunteers' or CPV) in November 1950 which was to deeply shock the United States and its allies. This intervention did not occur because the CCP was particularly exercised by the fate of the Korean revolution but because it felt its own revolution was threatened.

The decision to intervene militarily in the Korean War was not an easy one for the PRC's leadership. Indeed it was the subject of intense debate between June and October 1950 during which the risks of not intervening were weighed against the risks of intervening. Fissures in opinion occurred within the Politburo, not between the CCP and non-communists. It would seem that both Zhou Enlai and the leading military figure Lin Biao opposed Chinese intervention. Zhou believed that the first priority was the unification and reorganisation of China itself. It was therefore essential to avoid a major war against the US with all the disruption and destruction such a war would entail. Lin was less subtle. 'We have certainty of success in defeating the Nationalist troops', he declared. 'The United States is highly modernised. In addition it possesses the atomic bomb. I have no certainty of success [fighting the US].' Lin and Zhou were not natural allies; indeed they were later engaged in a life-and-death power struggle in the 1960s which ended in Lin's mysterious death in 1971. Their views were refuted by Gao Gang, the party boss in Manchuria. He argued that 'if North Korea is occupied by the United States and South Korea, we could not avoid an antagonistic confrontation with the US and the fruit of our economic efforts might be destroyed'. Mao's own analysis, unveiled in August 1950, was similar: 'If the US imperialists won the war, they would become more arrogant and would threaten us. We should not fail to assist the Koreans. We must lend them our hands in the form of sending our military volunteers there. The timing could be further decided, but we have to prepare for this.'[123] Mao had no love for Gao who he believed was a Soviet puppet; three years after the end of the Korean War he was to have him put to death. There were obviously genuine disagreements about substantive strategy rather than strategy simply being a vehicle for factional conflicts.

Despite Mao's public dismissal of the atomic bomb as a 'paper tiger' there was also an intense sub-debate as to the likelihood of the United States using it either against China or against Chinese forces in Korea. Lin obviously feared such an American response. Marshal Nie Rongzhen countered that 'they might use it, but remember America no longer enjoys an atomic monopoly ... so they might be less eager to use it nowadays'. Those who favoured intervention could find at least three other reasons for discounting American atomic power. First, the United States had a small stockpile of atomic bombs whilst China had a small industrial sector. Second, attacks on Chinese troop concentrations in Manchuria would be regarded as too dangerous by the Americans because of the geographical proximity of the area to the Soviet Union. Finally, Chinese and American forces would be locked in 'jigsaw pattern warfare' in Korea, thus putting American forces at too great a risk if nuclear weapons were used too near the battlefront.[124]

Mao's full risk analysis is revealed in the telegrams he sent in the autumn of 1950. Since these telegrams were addressed to different audiences – Stalin; Zhou negotiating for Soviet support in Moscow; Peng Dehuai preparing the CPV for intervention – it is possible to compare their common elements. The successful American amphibious landing at Inchon on 15 September had prepared the way for the rout of North Korean forces and the advance of American and South Korean forces towards the Chinese border demarcated by the Yalu river. On 2 October 1950 Mao cabled Stalin to inform him of the Chinese intention to intervene and to request Soviet military assistance. According to Mao there were three main factors to be taken into account.

First, 'if Korea were completely occupied by the Americans and the Korean revolutionary forces were substantially destroyed, the American invaders would be more rampant, and such a situation would be very unfavourable to the whole East'. Second, a Chinese intervention would have a high chance of success 'if our troops could annihilate American troops [already] in Korea ... the Korean problem will end in fact with [the] defeat of American troops although the war might not end in name, because the United States would not recognise the victory of Korea for a long period'.[125]

Mao's third argument, however, was that China was running an enormous risk. If 'Chinese forces fail to destroy American troops in large numbers in Korea, thus resulting in stalemate', it was likely the United States would declare war on China. If this happened, the PRC had to be 'prepared for the possible bombardments by American air forces of many Chinese cities and industrial bases, and for attacks by American naval forces on China's coastal areas'. Such an outcome could threaten the revolution on two fronts: indirectly, by dislocating 'China's economic reconstruction already under way' especially in Manchuria;[126] but, as Mao told Zhou, 'if we do not send troops, the reactionaries at home and abroad would be swollen with arrogance when the enemy troops press to the Yalu river border'.[127] If this situation arose and China had not intervened to save Korea 'the Soviet Union will not intervene either once China faces disaster'.[128] Mao could not be swayed from this line even when Stalin reneged on the provision of Soviet air support for Chinese forces. Stalin's actions, in the aftermath of Kim's defeat by the Americans, were marked by extreme caution. Having initially promised the Chinese air support if they intervened on Kim's behalf, he then welshed on the promise and emphasised the dangers to the Soviet Union of a new war. He told Zhou Enlai on 10 October 1950, two days after the United States Air Force (USAF) had mistakenly attacked an air base inside the Soviet Union: 'For you it is possible to help the Korean people, but for us it is impossible because as you know the Second World War ended not long ago, and we are not ready for the Third World War.'[129] At this stage Stalin even refused to send military equipment to the Chinese with which to fight a war. One week after the Chinese intervened in the Korean War Soviet military aid was sent, including the provision of air cover for Chinese forces. Even then extraordinary precautions were instituted to prevent Soviet involvement in the war becoming public.[130]

China made a massive military effort in Korea between 1950 and 1953. Over those three years it deployed 2.3 million troops in Korea and suffered over 360 000 casualties. In the long term China's intervention in the Korean War shaped the structure of the Cold War. First, this military effort convinced the United States of the existence of a Sino-Soviet military bloc with the intention and capability of using full-scale warfare as a means of furthering its aims. Second, it insulated China from any meaningful contacts with American governments until the early 1970s. Third, it increased both China's existing reliance on and distrust for the Soviet Union.

THE UNITED STATES AND THE FAR EAST

The optimism felt by American policy-makers in 1949 had been dented by the Soviet A-bomb but it was shattered in Asia. Although the United States had a long-standing interest in the Pacific, reflected in its preponderant role in the recent defeat of Japan, the area was relatively unimportant to most of those who dominated American policy-making in the immediate post-war period. If there was a sense that the enfeebled societies of Europe could not run their own affairs in the absence of American leadership, that leadership had little regard for Asian civilisation. At best Japan was regarded as a pale reflection of Germany in terms of economic importance. In a speech preparing the way for the launch of the Marshall Plan, Dean Acheson called for measures to push forward 'with the reconstruction of those two great workshops of Europe and Asia – Germany and Japan – upon which the ultimate recovery of the two continents so largely depends'. Yet it was notable that no Marshall Plan for Asia emerged. This was not because plans for such an approach did not exist. The State Department submitted a proposal to the State–War–Navy Coordinating Committee (SWNCC) in July 1947 for a crash $500 million programme to revive the 'great workshop' of Asia by 1950. The Department of the Army, intimately involved in the occupation of Japan, explicitly proposed an Asian Marshall Plan in February 1948. All could agree with the CIA's view that 'Japan is the key to the development of a self-sufficient war-making complex in the Far East'. Most accepted Kennan's view that any hope 'of having stable civilisation in Japan [depended on re-opening] ... some sort of empire toward the south'. This would 'involve the export from the US to Japan of such commodities as cotton, wheat, coal and possibly specialised industrial machinery; the export from Japan of such items as low-cost agricultural and transportation equipment, textiles and shipping services to South East Asia; and the export from the latter of tin, manganese, rubber, hard fibres, and possibly lead and zinc to the US.' Such a policy would involve a Japan 'friendly to the United States ... industrially revived as a producer primarily of consumers' goods and secondarily of capital goods ... reliant upon the US for its security from external attack'. Unlike Germany, however, Japan was a group of islands wholly under American control. The threat of subversion was limited.[131] A threat to Japan could only develop if there was a major crisis in the region: the only source of that crisis would be China which was wracked by a civil war between the CCP and the KMT. Yet although the Americans had been intimately involved in efforts to resolve that civil war at the very time the Marshall Plan was being launched for Europe, a decision to cut losses in China had been taken. George Marshall himself had returned from a year-long mission in China to take up the post of Secretary of State in January 1947. He had concluded that although the CCP were true communists, their links with the Soviet Union were tenuous and that, more importantly, whatever the outcome of the war, China was a quagmire from which neither the Soviets nor the Americans could seize advantage. Although there certainly were those in Congress, the press and some sections of the bureaucracy who believed that America should wholeheartedly support the KMT as anti communist crusaders, President Truman regarded them as 'grafters and crooks'. In August 1948, as the KMT was visibly losing the military struggle, Marshall rejected frenzied calls for American military aid to stem the tide of defeat.[132]

The Truman administration did not see the situations in Europe and Asia as intimately linked. In the autumn of 1948, however, a European parallel became the ground on which much of US policy for the next two years was argued over. The Soviet–Yugoslav split seemed to have some explanatory relevance for the reaction of indigenous, armed communist movements to Stalinist pressure. For those who drew this parallel it seemed sensible to pursue a 'wedge' strategy to ensure that the victorious CCP did not come under direct Soviet control. A Kennan-inspired document argued that there were implicit tensions between the Kremlin and the CCP since the former was 'certainly covetous of Manchuria's ... natural resources, both to deny them to Japan and to develop the Soviet Far East'. In any event 'as for the bulk of China proper, the Kremlin is hardly likely to view it other than as a vast poorhouse, responsibility for which is to be avoided ... in any war in the foreseeable future China could be at best a weak ally or worst an inconsequential enemy.'[133] The wedge strategy came in two forms. The soft form suggested that the US could exploit these tensions by keeping its lines of communication to China open, by such means as trade. The hard form preferred to isolate the CCP as a means of exacerbating the implicit Sino–Soviet tensions. It was this latter view which emerged as the preferred option. In July 1949 Truman declared he 'did not intend in any way, shape, or manner to offer any comfort to communism in China'. This approach was enshrined in a long government document, the China White Paper, published in the following month. Dean Acheson, who had succeeded Marshall as Secretary of State, suggested that American policy should be more ambitious. The US had discarded the KMT as a civil warrior but would continue to try and overthrow the CCP, 'through appropriate clandestine channels'. If at all possible the US would also attempt to separate the island of Taiwan, to which the KMT retreated after their final defeat, from the rest of China. Acheson warned, 'we must carefully conceal our wish to separate the island from mainland control'. Acheson's caution reflected the surviving aspect of the wedge strategy: taking 'the long view not of 6 or 12 months but of 6 or 12 years ... the inevitable [Sino–Soviet] conflict ... our one important asset in China' should not be lost by the risk that the US would 'substitute itself as the imperialist menace to China'.[134]

That the Truman administration felt the need to justify their actions since 1945 in such a public manner as the White Paper was a product of US domestic politics. Republicans found that bipartisanship over European policy had reaped them few electoral rewards. They were shocked when Truman narrowly defeated Thomas Dewey in the November 1948 presidential election. In the Far East there was, at least at a rhetorical level, a policy gap to be exploited. In private many right-wing Republicans actually believed that developments in East Asia were more important than, and not necessarily bound up in, European events. A leading spokesman of the China lobby, Walter Judd of Minnesota, imagined

> a dissident Bolshevism loose in Asia. It would be free to renounce Russian influence. It would pick up the slogan of Asia for the Asiatics. It would have Manchuria, half the base of Jap war industry. It would have in prospect the resources of Indonesia, not only for its side [but] as a denial to us. It could rally half of humanity. It could turn the underprivileged line from focus on the underprivileged *class to the underprivileged nations. It could renew the conflict of haves versus have-nots* on international lines.

It was in their public rhetoric that the Republicans presented a fully realised global vision of the Cold War, with the added ingredient of accidental or even deliberate subversion within the American state. As freshman Representative, Richard M. Nixon declared in May 1949: 'apologists for the Chinese communists in the United States, both in and out of the State Department ... [are deceived by the] fallacious theory that Chinese Communists are different from

Communists in other countries and will not owe their allegiance to the Russian bloc in the event they come to power in China.'[135] The rebarbative Republican attack left little room for subtlety in US public policy. Although Acheson tried to portray the Soviet Union as a land-grabber in China, he was forced to conclude, in a much publicised address to the National Press Club, that 'the consequences of . . . Russian action in China are perfectly enormous. They are saddling all those in China who are proclaiming their loyalty to Moscow, and who are allowing themselves to be used as puppets of Moscow, with the most awful responsibility which they must pay for.'[136]

At the end of 1949 Acheson remarked regretfully to Oliver Franks, the British ambassador in Washington, that he believed the Far East would take up most of his time in 1950. He was regretful because although Asian issues were becoming pressing he had not altered his belief in its status as a secondary theatre. The congruence of a changed atmosphere in domestic politics and an increasing concern with military and nuclear issues within the bureaucracy was transformed into a reshaping of national policy by the eruption of a crisis on the Korean peninsula between June and November 1950. Looking back, bitterly, in 1953, Acheson observed that:

> this Chinese Communist advance into North Korea . . . was one of the most terrific disasters that has occurred to American foreign policy, and certainly . . . the greatest disaster which occurred to the Truman administration. It did more to destroy and undermine American foreign policy than anything I know about – the whole Communists-in-government business, the whole corruption outcry, was really just window-dressing put upon this great disaster.[137]

For Acheson and his contemporaries, harried after February 1950 by the most effective, and most vicious, Republican conspiracy theorist, Joseph McCarthy, it was never to be glad confident morning again. American policy-making was to be changed by a sense of crisis. In a sense the change was ironic since, although there is little convincing evidence that the United States wanted a war in Korea, there were times when the bureaucracy Acheson led seemed to suggest that Korea would not be a bad laboratory for conflict with the Soviets. Korea interested American policy-makers because, as a former part of the Japanese empire, it had been occupied by and divided between both the Soviet Union and the United States. American forces were withdrawn in 1949. Although some, such as Kennan, thought that Korea would be better back under Japanese control, at least southern Korea seemed to have a reasonably effective pro-Western regime. As Acheson himself noted: 'there are . . . places where we can be effective. One of them is Korea, and I think that is another place where the line has been clearly drawn between the Russians and ourselves.' As early as March 1947 an interdepartmental study involving Acheson as Under Secretary drew attention to Korea's ambiguous position:

Korea would be a military liability ... [the US has] little strategic interest in maintaining troops or bases in Korea ... [yet] control of all Korea by Soviet or Soviet-dominated forces ... would constitute a strategic threat to US interests in the Far East ... an extremely serious political and military threat to Japan ... It is important that there be no gaps or weakening in our policy of firmness in containing the USSR because weakness in one area is invariably interpreted by the Soviets as indicative of an overall softening. A backing down or a running away from the USSR in Korea could very easily result in the stiffening of the Soviet attitude in Germany or some other area of greater intrinsic importance to us. On the other hand, a firm 'holding of the line' in Korea can materially strengthen our position in our other dealings with the USSR![138]

A relatively low-level study had already made the national–regional–global links which were to become national policy in 1950–51. At the end of 1949, however, a major reconsideration of US policy in Asia did little to resolve Korea's position. In his Press Club speech Acheson outlined an American strategy based on a 'defensive perimeter [which] runs along the Aleutians to Japan and goes to the Ryukyus ... to the Philippine Islands. ... So far as military security of other areas in the Pacific is concerned, it must be clear that no person can guarantee these areas against military attack.' Acheson was later pilloried by his enemies for having invited an attack on Korea by having excluded it from this defensive cordon. In fact the speech laid more stress on the

great difference between our responsibility and our opportunities in the northern part of the Pacific area and the southern part of the Pacific area. In the north we have direct responsibility in Japan and we have direct opportunity to act. The same to a lesser degree is true in Korea. There we had a direct responsibility, and there we did act ... that we should stop half way through the achievement of the establishment of this country, seems to me to be the most utter defeatism and utter madness in our interests in Asia.[139]

Korea's status as a potential battleground was seemingly confirmed by Senator Tom Connally, chairman of the Senate Foreign Relations Committee, in May 1950 when he told a reporter:

I'm afraid it's going to happen, whether we want it or not. I'm for Korea. We're trying to help her ... [but Russia] can just overrun Korea just like she will probably overrun Formosa. ... any position like that is of some strategic importance. But I don't think it is very greatly important. ... A lot of them [government policy-makers] believe this: believe that events will transpire which will manoeuvre around and present an incident which will make us fight. That's what a lot of them are saying: 'We've got to battle sometime, why not now?'

There were certainly those within the bureaucracy who thought the United States was manoeuvring itself into a dangerous position in the Far East. A State Department comment on NSC 48, the document upon which Acheson's Press Club speech was based, called it 'an imposing collection of logical absurdities

... "reduction" quite different from the "containment" of Soviet power ... made perfectly clear by the reference to a possibility of "rolling back" communism. ... This concept of "reduction" goes far beyond anything I have ever seen used to describe US policy towards the USSR, and clearly implies military action of some sort.'[140] Equally clear, however, was that the United States was not prepared for military conflict on the Korean peninsula.

Once the conflict broke out the dynamics of decision changed. The military leadership became much more important. This was especially true for the US commander in the Far East, General Douglas MacArthur. MacArthur was instrumental in three major decisions in 1950 which tended to make Korea the centre of American policy: the interposition of the US Seventh Fleet to prevent any invasion of Taiwan by the Chinese in June; daring amphibious landings at Inchon which defeated the North Koreans in September; and the decision to cross the 38th parallel and reunify Korea by force in October.[141] In August MacArthur dismissed the possibility of Chinese military intervention but 'prayed nightly' they would intervene so that he could beat them. When Chinese forces poured south in November 1950, sweeping aside American forces and threatening to reunify the peninsula in the opposite direction, Acheson had to fight increasingly hard to maintain a sense of limited conflict. MacArthur wanted to bomb Manchuria, institute a naval blockade of China and insert KMT forces into southern China. The JCS were willing to back him on the naval blockade, to 'remove restrictions on operations of Chinese nationalist forces and give such logistic support to these forces as will contribute effective operations against the Communists'; and to recommend the bombing of Manchuria if US forces in Japan or Okinawa were threatened. On 30 November Truman publicly declared that Strategic Air Command was 'to be prepared to dispatch without delay medium bomb groups to the Far East ... this augmentation should include atomic capabilities'. Acheson argued that blockade and the KMT would be ineffective and the bombing of China did not address the central issue: the 'danger in centring all our concern on the Chinese'.[142] In making this argument he was forced into the position of articulating a fully globalised view of the Cold War. As Gordon Chang has remarked: 'both Acheson and Truman [now] saw the Beijing regime, for all practical purposes, as an instrument of Moscow'.[143] More than that the Soviet campaign was not limited to the Far East. Acheson argued in May 1951:

Korea is not a local situation. It is not the great value of Korea itself which led to the attack. It isn't that they wanted square miles in Korea. But it was the spearpoint of a drive made by the whole Communist control group on the entire power position of the West – primarily in the East, but also affecting the whole world. Surely their purpose was to solidify Korea – but it was also to unsettle Japan, Southeast Asia, Philippines ... and to affect [the] situation also in Europe. That is what the war in Korea is being fought about.[144]

Certainly, any thought of a Sino-Soviet split had to be abandoned. An attack on China could well provoke a global war: 'China is the Soviet Union's largest and most important satellite. Russian self-interest in the Far East and the necessity of maintaining prestige in the Communist sphere make it difficult to see how the Soviet Union could ignore a direct attack on the Chinese mainland.' These realisations had important implications for American policy. The Soviet Union could not be allowed to pursue its global strategy by means of war in Korea: 'instead of doing what the enemy set out to do, the enemy has done the exact opposite. Nothing they could have done would be more calculated to defeat their own purpose. . . . It isn't a Korean war on either side.' The most important implication of this global rhetoric was the decision to accelerate the militarisation of NATO. Apart from the financial implications, this was a relatively uncontroversial approach in itself but it implied a massively controversial element: the rearmament of the Federal Republic of Germany (FRG). As Acheson had remarked when the Federal Republic was founded: 'You cannot have any sort of security in Europe without using German power.'[145] Yet this long-term assessment was mediated through the Korean crisis. The representative of the British Chiefs of Staff in Washington noted:

A year ago, American strategy was content to liberate Europe. Today it insists on defending Europe. . . . Though the decision to send American troops to Europe has been taken, and the announcement has been made by the President, there is always the danger that the Americans may whittle down, or even withdraw, their offer. It has been made in the rush of the self-righteous enthusiasm – at times approaching spiritual elation – which the Americans are experiencing as the champions, as they see themselves, of freedom against aggression in the action they have taken in Korea. This mood may, however, evaporate, and evaporate quite quickly.

The leader of the American troops sent to Europe, Dwight Eisenhower, confirmed that their despatch could have been nothing other than a first step.

From the very beginning, some of our troop dispositions were visualised as temporary emergency measures. I think that none of us have ever believed for an instant that the United States could over the long term (several decades) build a sort of Roman Wall with its own troops and so protect the world. Not only would the ultimate cost be excessive, equally important is the adverse reaction that sometimes springs up in any country where foreign troops are stationed. . . . In addition, we have our own political situation at home.[146]

Acheson told the Europeans that American aid to NATO was part of a 'single package' which included the rearmament of Germany. It was the fact rather than detail of such rearmament which concerned the Americans; thus they were willing to agree to French plans for Germany to be subsumed in a European Defence Community (EDC) rather than be allowed a national army.[147] In 1951 the Americans proposed that an Anglo-American–French committee should draw up plans for the conventional defence of Europe by NATO, whose forces would include a large West German contingent. The committee was greatly influenced by an intelligence assessment drawn up by Eisenhower's staff which suggested that by 1954 NATO would be faced by up to 180 Soviet and 70 satellite divisions and over 20 000 combat aircraft.[148] Many questioned these figures. Churchill, for instance, pointed out that they were merely an aggregate of those produced by various NATO intelligence agencies. However, even he was willing to accept the 'working hypothesis' that Western Europe was threatened by 80 Soviet divisions – a 'sombre' situation which demonstrated that the West would find it almost impossible to match Soviet conventional strength.[149] The result of these deliberations was the Lisbon force goals of February 1952 which called for a NATO force of 96 divisions and over 9000 combat aircraft in 1954. Since the United States, Britain and France all believed that they were already at the peak of their military commitment, the call for German rearmament as well as increased reliance on nuclear weapons grew even stronger.[150]

Acheson was able to prevent the spread of the Korean War because army and air force leaders believed that the military situation could be stabilised even if the war was confined to the peninsula and because Truman, angered by MacArthur's arrogance and political ambitions, dismissed the leading proponent of expansion.[151] The cost of capping the commitment was that the Truman administration could not abandon the war as it drifted into stalemate and that on a wider stage US policy became extremely inflexible. The administration thus bequeathed to its successors three problems: an undifferentiated global vision which made it difficult to make policy based on specific regional circumstances; a major war; and a large crisis-driven military establishment and defence budget which proved very hard to reduce. Paul Nitze said in July 1952 that: 'We can in the next several years gain preponderant power' but 'to seek less than preponderant power would be to opt for defeat. Preponderant power must be the objective of US policy.' Melvyn Leffler has commented: 'The price of preponderance – the cost of linking Western Europe, Japan and their dependencies to a US-led orbit – was an unlimited arms race, indiscriminate commitments, constant anxiety, eternal vigilance, and a protracted cold war.'[152]

NOTES

1 *New York Times* (17 April 1947). The term 'Cold War' was suggested to him by H. B. Swope, former editor of the *New York World*.
2 President Truman's message to Congress, 12 March 1947, *Documents on International Affairs*, 1947–8 (London, Royal Institute of International Affairs), pp. 2–7.

3 Speech by the United States' Secretary of State, General G. Marshall, at Harvard University, 5 June 1947, *Department of State Bulletin* (15 June 1947), pp. 1159–60.

4 A. Resis, ed., *Molotov Remembers: Inside Kremlin Politics, Conversations with Felix Chuev* (Chicago, Ivan R. Dee, 1993), p. 59.

5 David Holloway, *Stalin and the Bomb: The Soviet Union and Atomic Energy, 1939–1956* (New Haven, Yale University Press, 1994), p. 260.

6 Nikita Khrushchev, *Khrushchev Remembers: The Glasnost Tapes*, ed. Jerrold Schechter (Boston, Little Brown, 1990), pp. 72–3.

7 Holloway, *Stalin and the Bomb*, p. 291.

8 N. Novikov, 'US Foreign Policy in the Postwar Period', 27 September 1946, *Diplomatic History*, 15 (1991), pp. 527–37.

9 Dieter Staritz, 'The SED, Stalin, and the German Question: Interests and Decision-Making in the Light of New Sources', *German History*, 10/3 (1992), pp. 274–89.

10 'Full Text of J. V. Stalin's Speech delivered on February 9', *Soviet News*, 1370 (11 February 1946), pp. 1–4.

11 J. V. Stalin, *Report to the Eighteenth Congress of the Communist Party of the Soviet Union (Bolshevik) on the Work of the Central Committee*.

12 Gavriel Ra'anan, *International Policy Formation in the USSR: Factional 'Debates' During the Zhdanovschina* (Hamden, Archon Books, 1983), p. 123.

13 Dmitrii Volkogonov, *Stalin: Triumph and Tragedy*, ed. Harold Shukman (London, Weidenfeld and Nicolson, 1991), p. 531.

14 Matthew Evangelista, 'Stalin's Postwar Army Reappraised', *International Security*, 7/3 (1982/3), pp. 283–311.

15 William McCagg, *Stalin Embattled* (Detroit, Wayne State University Press, 1978), pp. 244–7.

16 Bruce Parrott, *Politics and Technology in the Soviet Union* (London, MIT Press, 1983), p. 104.

17 Vladimir Rudolph, 'The Execution of Policy, 1945–47', in Robert Slusser, ed., *Soviet Economic Policy in Postwar Germany* (New York, Research Program on the USSR, 1953), pp. 36–42.

18 Holloway, *Stalin and the Bomb*, pp. 240–1.

19 Holloway, *Stalin and the Bomb*, pp. 156–71.

20 Holloway, *Stalin and the Bomb*, p. 318.

21 Holloway, *Stalin and the Bomb*, pp. 244–50.

22 Thomas Cochran, William Arkin, Robert Norris and Jeffrey Sands, *Nuclear Weapons Data Book: Volume IV Soviet Nuclear Weapons* (Grand Rapids, Ballinger, 1989), pp. 79–81.

23 Ra'anan, *Zhdanovschina*, pp. 59–60.

24 Director of the Policy Planning Staff to Under Secretary Acheson, 23 May 1947, *FRUS* 1947, III, pp. 223–30.

25 Scott Parrish, *The USSR and the Security Dilemma: Explaining Soviet Self-Encirclement, 1945–1985* (Ann Arbor, University Microfilms, 1993), pp. 197–204.

26 Ra'anan, *Zhdanovschina*, p. 69.

27 Scott Parrish and Mikhail Narinsky, *New Evidence on the Soviet Rejection of the Marshall Plan: Two Reports* (Washington, CWIHP/Woodrow Wilson Center, 1994).

28 Parrish, *Marshall Plan*.

29 Michael Hogan, The *Marshall Plan: America, Britain and the Reconstruction of Western Europe, 1947–1952* (Cambridge, Cambridge University Press, 1987), pp. 52–3.

30 Alan Milward, *The Reconstruction of Western Europe, 1945–1951* (London, Methuen, 1984), Table 17, p. 101.
31 Alan Milward, 'Was the Marshall Plan Necessary', *Diplomatic History* 13 (1989), p. 252.
32 Irwin Wall, *The United States and the Making of Postwar France, 1945–1954* (Cambridge, Cambridge University Press, 1991), pp. 77–95.
33 Ambassador in France to Secretary of State, 31 March 1947, *FRUS* 1947, III, pp. 695–6.
34 Ambassador in France to Secretary of State, 12 May 1947, *FRUS* 1947, III, pp. 709–13.
35 John Young, *France, the Cold War and the Western Alliance, 1944–1949* (Leicester, Leicester University Press, 1990) p. 146.
36 Ambassador in France to Secretary of State, 7 August 1947, *FRUS* 1947, III, pp. 729–30.
37 Volkogonov, *Stalin*, p. 533; Parrish, *Marshall Plan*; Eugenio Reale, 'The Founding of the Cominform', in M. Drachkovitch, ed., *The Comintern: Historical Highlights* (New York, Praeger, 1966), pp. 253–68.
38 A. A. Zhdanov, 'The American Plan for the Enthralment of Europe', *For a Lasting Peace, For a People's Democracy!* (10 November 1947). See also Giuliano Procacci, ed., *The Cominform: Minutes of the Three Conferences 1947/1948/1949* (Milan, Fondazione Giangiacomo Feltrinelli, 1994).
39 Staritz, 'SED'.
40 Parrish, *Marshall Plan*.
41 Parrish, *Marshall Plan*.
42 Memorandum by the Director of the Office of European Affairs to Under Secretary Lovett, 11 July 1947, *FRUS* 1947, III, pp. 717–22.
43 Parrish, *Marshall Plan*.
44 Ambassador in France to Secretary of State, 20 December 1947, *FRUS* 1947, III, pp. 819–20.
45 Reale, 'Cominform'.
46 Zhdanov, 'American Plan'.
47 Parrish, *Marshall Plan*; Christopher Andrew and Oleg Gordievsky, *KGB: The Inside Story of its Foreign Operations from Lenin to Gorbachev* (London, Hodder and Stoughton, 1991); Charles Gati, *Hungary and the Soviet Bloc* (Durham, Duke University Press, 1986); Karel Kaplan, *The Short March: The Communist Take-over of Power in Czechoslovakia* (London, Hurst, 1986); Thomas Hammond, ed., *The Anatomy of Communist Takeovers* (New Haven, Yale University Press, 1975).
48 Milovan Djilas, *Conversations with Stalin* (Harmondsworth, Penguin, 1962), pp. 99–144.
49 Melvyn Leffler, *A Preponderance of Power: National Security, the Truman Administration and the Cold War* (Stanford, Stanford University Press, 1992), p. 152.
50 Hannes Adomeit, *Soviet Risk-taking and Crisis Behaviour: A Theoretical and Empirical Analysis* (London, Allen and Unwin, 1982), p. 79.
51 Raymond Poidevin, *Robert Schuman: Homme d'Etat, 1886–1963* (Paris, Imprimerie Nationale, 1986), pp. 208–28.
52 Georges-Henri Soutou, 'France', in David Reynolds, *The Origins of the Cold War in Europe: International Perspectives* (New Haven, Yale University Press, 1994), pp. 96–120.

53 James Forrestal, *The Forrestal Diaries: The Inner History of the Cold War*, ed. Walter Millis (London, Cassell, 1952), pp. 454–5 and Lucius D. Clay, *The Papers of General Lucius D. Clay, Germany, 1945–1949*, ed. Jean Smith (2 vols., Bloomington, Indiana University Press, 1974).
54 Adomeit, *Soviet Risk-taking*, p. 95.
55 Ambassador to the Soviet Union to Secretary of State, August 1948, *FRUS* 1948, II, pp. 999–1007.
56 PPS 37, in Thomas Etzold and John Lewis Gaddis, eds., *Containment: Documents on American Policy and Strategy, 1945–1950* (New York, Columbia University Press, 1978).
57 Staritz, 'SED'.
58 Leffler, *Preponderance*, p. 285.
59 Herman-Josef Rupieper, 'American Policy Toward German Unification, 1949–1955', in Jeffry Diefendorf, Axel Frohn and Hermann-Josef Rupieper, eds., *American Policy and the Reconstruction of Germany, 1945–1955* (Cambridge, Cambridge University Press, 1993), pp. 45–68.
60 Lord Inverchapel to Secretary of State, 13 January 1948, *FRUS* 1948, III, pp. 3–6.
61 The Vandenberg Resolution. Approved by the US Senate, 11 June 1948, *Congressional Record*, 11 June 1948, p. 7791.
62 North Atlantic Treaty, 4 April 1949, *Documents on International Affairs [DOIA]*, 1949–50, pp. 257–60.
63 NSC 7, 30 March 1948, in *FRUS* 1948, I (Part 2), pp. 546–50.
64 JCS 1844/13 Brief of Short Range Emergency War Plan (Halfmoon), 21 July 1948, in Etzold and Gaddis, *Containment*.
65 Samuel Williamson and Steven Rearden, *The Origins of US Nuclear Strategy, 1945–1953* (New York, St Martin's Press, 1993), p. 85.
66 NSC 20/4, 23 November 1948, in *FRUS* 1948, I (Part 2), pp. 663–9.
67 David Lilienthal, *The Journals of David E. Lilienthal* (7 vols., New York, Harper and Row, 1964–1983), II: *The Atomic Energy Years, 1945–1950*, p. 502.
68 Williamson and Rearden, *US Nuclear Strategy*, p. 107.
69 Lilienthal, *Journals*, II, p. 577.
70 Lilienthal, *Journals*, II, p. 632.
71 Lilienthal, *Journals*, II, p. 580.
72 PPS 43, 23 November 1948, in *FRUS* 1948, III, pp. 284–8.
73 Paul Hammond, 'NSC-68: Prologue to Rearmament', in Warner Schilling, Glenn Snyder and Paul Hammond, *Strategy, Politics and Defense Budgets* (New York, Columbia University Press, 1962), pp. 267-378.
74 NSC 68, 14 April 1950, *FRUS* 1950, I, pp. 237–92.
75 Hammond, 'NSC-68'.
76 NSC 114/3, 5 June 1952, *FRUS* 1952, II, pp. 20–47.
77 Sergei Goncharov, John Lewis and Xue Litai, *Uncertain Partners: Stalin, Mao and the Korean War* (Stanford, Stanford University Press, 1993), p. 27; Michael Yahuda, *China's Role in World Affairs* (London, Croom Helm, 1978), pp. 43–7.
78 Michael Hunt, 'Mao and Accommodation with the United States', in Dorothy Borg and Waldo Heinrichs, eds., *Uncertain Years: Chinese–American Relations, 1947–1950* (New York, Columbia University Press, 1980), p. 227.
79 Shi Zhe (trans. Chen Jian), 'With Mao and Stalin: The Reminiscences of a Chinese Interpreter', *Chinese Historians*, 5/1 (spring 1992), pp. 35–46.

80 Shi Zhe, 'With Mao'.
81 Goncharov *et al.*, *Uncertain Partners*, p. 49.
82 Hunt, 'Mao and Accommodation', pp. 185–233.
83 Shi Zhe, 'With Mao'.
84 Goncharov *et al.*, *Uncertain Partners*, pp. 1–75.
85 Chen Jian, *The Sino-Soviet Alliance and China's Entry into the Korean War* (Washington, CWIHP/Woodrow Wilson Center, CWIHP *Working Paper* No. 1).
86 Shi Zhe, 'With Mao'.
87 Chen Jian, *China's Entry*.
88 Chen Jian, *China's Entry*.
89 Goncharov *et al.*, *Uncertain Partners*, pp. 61–75.
90 Goncharov *et al.*, *Uncertain Partners*, pp. 38–51.
91 Bo Yibo (trans. Zhai Qiang), 'The Making of the "Leaning to One Side" Decision', *Chinese Historians*, 5/1 (spring 1992), pp. 57–62.
92 Goncharov *et al.*, *Uncertain Partners*, p. 122.
93 Sergei Goncharov interview with Ivan Kovalev, *Far Eastern Affairs* (1992), no. 1, pp. 100–16 and no. 2, pp. 94–111.
94 Goncharov *et al.*, *Uncertain Partners*, p. 123.
95 Kathryn Weathersby, *Soviet Aims in Korea and the Origins of the Korean War, 1945–1950: New Evidence from Russian Archives* (Washington, CWIHP/Woodrow Wilson Center, 1993).
96 Bruce Cumings, *The Origins of the Korean War* (2 vols., Princeton, Princeton University Press, 1981–90), I: *Liberation and Emergence of Separate Regimes, 1945–1947*, p. 188.
97 Goncharov *et al.*, *Uncertain Partners*, p. 131.
98 Cumings, *Korean War*, II: *The Roaring of the Cataract, 1947–1950*, p. 186.
99 Cumings, *Korean War*, II, p. 219.
100 Cumings, *Korean War*, II, p. 291.
101 Cumings, *Korean War*, II, pp. 226–7.
102 Goncharov *et al.*, *Uncertain Partners*, pp. 131–2.
103 Weathersby, *Soviet Aims*.
104 Cumings, *Korean War*, II, p. 348.
105 Weathersby, *Soviet Aims*.
106 Weathersby, *Soviet Aims*.
107 Goncharov *et al.*, *Uncertain Partners*, p. 135.
108 Weathersby, *Soviet Aims*.
109 Khrushchev, *Khrushchev Remembers: The Glasnost Tapes*, pp. 144–7.
110 Cumings, *Korean War*, II, pp. 237–90.
111 Gye-Dong Kim, 'Who Initiated the Korean War?' and Gregory Henderson, 'Korea, 1950', in James Cotton and Ian Neary, eds., *The Korean War in History* (Manchester, Manchester University Press, 1989), pp. 33–50 and 175–82.
112 Gye-Dong Kim, 'Who Initiated?', in Cotton and Neary, *Korean War*.
113 Cumings, *Korean War*, II, p. 506.
114 Goncharov *et al.*, *Uncertain Partners*, pp. 143–4.
115 Hak-Joon Kim, 'China's Non-Involvement in the Origins of the Korean War: A Critical Reassessment' in Cotton and Neary, *Korean War*, pp. 11–32.
116 Hao Yufan and Zhai Zhihai, 'China's Decision to Enter the Korean War Revisited', *China Quarterly*, 121 (March 1990), pp. 94–115.
117 Goncharov *et al.*, *Uncertain Partners*, pp. 148–9.

118 Goncharov *et al.*, *Uncertain Partners*, pp. 147–55.
119 Khrushchev, *Glasnost Tapes*, p. 147.
120 Edward Keefer, 'The Truman Administration and the South Korean Political Crisis of 1952: Democracy's Failure', *Pacific Historical Review* (1991), pp. 145–68.
121 Goncharov *et al.*, *Uncertain Partners*, pp. 152–8.
122 Goncharov *et al.*, *Uncertain Partners*, p. 157.
123 Goncharov *et al.*, *Uncertain Partners*, pp. 159–87.
124 Goncharov *et al.*, *Uncertain Partners*, pp. 164–7.
125 Mao to Stalin, 2 October 1950 and Mao to Peng, 23 October 1950, in Li Xiaobing, Wang Xi and Chen Jian, 'Mao's Dispatch of Chinese Troops to Korea: Forty-Six Telegrams, July–October 1950', *Chinese Historians*, 5/1 (1992), pp. 63–86.
126 Mao to Zhou, 13 October, in Chen Jian, *China's Entry*.
127 Mao to Zhou, 13 October, in Chen Jian, *China's Entry*.
128 Goncharov *et al.*, *Uncertain Partners*, p. 182.
129 Goncharov *et al.*, *Uncertain Partners*, p. 189.
130 Jon Halliday, 'Secret War of the Top Guns', *The Observer* (5 July 1992), pp. 53–4.
131 Michael Schaller, 'Securing the Great Crescent: Occupied Japan and the Origins of Containment in Southeast Asia', *Journal of American History*, 69/2 (September 1983) pp. 393–414.
132 Gordon Chang, *Friends and Enemies: The United States, China and the Soviet Union, 1948–1972* (Stanford, Stanford University Press, 1990), pp. 12–13.
133 NSC 34, 13 October 1948, in Etzold and Gaddis, *Containment*, pp. 240–7.
134 Chang, *Friends and Enemies*, pp. 60–1.
135 Chang, *Friends and Enemies*, pp. 25–6.
136 'Crisis in Asia', Remarks by Secretary Acheson made before the National Press Club, Washington on 12 January 1950, *Department of State Bulletin* (23 January 1950), pp. 111–18.
137 William Stueck, *The Road to Confrontation: American Policy Toward China and Korea, 1947–1950* (Chapel Hill, University of North Carolina Press, 1981), p. 3.
138 Cumings, *Korean War*, II, p. 46.
139 Acheson, 'Crisis'.
140 Cumings, *Korean War*, II, p. 167.
141 Thomas Christensen, 'Threats, Assurances and the Last Chance for Peace: The Lessons of Mao's Korean War Telegrams', *International Security*, 17 (1992), pp. 122–54.
142 Rosemary Foot, *The Wrong War: American Policy and the Dimensions of the Korean Conflict, 1950–1953* (Ithaca, Cornell University Press, 1985), pp. 88–130; Roger Dingman, 'Atomic Diplomacy During the Korean War', *International Security*, 13 (1988–9), pp. 50–91.
143 Chang, *Friends and Enemies*, p. 77–8.
144 Cumings, *Korean War*, II, p. 628.
145 Leffler, *Preponderance*, p. 322.
146 Herman-Josef Rupieper, 'German Unification'.
147 Norbert Wiggershaus, 'The Problem of West German Military Integration, 1948–1950', in Norbert Wiggershaus and Roland Foerster, *The Western Security Community* (Oxford, Berg, 1993), pp. 375–412.
148 PREM11/369, MC.33, 'Estimate of the Relative Strength and Capabilities of NATO and the Soviet Bloc Forces at Present and in the Immediate Future', Report by

Standing Group, 10 November 1951. Public Record Office, Kew.
149 PREM11/369, Winston Churchill to Minister of Defence, 13 March 1952.
150 PREM11/369, BC(P)(53) 3rd, 6 December 1953.
151 Foot, *Wrong War*, pp. 131–73.
152 Leffler, *Preponderance*, p. 19.

3

Theories of Victory, 1953–1962

THE SOVIET WORLD VIEW

Stalin's death transformed the possibilities for Soviet Cold War policy. All of the leading figures in the party had been deeply implicated in his regime. Political action for these senior figures had consisted of predicting, interpreting and serving the dictator's demands. Independent thought was not welcome; indeed it was dangerous. After 1953 political struggle within the top leadership was intense and could lead to humiliation but rarely death. Thus, after 1953, there was more scope for genuine political manoeuvring within the oligarchy. There was also the possibility that the 'secondary élite' would be allowed to develop competing ideas about the international system. Cold War policy became both the tool and the result of intra-Presidial struggle. Between 1953 and 1957 Soviet political life was marked by a succession of eclipses: of Beria in 1953, of Malenkov in 1955, of the anti-party group, and particularly of Molotov in 1957, and of Marshal Zhukov later in the same year. Disputes were primarily about power in the Soviet Union rather than international policy. The most notable proof is the struggle between Malenkov and Khrushchev, resulting in the fall of the former and the subsequent adoption of much of his foreign-policy programme by the victor. Khrushchev manufactured crises over Germany, which had been central to Soviet concerns since 1945, over Cuba, which had not, and attempted to contain a crisis, the Sino-Soviet split, which had massive ideological and pragmatic implications for the Soviet Union's world position. The most interesting aspect of these nine years, however, is the remarkable continuity of Soviet élite belief in the face of internal and external vicissitudes. The West was viewed as inherently hostile but malleable in the face of Soviet strength. What shifted was the 'time frame' for Soviet victory. In 1958 and 1962 Khrushchev believed the West could be forced into concessions by a 'short, sharp shock'. His assumptions were demonstrably falsified by events and thus were replaced by a belief in the gradual aggrandisement of socialism.

After Stalin's funeral, Beria, Malenkov and Molotov all spoke in favour of 'peaceful coexistence' between socialism and capitalism. Despite this public unity there were actually deep divisions amongst the new leadership. Not only did they distrust each other but they differed as to the role of the party. Molotov saw it as the vanguard of social transformation and all competing sources of authority as hostile. He portrayed a world deeply divided between socialism and capitalism and involved in a struggle which would end in violence. For him concessions would weaken the socialist camp, although declarations of peacefulness were a legitimate way of dividing the imperialists. In his memoirs Molotov accused Beria of being 'not particularly interested in the essential question of politics' and believing that Soviet 'strength exists such that no-one will touch us'. He also accused Khrushchev of being motivated more by Russian patriotism than Soviet ideology. Both Molotov and Khrushchev identified the interests of the world communist movement with Soviet state interests. Whilst these interests were identical for Molotov, they were overlapping but distinct for Khrushchev. As early as the July 1953 plenum Khrushchev's rhetoric stressed the international balance of power particularly between the USSR and the USA rather than the struggle between social systems.[1] Malenkov too was concerned with this balance of power. In 1953 he highlighted 'serious successes' in lowering international tension and argued that it would be 'a crime against humanity' to let them flare up once more. He did not use the non-traditionalist argument that the internal dynamics of capitalism had changed, but simply noted that Soviet military strength and possession of the H-bomb obliged the capitalist world to follow the path of peaceful coexistence. He received some support from Anastas Mikoyan who declared that all Soviet–American problems could be solved by negotiation and that trade should increase and an arms control process be set in motion. Malenkov was, however, opposed by Khrushchev and hard-liners such as Kliment Voroshilov who declared: 'we live in capitalist encirclement all the same'.[2]

Once he had defeated Malenkov in February 1955, Khrushchev was free to change his position and turn on the hard-liners. In 1957 the 'anti-party group', which included Molotov and, as a means of final disgrace, Malenkov, was condemned for resisting the policy of peaceful coexistence. This contrasted with previous succession struggles when the accusation had been softness in opposing imperialism. In March 1958 Khrushchev and Mikoyan explicitly renounced the doctrine of capitalist encirclement. 'All [are] to understand', they announced, 'that the Soviet Union long ago emerged from "capitalist encirclement", in both the geographical and political senses of the concept.' It was no longer clear 'who encircles whom, the capitalist countries the socialist states, or vice versa'. To a large extent their view of the international system rested upon a series of assumptions about the 'main adversary', the United States. Khrushchev had developed a dualistic view about the American élite. It was divided between die-hard anti-Soviet capitalists who would never show any flexibility and 'realists' who perceived Soviet strength and knew they must compromise in order to ensure their own survival. Khrushchev felt a need to be informed of these conflicting tendencies and re-established the institute, suppressed under Stalin, which analysed them in 1956.

Khrushchev claimed that even after 1957 he had to contend with the views of some of his Presidial colleagues who rejected the possibility that any imperialists could be realists. His opponents, led by Mikhail Suslov and Frol Kozlov, supported the Chinese view that the Soviet Union should use its military strength to pursue an aggressive strategy against capitalism and cause its collapse. According to an interview Khrushchev gave to *Time* magazine,

> his own idea always had been to have our two countries live together peacefully and compete economically not militarily ... 'Things were going well until one event happened. From the time Gary Powers was shot down in a U-2 over the Soviet Union, I was no longer in full control ... those who felt America had imperialistic intentions and that military strength was the most important thing had the evidence they needed, and when the U-2 incident occurred, I no longer had the ability to overcome that feeling'.

Yet Khrushchev's thinking was not separated from that of men like Frol Kozlov, however intense their political rivalries, by too great a distance. Whilst Khrushchev believed Soviet positions of strength would cause American 'realists' to make concessions, others on the Presidium believed concessions could be forced from recalcitrant monopoly capitalists by Soviet positions of strength. The main internal struggle, however, concerned the *form* of Soviet military power: the primacy of strategic rocket forces or 'balanced' armed forces.

Dualism was always the hallmark of Khrushchev's thought about the Cold War. In mid-1958 he could claim that 'alongside the active proponents of peace [in the West] there are still hotheads who not only dream of war but prepare for it. Unfortunately, such hotheads occupy high posts in several states.' A year later he could see the other side of the coin and remarked that '[even the most aggressive Western leaders] were not that stupid: they realise what the consequences for them might be if war is unleashed against the socialist countries ... [even Dulles] showed a more sober understanding of the evolved international situation in the last months of his life.'[3] Khrushchev certainly favoured the election of Kennedy rather than Nixon in November 1960. The Soviet embassy in Washington had reported in July 1960 that Kennedy was a 'typical pragmatist' and under his presidency there was 'a possibility of mutually satisfactory settlement ... on the basis of mutual willingness to avoid nuclear war'. Khrushchev himself announced in May 1961 that 'the coming to power of a new government in the USA has created in certain people a hope that the new leading officials of the United States will show a more reasonable approach to the solution of international questions'. Yet a month earlier he described the powers running the Kennedy administration as 'Rockefeller' (i.e. globally minded monopoly capitalists). By August 1961 Khrushchev had decided that America

> is a barely governed state ... Kennedy hardly influences the direction and development
> of policies ... [Congress is] very similar to our *Veche* of Novgorod ... Hence everything
> is possible in the United States ... War is also possible. ... When our 'friend' Dulles
> was alive there was more stability ... [he] would reach the brink, as he put it himself,
> but would never leap over the brink, and still retained his credibility ... [if Kennedy
> pulls back] he will be called a coward ... [he is] too much of a light-weight. And the
> state is too big, the state is powerful, and it poses certain dangers.[4]

It could be argued that Khrushchev's tergiversation was the product of factional struggle within the Kremlin or the 'hard cop, soft cop' tactics of his personal diplomacy. Kozlov certainly sneered at the possibility of 'relying on the mercy of god and the "good sense" of military maniacs'. Yet Khrushchev's thinking about the Cold War had a certain amount of internal consistency: the United States could be manipulated by the Soviet Union taking up positions of strength but due consideration had to be given to its military power.

At the absolute apogee of the Cold War on 26 October 1962 (the Soviets offered to withdraw their missiles from Cuba the next day) Khrushchev outlined his thinking, sharpened by a real fear of nuclear catastrophe:

> You can regard us with distrust, but, in any case you can be calm in this regard, that we
> are of sound mind and understand perfectly well that if we attack you, you will respond
> in the same way. But you too will receive the same that you hurl against us. And I think
> that you will also understand this ... We, however, want to live and do not at all want
> to destroy your country. We want something quite different: to compete with your
> country on a peaceful basis. We quarrel with you, we have differences on ideological
> questions. But our view of the world consists in this, that ideological questions, as well
> as economic problems, must be solved on the basis of peaceful competition, i.e. as this
> is understood in capitalist society, on the basis of competition. We have proceeded ...
> from the fact that the peaceful coexistence of the two different social-political systems
> now existing in the world is necessary, that it is necessary to assure a stable peace ... Let
> us normalise relations.[5]

What the Soviet leader did not add for his American audience were two important riders to his statement. 'It's said that we cannot believe the enemy', he told Fidel Castro in January 1963. 'We always held, hold and will always hold this position.'[6] Second, Khrushchev was convinced that the Soviet Union was winning the 'peaceful competition'.

In 1956 Khrushchev had declared that there were many possible roads to socialism including the election of communist governments in democratic elections. The two 'camps' were joined by the third 'zone of peace' made up of 'peace-loving European and Asian states which have proclaimed non-participation in blocs as a principle of their foreign policy' (a reference to the non-aligned movement initiated at the 1955 Bandung conference). According to Khrushchev it was the existence of the socialist world which made neutralism possible since the new correlation of forces restrained imperialist aggression against such states. The disintegration of the colonial system, of which non-alignment was a part, marked a new stage in the general crisis of capitalism. Soviet military power ensured that this crisis would proceed without the capitalist states lashing out and creating a general war. Khrushchev was particularly enthused by the role of charismatic Third World leaders. He concentrated on individual leaders such as Nasser of Egypt, Sukarno of Indonesia and Nkrumah of Ghana and made extravagant claims about their ideological development. Nasser was a 'hero of the Soviet Union' and Ben Bella led 'the determination of the Algerian people to embark upon the socialist path'. This enthusiasm could lead to embarrassment when such leaders suppressed communists, as the Iraqi dictator Abdul Karim Kassem did in 1959. Khrushchev's ideological laxity found little favour with men such as Suslov and Kozlov who wanted to see much more discipline and coordination. Attitudes to the Third World became more cautious after 1960. The need for violent revolution was stressed, the risks emphasised. Yet the general consensus remained that the collapse of colonialism would bring more and more countries into the Soviet orbit.

Just as Stalin's death freed his successors to reconsider the nature of the international system, it also unleashed a debate about the national security of the Soviet Union. The Soviet leadership and their supporting secondary élites began to ask: what is the purpose of military power? How much does the Soviet Union need? How can this military power be supported from the national economic base? From these questions a number of clear answers emerged. Military power was much more flexible than Stalin had allowed: since war between capitalism and communism was not inevitable both had more room for manoeuvre in a 'zone of uncertainty'. In order to maximise the possibility for success the Soviet Union needed to amass highly visible armed forces which could be used to cajole and deter enemies. It was at this point that consensus broke down. The form that the highly visible armed forces were to take had important implications. If the Soviet Union was to concentrate only on certain forms of weaponry, specifically ballistic missiles, the resource allocations needed were very different from those required by the effort to strive for large, modern 'multi-purpose' armed forces. Resource allocation translated into domestic political power. The issue was sensitive for both its internal Soviet and foreign-policy ramifications. The consensus view favoured large 'multi-purpose' armed forces but under the leadership of Malenkov and Khrushchev it was held at bay between 1953 and 1961 only to become dominant thereafter.

The first phase of the struggle to define the nature of war and the resources the Soviet Union should devote to its armed forces was central to the immediate post-Stalin struggle for power. The inevitability-of-war debate broke out soon after Stalin's death. As early as September 1953 Major-General Nikolay Talenskiy declared that Stalinist military theory (as opposed to Stalin's own political calculus), which dismissed the primacy of nuclear weapons, needed to be modified to take into account that 'the influence of surprise on the course of military operations can be significant'. Talenskiy argued that Soviet defence policy should be modified. In November 1953 a Leningrad journal ran an article claiming that although the uneven development of capitalism made war inevitable, 'Experience has shown and proved that we are in a position to prevent war, and to paralyse the action of the law.' The Soviet Union had to accept that the nature of the Cold War was defined by the existence of nuclear weapons, that the Soviet Union should give primacy to such weapons. Indeed concentration on nuclear weapons opened many possibilities for the conduct of international politics.

Malenkov championed this approach within the Soviet leadership. He argued that the destructiveness of nuclear weapons and the availability of long-range delivery methods meant that no country was invulnerable. Malenkov and his allies wanted to restrain the growth of the military budget, emphasising that the Soviet Union had sufficient strength, reduce the priority of heavy industry and shift resources towards a 'steep rise' in light industrial output. The low level of manufacturing technology could no longer be tolerated. Khrushchev, Molotov, Minister of Defence Nikolay Bulganin and Lazar Kaganovich argued that Soviet military power should be increased and that since heavy industry was the basis of that power it could not be diminished. A change in investment policy would inhibit military research and innovation and leave the Soviet Union helpless before the West. In March 1954 Bulganin claimed that complacency about military power was an 'irreparable error ... the most important thing in military affairs is the uninterrupted perfection of the armed forces. This is especially true of aviation, where technological progress is very rapid ... We cannot assume that the imperialists expend enormous material and financial resources on armaments only to frighten us'. This point was expanded by Dmitriy Shepilov, the chief editor of *Pravda*, in January 1955 when he argued that a change in priority towards light industry would mean that: 'we surrender the advantage of forcing industry forward, the development of heavy industry, machine construction, energy, [the] chemical industry, electronics, jet technology, guidance systems, and so forth, to the imperialist world ... It is hard to imagine a more anti-scientific, rotten theory, which could disarm our people more.' Malenkov's opponents poured vituperation on his head. He was undermining the security of the Fatherland by his complacency and incompetence. Although Anastas Mikoyan could argue that 'atomic and hydrogen weapons in the hands of the Soviet Union are a means for checking the aggressors and waging peace', Khrushchev, Molotov, Bulganin and Kaganovich all claimed that the reactionary forces of capitalism were preparing a new war in order to overcome their internal difficulties. Indeed Malenkov, who as chairman of the

Council of Ministers exercised direct supervision over the industrial ministries, was to blame for any shortcomings in the industrial base for the arming of the nation.

The dispute between those who believed in a Soviet Union concentrating on heavy engineering and large armed forces and those who wanted to see a concentration on high technology which could build advanced weapon systems was real. Yet during the interregnum the participants did not take up their real positions; they advanced those which were most advantageous in the internal power struggle. Khrushchev purged his erstwhile allies, Bulganin, Molotov, Kaganovich and Shepilov, after Malenkov's fall. As soon as Malenkov was stripped of his political power in February 1955, Khrushchev could take over his views. At the earliest possible opportunity after the Soviet Union launched the first ICBM and the first satellite, Khrushchev announced, 'we now have all the rockets we need: long-range rockets, intermediate-range rockets and short-range rockets'. In November 1957 he claimed a stockpile of 20 ICBMs. Once he had clamped down on the military by removing Zhukov as Defence Minister in 1957, Soviet rhetoric started to cite achievements in space and technology rather than the current stock of strategic weapons to show that the world correlation of forces was changing. Between November 1958 and October 1959 public statements by Khrushchev and military leaders were designed to create the impression that the Soviets were rapidly producing ICBMs. In November 1959 Khrushchev's statements became more ambitious. 'We have now stock-piled so many rockets, so many atomic and hydrogen warheads, that, if we were attacked, we would wipe from the face of the earth all of our probable opponents.' Khrushchev portrayed such weapons as 'country-busters': West Germany could be 'put out of commission' by eight warheads of 3–5 megatons. These statements continued into 1961. 'The Soviet Union has the world's most powerful rocketry', Khrushchev declared in March, 'and has produced the quantity of atomic and hydrogen bombs necessary to wipe the aggressors from the face of the earth.'[7]

Khrushchev twinned this 'rattling of rockets' with proposed reductions in the Red Army's conventional forces and a re-ordering of industrial priorities. He wanted to upgrade chemical production in relation to metallurgy. Machine-building heavy industry would still have first priority, but Khrushchev favoured those parts which would help agriculture and consumer goods. Early in 1957 Khrushchev launched a major reorganisation of industry. Power and personnel were to be transferred from central ministries to regional economic councils. Khrushchev's proposals were met with firm opposition in the Presid-ium. Khrushchev's Presidium rivals objected that he was siphoning off resources from heavy industry and the military–industrial competition with the West and accused him of underestimating the ease with which the USSR could overtake the United States economically. Molotov denounced Khrushchev's agricultural plans for weakening heavy industry and undermining the Soviet

Union's military might and international position. Molotov himself was overthrown as part of the Kremlin coup which destroyed the anti-party group, but Khrushchev's plans met continuing opposition in the Presidium from members such as Kozlov. Their position was strengthened when it became obvious that Khrushchev's ambitions for new technology and his new economic organisation had failed.

Khrushchev's problems were increased by the resolution of the fierce controversy on the nature of war within the Soviet military. Talenskiy had been removed from his post as the editor of a leading military journal for expressing his views. However, when Marshal Zhukov became Minister of Defence in February 1955, he opened Stalinist military theory up to scrutiny. The military were happy to accept the importance of nuclear weapons. At the beginning of 1955 a previously suppressed article by Marshal Rotmistrov was published. It clearly stated that 'surprise attack with the employment of atomic and hydrogen weapons ... is one of the decisive conditions for the achievement of success, not only in battles and operations, but even in wars as a whole'. In the aftermath of the 20th Congress, however, the development of military doctrine continued to stress 'decisive factors' in warfare such as 'quantity and quality of divisions' and the 'armament of the army'. Although Zhukov lost his place, his views were not abandoned. The military demanded nuclear weapons in abundance: 'atomic weapons ... with their carriers: intercontinental ballistic missiles; long-range aviation; surface vessels and submarines armed with rockets ... rockets for operational-tactical purposes and atomic artillery'. In other words not just strategic rocket forces but modernised, nuclearised all-arms formations.

The military went along with Khrushchev's enthusiasm for strategic arms. Zhukov's replacement, Rodion Malinovsky, spoke of 'the readiness of the Soviet armed forces to break up a surprise attack of the imperialists' at the 22nd Congress, and in 1962 wrote: 'the objectives of crushing nuclear attacks, together with groupings of the armed forces of the enemy, will be industrial and administrative centres, communications centres, and everything which aids wars'. Some military authors also called for a launch-on-warning capability: 'the first rockets and bombers on the defensive [side] would take off even before the aggressor's first rockets, to say nothing of his bombers, reached their targets'. In order to pursue such a nuclear policy the Soviet Union needed very large and extremely capable nuclear forces. Yet despite the rhetoric of the previous five years and the priority given to strategic rocket forces, existing achievements were not impressive. The Soviet Union's first technically successful ICBM, the SS-7, only started deployment in 1962. At the time of the Cuban missile crisis the Soviet Union only had about 20 missiles, the total Khrushchev had claimed in 1957, capable of hitting the United States: four SS-6s, the missile Khrushchev had made so much of in 1957, some training launchers and a handful of SS-7s in the process of installation. The Soviet nuclear submarines were in port with reactor problems in 1961. About 100 long-range bombers were operational. It has been calculated that in October 1962 the Soviet Union had about 220 warheads deployed against the United States whilst the Americans had over 4000 targeted on the Soviet Union, a ratio of 1:18.[8]

Two major options were open to the Soviet leadership. They could either negotiate with the United States to reduce this disparity or they could expand Soviet military power. There was a strand within Soviet thought which stressed negotiation. According to the defector Arkadiy Shevchenko, Khrushchev believed he could not only use disarmament negotiations to extract concessions from the West but also pursue a genuine form of arms control. Khrushchev, however, was forced to compromise with Malinovsky in 1961 and accept that all branches of the armed forces were important: multi-million-men armies and increased military budget allocations were required. On 25 June 1961 he expressed his personal view of the Cold War:

> In spite of the twenty years we lost because of the wars that were imposed upon us and the reconstruction that followed we have been able in 44 years to reach second place in the world. Britain the ruler of the seas, which had Africa and Asia, we have left behind. France we have left behind ... Now only America is left for us. It [*sic*] is like an already aged runner ... he had had ... first prizes. Then others were born and trained, and he is still running – he lives on yesterday's glory ... By now the scientists of America are studying and reporting to the government that the Soviet Union will have caught up with America in 1970. That is also our figure.[9]

Less than a fortnight later he shifted his ground to the orthodox view. The Soviet Union was a military superpower but it did not receive the respect it deserved from the capitalist nations. Indeed, far from accepting the inevitable, the West was trying to overawe the Soviet leadership with its own military power. In response the Soviet Union would have to prove its own military potential and in return overawe the West. 'The Soviet government has been compelled to instruct the Ministry of Defence to suspend temporarily the reduction of the armed forces planned for 1961 ... to increase defence expenditures by [34 per cent] ... these are forced measures.'[10]

THE AMERICAN WORLD VIEW

At the beginning of its term the Eisenhower administration attempted to define the differences in its approach to the Cold War to that of its predecessor. The key concept articulated by Eisenhower's Secretary of State John Foster Dulles was that 'emergency measures – however good for the emergency – do not necessarily make good permanent policies. Emergency measures are costly; they are superficial; and they imply that the enemy has the initiative. They cannot be depended on to serve our long-time interests. This "long time" factor is of critical importance.'[11] Most commentators focused, however, on another of Dulles's striking phrases: 'there is no local defence which alone will contain the mighty landpower of the Communist world. Local defences must be reinforced by the further deterrent of *massive retaliatory power*. A potential aggressor must know that he cannot always prescribe battle conditions that suit him. . . . The way to deter aggression is for the free community to be willing and able to respond vigorously at places and with means of its own choosing.'[12] The new administration's rhetorical enthusiasm for nuclear weapons seemed to be its most striking innovation. Indeed Dulles soon had to offer a gloss on his own statements. 'Massive atomic and thermonuclear retaliation' was 'not the kind of power which could most usefully be evoked under all circumstances'. The United States 'must not put itself in the position where the only response open to it is general war'. Massive retaliation did 'not mean that if there is a Communist attack somewhere in Asia, atom or hydrogen bombs will necessarily be dropped on the great industrial centres of China or Russia'. Dulles reiterated, however, that:

> the United States put forward a new concept, now known as that of the 'long haul'. It meant a steady development of defensive strength at a rate which would preserve and not exhaust the economic strength of our allies and ourselves. This would be reinforced by the availability of new weapons . . . No single nation can develop for itself defensive power of adequate scope and flexibility. In seeking to do so, each would become a garrison state and none would achieve security.[13]

The manner in which policy was articulated revealed both the primacy of the long haul and the difficulties the Eisenhower administration had in dealing with its implications.[14]

Political leaders were aware of the dangerous tendencies of their own national security establishment: a preference for more and better weapons systems, more covert action, wider horizons for military action. Increasingly, policy was implemented by men who had internalised the Cold War and had made it an unchallengeable paradigm. The paradigm was, however, shared by most political leaders. It was thus hard to imagine new directions for policy. Dulles's 1954 statements reflected a vigorous debate which had gone on throughout 1953 as the incoming administration had tried to write a national security directive to replace NSC 68. According to the NSC staff the debate broke down into two positions. One, usually emanating from the office of the Secretary of Defense and the Joint Chiefs of Staff saw 'the threat to the United States as the basic Soviet hostility to the United States and the Soviet's formidable military power. While acknowledging a sound US economy is essential, [it] believes the United States *must* first meet necessary security costs.' The other side, led by the civil departments, saw 'the threat to the United States as a dual threat – the external threat of Soviet power; the internal threat of weakening our economy and changing our way of life'. Both sides 'agreed that short of general war acceptable negotiated settlements with the USSR are the only means of substantially reducing the Soviet threat'. The

hawks argued that the chance of such settlements was remote and 'believed that
the best way of bringing the Soviets to agree to such settlements is to maintain
pressure against the USSR. . . . Settlements which reduce tensions without a
concurrent reduction of the Soviet threat could lead the free world dangerously
to relax its defence.' The doves, on the other hand, 'believed that the best way
to induce the Soviets to accept such settlements is for the United States to
forego pressures at least against the USSR itself; to attempt to reduce tensions
on secondary issues; and to try to convince the Soviet leaders that, if they
renounce aggression and domination of other peoples, the United States has no
intention of interfering with the internal organisation or the territorial integrity
of the USSR.' These debates were to some extent artificial since key officials
often straddled both positions. Dulles, for instance, 'with obvious emotion . . .
pointed out . . . we certainly couldn't throw the common defence system out of
the window because we had to balance the budget . . . it seemed significant to
him that there was never any talk of making any drastic cuts except in defence
expenditures'. On the other hand the Secretary of State was equally warm in
stating that 'in his view we could not reduce tensions with the USSR if in each
case we expected to gain all the advantage and the Soviets none. . . . that if you
subordinate the achievement of mutually acceptable settlements to improving
the power position of the United States as against the USSR, you will eliminate
all hope of settlements in Korea, Austria, Germany, etc.'[15]

The 'long haul' would mean that Europe was virtually a 'frozen front'.
Although the Defense Department argued that American forces in Europe
should be redeployed to the continental United States, the President was
almost disdainful of the suggestion. He reminded the NSC

> that if the Communists succeeded in gaining control of Europe the world balance of
> power would be hopelessly upset against us. It would be necessary to spend many more
> billions than we are now spending to redress the balance of power. In short, said the
> President, that Western Europe not fall to the Communists was a *sine qua non*.
> Therefore, anxious as he was to see European nations do more to provide for the
> common defence, we simply could not abandon what we had begun in Europe. On the
> contrary, what we must do is improve the morale of Western Europe. Bringing back our
> divisions in any abrupt way would not improve European morale but completely
> destroy it. Speaking with great emphasis, the President pointed out that the United
> States' divisions in Europe had done marvels in restoring Europe's faith in itself.[16]

Instead the potential growth in US conventional forces would be capped by
increased reliance on nuclear weapons 'used by all three services for tactical as
well as strategic purposes'.[17] The major area in which change would have been
possible was Germany. This change could have been expressed in a 'Potsdam
deal' with the Soviets, an attempt to destabilise East Germany or a change of
policy on German rearmament. The administration, however, reaffirmed that a
'united Germany, disarmed or neutralised by four-power agreement, would
jeopardise [US interests] by tending to separate Germany from the West and

placing excessive military burdens on the US and free Europe'. The administration also reaffirmed support for a unified Germany with 'full sovereign
rights, including the right to affiliate itself with the West' in the expectation
that the Soviet Union was 'unlikely to accept unity on these terms at this
time'.[18] Although four-power talks seemed to be in the offing after Stalin's
death in March 1953, and attracted considerable enthusiasm in Western
Europe,[19] Dulles and Eisenhower believed, 'This was not the time to be soft. If
we keep our pressures on, psychological and otherwise, we may either force a
collapse of the Kremlin regime or else transform the Soviet orbit from a union
of satellites dedicated to aggression, into a coalition for defence only.'[20] A
golden opportunity for rollback was presented by the July 1953 workers'
uprising against the communist state in Berlin. Although the Americans went
some way to exploit the uprising by radio broadcasts and a large-scale food
programme for East Germany,[21] in the end the USA veered away from decisive
action. The State Department concluded that 'we should never consider
Eastern Europe can be liberated by political warfare devices no matter how well
planned and energetic they may be'.[22]

With so little perceived room for manoeuvre, the agreements envisaged by
the doves in 1953 were bound to be confined to secondary issues. These issues
were addressed during 1955 when a successful four-power negotiation which
reunited Austria as a sovereign state was followed by a summit meeting in
Geneva. The Austrian State Treaty was a practical agreement which organised
the withdrawal of military forces from Austrian territory by the end of 1955.[23]
The Geneva summit was far more ambitious. The leaders agreed to explore the
idea of a security pact, arms limitation and a demilitarised zone in central
Europe. They also subscribed to the 'spirit of Geneva', calling for 'freer contacts
and exchanges as are to the mutual advantage'.[24] The most striking American
proposal was Eisenhower's 'open skies' offer, permitting free aerial reconnaissance over the Soviet Union and the United States. Khrushchev dismissed
'open skies' as 'nothing more than a bald espionage plot'.[25] For the Americans it
had a propaganda value and met Eisenhower's uneasiness that the technology
for regular overflights of the Soviet Union was soon to be placed in his hands.
As he remarked about a later Russian protest about balloon reconnaissance
probes: 'I don't blame the Russians at all. I've always thought it was a sort of
dirty trick.'[26] The 'spirit of Geneva' counted for little. Even though American
leaders were struck by the subsequent denunciation of Stalin by Khrushchev in
the so-called Secret Speech, they continued to see any lessening of hard-line
positions as either an opportunity for the United States or evidence of new
dangers. Commenting on the Secret Speech, Dulles observed that: 'these events
afforded the US a great opportunity, both covertly and overtly, to exploit the
situation to its advantage. Stalin had been the chief theoretician of the Soviet
Union. He had been its great war hero in addition to his more familiar role as
Dictator . . . for 25 years. . . . It would obviously be very difficult to create a new

tradition.'[27] Although Dulles characterised Khrushchev as 'the most dangerous person to lead the Soviet Union since the October revolution', 'an emotional drunk given to irrational acts', he was actually more optimistic than many of his advisers. He continued to favour the policy of engagement.[28] Such engagement was the other side of the 'long haul'. It would not be too much to say that this was a theory of victory. Yet in practical terms Dullesian optimism suggested policies similar to those of more pessimistic Cold Warriors.

By the mid-1950s the United States had built a large bomber force equipped with a plentiful supply of nuclear weapons. Its primary objective was to attack over 600 Soviet air bases with nuclear weapons. By the beginning of 1955 H-bombs were entering operational service. In February 1955 the Soviet nuclear industry was targeted with 15 of these weapons.[29] Unfortunately, analysts were beginning to conclude that 'the atomic offensives do not provide a high degree of assurance of neutralising the Soviet atomic capability'. A report noted that 'even under the improbable assumption that only 5 per cent of the [Soviet] aircraft survived [a US nuclear strike], seventy-five weapons could be lifted against the US'.[30] Although this situation had been anticipated by some commentators, such as the Yale academic Bernard Brodie, from the outset of the nuclear age, the reality of the American continent vulnerable to a nuclear attack concentrated minds in much the same manner as the Soviet A-bomb had affected the Truman presidency. Increasing uneasiness was exacerbated by the paucity of hard intelligence about the Soviet nuclear forces. The tendency to see Soviet developments as a mirror of American programmes led to a number of intelligence estimates positing a large and effective Soviet bomber force. When the Soviets offered visible evidence of their nuclear prowess, as they did between August and October 1957 by launching the world's first ICBM, its first earth satellite, *Sputnik*, and by testing high-yield thermonuclear weapons, this technical challenge could be seen as a much wider systemic challenge.[31] In a document known as the Gaither report the President's scientific advisers drew a critical picture of the American political–scientific–defence system whilst lauding Soviet achievements. In the US, 'the new weapon systems ... have caused management problems which have been difficult to resolve within existing legislative and organisational restrictions. We have lost the ability to concentrate resources, to control performance and expenditures, and to change direction or emphasis with the speed a rapidly developing international situation ... make necessary.' On the other hand

the GNP of the USSR is now more than one-third that of the United States and is increasing half again as fast. ... This growing Russian economic strength is concentrated on the armed forces and on investment in heavy industry ... an allocation of $57 billion per annum, which is roughly equal to our country's current effort. If the USSR continues to expand its military expenditures throughout the next decade, as it has during the 1950s, and ours remain constant, its annual military expenditures may be double ours.

The advisory committee suggested that a minimum of an extra $19 billion be added to the defence budget between 1959 and 1963, with, possibly, another $25 billion expended on ballistic missile defence and shelter programmes.[32] At the same time the US army attempted to revise military doctrine. The implication of the proposed change would be greatly expanded conventional forces. The rock on which all these initiatives broke was Eisenhower's stubborn refusal to change his views.[33] He insisted, with some asperity, to both Congressional and military leaders that neither Soviet military developments or threats of aggression changed anything. Congress was informed that: 'the Soviets are engaged in confronting the US with a series of crises ... the mounting burden [of responding to each] would call for full mobilisation and eventually a garrison state ... Berlin should not throw us off balance and render us hysterical ... nothing more is needed [in terms of military force].' The President, 'expressed his disgust with the idea of considering ourselves weak after nine years of gigantic efforts to strengthen our defences'.[34]

This stance became increasingly untenable on two counts. First, it made the government vulnerable to persistent charges of inertia and complacency from both Democrats and right-wing Republicans. Second, Eisenhower's efforts on the diplomatic front misfired badly. In 1959 Khrushchev was invited to Camp David in an attempt to re-ignite the 'spirit of Geneva'. Unfortunately the resulting four-power summit in Paris in May 1960 was wrecked by the Soviet response to the downing of a U-2 spy plane over their territory at the beginning of the month.[35] The political problems of 1959–60 meant that any successor administration would have to strike out in a new direction. The eventual winner of the 1960 election, John Kennedy, used the 'missile gap' as a major plank in his campaign but he was also genuinely critical of Eisenhower's performance. Some advisers such as Robert McNamara, the new Defense Secretary, believed the previous administration had been hopelessly unsystematic. Others, most notably the President's brother, Bobby, believed Eisenhower had been too passive. Even the 'old guard' argued that, although there was no imminent threat, the Soviets were on an upswing.[36] In June 1961, during a bruising encounter in Vienna, Kennedy attempted to warn Khrushchev against such overconfidence.[37] The administration was, however, itself confident that rationalised planning would ensure continuing American strategic superiority.[38] Within months two Eisenhower technical programmes came to fruition. The first three nuclear-powered submarines, armed with Polaris ballistic missiles, powered by solid fuel and thus launchable from under water, went into service, and the first effective spy satellites covered the Soviet Union. Satellite intelligence 'caused a sharp downward revision in [the] estimate of present Soviet ICBM strength'. The CIA now estimated that 'ICBM strength is in the range of 10–25 launchers from which missiles can be fired against the US. ... Although Soviet propaganda has assiduously cultivated an image of great ICBM strength ... the present ICBM force poses ... only a limited threat

to US-based nuclear striking forces.'[39] The impact of this information amounted to more than a technical re-evaluation: it cast doubt on the whole Soviet
system. The pessimism of the Gaither report was misplaced: the Soviets were
technological incompetents who blustered to cover their own failings. Civilian
officials in the Pentagon also continued to doubt the strength of Soviet
conventional forces. Once the inadequacies of American strategy had been
overcome, the United States would be in an extremely strong position. Not
only did the President need more nuclear options, the United States needed
more and better conventional forces.[40] Provision of such mixed forces, which
Truman had reluctantly approved to meet the Korean crisis and Eisenhower
had tried to cap, seemed less and less of a problem. Kennedy was moving
towards the rejection of balanced budgets as a sound indicator of economic
policy and McNamara promised huge efficiency savings at the Pentagon. The
administration was thus happy not only to add an extra 10 Polaris SSBNs and
400 Minuteman ICBMs into the defence budget[41] but to add over 100 000 men
to the army and four tactical combat wings to the USAF.[42]

THE FAR EASTERN CRISIS

As the Eisenhower administration progressed, the fluid areas in international
relations tended to be interpreted in a pessimistic fashion. This was particularly
true of Asia. In the Far East the major problem left from the Truman
administration was the war in Korea. As the major study initiated by the
administration pointed out, the time was ripe for finding some way out of the
conflict. Although 'the USSR and Communist China [were] united in their
intention to expel the West from Asia, in Korea, they have appeared for the past
year to be reconciled to the existing military stalemate'. Meanwhile there had
been the 'March 30 radio declaration of the Chinese Communist authorities
proposing resumption of armistice negotiations'. Other considerations
included: 'the increase in communist military capabilities . . . the improvement
in the capabilities of ROK forces, some loss in the effectiveness of US forces
resulting from rotation and stalemate, the death of Stalin and the transfer of
power to Malenkov . . . developments in atomic weapons, developments in the
attitude of our allies and in American public opinion'.[43] Initially, Dulles had
hoped that the US could triumph before an armistice was reached: 'I don't
think we can get much out of a Korean settlement until we have shown – before
all Asia – our clear superiority by giving the Chinese one hell of a licking.' Once
talks had been started, however, Eisenhower soon made clear his grasp of
political realities. It would be 'impossible to call off the armistice now and go to
war in Korea. The American people would never stand for such a move.'[44]
Although the administration gave serious consideration to the possibility of
expanding the war, its actions were fairly limited.[45] The KMT were 'unleashed'
by the withdrawal of the Seventh Fleet from the Formosa Strait. In fact, the

Eisenhower administration, although more open to the China lobby in the Republican Party, shared the view of its predecessor that the Taiwanese regime was corrupt, ineffectual and dangerously destabilising. It insisted on an agreement to limit offensive operations and attempted to close down CIA-supported covert operations by a KMT faction on the Burma–China border.[46] Like their predecessors, Eisenhower and Dulles were interested in a wedge strategy, but like them they favoured the hard variant. Dulles believed: 'The best way to get a separation between the Soviet Union and Communist China is to keep pressure on Communist China and make its way difficult so long as it is in partnership with Soviet Russia. Tito did not break with Stalin because we were nice to Tito. It seems to me that if China can win our favours while she is working closely with Moscow, then there is little reason for her to change.' A research project known as Solarium, set up to advise the President on new methods of waging the Cold War, regretfully concluded that, as in Europe, there was little hope of 'rollback or liberation' in Asia. The China panel, led by George Kennan, did see forthcoming strains in the Sino-Soviet relationship but could not believe these would redound to the favour of the USA. China was assembling independent prestige, not least through its performance in Korea, and would remain a threat to South East Asia. 'A Communist China, even independent of Moscow, predominant in the power equation in the Far East and attracting Asian support, is very much against our interest.' Matthew Ridgway, the former commander of UN forces in Korea, did suggest, in 1954, that the USA could 'bring Red China to a realisation that its long-range benefits derive from friendliness with America, not with the USSR, which casts acquisitive eyes on its territory and resources; that these benefits could reasonably be expected in time, if Red China would mend its ways, abjure its offensively aggressive actions towards the West, and takes steps to remove the stigma of "aggressor" with which it is now branded.' His views were talked down in the NSC and although Eisenhower had some sympathy he was unwilling to recast policy on this basis.[47]

At the end of the Korean War, as before it, the CCP was motivated by a multifaceted search for legitimacy. It wanted to build an economically and militarily strong China by mobilising the populace. It wanted to secure the safety of its borders against KMT infiltration and American influence. It wanted to overturn the humiliating secret protocols to the Sino-Soviet treaty Stalin had imposed in 1950 and to seek a more equitable partnership, at least in the medium term, with the Soviet Union. It wanted to attain a special status as a leader of the international communist movement. It wanted to secure international legitimacy by replacing Taiwan and its KMT government as the China recognised in the UN. It wanted to finally gain complete victory in the Chinese civil war by seizing Taiwan and extirpating the KMT. All of these objectives had been made harder to achieve by the PRC's role in the Korean War. China found itself locked into a trilateral relationship with the Soviet

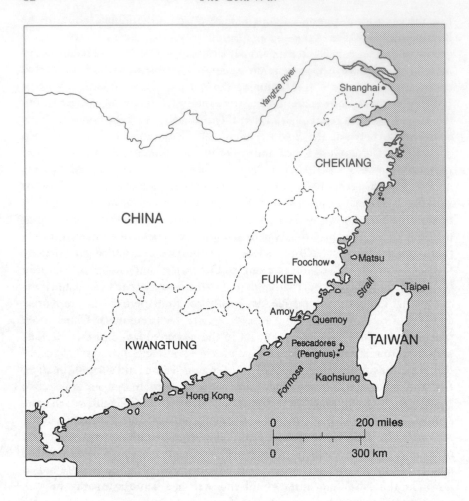

Map 4 The offshore islands

Union and the United States. Korea had reshaped the attitudes of the American political and foreign-policy establishment to such an extent that there was an almost visceral hatred of the PRC which, if anything, outweighed distaste for the Soviet Union. The CCP needed the Soviet Union to be successful enough in recasting the international system to force or influence the United States to accept the PRC on grounds of pragmatism. In doing so the CCP had to avoid too much reliance on the Soviet Union, which active conflict with the United States would bring, since it suspected that the CPSU leadership were little more than European 'neo-imperialists'. In attempting to achieve these objectives the PRC succeeded in maintaining the alienation of the United States whilst alienating the Soviet Union. It also managed to inject an element of acute uncertainty into Cold War relations through its alarming rhetoric and, arguably misunderstood, actions.

Any increase in security China had gained through Zhou's subtle diplomacy was lost through the continued primacy of the Taiwan issue. Taiwan was an issue apart for the CCP leadership. 'The civil war against Chiang Kai-shek never ended in the coastal regions' they noted in July 1954.[48] According to the PRC, between 1950 and 1954 the KMT launched '41 raids on the mainland, employing 28 000 men, and flew 977 bombing and strafing and reconnaissance missions over coastal regions'. Zhou noted: 'we are, of course, willing to coexist peacefully along with the United States', but he deliberately excluded Taiwan. 'Up to the present the United States is still occupying our territory, Taiwan. They are attempting to prevent the Chinese people from liberating it, and using [the] traitorous Chiang Kai-shek clique to threaten our country.'[49] Indeed Mao was sceptical about achieving any accommodation with the Americans. He cabled Zhou at Geneva to tell him that: 'in order to break up the collaboration between the United States and Chiang and to keep them from joining military and political forces [a US–Taiwan defence treaty was under negotiation], we must announce to our country and the world the Liberation of Taiwan. It was improper of us not to raise the slogan in a timely manner after the cease-fire in Korea. If we continue dragging our heels now, we should be making a serious political mistake.'

Taiwan provided a rallying point around which to mobilise the people. In July 1954 the CCP launched a massive 'Liberate Taiwan' propaganda campaign aimed at both the internal and international audience. In September 1954 the PLA began shelling the KMT-controlled island of Quemoy just off the mainland coast opposite Amoy. These actions were the start of what was consciously seen as a 'long-term and complex struggle'. The CCP leadership believed that, 'we are not able to liberate Taiwan without a powerful navy and air force and need time to build them up'. Eventually 'we will be able to complete the historical task of the liberation of Taiwan through a long-term struggle as we grow in strength and achieve victories one by one in the military, political, and diplomatic fields'. In the short term, however, 'the direct target of our military struggle is Chiang Kai-shek and his cohorts in Taiwan. The United States should not be treated as our direct target; we should confine the conflicts with the United States to the diplomatic arena only.' In the long term both Mao and Zhou hoped that the United States' will to defend Taiwan could be undermined. In 1956 Zhou noted that, 'even in the United States' ruling circles, some people who are more sober-minded are beginning to realise that there is no future for the policy of cold war'. Even though those who were 'in a powerful position, particularly those who handle foreign policy are still obstructing this change' there were others 'in American industrial and commercial circles, who are dissatisfied with the US policy' since it disrupted lucrative international trade.[50] Chinese military action was actually launched against the KMT-held Dachen islands hundreds of miles north of Taiwan, and in doing so Mao ordered that 'only after verifying that there are no US ships or planes present can we launch the attack on the Dachens. Otherwise, do not initiate any military action'. Mao believed that China could afford to, indeed had to, needle the United States in this fashion: not only would resolute Chinese action discourage any real American support for Chiangist ambitions on the mainland but 'if we show any fear, the enemy will consider us weak and easy to bully. In other words, if we give them an inch, they will take a mile and intensify their military expansion. Only by adopting an unyielding, resolute, and calm stance can we force the enemy to retreat.'[51]

Despite Mao's belief in fortitude, however, the obvious reality was that the United States had moved substantial forces around Taiwan. The PRC had neither the military power to defeat those forces nor the diplomatic strength to cause their withdrawal. Both military–industrial and diplomatic power had to be drawn from the Soviet Union. At the time of the 1954 Geneva conference the Chinese and the Soviet delegations had worked in close cooperation. The post-Stalin leadership seemed willing to mitigate the hateful secret protocols attached to the Sino-Soviet treaty. Yet the basic distrust of the Stalin period remained, and as it became clear to the Chinese that the Soviet leadership would not exert itself to deal with what the Chinese leadership saw as their most important problems, that distrust matured into outright hostility.

In December 1952 Zhou had launched, after the delays he feared the Korean War would cause, China's first five-year plan. Its chief aim was to industrialise China through state control over economic expansion, central planning and the socialisation of enterprises. Zhou estimated that it would take three such five-year plans to transform China into a true industrial power. Such industrialisation had a direct bearing on China's foreign policy. In December 1955 Mao urged: 'speed up the tempo and accomplish the overall task . . . If we can fulfil the overall task during the transition period ahead of the schedule, taking care of the battlefield should be easy . . . though we have a large population we have not yet demonstrated our strength. One day when we catch up with Great Britain and the US, Dulles will respect us.'[52] Zhou hoped that the nation-wide imposition of austere living standards would finance the plan, but the other key element in its achievement was Soviet aid.

Soviet aid proved to be something of a mixed blessing, however. It was certainly substantial. Between 1950 and 1957, 8.1 billion roubles worth of industrial aid was assigned to the PRC. The Soviets were involved in building 211 large-scale industrial enterprises and other similar projects. In 1958 another 47 were started and in 1959 a further 58. It was intended that a total of 20 billion roubles should have been spent on China's industrial infrastructure by 1967, that is by the time the third five-year plan would be drawing near to completion. Yet in 1957 only 37 of these projects had actually been completed.[53] The Chinese were dissatisfied with this effort. In March 1958 Mao announced that the application of Soviet planning to China had been partially incorrect. 'It was imported uncritically', he claimed. 'We are now capable of undertaking the planning and construction of large enterprises ourselves. In another five years we shall be capable of manufacturing the equipment ourselves.'[54] In retrospect he was more straightforward: Soviet products were 'heavy, crude, high priced, and they always keep something back'.[55]

By far the most important set of projects from the Chinese point of view was aimed at giving them nuclear weapons. The Soviets and the Chinese had done their first nuclear deal in 1951 when the PRC agreed to supply uranium to its ally. At the end of 1954 the Chinese demanded help in producing their own atomic weapons. The Chinese intended to make a large nuclear effort with or without Soviet help. In Mao's words: 'now the Soviet Union is giving us assistance, we must achieve success [but] we can achieve success even if we do this ourselves'. The Chinese leadership's insistence on attaining a nuclear capability tied in with its wider analysis of international affairs. Echoing Mao's views on international relations whilst tying nuclear weapons directly to the Taiwan issue, Deng Xiaoping commented in 1957: 'the Soviet Union has the atom bomb. Where does the significance lie? It lies in the fact that the imperialists are afraid of it. Are the imperialists afraid of us? I think they are not ... the United States stations its troops in Taiwan because we have no atom bombs or guided missiles.' Mao was delighted by the programme. In June 1958 he announced that 'I consider it entirely possible for China to develop atomic bombs, and intercontinental missiles within ten years.' The Soviets provided an experimental nuclear reactor, facilities for processing uranium, a cyclotron and part of a gaseous diffusion plant. In addition they sent China jet bombers capable of carrying atomic weapons, the plans for a conventionally powered guided-missile submarine and the designs for ballistic missiles (including the type they themselves deployed in Cuba in 1962). In October 1957, after long drawn-out negotiations in Moscow, the Soviet leadership agreed to sell China full information on the design of nuclear weapons and more advanced ballistic missile technology and, most remarkably, to send it an atomic bomb. Almost immediately, however, the Soviets decided they had made a bad mistake and in the spring of 1958 insisted that any Soviet weapons provided to China should be under effective Soviet control. In June 1959 they formally resiled from the agreement.[56]

The nuclear issue was probably the key factor in Sino-Soviet relations. Not only did the Soviet Union fail to deliver on its promises to make China a nuclear power, it refused to use its own perceived nuclear superiority to further China's central interests, specifically in forcing the United States to compromise over Taiwan (a failure exacerbated by continuing Sino-Soviet disputes over areas of their own borders such as Mongolia). When the PRC provoked another conflict over the offshore islands in 1958,[57] Mao ensured his talks with Khrushchev, before the PRC acted, 'did not contain a word' about Chinese intentions. Mao was disingenuous when he claimed: 'I simply did not calculate that the world would become so disturbed and turbulent from firing a few rounds [about 41 000] of artillery at Quemoy and Matsu.' China faced a direct nuclear threat from the United States which had installed nuclear-capable missiles on Taiwan. Khrushchev publicly backed the Chinese, but his intervention, sending a letter to Eisenhower which contained the phrase 'an attack on China is an attack on the Soviet Union', came a day after the Chinese had proposed negotiations directly to Washington.[58] By 1958 an ambiguous nuclear guarantee was regarded as completely insufficient by the Chinese leadership: they wanted aggressive diplomacy backed by threats. A senior CCP leader, Chen Yun, castigated the Soviet Union for its 'US phobia': If formerly, 'at the time after the October Revolution Lenin, the Soviet Communist Party, and the Soviet people, confronted with the encirclement of the capitalist world and the armed intervention of fourteen countries, were not afraid, why should there be any fear toward imperialism when the socialist camp has absolute superiority?' The CCP needed acute conflict between the Soviet Union and the United States if the latter was to be rendered malleable. Instead the Soviet Union showed signs of compromising with the United States, most notably over a nuclear test ban which obviously aimed at China's programme.[59]

Chinese aggression, which rhetorically at least was extreme, was partly a function of changes within the CCP leadership itself. As Khrushchev claimed in 1960, Mao started to resemble Stalin, creating a paranoid dictatorship. Mao's method of asserting his own power was to mobilise mass movements dependent on his charisma: first the 'Hundred Flowers' movement and then, in 1958, the Great Leap Forward. The GLF was an economic catastrophe which plunged China into famine in 1960–61. Those who criticised Mao's economic inanity, most notably the former commander of the CPV, Peng Dehuai, were purged.[60] Mao introduced a positively apocalyptic strand into Chinese threat assessments. In 1958, having conceded war was unlikely, and just before the shelling of Quemoy and Matsu was begun, he commented, 'if they strike they strike [with atomic weapons]. We will exterminate imperialism and once again construct ... if war breaks out it is unavoidable that people will die. We have seen wars kill people. Many times in China's past half the population has been wiped out ... We have at present no experience with atomic war. We do not know how many must die. It is better if one-half are left, the second best is one-third ... After several five-year plans China will then develop and rise up. In place of the totally destroyed capitalism we will obtain perpetual peace. This will not be a bad thing.'[61] There was a reality which underlay the chilling rhetoric. Mao was already thinking of building a huge military–industrial complex protected from nuclear attack in the remote south-west of China. In the early 1950s he had sent Deng Xiaoping to start building a transport infrastructure in the difficult terrain of Szechwan.[62] The concept was formally launched to a mass audience by Lin Biao ten years later when he told a party audience in January 1962 that China should construct a 'third front' invulnerable to possible attack from Taiwan.[63]

By 1963 the CCP under Mao had set itself up in opposition to both the United States and the Soviet Union. In Mao's September 1962 formulation: although 'the contradiction between the people of the whole world and imperialism is the primary one . . . there are also the contradictions between the peoples of all countries and [Soviet] revisionism'.[64] In the mid-1950s Chinese foreign policy had been dominated by strategy rather than ideology. That strategy was certainly ideologically reified into Cold War policy but it was based on the attempt to achieve concrete objectives. In the late 1950s Mao Zedong reasserted his supreme role in all areas of policy. At the centre of his belief system was the conviction that his judgements shaped objective reality rather than vice versa. Anyone who failed, even implicitly, to acknowledge this truth was a deadly enemy. There were those who adapted to, indeed gloried in, this new dispensation, most notably Mao's wife, Jiang Qing, and the general Lin Biao. The Cultural Revolution was a product of the implosion of the civil war leadership into vicious factionalism. That leadership was an enclosed political and social elite who lived together in the Zhongnanhai compound next to the Forbidden City in central Peking. The origins of the Cultural Revolution thus lay in a highly personalised struggle for power. Mao and his temporary allies used the techniques of mass mobilisation to create hysteria and generational conflict in order to destroy existing government and party structures and thus concentrate power in their own hands. The Cold War did, however, have some role to play in sparking the Cultural Revolution. First, Mao was heavily influenced by his thinking on Soviet revisionism and the 'failure' of the rationalists such as Zhou, Liu Shaoqi and Deng Xiaoping to combat it. They continued to put forward their views as they had done in the 1950s, thus confirming Mao's paranoid view that they were traitors. In 1962 Mao commented: 'I think right wing opportunism should be called revisionism.'[65] He became increasingly convinced that since the Soviet Union had once been a socialist country which had been corrupted by bourgeois mores, capitalist economics and imperialist foreign policy any socialist country, including China, could regress.[66] The senior figures in the party did not take this seriously. Liu acknowledged in November 1963 that 'the current principal task is to oppose foreign revisionism' but he contradicted Mao's December 1963 statement that 'the heart and soul of the general line of peaceful coexistence pursued by the leaders of the CPSU is Soviet–US collaboration for the domination of the world'. In Liu's opinion 'the US and the USSR may make some compromises on a few unimportant questions affecting their current interests [but] . . . the principal enemy of the United States and its principal rival is the Soviet Union. That is the country they fear most: it is not China.' In addition his recipe for combating the domestic consequences of revisionism was hardly radical: more work to write 'our own history, political economy,

international relations, literary theory, legal studies and world history ...
especially with regard to our modern history from the Opium War to the
completion of land reform; all the countries which have not yet succeeded in
revolution want to learn from us.' Zhou spoke up for the Mao line in 1964 in his
report on the work of the government.[67] Yet Zhou was closely associated with
the failure of China's export of revolution to the 'intermediate zone'. Mao
regarded the zone as vital since it was the arena of conflict with both
imperialism and revisionism but Chinese policy in Africa and Asia met with a
number of embarrassing setbacks. A Chinese plot to murder the president of
Burundi was foiled in 1965 and that country broke off diplomatic relations.
Similar fiascos occurred in Ghana, Dahomey and the Central African Republic.
The attempt to assemble another non-aligned conference, a 'second Bandung',
in Algiers failed, largely because of Chinese diplomatic incompetence. The
PRC's accumulation of votes in the UN General Assembly for its own
recognition actually fell. A Chinese-supported communist coup in Indonesia,
predicated on murdering the high command of the army, failed; the PKI was
wiped out as a political force and the Indonesian security forces massacred
hundreds of thousands of ethnic Chinese during the backlash.[68] Zhou's attempt
to secure the southern border through diplomacy also seemed to have failed.
There, a security crisis was created by direct American military intervention in
Vietnam.[69] In Mao's words, the rationalists 'became flabby and weakened; it
was surrender to the bourgeoisie'.[70]

There was an increasing tendency within the US administration to see China
as more of an immediate threat than the Soviet Union. This perception was
largely a product of conflict between the PRC and the Taiwanese regime. The
shelling of the island of Quemoy by Chinese artillery in September 1954
sparked off a nine-month crisis which encompassed the signature of a US–
Taiwan mutual defence treaty and a Congressional resolution which gave the
administration a free hand in the use of force to defend Taiwan. For Dulles 'the
Chinese Communists had already begun to probe and were exposing ...
indecision. ... The US could not afford to back down from any position which
it assumed, or be exposed in a bluff.' What seemed interesting about the crisis
on a wider front was that 'Soviet government does not have controlling
influence over Chinese actions and even degree of influence is problematical'.
US officials noted the 'extreme caution of Soviet Press on Formosa question
which, while justifying morally Chinese position and quoting with approval
Chinese statements on subject, has been careful not to commit even indirectly
Soviet Union to any military support of Chinese policy'.[71] In 1955 Eisenhower
admitted his uncertainty about the nature of Sino-Soviet relations:

> I do not believe Russia wants war at this time – in fact, I do not believe that if we became
> engaged in a rather bitter fight along the coast of China, Russia would want to intervene
> with her own forces. She would ... pour supplies into China in the effort to exhaust
> [the] US and certainly would exploit the opportunity to separate us from our major

allies. But I am convinced that Russia does not want . . . to experiment with means of defence against the bombing we could conduct against her mainland. At the same time I assume that Russia's treaty with Red China comprehends a true military alliance, which she would have to repudiate or take the plunge. As a consequence of this kind of thinking, she would be in a considerable dilemma.[72]

Three years later, when the crisis re-erupted, the Americans were no nearer resolving this confusion. In September 1958 Dulles admitted, during Khrushchev's visit to Peking: 'I can't even guess intelligently whether the Russians egged the Chinese on, whether Khrushchev began to boast about how powerful they were and how we always gave in when they threatened and Mao said if that's the case I might as well pick up something as long as you will make the threat to back us up, or whether the Chinese pressed the Soviet and the Soviet reluctantly gave in'. The Director of the CIA confirmed that the United States actually had little information about the state of Sino-Soviet relations, although he suspected that Moscow was increasingly unwilling to cooperate on nuclear weapons, grant large-scale credits or push too far on Taiwan.[73]

In the last year of his life John Kennedy was much exercised by the Chinese threat. In the aftermath of the Cuban missile crisis it seemed possible that the Soviet Union would show more interest in direct negotiations on nuclear arms control. Indeed Khrushchev wrote directly to Kennedy on 10 December 1962 to suggest that the United States, the USSR and Great Britain might reach an agreement banning the testing of nuclear weapons. Kennedy was genuinely interested in a Soviet–American *rapprochement*, especially on the nuclear issue. He made the case for such a course during one of his greatest orations, delivered at the American University in Washington on 10 June 1963. Yet the main context in which Kennedy placed this *rapprochement* was the growing threat from China.[74] In his reply to Khrushchev, Kennedy asked the Soviet leader to tell him 'what you think about the position of the people in Peking on this issue'. In an NSC meeting in January 1963 he observed that: 'If the Soviets want this [test ban treaty] and it can help in keeping the Chinese Communists from getting a full nuclear capacity, then it is worth it.' At one level the Americans were interested in a policy of divide and rule. As Earle Wheeler, the chairman of the JCS, expressed it in August 1963, it was 'always a sound military principle to divide your enemies if you can, or to contribute to any division that there might be between them'. On the other hand, Kennedy had come to regard the Chinese as a potential 'loose cannon' in world politics, not only because of their incipient nuclear capability but also because of their regional ambitions.[75]

THE GERMAN QUESTION

In the decade after Stalin's death Germany had a dual importance. It retained its role as the most visible Cold War battlefield. The fate of Germany was of

enormous symbolic importance for both the Soviet Union and the United
States: the protection of their respective German states reinforced claims to
bloc leadership. Germany continued to be regarded as crucial in economic and
military terms. Since 1950 the USA had seen the rearmament of West
Germany as a keystone in NATO's architecture. The FRG's economic performance, unexpected in 1950 when unemployment was over two million and
economic viability seemed 'as remote as ever',[76] further strengthened this
perception in Washington. The West German 'economic miracle' was at its
most pronounced in the 1950s. The compound annual growth in gross
domestic product was 9.4 per cent between 1950 and 1955 and 8.3 per cent
between 1955 and 1960, compared to 3 per cent and 2.5 per cent respectively in
Britain.[77] The denial of a united Germany allied to the opposite camp also
remained vital to both superpowers. Although Germany's role as prize continued into the 1960s an equally important development emerged in the early
1950s. The FRG and the GDR which had both been set up in 1949 started to
develop independent political agendas which their allies were forced to accommodate. For both German powers, diplomacy in the 1950s was a diplomacy of
weakness. Neither had a functioning military establishment in place until after
1960. Neither had the full legitimacy of UN membership; both had foreign
forces with quasi-legal rights stationed on their own territory. As a result the
governments of Konrad Adenauer and the communist regime led by Walter
Ulbricht trod carefully in their dealings with their patrons, their allies and,
most delicately of all, with each other. The essential difference between them,
however, remained. The FRG was a viable state. The GDR was under constant
threat of internal political disintegration or economic collapse. The relative
strengths of the two states provided the context for Germany's two defining
crises of this period: the 'uprising' in the East of June 1953 and the construction
of the Berlin Wall in August 1961.

The United States had decided that German rearmament was vital for the
security of Western Europe in June 1950. Its insistence on this step was a
running sore for NATO between 1950 and 1954, largely because of French
unhappiness with the idea. In 1950 Dean Acheson had insisted that if Europe
was to be effectively defended it needed German units participating in a
'common defence force under unified command'. These units would be equipped by America and 'their numbers would have to be considerably less than
those of the French forces'.[78] Robert Schuman had objected to these proposals on
the grounds that NATO's publicly announced need for troops would put the
Germans in a powerful political position. Schuman, the French Foreign Minister, wished German rearmament to occur after France had been fully rearmed,
Acheson wanted it to occur immediately.[79] Many in the French foreign élite were
not as sanguine as Schuman.[80] René Massigli declared that: 'the decision to rely
on the Germans would ... inevitably lead to a "preventive war" being launched
by the Americans within the next two years ... the Germans had only one

interest and that is the unification of Germany; and they can only achieve this either by going Communist or through a preventive war; therefore as soon as the Americans have built up substantial German armed forces and begun to rely on them, they will be led by the Germans into a preventive war.'[81] Bidault, out of office, commented that France 'resented the hustling methods adopted by the United States'.[82] Schuman was thus left to find 'a formula which would be somewhere between "yes" and "no", which would be sufficient to gain the approval of the French Assembly and yet would also be enough to persuade the Americans and their Congress to [proceed] with the rest of their plans [to send American forces to Europe]'.[83] This 'formula', suggested by Jean Monnet, and launched by René Pleven on 24 October 1950 was for a federalised system with a European Ministry of Defence controlling a European army made up of relatively small national units. The remaining sticking point was when German units would actually begin to form in the course of negotiations for such a complex body. The European Defence Community (EDC), as the plan became, was little more than a diplomatic finesse of what the Americans demanded and some French ministers believed to be necessary.

By the time the French government brought itself to accept the EDC it did so only partly in response to the Soviet threat. It seemed to offer the advantages of a guarantee against German militarism. It bound the FRG into the West by preventing it from aligning with the Soviet Union or, indeed, becoming a pivotal country capable of balancing between East and West and using the leverage so gained to France's detriment. In addition a combination of the EDC and the ECSC opened the way to some form of European political body largely under French control. France's position would be maintained since Germany would be kept out of NATO as long as France kept control of large armed forces overseas.[84] These ideas appealed to Schuman and his advisers but some ministers in the government still seemed to favour a Franco-Soviet agreement on Germany. As such, it was an issue to be exploited by the Soviet Union. The Soviets remained in complete control of GDR foreign policy and insisted on the continuance of the 'zigzag' course. The East German state was to some extent consolidated but was still portrayed as a temporary entity. For the Soviets Germany was the wedge which would continue to disrupt the Western alliance. The last phase of this strategy was initiated in March 1952 when the Soviet Union put forward proposals for a united and neutralised Germany. Schuman regarded the Soviet *démarche* with alarm since it raised the possibility that the whole concept of reunification would become a Soviet preserve and patriotic Germans would be drawn inexorably to the East. Schuman believed that France's response should be to accelerate the FRG's integration into the West.[85] By April 1952 Stalin had decided that the gambit was a failure. He told the SED leadership that, 'in reality there is an independent state being formed in West Germany. And you must organise your own state. The line of demarcation between East and West Germany must be seen as a frontier and not as a simple border but a dangerous one. One must strengthen the protection of this frontier.'[86] This first step was to raise and arm a proper army, rather than the existing paramilitary forces. Economic reforms were to be instituted, although still with caution. Yet, as some French diplomats recognised at the time, the realisation of the EDC was becoming less and less likely. Although the treaties were duly signed in May 1952, de Gaulle, who was in opposition at the time, denounced the EDC the next month. His condemnation was echoed by political leaders from across the political spectrum. The French political system was split by the EDC on non-Cold War lines. A loose coalition of Christian Democrats, radicals and socialists faced an even more diverse coalition of Gaullists, communists, socialists and radicals.[87] The opposition to the EDC thus stretched from the far right to the far left. In fact disillusion that the defence of the West seemed to entail constant French concessions on Germany and dependence on American military aid was widespread within the government itself.[88]

In 1953 the power struggle in the Soviet Union which took place after Stalin's death crystallised over East Germany. All of the leading members of the Presidium agreed that Germany had to be stabilised, but they disagreed how this should be done. Malenkov was willing to accept either a reunified Germany or the formal recognition of the GDR, as long as the Soviet Union did not have to pay the costs of socialist transformation. Khrushchev, on the other hand, claimed a neutral capitalist Germany would become a bastion of imperialism. Their hand was forced by East Germany's own weakness. Walter Ulbricht, perhaps aware that the new Soviet regime were ready to sacrifice him, proved an enthusiastic constructor of socialism. Small business owners were persecuted and attempts were made to collectivise agriculture. Agricultural reform had an important short-term impact since it caused serious food shortages. Within months of Stalin's death the Soviet government had realised that the 'cold exercise of power' by Ulbricht constituted 'a serious danger for the continued political existence of the German Democratic Republic'. In the first four months of 1953 approximately 120 000 people left the GDR for the West. Ulbricht was summoned to Moscow and ordered to desist. Obeying orders, the SED announced a 'new course', abandoning collectivisation, reducing pressure on private enterprise and easing attacks on religious activity. This announcement was so badly botched, however, that 'broad segments of the population', in the words of an internal SED report, 'did . . . not understand the party's new course, [and] viewed it as a sign of weakness or even as victory by the Americans or the Church'. On 16 June construction workers staged a demonstration in Berlin and called for a general strike. The next day anti-regime protests took place in most cities. The Soviet reaction was swift: tanks and troops of the Group of Soviet Forces in Germany (GSFG) were sent in to quell the disturbances. The SED's control remained precarious, however, not least because it was exploited by the Americans who distributed food to any inhabitant of eastern Germany who crossed to West Berlin to collect it. The regime reasserted its authority in July 1953: Ulbricht's rivals in the Politburo were purged, the 'new course' was reaffirmed by the intensive use of propaganda, mass arrests occurred and the Stasi were able to isolate and neutralise any further protests.[89] The sudden destabilisation of the GDR gave Ulbricht, paradoxically, much greater leverage in Moscow: if the Soviets wanted stability in Germany they had to give full backing to the incumbent SED leadership and the East German state. Beria had wanted to trade German unification for neutralisation. He argued in the Presidium that the GDR could abandon socialism and re-unite in a 'peace-loving' Germany. He was arrested on 26 June and subsequently shot. Beria's demise was the result of his record as Stalin's secret-police chief rather than his German machinations. Nevertheless, his fall ended any possibility of the creation of a genuinely neutral Germany. The emergency measures of the summer of 1953 drove the Soviet Union's German policy into a cul-de-sac. They temporarily stabilised the GDR but did nothing to destabilise the FRG.[90]

The EDC treaty was finally rejected by the French National Assembly in August 1954 but without provoking the expected crisis.[91] When the EDC finally failed in the summer of 1954 there was never, despite Dulles's publicly expressed anger with France,[92] any real intention to abandon the forward defence of Europe. James Conant, the High Commissioner in Germany, was a lonely voice in suggesting that it would be preferable to have 'the withdrawal of all but token [US] forces from Europe and a so-called peripheral defence rather than a German national army'.[93] Instead the State Department favoured any alternative route the Europeans could follow 'promptly and with determination'. Preferably, 'Germany should be invited to accede to the North Atlantic Treaty . . . undertaking to follow in her initial contribution the size and composition of forces specified in the EDC Special Military Agreement (this excludes submarines and strategic bombers) [and to] state . . . that she would not produce atomic and thermonuclear weapons, [or] military aircraft.' There had always been a fall-back position to isolate France by creating a US–German–British defence pact which would oversee the 'prompt institution of the "interim measures" programme for actually getting under way the preliminary training of German forces' until the FRG could be levered into NATO.[94] A new policy was quickly hammered out at meetings in London and Paris: a new body, the Western European Union, provided a vehicle for the FRG's membership of NATO in 1955.[95] This new arrangement, shorn of its supranational aspects, was actually much closer to the arrangement desired by Adenauer as well as the British and American governments in 1950.[96] By the end of 1956 the Soviet Foreign Ministry could gloomily report that the FRG was 'becoming a major American partner' and that the 'activisation of the course towards German reunification on a bourgeois basis' had begun.[97]

Since his election as Chancellor of the FRG in 1949, Adenauer's fundamental purpose had been to anchor the FRG in the West, politically,
economically and militarily, whilst reunification remained a distant, if not
impossible, project.[98] With the FRG safely enmeshed in NATO, Adenauer
proposed that the three Western powers should take the initiative on the issue
of unification. He did so, however, on the basis that although the Soviet Union
had legitimate security interests it would be a permanent threat.[99] In June 1955
Adenauer was able to carry forward his policy personally when the Soviet
leadership offered to normalise relations with the FRG. Adenauer journeyed to
Moscow in September 1955 to sign the treaty which established diplomatic
relations with the USSR.[100]

The Moscow visit was the imprimatur on a highly successful policy of
establishing the FRG as a viable state. Paradoxically, it also marked the
beginning of West German disillusionment with that policy. The price of a
rearmed FRG was a rearmed GDR incorporated into the Warsaw Pact
organisation, also established in 1955 to supersede the individual treaties of
'alliance' which bound the ruling communist parties of Eastern Europe to the
Soviet Union. By the end of 1956 Adenauer had become much more concerned
about the American security guarantee to the FRG. In December 1953 the
American government had approved a plan to cut the number of men in the
armed forces by 600 000 by 1957, with the deepest cuts falling on the army. In
December 1954 NATO adopted a new strategic directive which envisaged the
use of tactical nuclear weapons in the defence of Europe. In June 1955 the first
NATO summer exercise under the new directive demonstrated that any
defence of Europe would involve the devastation of Germany. In the summer
of 1956 details of military planning were leaked to the press under the title of
the 'Radford plan', named for the chairman of the US JCS, Admiral Arthur
Radford. In October 1956 a political crisis overtook the German rearmament
programme, when delays in implementation were revealed. The Minister of
Defence, Theodor Blank, was forced to resign and was replaced by the Minister
of Atomic Affairs, Franz-Josef Strauss. These twin political crises had a
profound effect on Adenauer. Although the FRG had disclaimed the right to
build nuclear weapons on its territory in 1954, the Chancellor denounced the
US–Soviet dominance of nuclear power as intolerable, bemoaned the lack of
FRG influence in NATO and decided that the Bundeswehr should be equipped with nuclear weapons.[101]

In November 1956 Soviet forces crushed the popular reform communist
regime which had emerged in Hungary, demonstrating how vulnerable Germany might be to limited military action in central Europe.[102] In December
1956 the United Kingdom persuaded NATO to adopt a new military doctrine
which stressed even further the need to use nuclear weapons in any European
conflict.[103] In April 1957 the US embassy in Bonn reported that 'within past few
weeks subject of Atomic Weapons has come from relative obscurity to be

number one topic in press and, at the moment, in election campaign. Repercussions are already widespread and threaten to grow in number, variety and seriousness.'[104] Although Adenauer won the elections, the Soviets did all they could to keep the pot boiling by using the Poles to propose in the UN during October 1957 that the FRG, the GDR, Poland and Czechoslovakia become a nuclear-free zone.

It was in this already tense situation that the next German crisis, over Berlin, developed in November 1958. Whatever the worries of the West German government, those of the communist élite in the East were much more pressing. The major crisis of the East German state was that many amongst its population wanted to leave. The SED leadership was divided about how to tackle the Berlin issue. In May 1958 the head of the SED's International Department reported, 'some German comrades believe, for example, that the Berlin question cannot be resolved as long as Germany is not united. Others, on the other hand, believe that the Berlin question can be gradually resolved by starting now to carry out a determined line of political and economic conquest of West Berlin so as to create the preconditions for the unification of Berlin in the future.'[105] In the course of 1958 the latter view came to dominate as Berlin became a 'bleeding ulcer' for the GDR. In December 1957 the GDR had introduced a passport law to cut down emigration to the West. In July 1958 the Fifth SED Congress had vigorously endorsed the construction of socialism. Many of those now completely disillusioned with East German society were its best-qualified and productive citizens. They found a possible escape through Berlin. In 1957 about 60 per cent of emigrants left through West Berlin; in 1958 the figure was over 90 per cent.[106] Ulbricht saw West Berlin as a major threat to the survival of the GDR. The Soviet leadership was only too aware of the GDR's fragility. There had, for instance, been clashes between Soviet troops and German demonstrators at the time of the Hungarian uprising in November 1956.[107] In August 1958 Yuriy Andropov, head of the Central Committee department for dealing with communist parties, reported that the most talented people were being bled out of East Germany by hostility to the political system as well as by economic hardship.

In November 1958 a new Berlin crisis was activated by Khrushchev. He called upon the Potsdam powers to renounce their role in Berlin in favour of East Germany. On 27 November he threatened to transfer Soviet rights in the city and access routes to the GDR within six months. The Soviets had a range of objectives. They wished to disrupt the FRG's integration into NATO and stabilise the GDR. There were certainly 'Berlin firsters' in the Soviet foreign-policy apparatus who believed that success in dislodging the Western powers from West Berlin would be a major victory in itself. In 1959, however, wider political objectives seemed within reach. The willingness of the United States, Britain and France to negotiate on Berlin's status suggested that the FRG might be partially abandoned by its allies. Khrushchev withdrew his ultimatum in March 1959 and replaced it with a draft peace treaty to be considered at the Paris conference of May 1960, a four-power American–Soviet–British–French summit from which Adenauer was excluded. This proved to be a false dawn: no Western countries broke ranks and acceded to any Soviet proposals.

Nevertheless, the Berlin crisis was a defining moment for both the FRG and the GDR. It convinced the SED of the need to create an even more closed society; it convinced many western German political leaders that the FRG must pursue a more active policy to prevent that closed society becoming a reality. Between 1958 and 1963, however, FRG policy was actually thrown into a state of paralysis. Adenauer was taxed by fear of American betrayal, an even greater fear of a nuclear exchange and an inability to suggest how the West should mix adamantine resolve and diplomatic flexibility. As early as 26 November 1958 the Chancellor was shocked by the suggestion of the US Secretary of State, John Foster Dulles, usually his favourite American foreign-policy-maker, that GDR border officials might act as 'agents' of the Soviet Union rather than representatives of a sovereign state.[108] The Chancellor's anxieties were increased further by what he saw as the British Prime Minister, Harold Macmillan's, willingness to abandon Berlin in his search for a great power summit which included Britain and France.[109] What Adenauer feared most, however, was the possible use of nuclear weapons in Germany. Thus he insisted that the Western allies take no physical positions in Berlin or its access routes from which they could be forced to retreat.[110] The tension created by a desire for a strong line and the avoidance of risk caused diplomatic inertia. The head of the reunification desk in the German Foreign Ministry 'admitted frankly Fedrep still groping for ideas [to] counter Soviet manoeuvres'.[111] Adenauer himself told the Americans that 'he thought there might be need for an interim or provisional solution of the problem of Berlin . . . he had no answer to the problem himself'.[112] Thus the 1958 FRG–Soviet trade treaty was renewed for another three years on 31 December 1960, although West Berlin was only implicitly included, but a GDR attempt to restrict West Berliners from entering the East provoked the threat of a trade embargo unless the policy was reversed.[113]

The threat of embargo had a disproportionate impact on Ulbricht. It loomed large in his assessment of the German situation delivered at a meeting with Khrushchev at the end of November 1960. He put forward a plan to insulate the GDR from the West by tying its economy to that of the Soviet Union. Ulbricht complained that Khrushchev had reneged on his 1958 promise to sign a peace treaty with the GDR, yet he was terrified of actually signing such a treaty because the FRG could undermine the GDR economy.[114] On the basis of this analysis Ulbricht argued that the GDR's economic failure should be compensated for by political action.[115] In the first six months of 1961 over 100 000 people fled from the GDR. In July 1961 another 30 000 left.[116] Over the summer of 1961, Ulbricht, believing the Soviet Union would support him economically, was able to persuade a somewhat dubious Khrushchev to take decisive action. On 13 August 1961 a makeshift barricade was thrown up to prevent Germans travelling between the two halves of Berlin. This action solved the GDR's short-term problem but devalued Berlin as a lever in Soviet Cold War policy. Soviet unwillingness to endorse a clear two-Germanies policy was demonstrated by their failure to conclude a peace treaty with the GDR.[117]

Although the Wall became the most famous symbol of the Cold War, immediate reactions were muted.[118] Indeed, Adenauer had fallen back on his old cry of unity and strength of the West and attempted to minimise the crisis.[119] He rejected the trade embargo that Ulbricht had expected. An embargo on large-diameter steel pipes for the Soviet oil industry, proposed in July 1961, was only implemented in December 1962. Although Adenauer, on the eve of his retirement in October 1963, denounced Kennedy's decision to sell grain to the Soviet Union to compensate for a series of poor harvests, and argued that food should only be delivered if the Soviet Union was willing to dismantle the Wall, the Foreign Minister, Gerhard Schröder, remarked that it was unrealistic to believe that the Soviet Union would be influenced by economic pressure.[120] Governmental inaction after August 1961 did, however, create an opportunity for new ideas on German–Soviet–German relations to emerge. The mayor of Berlin and the SPD's candidate for Chancellor in the September 1961 federal elections, Willy Brandt, called for much stronger action, such as an embargo. On 16 August 1961 Brandt wrote an angry letter to Kennedy denouncing American inaction.[121] Three days later he told Lyndon Johnson that 'the 13th of August could play a very great role in future German developments. He did not know yet exactly what they would be.'[122] Although Brandt lost the elections to Adenauer, his view that the Berlin crisis was a key event in German development was to prove more influential in the coming decade.

Neither was the Wall entirely to the Soviet advantage. As Khrushchev himself later pointed out, Soviet declaratory policy had originally envisaged a 'free city' from whence disruption of the FRG could have been launched. To cover the construction of the Wall, which led to a 16-hour confrontation between American and Soviet tanks at a Berlin checkpoint on 26 October, the Soviets felt the need to make direct threats. 'Your generals talk of maintaining your position in Berlin with force. This is bluff. If you send in tanks, they will burn and make no mistake about it. If you want war, you can have it, and remember it will be your war. Our rockets will fly automatically.'[123] In the wake of such threats Kennedy was unlikely to listen to Khrushchev's subsequent argument that Europe was 'fraught with danger for the whole world only because most extreme aggressive militarist forces in West Germany are interested in this' or his pleas to reach agreement on West Berlin since it was a 'dangerous hotbed of collision' used by an 'old-aged man who both morally and physically is with one foot in the grave [sic]'.[124]

THE CUBAN CRISIS

For the Soviets the lessons of 1961 were reinforced by the Cuban crisis of 1962. Fidel Castro was a new type of revolutionary when his 26th July movement seized power in Cuba at the end of 1958. Unlike revolutionary leaders in Asia he had not been part of a movement which fused anti-Western nationalism, a relationship with the Russians and a response to the October revolution. Cuba too was a new type of Cold War environment. It had a long history of economic and political entanglement with the United States dating back to the 1890s. Even when the USA had adopted an 'isolationist' stance with regard to Europe it had intervened vigorously and freely in Cuba's affairs, as at the time of the 1933 revolution which brought the then Sergeant Fulgencio Batista to prominence.[125] The relationship between the small group which gathered around Castro after Batista seized power in a coup in 1952 and the United States was, whilst essentially hostile, based on an understanding of the bilateral Cuban–American relationship and its workings since 1902. Between 1959 and 1961 a trilateral Cuban–Soviet–American relationship came to be superimposed upon this existing, rather hysterical, relationship. The merging of these two currents gave the Cuban revolution its peculiarly destabilising influence upon the Cold War. Briefly, in 1962, the island became the focus of the Soviet–American conflict. Soviet policy at the time of the Cuban missile crisis demonstrated Castro's relative impotence in dealing with the international environment. Yet the existence of a Soviet ally across the Straits of Florida wilfully combined in 1962 with a widespread realisation of America's vulnerability to nuclear weapons and a new age of television diplomacy did much to create a new stage in the Cold War: a populist Cold War which leaked beyond the control of the relatively circumscribed American foreign and security policy élite.

Castro was a self-proclaimed revolutionary but not a communist. Cuba did possess a communist party with close links with Moscow: the Popular Socialist Party (PSP). Its relations with Castro were poor. In 1956 its leadership denounced Castro's insurgency in the Sierra Maestra as 'putschism': secret plotting to overthrow the government which merely served the 'purpose of maintaining the existing regime'.[126] Castro certainly wished to lead a revolution. In its aftermath happiness for the Cuban people would be achieved by measures such as the rise in agricultural prices, extended credit, debt cancellation, increased employment, raised salaries, a reduced working week and unemployment benefit – measures which Castro attributed to Franklin Roosevelt and the New Deal. This is not to say that Castro was unaware of the Soviet Union as a model. He was an enthusiastic consumer of popular histories of Soviet success.[127] His brother Raul was a member of Soviet front organisations and had had some contacts with the KGB.[128] In the end it was Che Guevara, one of Castro's closest companions, who began to develop the idea of aligning the Cuban revolution with world revolution.[129]

When Batista resigned and fled on the last day of 1958, a new regime, which at first sight seemed broad-based, was set up. As a Soviet analysis pointed out, however, all of the real power lay in Castro's hands. The PSP, initially excluded from power, worked hard to convince their contacts in the International Department of the Central Committee that Castro should be nurtured. He was, the PSP leadership claimed, progressive, anti-imperialist and a national demo-crat with good socialist potential. If the Soviet Union offered the Cuban revolution economic and military aid, the influence of the communists would be increased. Initial Soviet analyses saw the 'main aims of the revolution' as a series of economic measures which would effectively weaken the dominance of American companies and the old élite. Such measures, although certainly not communistic, were not inconsistent with a 'bourgeois democratic revolution' and could lead to the 'objective prerequisites' of a socialist revolution if a Marxist-Leninist party was able to secure a large measure of influence in the new regime. The International Department was informed by the PSP leader Blas Roca that through the role of Carlos Rafael Rodriguez, the only prominent PSP member to join Castro in the Sierra Maestra, the PSP could be active in wielding revolutionary power.[130] It was certainly the case that Castro wasted no time in denouncing the United States. Castro, however, faced a major problem in his defiance. The Cuban economy was largely based on sugar monoculture. Most of this sugar was exported to the United States and the proceeds were used to buy basic commodities such as oil.

The initial American response to Castro's seizure of power was reasonably cautious. The director of the CIA, Allen Dulles, told Congressmen that 'when you have a revolution you kill your enemies . . . it will probably go much too far, but they have to go through this'. Yet the combination of Castro's anti-Americanism and economic weakness was bound to antagonise groups with political power in the United States. The two most obvious solutions to the regime's problems were to confiscate land and industrial assets and to seek another market for Cuban sugar. As early as 1959 unofficial opposition groups were operating from the USA. One of their tactics was to send World War Two vintage bombers from Florida to drop incendiary bombs on cane fields. During one of these raids the popular commander of the Cuban army, Camilio Cienfuegos, flying in a light plane, was killed, probably shot down mistakenly by a Cuban fighter. Ties with the Soviet Union seemed desirable to defend the revolution both militarily and politically.[131] In February 1960 the Politburo member Anastas Mikoyan arrived in Cuba to explore such a relationship. Mikoyan supported the idea of offering significant aid to Castro's regime. He recommended a three-point programme. The Soviet Union would accept sugar from Cuba and in return supply it with oil. The Soviet Union would also offer further technical and economic assistance to Cuba. Finally, active consideration would be given to offering the Cubans military training and weapons.[132] Mikoyan's visit was the turning point in transforming the Cuban revolution into a Cold War conflict. For the Soviets the island became an area of strategic and rhetorical importance. The overthrow of the Castro regime became a high priority for the Eisenhower administration. Castro's rhetoric took on an apocalyptic cast which caused increased tension amongst the decision-makers of both superpowers.

In March 1960 a ship carrying arms exploded, probably accidentally, in Havana harbour. Castro immediately accused officials of the American government of sabotage.[133] In the same month Eisenhower did indeed give orders for the CIA to start training the Cuban exiles who were to overthrow the revolution. Within the Soviet leadership there continued to be splits over Cuban policy. Khrushchev and Mikoyan saw Cuba as an important asset in the struggle for influence with the United States. As early as September 1960 Khrushchev privately expressed the view that Cuba could become 'a beacon of socialism in Latin America'.[134] Mikoyan had stressed during his visit the need to confiscate private property. Castro made an important step in this direction in June 1960 when he nationalised the petroleum refining industry after it refused to refine the oil which started to arrive from the Soviet Union in April.[135] Other Soviet leaders, most notably Boris Ponomarev, the head of the International Department, continued to argue that Castro was not a socialist and could not be trusted. In material terms aid to Cuba was kept low-key. Military aid began to arrive in July but this aid was kept secret.[136] In the same month, however, Khrushchev and Castro rhetorically inflated the Cold War importance of the Cuban revolution. On 9 July 1960 Khrushchev used Cuba as part of his continuing campaign to exaggerate the Soviet Union's nuclear capability. He declared:

> One should not forget that now the United States is no longer an unreasonable distance from the Soviet Union, as it was before. Figuratively speaking, should the need arise Soviet artillerymen can support the Cuban people by missile fire, if the aggressive forces from the Pentagon dare to intervene in Cuba. We have the capability of landing missiles precisely on a given square at a distance of 13 000 kilometres ... the Soviet Union is raising its voice and extends the hand of friendship to the people of Cuba in their fight for independence.

Later in the month Castro promised to spread revolution 'the length of the Andes'.[137]

As Khrushchev had predicted, the United States would give Castro nowhere else to turn except the Soviet Union. One of Eisenhower's last acts as President was to cut economic relations with Cuba and one of Kennedy's first important decisions was to sanction a CIA-organised invasion of Cuba by Cuban exiles. The senior members of the Eisenhower and Kennedy administrations showed considerable restraint and caution in the central strategic relationship with the Soviet Union. They showed a corresponding lack of caution in their dealings with third countries when the military relationship was not directly involved. This substratum of US Cold War policy developed, first, because of fear about the likely course of industrialisation in the Third World and, second, because of the frustrations of 'rollback' in Europe.[138] Kennedy brought a difference of style rather than substance: the Eisenhower men tended to be more paternalist and more cautious, the Kennedy men more sympathetic to indigenous leaders but more interventionist: 'liberals with machine guns'. By inclination Eisenhower and Kennedy were as keen to deploy American military and paramilitary power as their most gung-ho subordinates. Eisenhower had ordered the CIA overthrow of President Jacobo Arbenz Guzman of Guatemala in June 1954 after he had expropriated the funds of the United Fruit Company and accepted arms from the Soviet bloc. The Guatemalan coup was an exhilarating experience for its authors.[139] However, the invasion of Cuba at the Bay of Pigs on the south of the island, launched in April 1961, was a complete fiasco. This episode quelled some of the doubts in the Soviet leadership about the usefulness of the Cuban revolution. Not only was the Cuban regime irreparably divided from the United States but it had proved it could mobilise support and withstand challenges to itself.[140] In the summer of 1961 the PSP was allowed to grow in influence, particularly in the field of suppressing literary and artistic dissent. In May Castro declared that it was in the vanguard of the revolution and should be accorded a leading role. He engineered the creation of a new party combining the PSP and the 26th July movement controlled by him and his close supporters. In December 1961 he announced, 'with complete satisfaction and confidence, that I am a Marxist-Leninist and shall remain so till the last days of my life'.[141]

Cuba thus became an asset not only for the Soviet Union but for Khrushchev, who, at an early stage, had argued that Castro would be useful. What was less clear was how the Soviet Union could use this asset. Some members of the Soviet government continued to insist that Castro's post-Bay of Pigs actions were precipitate, not only threatening the internal stability of the revolution but inviting an American intervention which would put the Soviet Union in a very difficult position.[142] The Kennedy administration was committed to the overthrow of Castro by all means short of outright invasion. At the end of 1961 Robert Kennedy had been placed in charge of the 'Cuba Project' to 'help the people of Cuba overthrow the Communist regime from within Cuba and institute a new government with which the United States can live in peace'. In achieving this goal it was acknowledged that 'to cause the overthrow of the target government, the US will make use of indigenous resources, internal and external, but recognises that final success will require decisive US military intervention'.[143] The next move in Cuba fell very much within Khrushchev's domain. If he wanted to use the Cuban revolution, action had to be taken whilst Cuba was still an asset. The Soviets made a clear decision to act exactly a year after the Bay of Pigs.

Cuba was chosen as a suitable place to demonstrate Soviet power rather than for the good of the Cuban revolutionaries. As the crisis developed Khrushchev very quickly passed from Cuba itself to wider diplomacy.[144] Berlin had failed to provide a foreign-policy coup for Khrushchev. The one positive lesson he drew from it, however, was that his oft-repeated faith in the deterrent power of Soviet nuclear weapons had been vindicated: American leaders were unwilling to push any crisis to the brink. The deployment of missiles in Cuba was Khrushchev's personal project, hatched in May 1962. It was prompted by a negative concern for Cuba. Khrushchev feared that the USA and its allies would make the USSR and its allies retreat in some regions of the world and that, after the relative failure of German policy in the previous three years, he would be made the scapegoat for any setbacks. He was much exercised by Stalin's dying expression of contempt for his successors: 'When I'm not around they'll strangle you like kittens'. The Cuban missiles were 'an easy solution . . . a sort of cure-all'.

Some Soviet leaders saw the deployment of missiles in Cuba as a means of changing the strategic balance. Yuriy Andropov argued that 'we shall be able to sight them at the soft underbelly of the Americans'. Malinovsky pointed out that there were American missiles already in Turkey which could destroy Kiev, Minsk and Moscow. Indeed the missiles in Cuba were far from being a political symbol. If the planned deployment of 24 SS-4 and 16 SS-5 launch systems had actually taken place (42 SS-4s and 20 nuclear warheads reached Cuba) it would have tripled the Soviet missile force threatening the United States.[145] More caution was shown by Anastas Mikoyan, who argued that it would be overly provocative, and Andrey Gromyko, who commented: 'it will cause a political explosion in the USA. This has to be taken into account.' General Moskalenko, head of strategic missile forces, and General Golikov, head of MPD, objected and were removed.[146] Khrushchev believed that if the missiles were delivered secretly and the Americans were presented with a *fait accompli* they would have no choice 'but to swallow this bitter pill'. Indeed in the United States there had been an initial unwillingness to accept the reality of the deployments. They indicated a propensity to take risks which US officials regarded as unreasonable given the strategic balance. On 5 October, McGeorge Bundy said 'he felt the Soviets would not go that far, that he was satisfied that no offensive weapons would be installed in Cuba because of the world-wide effects'.[147]

Soon, however, Khrushchev began to realise the enormity of his miscalculation. According to his adviser Oleg Troyanovskiy, by the 'end of September . . . Khrushchev said "Soon hell will break lose . . . Now it's too late to change anything." I gathered the impression that by that time he had realised the risks involved in the operation. However, it was really too late to call it off.' By the time Kennedy announced the United States would 'quarantine' Cuba on 22 October 1962, the first acquaintance of Khrushchev and others with the content of the President's speech evoked relief rather than anxiety. 'The sea blockade . . . was received like something intangible . . . a step leaving a lot of room for political manoeuvring . . . It did not look like an ultimatum or a direct threat to

attack Cuba.' So cautious had Khrushchev become that when 'Vasiliy Kuznetsov advanced, although very cautiously, an idea of countering the pressure the
Americans brought to bear on the Soviet Union in connection with Cuba by
putting pressure on West Berlin it provoked a sharp ... reaction by Khrushchev. The latter said in a peremptory manner that he could do without such
advice and that we had no intention to add fuel to the conflict, the more so to
expand its geographic boundaries.'[148]

During the crisis Kennedy and his advisers shifted from seeing the significance of linkages in the crisis based on global prestige to seeing them as
based on a bilateral quid pro quo. At the beginning of the crisis it was assumed
Cuba was linked to Berlin. The CIA analysis suggested, 'Moscow clearly is
seeking to portray Berlin as a hostage to Cuba ... [it] must have anticipated
[opportunities] to bring the Western Powers into serious negotiations on Berlin
and German questions ... [which] underscore the importance Moscow atta-
ches to demonstrating alleged shift in world balance of power in favour of the
bloc which, in the Soviet view, will eventually oblige the West to come to an
accommodation on Berlin.'[149] Dean Rusk concurred:

> Khrushchev may feel it's important for us to learn about living under medium-range
> missiles, and he's doing that sort of balance that, uh, that political, psychological
> (plank?). I think also that, uh, Berlin is, uh, very much involved in this. ... they may be
> thinking that they can either bargain Berlin and Cuba against each other, or that they
> could provoke us into a kind of action in Cuba which would give an umbrella for them
> to take action with respect to Berlin. In other words, like the Suez–Hungary combi-
> nation.[150]

The most forceful voices in the early meetings of the Executive Committee
of the National Security Council (ExComm) insisted on the central importance
of global linkage. Treasury Secretary Douglas Dillon insisted that:

> the Soviet Union has now deliberately initiated a public test of our intentions that can
> determine the future course of world events for many years to come. If we allow the
> offensive capabilities presently in Cuba to remain there, I am convinced that sooner or
> later and probably sooner we will lose all of Latin America to Communism because all
> credibility of our willingness to effectively resist Soviet military power will have been
> removed ... we can expect similar reactions elsewhere, for instance in Iran, Thailand
> and Pakistan.[151]

Even more brutally Dean Acheson decreed: 'Khrushchev had presented the
United States with a direct challenge, we were involved in a test of wills, and
the sooner we got to a showdown the better. He favoured clearing the missile
bases out decisively with an air strike.'[152] As the crisis progressed, however,
others began to suggest that global prestige was not the key issue. Robert
McNamara has recalled: 'the *possibility* of what I call "blundering into disaster"
preoccupied me during the missile crisis, not the alleged *probability* of this or
that event. What the missile crisis impressed on me was that, yes, we *could*
stumble into a nuclear war; that such an event, however "limited", was totally

unacceptable; and thus that it must be avoided.'[153] If this was the case, a mutually acceptable deal rather than unilateral American action seemed preferable.

At one level the missile crisis developed as a Soviet–American confrontation in which the Cubans played relatively little part. Once the missiles were discovered and the United States imposed a blockade on Cuba, Khrushchev started by reaffirming Soviet–Cuban solidarity in the defence of the island. On 23 October 1962 he wrote to Castro rejecting 'the brazen demands of the US government to control the sending of weapons to Cuba . . . the Soviet government has expressed the most determined protest against the piratical measures of the United States government – and declares its determination to fight actively . . . we have issued instructions to our military personnel in Cuba to adopt the necessary measures to be completely ready for combat.'[154] On 26 October Castro tried to persuade Khrushchev to continue with this confrontational stance. Claiming 'that aggression is almost imminent within the next 24 or 72 hours' he delivered the chilling message that the most likely form of aggression was 'an air attack against certain targets [i.e. the ballistic missiles] with the limited objective of destroying them' and that 'the Soviet Union must never allow the circumstances in which the imperialists could launch the first nuclear strike against it'.[155] By this stage of the crisis, however, Castro was effectively 'outside the loop'. In his own words: 'Neither we nor the Soviet soldiers were aware of the messages sent by Khrushchev [to Kennedy offering to settle the crisis] on the 26th and the 27th. You see, I think Khrushchev was far more informed than we were. He was already proposing a solution, and we knew nothing. Kennedy immediately accepted Khrushchev's proposition . . . because it was exactly what he was demanding.'[156] Yet whilst Cuba itself was excluded from the high diplomacy of the Cuban missile crisis Castro remained influential in Cuba itself, even with the Soviet forces based there. These forces were equipped with a small number of short-range tactical missiles armed with nuclear warheads intended for use against a full-scale American invasion. This eventuality never arose but the Soviet forces did shoot down an American U-2 reconnaissance aircraft on the morning of 27 October without permission from the Kremlin. According to General Georgiy Voronkov, 'the Soviet armed forces thought they were there to protect Cuba, and at a given point the overflights – both the low-level overflights and the high-level overflights – combined with the apparent imminence of attack and war, caused the situation . . . to bubble over. So when the U-2 appeared on the radar screen . . . he gave the order to shoot it down. Events had reached such a point that he believed war had either broken out or was about to break out'. In Castro's recollection he egged the Soviet commanders on:

> we contacted the Soviet command . . . I told them we had reached this decision: we cannot tolerate these low-level overflights . . . because any day at dawn they're going to destroy all these units . . . a decision taken on the afternoon and evening of the 26th of

October ... All our batteries fired on all low-level flights on the morning of the 27th when the planes appeared at their usual time ... Now, we didn't have ground-to-air missiles. I explained to the Soviet commander the seriousness of these overflights, and I explained our point of view, to persuade them that our order had been correct ... Obviously, we couldn't give them any orders, but we cannot say they were solely responsible.[157]

In the event the American leaders in ExComm decided that the shootdown was not sufficient reason to abandon the settlement they and the Soviets were in the process of working out, but the dangers of uncontrolled escalation were obvious.[158] The deal offered by the Americans was that in return for the removal of the missiles they would publicly promise not to invade Cuba and secretly remove IRBMs which had been deployed in Turkey to signal American determination after the Vienna summit.[159]

The failure of the Cuban gambit was a hard blow for the Soviets. When the Presidium and other senior Soviet leaders met on 28 October no-one had any substantive comments to make except Khrushchev. He defended his decision to withdraw the missiles on the grounds that it was a Brest-Litovsk: a forced compromise with the imperialists. Khrushchev attempted to turn the reverse into a diplomatic breakthrough, playing on a shared sense of relief that the crisis had not escalated into war.[160] He called upon Kennedy to initiate '*détente* between Nato and the Warsaw treaty countries' and expressed a willingness 'to exchange views on this question with you and to find a reasonable solution'. Khrushchev was probably sincere when he declared: 'we ... appreciate your cooperation in the elimination of the crisis and your understanding of the necessity for reciprocal concessions and compromise so that the conflict might be prevented from going beyond the limits that might really break into a thermonuclear war ... the sooner we clear away the roadblock, the wind-fallen wood, which has piled up in the international relations, and make clear the roads to correct mutual understanding the better it would be.'[161]

Most Soviet leaders took quite a different lesson about the future course of the Cold War from the Berlin and Cuban crises. As Mikoyan told Fidel Castro, 'the Americans' appetites are growing. When I was talking with McCloy, he said with a smile that it would not be a bad idea if we also removed anti-aircraft rockets from Cuba. Yet that weapon is defensive, not offensive. Half an hour before I left New York, those swindlers ... sent Comrade Kuznetsov a letter alleging that the Americans had forgotten to raise the question of certain weapons ... To be sure, the appetite comes with eating but we are going to stand firm against that.'[162] Vasiliy Kuznetsov himself told John McCloy, the epitome in Soviet eyes of the monopoly capitalist, that 'the Soviet Union would never again face a 4-to-1 missile inferiority'. In the longer term most Soviet leaders were confirmed in their belief that the Soviet position needed further strengthening in the face of a malign enemy. According to Malinovsky, the leadership had 'no facts to indicate the abandonment by US imperialist circles of the policy of war ... preventive war against the Soviet Union all along has been within the range of possibilities envisaged by the Pentagon'. As ever, Mikhail Suslov delivered the harshest verdict: '[the imperialists] backed down every time, breaking their head on the solidarity and might of the socialist camp'. He added that all peace-loving forces on Earth must preserve vigilance and strengthen their solidarity, so as to strengthen not weaken the struggle against aggressive force.

In terms of immediate policy Khrushchev declared that 'in the interest of preserving the gains of socialism, we are ready to make and we do make reasonable political compromises'. After 27 October 1962 the shock of the missile crisis ensured that Cuba returned to its role as an irritant in the Soviet–American relationship rather than being at the centre of it. Castro felt that he had been betrayed by Khrushchev, as the Soviet leader was willing to withdraw all weapons which the Americans defined as offensive, light bombers as well as missiles, from the island in return for an ambiguous 'gentleman's' agreement' with Kennedy that there would be no American invasion. The Cubans launched their own diplomatic effort in the form of five demands: an end to economic sanctions, an end to subversive activity, an end to anti-Cuban naval activity, an end to violations of territorial waters and airspace and an American withdrawal from their naval base at Guantanamo in the south-east of Cuba, but were effectively ignored by both superpowers.[163] Khrushchev, however, did not want to abandon his Cuban alliance. Welcoming Castro to Red Square in April 1963, he portrayed Cuba as both a validation of the October revolution and his own policy of 'peaceful coexistence'. 'Revolutionary Cuba [was] a beacon that shows the way to progress, freedom and happiness to all peoples of Latin America', in Khrushchev's rhetorical imagination. One former Soviet diplomat has suggested, however, that he regarded Cuba as a new Albania. Albania was a 'base in the Mediterranean' whose army was trained and equipped by the Soviet Union and was supposed to serve as 'a pearl that would be attractive to the Muslim world, especially for countries in the Middle East and Africa'. Cuba was to play the same role in the Caribbean for Latin America.[164] Khrushchev dispatched Mikoyan to Cuba in November 1962 to restore the broken relationship. He was largely successful because of Cuban dependence.[165] As Castro explained: 'The entire life of the country, the energy of the country, depended on the Soviets. Who else was going to supply us? ... The USSR supplied the oil, they supplied the weapons. After the October crisis we did have one victory, which was weapons free of charge ... So we didn't want to make relations bitter. Who could profit from that? ... We simply had to control that anger.'[166] In the initial aftermath of the crisis Khrushchev continued to insist that the Soviet Union would defend Cuba. In May 1963 a joint agreement declared that 'the organisers of aggression must understand that an invasion of Cuba will bring mankind to the brink of a destructive thermonuclear war'. In reply to Chinese sneers in July that not only had the saga of Soviet missiles in

Cuba been a 'venturesome blunder' but that the Soviet Union had 'capitulated to American imperialism', the CPSU Central Committee issued a statement reiterating that 'if the US imperialists break their word and invade the territory of Cuba, we shall come to the assistance of the Cuban people ... from Soviet territory, just as we would have helped from Cuban territory ... it would take somewhat more time for the missiles to reach their targets, but this would not affect their accuracy.' This was just empty bluster after the events of October 1962 and was recognised as such by the Soviet leadership, who had abandoned all such rhetoric by the end of 1963.[167] Khrushchev ceased to believe that the Soviet Union should make any gestures towards the Chinese and their virulent Cold War rhetoric.

For the Americans the bargaining over prestige during the crisis was qualitatively different from that which had started the crisis. It is notable, however, that the usual assumptions only broke down under enormous pressure. Once the immediate threat of the missiles had been removed the Americans returned to more conventional thought patterns. The State Department's review of the crisis concluded:

> The short-run effects would be very favourable to the US. Unquestionably the US will emerge from this confrontation with increased prestige. The Soviet action should demonstrate once again the offensive nature of Soviet motivations more clearly than anything we could say. It should also demonstrate that the Soviets are not prepared to risk a decisive military showdown with the US over issues involving the extension of Soviet power. We should be clear, however, that this is not to be confused with Soviet willingness to 'go to the mat' over an interest vital to Soviet security.[168]

If officials had reflected on this last comment, and applied it to the United States, they may have concluded that Cuba, and by implication many other countries, was not vital to American security. More influential was the view of the Defense Department that, 'the Soviet setback in Cuba was more than a local one. And not because of the importance of the base in Cuba. Retreat in Cuba suggests retreat closer to home. The lesson for us should be clear. No matter how valueless an overseas base the time to give it up is before or well after a crisis – not during it – if we want to have allies believing that association with us is in their interests.'[169]

NOTES

1 James Richter, *Reexamining Soviet Policy Towards Germany During the Beria Interregnum* (Washington, CWIHP/Woodrow Wilson Center, *CWIHP Working Paper* No. 3).

2 Parrott, *Politics and Technology*, pp. 127–31.

3 Parrish, *Security Dilemma*, p. 358.

4 Vladislav Zubok, *Khrushchev and the Berlin Crisis, 1958–1962* (Washington, CWIHP/Woodrow Wilson Center, *CWIHP Working Paper* No. 6).

5 Khrushchev to Kennedy, 26 October 1962, in *Problems of Communism*, XLI (1992), pp. 37–45.

6 Vladislav Zubok, 'The Missile Crisis and the Problem of Soviet Learning', *Problems of Communism*, XLI (1992), pp. 19–23.

7 Christoph Bluth, *Soviet Strategic Arms Policy before SALT* (Cambridge, Cambridge University Press, 1992), pp. 40–120.

8 Steven Zaloga, *Target America: The Soviet Union and the Strategic Arms Race, 1945–1964* (Novato, Presidio, 1993), p. 213.

9 Robert Slusser, *The Berlin Crisis of 1961: Soviet–American Relations and the Struggle for Power in the Kremlin, June–November 1961* (Baltimore, Johns Hopkins University Press, 1974), pp. 10–20.

10 Slusser, *Berlin*, pp. 38–61.

11 John Foster Dulles, 'The Evolution of Foreign Policy', speech made before the Council of Foreign Relations, New York, 12 January 1954, *Department of State Bulletin (25 January 1954)*, p. 107.

12 Dulles, 'The Evolution of Foreign Policy', p. 108.

13 John Foster Dulles, 'Policy for Security and Peace', *Foreign Affairs*, 32/3 (April 1954).

14 Dwight D. Eisenhower, 'Farewell Radio and Television Address to the American People by President Eisenhower January 17, 1961', in Robert Branyan and Lawrence Larsen, eds., *The Eisenhower Administration, 1953–1961: A Documentary History* (2 vols., New York, Random House, 1971), II, pp. 1375–6.

15 Memorandum of discussion at the 165th meeting of the National Security Council, Wednesday, 7 October 1953, *FRUS* 1952–54, II, pp. 514–34.

16 Memorandum of discussion at the 165th meeting of the National Security Council.

17 PREM11/369, WU.1072/180G, 'Record of the Restricted Meeting of Ministers of North Atlantic Council on December 16, 1953', PRO, Kew.

18 Hans-Jurgen Grabbe, 'Konrad Adenauer, John Foster Dulles, and West German–American Relations', in Richard Immerman, ed., *John Foster Dulles and the Diplomacy of the Cold War* (Princeton, Princeton University Press, 1990), pp. 112–13.

19 M. Steven Fish, 'After Stalin's Death: The Anglo-American Debate Over a New Cold War', *Diplomatic History*, 10 (1986), pp. 333–55.

20 Christian F. Ostermann, 'The United States, The East German Uprising of 1953, and the Limits of Rollback', *CWIHP Working Paper* No. 11 (December 1994), pp. 12–13.

21 Ostermann, 'East German Uprising of 1953', p. 24.

22 Ostermann, 'East German Uprising of 1953', pp. 37–8.

23 Austrian State Treaty, 15 May 1955, *DOIA* 1955, pp. 226–38.

24 Geneva Summit Conference Directive to the Foreign Ministers, 23 July 1955, *DOIA* 1955, pp. 48–9.

25 John Lewis Gaddis, 'Learning to Live with Transparency', in *The Long Peace* (New York, Oxford University Press, 1987), pp. 198–200.

26 Diary entry by President's Press Secretary, 24 January 1956, *FRUS* 1955–57, XXIV, p. 44.

27 Telegram from embassy in the Soviet Union to Department of State, 9 April 1956, *FRUS* 1955–57, XXIV.

28 Memorandum of discussion of the 280th Meeting of the NSC, 28 June 1956, *FRUS* 1955–57, XXIV, pp. 118–123.

29 Briefing of Weapons Systems Evaluation Group Report No. 12, in David Rosenberg, ' "A Smoking Radiating Ruin at the End of Two Hours": Documents on American

Plans for Nuclear War with the Soviet Union, 1954–1955', *International Security* 6 (1981/2), p. 31.

30 Briefing of WSEG Report No. 12, p. 32.

31 Memorandum of discussion at the 339th Meeting of the NSC, 10 October 1957, *FRUS 1955–57*, XXIV, pp. 161–6.

32 Deterrence and Survival in the Nuclear Age. Science Advisory Panel of the Security Resources Board (The Gaither Report), 7 November 1957, in *Documents of the NSC, 1947–1977* (Washington, University Publications of America, 1980), Reel 4.

33 Memorandum of discussion at the 339th Meeting of the NSC, 10 October 1957, *FRUS 1955–57*, XXIV.

34 Memorandum of conference with the President, 6 March 1959, and Memorandum of conversation with the President, 9 March 1959, in William Burr, ed., *The Berlin Crisis, 1958–1962* (Alexandria, Chadwyck-Healey/National Security Archive, 1994), Docs. 908 and 920.

35 Memorandum of conference with the President, 19 July 1960, *Berlin Crisis*, Document 1933.

36 Notes on discussion of the thinking of the Soviet leadership, 11 February 1961, *Berlin Crisis*, Doc. 1994.

37 Memorandum of conversation between President Kennedy and Premier Khrushchev, at the Vienna Summit, 3 June 1961, in Laurence Chang and Peter Kornbluh, eds., *The Cuban Missile Crisis, 1962* (New York, The New Press, 1992), Doc. 1.

38 NIE-8–61, 7 June 1961 in Donald P. Steury, ed., *Intentions and Capabilities: Estimates on Soviet Strategic Forces, 1950–1983*, Doc. 9.

39 NIE-8/1-61, in Steury, *Intentions and Capabilities*, Doc. 10.

40 John Lewis Gaddis, *Strategies of Containment: A Critical Appraisal of Postwar American National Security Policy* (Oxford, Oxford University Press, 1982), pp. 215–16.

41 Gaddis, *Strategies of Containment*, p. 218.

42 Jeffrey Record, *Revising U.S. Military Strategy* (Washington, Pergamon-Brassey's, 1984), pp. 101–3.

43 NSC 147: Analysis of Possible Courses of Action in Korea, 2 April 1953, *Documents of the NSC, 1947–1977*, Reel 3, Frames 664–723.

44 Foot, *The Wrong War*, pp. 204–31.

45 Rosemary Foot, 'Nuclear Coercion and the Ending of the Korean Conflict', *International Security*, 13 (1988–9), pp. 92–112.

46 Nancy Bernkopf Tucker, 'John Foster Dulles and the Taiwan Roots of the "Two Chinas" Policy', in Immerman, *Dulles*, pp. 235–62.

47 Chang, *Friends and Enemies*, pp. 109–113.

48 Gordon Chang and He Di, 'The Absence of War in the US–China Confrontation over Quemoy and Matsu in 1954–1955: Contingency, Luck, Deterrence?' *American Historical Review*, 98 (1993), pp. 1500–24.

49 Yahuda, *China's Role*, pp. 69–70.

50 Yahuda, *China's Role*, p. 66.

51 Chang and He, 'Quemoy'.

52 Yahuda, *China's Role*.

53 Mineo Nakajima, 'Foreign Relations: From the Korean War to the Bandung Line', in Denis Twitchett and John Fairbank, eds., *The Cambridge History of China* (15 vols., Cambridge, Cambridge University Press, 1978–91), XIV, pp. 259–92.

54 Allen Whiting, 'The Sino-Soviet Split', in *The Cambridge History of China*, XIV, pp. 478–538.

55 Yahuda, *China's Role*, p. 152.

56 Robert Norris, Andrew Burrows and Richard Fieldhouse. *Nuclear Weapons Databook*, vol. V: *British, French, and Chinese Nuclear Weapons* (Boulder, Westview, 1994), pp. 330–7.

57 Li Xiaobing, Chen Jian and David Wilson, 'Mao Zedong's Handling of the Taiwan Straits Crisis of 1958: Chinese Recollections and Documents, *CWIHPB*, 6–7 (1995), pp. 208–26.

58 Vladislav Zubok, 'Khrushchev's Nuclear Promise to Beijing during the 1958 Crisis', *CWIHPB*, 6–7 (1995), pp. 219–27.

59 Whiting, *The Cambridge History of China*, XIV.

60 Harrison Salisbury, *The New Emperors: Mao and Deng: A Dual Biography* (London, HarperCollins, 1992), pp. 176–87.

61 Whiting, *The Cambridge History of China*, XIV.

62 Salisbury, *Mao and Deng*, pp. 124–33.

63 Barry Naughton, 'The Third Front: Defence Industrialization in the Chinese Interior', *China Quarterly*, 115 (1988), pp. 351–86.

64 Yahuda, *China's Role*, pp. 123–4; Whiting, *The Cambridge History of China*, XIV.

65 Yahuda, *China's Role*, p. 172.

66 Thomas Robinson, 'China Confronts the Soviet Union: Warfare and Diplomacy on China's Inner Asian Frontiers', *The Cambridge History of China*, XV, pp. 218–304.

67 Yahuda, *China's Role*, pp. 178–81.

68 Robinson, *The Cambridge History of China*, XV.

69 Robinson, *The Cambridge History of China*, XV.

70 Yahuda, *China's Role*, p. 174.

71 Telegram from ambassador in the Soviet Union to Department of State, 27 January 1955, *FRUS* 1955–57, II, pp. 147–9.

72 President Eisenhower to Supreme Allied Commander, Europe, 1 February 1955, *FRUS* 1955–57, II, pp. 189–93.

73 Chang, *Friends and Enemies*, pp. 199–202.

74 Michael Beschloss, *Kennedy v. Khrushchev: The Crisis Years, 1960–63* (London, Faber and Faber, 1991), pp. 576–602.

75 G. Chang, 'JFK, China, and the Bomb', *Journal of American History*, 74 (1988), pp. 1287–1310.

76 H. Yasamee, 'A Chair in the Smoking Room: The German Question in 1950', in *Foreign and Commonwealth Office, Occasional Papers* No. 3 (London, FCO, 1989), p. 30.

77 Michael Porter, *The Competitive Advantage of Nations* (London, Macmillan, 1990), Table 7–1.

78 Sir Gladwyn Jebb to Kenneth Younger, 12 September 1950, *Documents on British Policy Overseas (DBPO)*, (London, HMSO, 1989), Series 2, vol. III, Doc. 9.

79 Sir Gladwyn Jebb to Kenneth Younger, 17 September 1950, *DBPO*, Doc. 32.

80 Sir Oliver Harvey to Ernest Bevin, 11 October 1950, *DBPO*, Doc. 63.

81 Minute from Evelyn Shuckburgh to Sir Roger Makins, 21 September 1950, *DBPO*, Doc. 38.

82 Sir Oliver Harvey to Ernest Bevin, 7 October 1950, *DBPO*, Doc. 57.

83 Sir Oliver Harvey to Ernest Bevin, 11 October 1950, *DBPO*, Doc. 64.

84 Soutou, 'France'.

85 Soutou, 'France'.

86 Minutes of conversation between Comrade Stalin and the leaders of the SED: W. Pieck, W. Ulbricht, and O. Grotewohl, 7 April 1952, *CWIHPB*, 4 (1994), p. 48.

87 Soutou, 'France'.

88 Philippe Melandri, 'Europe and America, 1948–1950: An Unequal Relationship', in Wiggershaus, *Western Security Community*, pp. 289–312.

89 Ostermann, 'East German Uprising of 1953'; Richter, *Beria Interregnum*.

90 Richter, *Beria Interregnum*.

91 Memorandum by the Joint Chiefs of Staff to the Secretary of Defense, 25 June 1954 in *FRUS* 1952–4, V, Part 1, pp. 994–5; John Foster Dulles, Statement on French Rejection of EDC, 31 August 1954, in *DOIA*, 1954, pp. 19–21; Secretary of State to Acting Secretary of State [Eden telegram], 7 September 1954 in *FRUS* 1952–4, V, Part 2, p. 1151; Secretary of State to Foreign Secretary Eden, 8 September 1954 in *FRUS* 1952–4, V, Part 2, p. 1155; US Position on Alternative to EDC: Paper prepared by the Director of the Office of European Regional Affairs, 10 September 1954, in *FRUS* 1952–4, V, Part 2, pp. 1164–70.

92 Statement by the American Secretary of State, Mr John Foster Dulles, on the French National Assembly's rejection of the European Defence treaty, 31 August 1954.

93 Hans-Jurgen Grabbe, 'Konrad Adenauer', p. 113.

94 Paper prepared by the Director of the Office of European Regional Affairs, 'U.S. Position on Alternative to EDC', 10 September 1954, *FRUS* 1952–54, V, pp. 1164–6.

95 The Paris Agreements, 23 October 1954, in *DOIA*, 1954, pp. 28–33.

96 David Clay Large, 'Grand Illusions: The United States, the Federal Republic of Germany, and the European Defense Community', in Diefendorf *et al.*, *Reconstruction of Germany*, pp. 379–84.

97 Zubok, *Berlin Crisis*.

98 United States Mission, West Berlin to State Department, 24 October 1957, *Berlin Crisis*, Doc. 36.

99 Memorandum of a conversation between Konrad Adenauer and John Foster Dulles, 7 May 1955, *Berlin Crisis*, Doc. 7.

100 Memorandum of a conversation between Konrad Adenauer and John Foster Dulles, 14 June 1955, *Berlin Crisis*, Doc. 15.

101 Memorandum of conversation between Konrad Adenauer and Robert Murphy, 4 October 1956, *Berlin Crisis*, Doc. 23.

102 David Bruce to State Department, 24 October 1957, *Berlin Crisis*, Doc. 36.

103 Memorandum of conversation between John Foster Dulles and Sir Roger Makins, 29 June 1956, *FRUS* 1955–57, IV, pp. 84–99; DCKN5/2, Directive to the NATO Military Authorities from the North Atlantic Council, Cambridge, Churchill College Archives Centre, Dickson Papers; Jan Melissen, *The Search For Nuclear Co-operation: Britain, the United States and the Making of an Ambiguous Alliance, 1952–1959* (Groningen, Styx, 1993), pp. 93–115; David Schwartz, *NATO's Nuclear Dilemmas* (Washington, Brookings, 1983), p. 59.

104 David Bruce to State Department, 22 April 1957, *Berlin Crisis*, Doc. 30.

105 Hope Harrison, *Ulbricht and the Concrete "Rose": New Archival Evidence on the*

Dynamics of Soviet-East German Relations and the Berlin Crisis, 1958–1961 (Washington, CWIHP/Woodrow Wilson Center, *CWIHP Working Paper* No. 5), p. 5.

106 Hope Harrison, *Concrete "Rose"*, pp. 16–17.

107 Zubok, *Berlin Crisis*, pp. 6–7.

108 David Bruce to State Department, 14 January 1959, *Berlin Crisis*, Doc. 626.

109 Foy Kohler to Christian Herter, 21 September 1959, and Dwight Eisenhower to Harold Macmillan, 18 March 1960, *Berlin Crisis*, Docs. 1630 and 1850; Richard Aldous, ' "A Family Affair": Macmillan and the Art of Personal Diplomacy', in Richard Aldous and Sabine Lee, eds., *Harold Macmillan and Britain's World Role* (London, Macmillan, 1996), pp. 9–36.

110 Memorandum of conversation between Konrad Adenauer and John Foster Dulles, 8 February 1959, *Berlin Crisis*, Doc. 741.

111 David Bruce to State Department, 22 January 1959, *Berlin Crisis*, Doc. 656.

112 *Berlin Crisis*, Doc. 741.

113 Angela Stent, *From Embargo to Ostpolitik: The Political Economy of German–Soviet Relations, 1955–1980* (Cambridge, Cambridge University Press, 1981), pp. 68–92.

114 Record of meeting of Comrade N. S. Khrushchev with Comrade W. Ulbricht, 30 November 1960. Annex A to Hope Harrison, *Concrete "Rose"*.

115 Letter from Ulbricht to Khrushchev, 18 January 1961, and letter from Ambassador Pervukhin to Foreign Minister Gromyko. Appendices B and D to Hope Harrison, *Concrete "Rose"*.

116 Hope Harrison, *Concrete "Rose"*, p. 44.

117 Hope Harrison, *Concrete "Rose"*, pp. 27–66 and Zubok, 'Berlin Crisis', pp. 16–27.

118 Letter from Ulbricht to Khrushchev, 15 September 1961. Appendix I to Hope Harrison, *Concrete "Rose"*.

119 Memorandum of conversation between Konrad Adenauer and Lyndon Johnson, 19 August 1961, *Berlin Crisis*, Doc. 2364.

120 Angela Stent, *From Embargo to Ostpolitik*, pp. 93–126.

121 Willy Brandt to President Kennedy, 17 September 1961, *Berlin Crisis*, Doc. 2340.

122 Memorandum of conversation between Willy Brandt and Lyndon Johnson, 19 August 1961, *Berlin Crisis*, Doc. 2369.

123 Bluth, *Soviet Arms Policy*, p. 69.

124 Khrushchev, oral communication, 10 December 1962, in *Problems of Communism*, XLI (1992).

125 Marifeli Perez-Stable, *The Cuban Revolution: Origins, Course and Legacy* (New York, Oxford University Press, 1993).

126 Yuri Pavlov, *The Soviet–Cuban Alliance, 1959–1991* (New Brunswick, Transaction Publishers, 1994), p. 3.

127 Robert Quirk, *Fidel Castro* (New York, W. W. Norton, 1993), pp. 64–6.

128 Pavlov, *Soviet Alliance*, p. 10.

129 Quirk, *Fidel*, pp. 149–76.

130 Pavlov, *Soviet Alliance*, pp. 5–6.

131 Quirk, *Fidel*, pp. 266–73.

132 Pavlov, *Soviet Alliance*, pp. 6–13.

133 Quirk, *Fidel*, p. 301.

134 Pavlov, *Soviet Alliance*, pp. 13–29.

135 Quirk, *Fidel*, pp. 316–19.

136 Pavlov, *Soviet Alliance*, p. 21.

137 Quirk, *Fidel*, pp. 322–55.
138 Memorandum of discussion at 301st Meeting of the NSC, 26 October 1956, *FRUS* 1955–57, X, pp. 124–133. Gaddis, *Strategies of Containment*, p. 208.
139 Stephen Rabe, 'Dulles, Latin America, and Cold War Anticommunism', in Immerman, *Dulles*, pp. 159–87.
140 Pavlov, *Soviet Alliance*, p. 21.
141 Quirk, *Fidel*, p. 395.
142 Pavlov, *Soviet Alliance*, pp. 21–2.
143 Richard Reeves, *President Kennedy: Profile of Power* (London, Papermac, 1994), p. 343.
144 William Taubman, 'The Correspondence: Khrushchev's Motives and His Views of Kennedy', *Problems of Communism*, XLI (1992), pp. 14–18.
145 Zaloga, *Target America*, p. 204.
146 Zaloga, *Target America*, pp. 201–3.
147 Memorandum of discussion between John McCone and McGeorge Bundy, 5 October 1962, in Mary McAuliffe, ed., *CIA Documents on the Cuban Missile Crisis 1962* (CIA, Washington, 1992), Doc. 42.
148 Oleg Troyanovski, 'The Caribbean Crisis: A View from the Kremlin', *International Affairs* (April–May 1992) pp. 147–57.
149 CIA Memorandum: Probable Soviet MRBM Sites in Cuba, 16 October 1962, in Mary McAuliffe, *CIA Documents on the Cuban Missile Crisis 1962*, Doc. 46.
150 Transcript of the First Executive Committee Meeting, 16 October 1962, *Cuban Missile Crisis*, Doc. 15.
151 Douglas Dillon memorandum for the President, 17 October 1962, *Cuban Missile Crisis*, Doc. 18.
152 Minutes of the Executive Committee, 19 October 1962, *Cuban Missile Crisis*.
153 James Blight *et al.*, 'The Cuban Missile Crisis Revisited', *Foreign Affairs*, 66 (1987), pp. 176–7.
154 Khrushchev to Castro, 23 October 1962. From transcript of Fidel Castro's remarks at the Havana Conference on the Cuban Missile Crisis, 11 January 1992, *Cuban Missile Crisis*, Doc. 83.
155 Castro to Khrushchev, 26 October 1962, *Cuban Missile Crisis*, Doc. 45.
156 James Blight, Bruce Allyn and David Welch, *Cuba on the Brink: Castro, the Missile Crisis and the Soviet Collapse* (New York, Pantheon Books, 1993), p. 359.
157 Blight *et al.*, *Cuba on the Brink*, pp. 101–123.
158 Blight *et al.*, 'The Cuban Missile Crisis Revisited', pp. 177–8.
159 Memorandum for McGeorge Bundy on Deployment of Turkish IRBMs, 22 June 1962, *Cuban Missile Crisis*, Doc. 2.
160 Troyanovski, 'Caribbean Crisis'.
161 Khrushchev to Kennedy, 30 October 1962, *Problems of Communism*, XLI (1992).
162 'Dialogue in Havana: The Caribbean Crisis', *International Affairs* (October 1992), pp. 108–28.
163 Blight *et al.*, *Cuba on the Brink*, pp. 214–16.
164 Pavlov, *Soviet Alliance*, p. 63.
165 'Dialogue in Havana: The Caribbean Crisis'.
166 Blight *et al.*, *Cuba on the Brink*, p. 245.
167 Pavlov, *Soviet Alliance*, pp. 56–7.

168 Robert Komer to McGeorge Bundy, 29 October 1962, *Cuban Missile Crisis*, Doc. 80.

169 Walt Rostow to George Ball, 15 November 1962, *Cuban Missile Crisis*, Doc. 81.

4

The Balance of Power, 1963–1972

THE AMERICAN WORLD VIEW

The nebulous concept of credibility came to be at the centre of American Cold War policies in the 1960s. It did so in the context of two main issues: first, the implications of an emerging nuclear balance; second, the ability of the United States to show 'firmness' in non-Western countries not already in the Soviet or Chinese orbit. The years between 1963 and 1972 saw the 'great inversion' in American foreign policy and the attempts to escape from it. The desire to show 'firmness' was translated from an abstract concept into a concrete commitment to one country – South Vietnam. Between 1965 and 1972 American Cold War policy was effectively mortgaged to the fate of that Asian country. Vietnam ceased to be an arena for Cold War conflict; instead the Cold War became a means of dealing with the Vietnam War. At the same time American policy-makers wrestled with the problem of nuclear credibility. What were the implications of rough parity between the United States and the Soviet Union in strategic nuclear weapons and delivery systems? Did such parity simply necessitate a restructuring of American nuclear forces to render them more flexible and less vulnerable? Or was it the precursor of a newly emerging structure of world politics? In this new structure the Soviet Union and the United States would still engage in hostile competition but the aim would no longer be victory but an enduring balance. If such a balance was to be achieved, deliberate and direct collaboration would be needed. At the beginning of the 1970s it seemed to some American leaders that the solution to both the short- and long-term challenges to American foreign policy could be overcome by direct negotiations with the Soviet Union.

VIETNAM AND THE COLD WAR

By 1961 American attention in the Far East had started to shift away from Taiwan to South East Asia. The post-mortem for the Bay of Pigs fiasco concluded:

> where we inherited Communist enclaves of power in the Free World ... we have, initially, not done terribly well. Laos, at best, will yield in the short run a muddy and

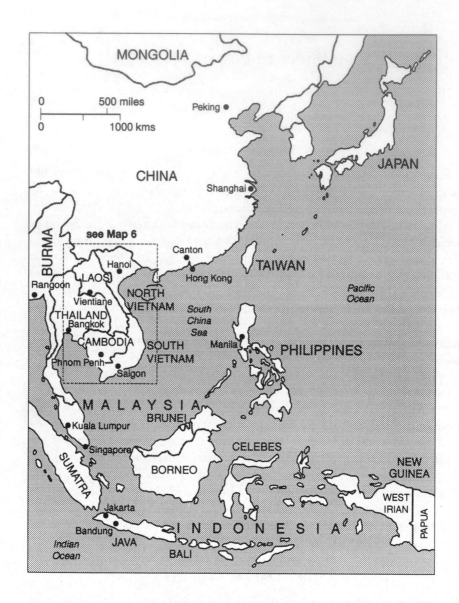

Map 5 South East Asia

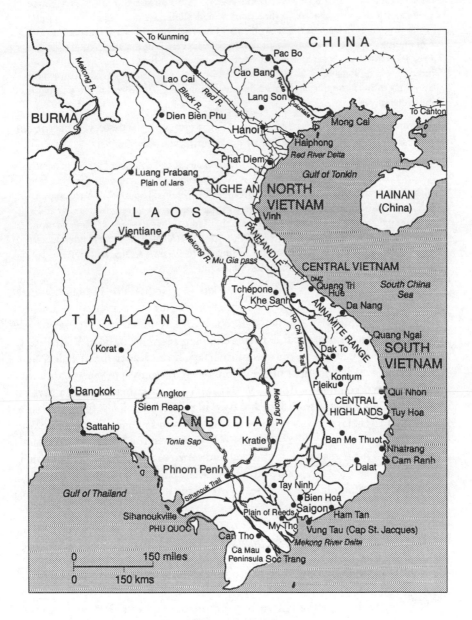

Map 6 Indochina

weak Free World position; in Cuba our first effort at a solution failed. There is building up a sense of frustration and a perception we are up against a game we can't handle. This frustration and simple anger could lead us to do unwise things or exert scarce national effort and resources in directions which would yield no significant results, while diverting us from our real problems. There is one area where success against Communist techniques is conceivable and where success is desperately required in the Free World interest. That area is Viet-Nam. A maximum effort . . . military, economic, political and diplomatic . . . is required there . . . a clean cut success in Vietnam would do much to hold the line in Asia while permitting us . . . to learn how to deal with indirect aggression.[1]

Vietnam was thus regarded as part of a general process, yet of special significance in itself. In the words of an Eisenhower-era analysis:

Viet-Nam assumes a special importance in US policies and courses of action in South East Asia because of its exposed position as an outpost of the free world face-to-face with a powerful and threatening communist regime occupying part of its territory, and because Viet-Nam is the principal country in the Area where a free government and a communist regime compete directly for the same territory and a whole nation. Moreover, the US has made a substantial investment in Viet-Nam's independence, and with such success, that the most determined efforts are justified to preserve the integrity and strengthen the position of the country.[2]

The Vietnamese conflict had had its roots in responses to French colonial rule. These responses included the formation of anti-French organisations of which the Indochinese Communist Party (ICP), founded in 1930, was one. Even among members of the ICP there remained a strong strand of Vietnamese nationalism. Ho Chi Minh, the communists' political leader for instance, had left Indochina as an opponent of the colonial regime some five years before the October 1917 revolution in Russia. Vo Nguyen Giap's father had taken part in anti-French uprisings in the 1880s and died in prison after arrest for subversive activities in 1919. Giap himself joined an underground nationalist group before joining the ICP in 1937.[3] The leaders of ICP (renamed the Viet Nam Workers' Party in 1951) formed a small, long-lived and remarkably cohesive group which emerged in the 1930s. It was, however, marked by factional in-fighting, sometimes based on regional loyalties.[4] One of the most notable features of the ICP leadership was that this group, locked into factional struggles and provincial loyalties with little relevance beyond Vietnam, developed a collective ideology which stressed the need to project Vietnam on to the world stage as part of their own struggle. This projection made Vietnam an important part of the Cold War after 1950 and the pivot upon which it swung between 1967 and 1972.

At a very early stage the ICP developed the concept of a protracted armed struggle leading to nationalist-socialist revolution. The party could draw on a heritage of national myth which stressed the homogeneity and qualities of resistance of the 'twenty-odd million descendants of the Lac and the Hong'.[5] It sedulously used the stories of the Trung sisters, who heroically, although unsuccessfully, resisted Chinese occupation between AD 39 and AD 43, and Le Loi who defeated Chinese forces in a war between 1418 and 1427. According to Giap the 'liberation war led by Le Loi ended victoriously after ten years of hard struggle. For this reason our people inherently possess a tradition of persistent resistance, and art of defeating the enemy in protracted wars.'[6]

Yet despite this rhetoric Vietnam was, in fact, a deeply fragmented society. In 1940 the Japanese had allowed the colonial regime to continue to function in the territory, whilst they used Indochina as a military base. The Japanese, in the death throes of their own war effort, then overthrew the French in March 1945. Even those who, broadly speaking, were anti-French were divided amongst themselves. Ho Chi Minh admitted as much in his message to the founding meeting of the Vietnam Independence League (Viet Minh), a broad-front organisation established by the ICP in June 1941 to widen its appeal. The VNQDD (Vietnamese Nationalist Party), founded in 1927, was based on and allied to the KMT, which occupied northern Vietnam in 1945. There were various Dai Viet (Greater Vietnam) organisations, the most important of which was the Greater Vietnam People's Party founded in 1939. It was élitist, with little more than 1000 members, but included leading officials who admired Japan as a model for Vietnam and thus prospered in the period of Japanese dominance.[7] In the south Cao Dai and Hoa Hao sects flourished. Cao Dai was the Supreme Being, the 'high tower', of a sect established in the 1920s. A syncretic mix of Confucianism, Buddhism and Christianity, it had as many as 300 000 adherents by 1939. The Hoa Hao sect was a form of purified Buddhism founded by a faith healer named Huynh Phu So in the 1930s. In 1942 it had 40 000 followers. These sects thrived under the Japanese and raised significant paramilitary forces. In late 1947 the Cao Dai militia numbered about 30 000 men, the Hoa Hao, 10 000. Both broke with the ICP in the same year. Huynh Phu So was murdered by a Viet Minh commander in April.[8] The Viet Minh used decapitation tactics against the secular parties as well, ousting the leadership of the VNQDD and assassinating the leader of the Greater Vietnam People's Party in 1946.[9]

The ICP's success over its rivals can largely be attributed to the manner in which it combined awareness of the outside world with an ability to build up its own apparatus. The party had to be ready whenever international events gave it an opening. Once that opening had arrived, however, success or failure would rest upon indigenous action.[10] The first communist armed force, the National Salvation Army of 1940, amounted to 125 guerrillas, mainly non-Vietnamese Montagnards (the French term for ethnically distinct mountain tribes), under the leadership of a 'local bandit'. Giap trained about 40 Vietnamese cadres, guarded by 500 Montagnards, in Cao Bang province between mid-1942 and mid-1944.[11] When Giap founded the first Armed Propaganda Brigade in December 1944, it had 34 members. Although the Vietnamese revolution was supposed to be part of the 'wave of new democratic revolution' the ICP leadership was willing to adapt to new international situations. Instead of remaining part of the world revolution, the Viet Minh decided to reinvent itself as a wholly anti-Japanese force in the expectation of an allied invasion. In this way it could 'profit by the antagonism between the Chinese and the Americans and the British and the Gaullist French to obtain aid from outside, sign agreements with the allies and bring them to recognise our national independence'. Once the Japanese occupying forces had been fully engaged by an allied invasion, the Viet Minh would rise up and seize power. These hopes were upset by the use of the atomic bomb on Japan rather than the gradual destruction of its outposts. Instead, the party leadership declared an uprising in August 1945, seized Hanoi, and a month later declared the formation of a Democratic Government of Vietnam.[12] The ICP had about 5000 members in total when it seized power.[13]

It attempted to cooperate with the new powers operating in Indochina: Britain, Nationalist China and the United States. The initial aim was to prevent the return of the French, but once it became clear that the British occupation forces, at least, would facilitate this, the Viet Minh even attempted to reach an arrangement with the colonial authorities. The Soviet Union seemed to have little to offer the ICP in the short term. Indeed, Moscow insisted that the ICP follow the lead of the PCF which, in line with its popular-front strategy in France, opposed any open hostilities without Soviet permission. The ICP had to try and communicate with the Soviet Union via Paris. The Viet Minh government was in danger of being outflanked by radical groups, especially in the south, such as the Trotskyite International Communist League which demanded 'arms for the people'.[14] The ICP leadership made overtures to the Americans. Ho Chi Minh even appealed directly to President Truman to seat the Viet Minh government rather than France on the United Nations Advisory Committee for the Far East.[15] Throughout 1946 the Viet Minh attempted to achieve their aims through negotiations with France. The French, however, had no intention of doing anything other than reassuming full control of the whole of Indochina.[16] In December 1946 Ho was still attempting to project himself to the Americans as a friend whose communism was of a non-militant, non-threatening variety. It was only in May 1947, at the final breakdown of all communications with the French, that Ho became more openly bellicose.

The descent of Indochina into war did not dampen the determination of the ICP leadership to internationalise the struggle.[17] The Viet Minh was, however, cut off from outside assistance. The bulk of its aid had to come through China: but Vietnam was a priority neither for the CCP nor the KMT. The French initiated open warfare in November 1946 when they shelled the Vietnamese quarters of Haiphong. In December 1946 and January 1947 fierce fighting drove the Viet Minh out of Hanoi into the northern rural area of the Viet Bac. Here they held out against French attacks. At the end of 1946 Giap had an army of about 50 000 men, with, perhaps, another 30 000 spread about in regional and guerrilla units. The party had about 20 000 members (all of these figures are extremely tentative). They faced a French army of 115 000. Giap could prepare his army psychologically but had little in the way of *matériel*: no heavy artillery, planes, tanks. The PAVN began to build its own light weapons in 1949 but it remained, essentially, a survival force.[18]

The conflict only widened into a Cold War struggle, rather than a colonial war, once the ICP could appeal to the CCP for aid after the proclamation of the PRC in October 1949. The ICP and the CCP had long-standing ties. Vietnamese communists had been active in China since the 1920s. Ho himself spent a great deal of time in China in the 1930s, he spoke fluent Chinese and had fought in the Chinese civil war. In late 1949 the ICP sent a representative, Hoang Van Hoan, to establish a direct link with the CCP leadership.[19] On 15 January 1950 the Viet Minh formally requested that China give diplomatic recognition to the DRV. Mao, in Moscow, responded with alacrity and extended recognition. Mao was much concerned with securing China's southern borders. In particular, he wished to prevent the French colonial regime, which had been aided by the KMT in 1945, from assisting the remnants of KMT forces in southern China.

In January 1950 Ho himself went to Peking to ask for Chinese and Soviet assistance. Mao broached the Vietnamese request with Stalin. The Soviet leader, however, was ignorant of the developing Vietnamese situation and suspicious of Ho's motives. He told Mao that the Soviet Union wanted no direct involvement in Vietnam; he would send some aid but the main burden would fall on the Chinese. The Soviet Union did not recognise the DRV until the end of January 1950.[20] The CCP transported Ho to Moscow at the beginning of February 1950. There, according to Khrushchev, he was treated with contempt. 'I remember', the ex-Soviet leader wrote in 1969, 'Ho Chi Minh coming to Moscow to ask for material help, arms and other kinds of assistance, for the Vietnamese struggle against the French occupiers. Stalin didn't believe the Vietnamese could prevail, so he treated Ho insultingly.' Khrushchev also recalled that 'later, Stalin often said he regretted [recognising the DRV]. "We were too hasty," he said. "It's too early for recognition." Stalin did not believe in the possibility for Ho's movement.' The ICP wanted to turn Ho's visit to Moscow into a propaganda coup. Thus 'Ho wanted very much to have his visit announced in Moscow and be officially received as the president of Vietnam.' In 'another disappointing, offensive incident' Stalin told Ho: 'the time for that has passed. You have already come to Moscow incognito, so there is no possibility of announcing your arrival.'[21]

These snubs did not prevent the Viet Minh projecting itself into the vanguard of international revolution.[22] Although Stalin was willing to offer very little in the way of military aid to the Vietnamese communists,[23] the Chinese did make a significant contribution. The opportunity offered by outside aid led the ICP to enunciate ambitious war aims: 'our strategic objective', Giap declared, 'is to reconquer the entire territory of Indochina, the territory of all three countries, Vietnam, Cambodia and Laos'.[24] In April 1950 the ICP leadership formally asked for Chinese military advisers to be sent to Vietnam. They were dispatched at the end of June, just after the outbreak of the Korean War. The 79 officers of the Chinese military aid group were led by General Chen Geng, an acquaintance of Ho's since the 1920s. Between April and September 1950 the Chinese also delivered 14 000 small arms, 1700 machine guns, 150 artillery pieces, food, ammunition and communications equipment to the Viet Minh. Chinese advisers played a large part in planning the battle of Cao Bang in October 1950. Indeed, although it refused to respond to a Viet Minh request for Chinese troops to be sent into Vietnam in July 1952, the CCP continued to play a major part in the strategic direction of the war right down to the Dien Bien Phu campaign in 1954. The Chinese encouraged the Vietnamese to stick to their ambitious war aims. In August 1953, when Giap persuaded the VWP Politburo to shift the emphasis of operations from the north-west to the Red River delta in the north-east, the CCP Central Committee intervened to maintain existing strategic priorities. These interventions laid the roots of future tensions. The Chinese complained about the qualities of Vietnamese troops and Chen Geng criticised Giap as lacking in 'Bolshevik-style self-criticism' and being 'slippery and not very upright and honest'.[25]

The Viet Minh leadership identified the United States as the primary enemy. As early as September 1947 Truong Chinh had warned 'there might be intervention by a third country which would first help the French colonialists to fight us; then oust them'.[26] Indeed, in February 1950 the French government recognised that it could not continue the struggle alone. In October 1950 the French expeditionary force suffered a major defeat at Cao Bang and the Minister for Overseas Territories, Jean Letourneau, reported that France faced the real possibility of losing the war. Alarmed by the possibility of defeat, the French gave the Indochinese war overriding priority.[27]

The American strategic assessment of Indochina had, however, little to do with France. US strategic planners believed Indochina was vital to the security of Japan, Australia and India. They also valued it as a source of strategic minerals and a communications cross-roads. They feared that if Vietnam was lost all other states on mainland South East Asia would become vulnerable to communist takeover. Indeed revolution would probably spread to Malaya, Indonesia and the Philippines. This would in turn exclude the United States from the eastern Pacific whilst cementing the Sino-Soviet alliance and increasing its war-making potential. France's role in Indochina was seen as a problem. In the long term it would be better if France was excluded from the area. Yet in the medium term this was not regarded as a practicable option: French armed forces of approximately 140 000 men were in the field.[28] If a small US force was sent to Indochina, the commitment would, in all probability, escalate. The best solution, it seemed, was 'to establish such conditions in Indochina [so] that no foreign armed forces other than the French will be required for the maintenance of internal security against the Vietminhs'. This could be done through a carefully controlled military aid programme and pressure on the French to institute political reforms, leading to independence for the countries of Indochina.[29]

The Americans had manoeuvred themselves into a difficult position. They believed they needed France to fight the war in Indochina and gave them increasing amounts of *matériel* aid to do so. Yet the need to keep the French fighting and the aid flowing militated against any serious pressure on France to pursue new political solutions. The Americans watched, with growing disgust, what they regarded as France's inept military and political performance in Indochina. By 1953 President Eisenhower concluded that the war was like 'pouring money down a rathole'. The US army's Chief of Staff, Lawton Collins, believed it was time 'to put the squeeze on the French to get them off their fannies'.[30] American pressure led to more aggressive French military operations, the so-called Navarre Plan, and indirectly to the parachute drop on to Dien Bien Phu which spelled final defeat for the French armies. Even before Dien Bien Phu, military defeat had forced France to the negotiating table in Geneva, at a peace conference jointly chaired by Britain and the Soviet Union. Yet the Americans had concluded that 'there is no negotiated settlement of the Indochina problem which in essence would not be ... a face saving device to cover a French surrender'. Eisenhower told Churchill that if Indochina passed into communist hands

> the ultimate effect on our ... global strategic position with the consequent shift in the power ratio throughout Asia and the Pacific could be disastrous. ... It is difficult to see how Thailand, Burma and Indonesia could be kept out of Communist hands. ... The economic pressure on Japan which would be deprived of non-Communist markets and sources of food and raw material would be such ... that it is difficult to see how Japan could be prevented from reaching an accommodation with the Communist world which would combine the manpower and natural resources of Asia with the industrial potential of Japan.[31]

Britain, however, had no interest in becoming involved. Churchill replied 'In no foreseeable circumstances ... could British troops be used in Indo-China ... and if we were asked our opinion we would advise against United States' local intervention.'[32] Eisenhower was not willing to ask Congress for authority for American intervention without full allied support. As a result the Geneva accords effectively created a communist state in North Vietnam and installed a regime under Ngo Dinh Diem in the south. France was determined to remain the premier Western influence in Vietnam but the United States was equally determined to push them out.[33] In this the Americans were largely successful but the organisation they set up in September 1954, the South-East Asia Treaty Organisation (SEATO), to guarantee South Vietnamese independence, was largely a sham. Britain insisted that as 'the sectors of the SEATO front are so

widely divided and different in conditions, it is better ... to operate nationally'.[34] There was never any hope of a Far Eastern NATO. Indonesia, the
second most populous state in Asia after China, had hosted the first conference
of the non-aligned movement in 1955. Over the next decade its internal politics
appeared perilously unstable. An inter-island civil war broke out in 1958. The
Americans gave covert aid to the anti-government rebels who lost. Although
the Kennedy administration successfully pressurised the Dutch government to
cede western New Guinea (West Irian), in 1963 another NATO ally, Britain,
became involved in a war with Indonesia over northern Borneo. In 1965 the
Indonesian Communist Party launched a botched coup which led to large-scale
massacres of ethnic Chinese. Even in Japan new security arrangements
appeared to be threatened by political instability. In 1957 the Americans bowed
to Japanese pressure to revise the security agreement they had imposed in 1951.
Bases in Japan would be maintained but the Japanese government would have
to be consulted before they were used. A new security treaty was signed in
January 1960 but was greeted by demonstrations and strikes in Japan. Socialist
deputies were ejected from the Diet to ensure ratification and the Prime
Minister, Nobusuke Kishi, was stabbed by a right-wing extremist.[35]

Mao too saw the 1954 Geneva conference as having enormous international
significance. During the Dien Bien Phu campaign he was willing to accept the
threat of American intervention, which the Chinese, rightly, believed to be
hollow, and accelerate the flow of military aid (200 trucks and 3000 artillery
pieces were delivered for use in the campaign) in order to achieve victory. In
light of this victory, the leader of the DRV delegation to Geneva, Pham Van
Dong, made a series of maximalist demands in line with previously stated
policy: an immediate truce followed by a plebiscite (organised to secure a VWP
victory). He refused to admit that Vietnamese troops were fighting in Laos and
Cambodia and argued that those countries should be dealt with in the same way
as Vietnam. By 1954, however, China's strategic aims were changing. The CCP
leadership was willing to abandon their Vietnamese clients, once the latter's
military efforts had brought the PRC, still unrecognised as a country by the
United Nations, to the conference table as a great power.[36] On 15 June, when
the Chinese, Vietnamese and Soviet delegations met together in Geneva, and
on 3–5 July when Zhou met with Ho and Giap in southern China, the Chinese
pressured the Vietnamese to give way. Zhou accused the Vietnamese of causing
deadlock by refusing to admit that their forces were in Laos and Cambodia and
proposed that those two countries should be neutralised, with all foreign forces,
including the Viet Minh, withdrawing. Although Zhou declared that 'with the
final withdrawal of the French all China will be yours' he made it quite clear
that the PRC was not willing to run the risk of direct American intervention on
its southern borders.[37]

Zhou Enlai explained in August 1954 that it was better for China to have 'an
area of collective peace in Indo-China and its surrounding countries' than to

have a communist Vietnam.[38] In the long run he believed that South Vietnam would not prove to be a viable state. To fight on behalf of the Vietnamese risked provoking American intervention and the emergence of another Korea-style struggle. Such a war would threaten the Chinese provinces of Yunnan and Kwangsi, in the same way as Manchuria had been threatened during the Korean conflict, and tax China's resources. As Zhou told Khrushchev: 'we've already lost too many men in Korea – that war cost us dearly. We're in no condition to get involved in another war at this time.'[39] He regarded the most important aspect of the Geneva accords as 'the provisions on the cessation of introduction . . . into Indo-China from outside . . . [of] fresh troops and military personnel.[40] Such provisions would avert the danger of the 'American plot of organising a South-East Asian military bloc . . . to use Asians to fight Asians since the countries which actually bordered China – Vietnam and Laos – would either be allied or non-aligned'.[41]

Thus the new DRV policy announced by Ho in July 1954 was virtually forced on him by the withdrawal of his main military and diplomatic backer, China. Ho conceded that: 'In the new situation we cannot maintain the old programme . . . we must secure a vast area, where we will have ample means for building, consolidating, developing our forces so as to exert influence over other regions and thereby advance towards reunification. The setting up of regrouping zones does not mean partition of the country; it is a temporary measure leading to reunification.' There was opposition to this policy in the VWP: Ho denounced those who saw the French as the only enemy and thus called for the immediate overrun of the south as 'leftist deviants' who saw 'only the trees, not the whole forest . . . only the French – not the Americans'. In the future 'the US imperialists . . . [will be] the direct enemy of the Vietnamese, Cambodian and Lao peoples . . . the brunt of our attack and that of the world's peoples should be focused on the United States'.[42]

After 1954 the North Vietnamese had little choice but to limit their part in the Cold War to the 'diplomatic struggle' for a united Vietnam. In July 1955 when Ho Chi Minh visited Moscow and Peking he was promised limited economic aid but no military aid or diplomatic support for unification.[43] Indeed in Moscow Ho was forced to agree to a number of extremely mild statements about the situation in South East Asia. In September 1955 the Vietnam Fatherland Front was established to try and unite all groups opposed to the Diem regime in the south. Cadres attempted to cooperate with anti-Diem sects but with little immediate success, as the GVN managed to suppress much of their paramilitary power in 1955–6. Despite their relative inactivity the North Vietnamese saw themselves as full participants in the Cold War. In contrast the Diem regime in the south, despite its declaratory adherence to the concept of a united Vietnam, eschewed any effort at reunification and concentrated on strengthening its power base on the basis of *de facto* partition.

All North Vietnamese leaders agreed that the objective was the 'liberation' of South Vietnam: some also dreamed of the creation of a 'greater Indochina' incorporating Laos and Cambodia. As early as June 1956, a month after the Deputy Foreign Minister Andrey Gromyko had once again failed to exert Soviet diplomacy on the DRV's behalf, the Politburo agreed that reunification through diplomacy was impossible. However, support for different methods of securing the agreed objective of reunification provoked a fierce struggle within the VWP during the mid- and late 1950s.[44] Giap attempted to modernise the army by rationalising its equipment – a *mélange* of French, Japanese, Chinese and American items – with limited Soviet aid in the form of light tanks and heavy artillery. On the other hand the Party Secretary Truong Chinh favoured the idea of a peasant militia and people's war tied in with his communal agrarian reforms. This conflict was seemingly resolved in Giap's favour in September 1956 when Chinh stepped down from his post. Both Giap and Chinh, however, were essentially 'North Vietnam firsters'. In the autumn of 1956 the political commissar in the south, Le Duan, demanded a southern-based revolution. Paradoxically, Giap – who most obviously wanted to declare Vietnam's allegiance by importing military equipment from Russia and China – advocated a low-key way forward in terms of North Vietnam's Cold War profile, whereas the champion of the indigenous Vietnamese revolution proposed a policy which would quickly re-establish Vietnam as a battleground.

In late 1956 the Vietnamese leadership, despite its political, policy and personal divisions, set a course to achieve its primary goal: a unified Vietnam ruled by the VWP, whatever the international situation. When the Presidium member Kliment Voroshilov visited Hanoi in May 1957 he once again emphasised the Soviet preference for peaceful reunification and gave no support to a more violent strategy in the south.[45] By 1957, however, the Chinese and the Soviets were involved in a struggle for influence within the communist bloc. North Vietnamese support became an important factor in this struggle. Thus, neither the Soviets nor the Chinese could afford to alienate the Vietnamese completely. Conversely, the Vietnamese leadership wanted to draw support from both; not least because the bulk of military supplies from the USSR would have to be transported via China.

From mid-1957 the VWP was committed to the progressive takeover of the south. Yet it had to balance, on the one hand, the caution of both the PRC and the Soviet Union and, on the other, the successes of the Diem regime in repressing subversive activity. Action could not be so fast as to alienate support, so overt as to invite a massacre of communist supporters, or so slow as to allow Diem's security apparatus to pick off the revolutionaries piecemeal. Judging the relative importance of these competing influences continued to provoke intense political conflict within the VWP's leadership. Although the first military units were organised in the south in October 1957, Giap's supporters continued to urge caution. It was, however, Le Duan who was ascendant both politically and strategically. He secretly visited the south in 1958 to assess the revolutionary situation.[46] His plans were put into definitive form in May 1959 at the 15th Plenum of the Central Committee. At the same time a unit known as Line 559 was formed to serve as both a proto-high command for the war in the south and to provide logistic and technical support for southern revolutionaries.[47] Ho set out on an extended tour to gain both Soviet and Chinese support for this more aggressive line. He spent most of July in the USSR, which in November announced a three-year economic support agreement for North Vietnam, and most of August in the PRC. Ho may have been helped in his efforts by the reassertion of executive power in China by Mao at the Lushan conference. According to the official Vietnamese account, released in 1979, as late as May 1960 the Chinese were arguing that only political not military support should be given to the overthrow of the Diem regime. At most there should be a guerrilla war based on southern 'self-reliance' rather than any large-scale military operations. In June in Bucharest and in November in Moscow, however, at gatherings of the communist movement, both China and the Soviet Union gave the go-ahead to a 'national liberation struggle'. Zhou Enlai linked the 'struggle for the peaceful reunification [of Vietnam]' to the 'stormy struggle against American imperialism'.[48]

Although an important step forward had been taken at the initiative and urging of the VWP, its leadership still had to exercise a degree of caution. The primacy of the political struggle did not mean, however, that there could be any goal short of outright victory even if Diem offered concessions.[49] In July 1960 about 4000 southerners, trained and armed in the north, were reinfiltrated into South Vietnam.[50] Although the military struggle was, in fact, directed by the North Vietnamese COSVN, a popular-front organisation, the National Liberation Front (NLF) was organised in 1959–60 and unveiled along with its People's Liberation Armed Forces (PLAF – the Viet Cong) in December 1960, to give the revolution a specifically southern face.[51]

To the Americans the commencement of guerrilla warfare by the DRV against South Vietnam at the beginning of 1960 was a clear threat. Although high-level estimates tended to state baldly that the 'foreign policy [of the DRV] is subservient to the bloc'[52] some analysts on the ground were less sure about what was going on. Ambassador Durbrow in Saigon admitted he was not sure why the North Vietnamese had acted. Was it because of a Chinese master plan to exert pressure on non-communist countries on its southern rim? Or were the North Vietnamese themselves fearful that economic development would undermine support for their southern organisation?[53] Neither was Vietnam's exact position in the communist world clear. The embassy reported:

> In its relations with the communist bloc countries the DRV has generally supported the Soviet propaganda line despite the fact that Communist China provides NVN with more economic aid than does the USSR and owing to geographic propinquity exercises a strong influence on DRV domestic politics. There are indications that Moscow-oriented leaders of the DRV are concerned over increasing Communist Chinese

influence and would like to see a greater degree of Russian interest in NVN to balance
the influence of Communist China.[54]

A presidential task force, headed by Roswell Gilpatric, concluded, however,
that 'stronger US actions [were needed to] . . . assist the Vietnamese to become
a polarising spirit against Communism in the Southeast Asia region'. These
actions included expanding the ARVN, supplying more US aid and sending
US advisers to directly participate in anti-guerrilla warfare.[55] Some of Kennedy's advisers favoured the creation of a neutral zone in South East Asia
achievable, it was argued, because Sino-Russian antagonism created a sufficient
US–USSR commonality of interest in the region.[56] Nevertheless these advisers
too tended to look at the global structure rather than arguing that the conflict
was driven on by factors indigenous to Vietnam. The dovish school of thought
was, in any case, very much in the minority. At the end of 1961 a report by
Maxwell Taylor and Walt Rostow, sent by Kennedy to assess the situation on
the ground, conflated activity in Vietnam into a joint Sino–Soviet threat. They
concluded:

> the United States must decide how it will cope with Khrushchev's 'wars of liberation'
> which are really para wars of guerrilla aggression. This is a new and dangerous
> Communist technique which bypasses our traditional and military responses. . . . the
> Communists are pursuing a clear and systematic strategy in Southeast Asia. It is a
> strategy which bypasses US nuclear strength, US conventional naval, air and ground
> forces. . . . The strategy is a variant of Mao's classic three stage offensive.[57]

Faced with this supposed Khrushchevite–Maoist threat, Kennedy expanded
the numbers of US advisers from 400 to 16 000.

In the aftermath of the initial insurgency there followed a two-year period of
increased VWP enthusiasm for their armed struggle[58] matched by continued
Soviet and Chinese caution. A high-level Chinese military mission arrived in
December 1961 and, according to a Chinese source, in mid-1962 'Ho Chi Minh
and Nguyen Chi Thanh came to China and requested military assistance for the
people of South Vietnam. The Chinese government immediately provided
90 000 weapons for the people of South Vietnam.' A high-level Soviet military
delegation arrived at the end of 1962 and a political mission led by Yuriy
Andropov in January 1963. Yet until 1963 the Vietnamese seem to have been
reliant mainly on their own resources.[59] The US JCS reported that 'availability
of weapons appears to be a continuing problem' and noted that the 'primary
source of arms' was American-supplied weapons captured from the ARVN.[60]
To some extent Vietnamese ambitions were trimmed to fit the support and
resources available. The Laotian government had moved against the Pathet Lao
leadership in Vientiane and its military forces on the Plain of Jars in May 1959,
many of whom crossed over into North Vietnam. This enabled the VWP to
exert much closer control over the Lao People's Party. In January 1961 Pathet
Lao and neutralist forces were reorganised, equipped by the Vietnamese with

Soviet weapons and subordinated to Vietnamese officers for both training and operations.[61] China's opposition to an all-Indochina revolution under VWP suzerainty, however, ensured it did not become the primary strategy.

Initially, the North Vietnamese leadership discounted both the likelihood and the decisiveness of American intervention.[62] However, as US intervention did indeed increase in 1962, the proponents of the war in the south shifted their emphasis to the necessity and possibility of holding off the Americans rather than the attempt to avoid such conflict altogether. Neither American support for the Diem regime nor its active acquiescence in his overthrow and murder in November 1963 altered North Vietnamese intentions. American intervention to stiffen South Vietnamese political and military resistance to the insurgency had the effect of causing COSVN to intensify its military activity, in an attempt to destroy the so-called 'strategic hamlets', and in consequence to increase its reliance on Soviet and Chinese supply. At the end of 1963 the dominant view in the Vietnamese leadership continued to be that a war could be fought and won without direct American military intervention. Whatever the Americans chose to do, the Vietnamese leadership was certain that the global and regional importance of the war had to be inflated by propaganda in order to 'isolate the enemy in the international arena'.[63]

Throughout 1963 Kennedy was intermittently troubled by the threat of communist insurgents to South Vietnam. This concern culminated in American encouragement of and collusion in a coup which overthrew the South Vietnamese leader, Ngo Dinh Diem, in November 1963. Diem was thus murdered only a few weeks before Kennedy. When Lyndon Johnson became President he was faced with the need to address the Vietnam situation for both short- and long-term reasons. In the short term it had become clear that the government of Vietnam, notwithstanding Diem's demise, was losing a war against political and military forces motivated and controlled by North Vietnam. At the same time Vietnam was also seen as a key element in the now unconcealed Sino-Soviet split. China was seen as a more aggressive power than the Soviet Union. According to Michael Forrestal in the State Department:

> Communist China shares the same internal political necessity for ideological expansion today that the Soviet Union did in the time of the Comintern and the period just following the Second World War ... This will impel her ... to achieve ideological successes abroad ... our objectives should be to 'contain' China for the longest possible period ... and at the same time strengthen the political and economic structure of the bordering countries ... We should delay China's swallowing up of Southeast Asia until (a) she develops better table manners and (b) the food is somewhat more indigestible.[64]

As a result, American involvement in Vietnam was variously seen as a means of driving a wedge between the Soviet Union and China or even as a means by which American-Soviet relations could be improved. Dean Rusk was 'quite convinced ... that the Russians as Russians are concerned about the prospect of living next to a billion Chinese armed with nuclear weapons'. He believed there was 'no real reason for a basic difference between the US and the USSR on Vietnam . . . At the other end of the spectrum was Peking which was adamant against negotiations.' His Assistant Secretary of State, Harlan Cleveland, argued that the United States was right to pursue a 'double-headed approach' combining the military punishment of North Vietnam and attempts to nego- tiate since 'it might drive the wedge more deeply between the Chicoms and the USSR. As military escalation increases, so will the Soviet Union's concern about the dangers of war in Asia. And so long as we are at the same time offering an opportunity for a negotiated settlement based on stabilising the status quo [in South Vietnam], Russian interests should coincide even more closely with our own in wanting to see an end to the affair.'[65]

Although American policy in Vietnam was calculated on its impact on the balance of Cold War power, Johnson, in fact, inherited from his predecessors a more visceral approach to the problem. 'I am', he declared soon after assuming office, 'not going to be the President who saw Southeast Asia go the way China went.' Although some CIA analysts warned that 'once outside powers do become involved [in Third World conflicts], whether by accident or design, crises can develop which will engage their prestige to a degree incommensurate with the intrinsic or strategic value of the area itself', this was not the view of the Johnson administration's top officials. Senator Mike Mansfield, the Senate majority leader, advised Johnson, as he had Kennedy, that 'present policy says that there is a war that can be won in South Vietnam alone. It says that the war can be won at a limited expenditure of American lives and resources somewhere commensurate with our national interests in South Vietnam. Both assumptions may be in error. There may be no war to be won in South Vietnam alone. There may only be a war which in time involves US forces throughout South-East Asia, and finally throughout China itself in search of victory.' Mansfield's prescription was the search for a truce, rather than victory in Vietnam. This could result in the stabilisation of South East Asia 'at a price commensurate with American interests. That peace should mean in the end a Southeast Asia less dependent on our aid resources and support, less under our control; not cut off from China but still not overwhelmed by China.'[66] Mansfield, and those who thought in the same vein, were, however, accused by State Department officials of setting 'neutralist hares running with self-fulfilling prophecies that dis- hearten those [in Asia] who wish to fight'. The administration needed to reaffirm its resolute policy because 'what gives these lofty, unrealistic thoughts of a peaceful neutralist Asia their credibility is fundamental doubts about our ultimate intentions . . . We must give them [the Communists] reason to assume that we are prepared to go as far as necessary to defeat their plans and achieve our objectives.'

This central concern with credibility was to the forefront of American thinking in August 1964 and the ensuing months when Johnson decided to launch air strikes against North Vietnam. It was even clearer a year later when the President decided to send American ground combat troops to fight in South Vietnam. Johnson made this decision with the overwhelming support of his closest advisers. There were, however, sceptics within the government who forced some kind of debate. In May 1965 Clark Clifford issued a warning to the President against tying American credibility to South Vietnam: 'My concern is that a substantial build-up of US ground troops would be construed by the Communists, and the world, as determination on our part to win the war on the ground. ... This could be a quagmire. It could turn into an open end commitment on our part that would take more and more ground troops, without a realistic hope of ultimate victory.'[67] The most persistent critic of US policy, the Assistant Secretary of State, George Ball, forced the credibility issue to be rehearsed in full. On 21 July Ball argued in front of the NSC that 'we cannot win ... The war will be long and protracted. The most we can hope for is a messy conclusion ... if the war is long and protracted ... we will suffer because the world's greatest power cannot defeat guerrillas.' He was denounced in turn by the President, the National Security Adviser, McGeorge Bundy, and the Secretary of State. The President objected: 'wouldn't all these countries say that Uncle Sam was a paper tiger, wouldn't we lose credibility breaking the word of three presidents? ... it would seem an irresponsible blow'. Bundy objected: 'George's analysis gives no weight to losses suffered by the other side. The world, the country, and the Vietnamese people would have alarming reactions if we got out.' Rusk was the most forthright: 'If the communist world found out that the United States would not pursue its commitment to the end, there is no telling where they would stop their expansionism.'[68]

By 1965 the DRV leadership had performed a remarkable feat. Not only had they made Indochina the focus of the USA's Cold War policy but they engineered a fragile coalition between the USSR and the PRC at the very moment that the two communist great powers were at the height of their hostility. Unsurprisingly, given the magnitude of the achievement, it was a fragile one. The North Vietnamese, however, managed to perpetuate it long enough to force the United States out and to conquer South Vietnam in 1975. Two factors were at the root of the DRV's success: first, the military perform-ance of its troops and sponsored guerrilla forces in Vietnam itself; second, its ability to promote the potent symbolism of the Vietnamese revolution to the Chinese, and thus to the Americans, as the vanguard of a new wave of communist revolution in Asia, and to the Soviets as an accomplished socialist revolution under threat, a bulwark against counter-revolution.

In the summer of 1964 minor clashes between American naval forces supporting the regime in Saigon and DRV coastal defence vessels provoked US air attacks on the north. They also provoked a major American commitment, the Gulf of Tonkin resolution, to further support Saigon against Hanoi. The DRV leadership was aware of the risks it was running in reaffirming and intensifying its war in the south. In its view the military successes of revolutionary forces would force the Americans to escalate the war. The enemy would increase the activity of special forces not only in South Vietnam itself but in Laos, Cambodia and the DRV. In all probability it would introduce regular American ground forces to fight the war in the south and vigorously attack the north from the air in order to bring about a negotiated settlement to the war which preserved the *status quo ante bellum*. On the other hand, Soviet support for the war in the south was now forthcoming. The overthrow of Khrushchev as Soviet leader brought to power men who were less sceptical of Vietnamese aspirations. In November 1964 Pham Van Dong led a delegation to Moscow and was promised military aid. In February 1965 Andrey Kosygin travelled to Hanoi to make Soviet support public. Because of the importance the United States attached to South East Asia and the PRC, Vietnam had become the nodal point for the Soviet Union's struggles with both countries. In consequence the Soviet Union would 'not remain indifferent to ensuring the security of a fraternal socialist country and will give the DRV the necessary aid and support'.[69] Although such Soviet support was not popular in the PRC, there seemed little possibility of the latter shutting down its own effort to succour Vietnam. Thus the Vietnamese believed, whatever military action the United States took, the Americans would not invade North Vietnam or attack the supply centres in south China. 'They see all the more danger, because they will come up against the socialist camp, with China and its 700 million people who now have the atomic bomb. They also know that they don't have enough troops and that they would not be supported by Britain, France, Germany and Japan.'[70] In April 1965 DRV fighter aircraft began to engage US aeroplanes. SAM sites were under construction by the Soviets.[71] In June 1965 Chinese troops moved into the DRV to secure the border and to provide logistical support for its military efforts.[72] In July 1965 the formal American decision to deploy a large number of ground combat troops to wage war in South Vietnam set the seal on its role as the fulcrum of the Cold War.

The Johnson administration's decision to introduce American ground combat troops into Vietnam was a double blow for Chinese leaders. On one level it upset Zhou's hopes for a 'zone of peace' in South East Asia. It was bound to provoke another debate such as the 1950 discussions which led up to China's intervention in Korea. In 1965, however, it also fitted neatly into the apocalyptic Maoist analysis of world politics. Mao told Japanese Communist Party leaders in January 1966 that 'a war between China and America is inevitable ... within two years at the latest ... America will attack us from four points, namely the Vietnam frontier, the Korean frontier and through Japan by way of Taiwan and Okinawa. On such an occasion, Russia with the Sino-Russian defence pact as its pretext, will cross the frontier from Siberia and Mongolia to occupy China.'[73] Here Mao was using a doom-laden threat assessment for political purposes. In fact the Chinese and Americans signalled to each other in April 1966 that neither would attack the other. Mao had, in any case, already decided in June 1965 that it was extremely unlikely that the Americans would invade North Vietnam in the way they had invaded North Korea. He rejected two lines of advice: one emanating from Liu and Deng that intervention in Vietnam would lead to bigger military budgets and thus slower economic growth and should be avoided; the other from Luo Ruiqing, the PLA's Chief of Staff, that there was a major threat to Chinese security emerging in Vietnam and that China had to take 'united action' with the Soviet Union to oppose it. All three were subsequently purged. Liu and Deng were already marked men; Luo failed to understand that Mao was more interested in combating internal revisionism and politicising the PLA than choosing the most efficient military options. Nevertheless, a massive military mobilisation did take place. Military production and arms transfers to the North Vietnamese were started, PAVN forces were trained in China, up to 50 000 PLA road-and-rail construction forces and anti-aircraft divisions were sent into North Vietnam. Most strikingly, the 'third front' concept was put fully into action. In May 1964 Mao insisted on a concentration on heavy industry. Immediately after the Gulf of Tonkin incident he called for a drastic acceleration of inland construction programmes on the basis that large-scale war was an immediate possibility. These facilities were constructed in remote areas of western China in locations such as caves, to protect them from nuclear attack. They were an example of Cultural Revolution action using politicised PLA personnel and 'human wave' construction techniques. Between 1965 and 1971 well over half of China's total national investment was expended on these projects.[74] They produced real outcomes such as the China–Vietnam transport infrastructure and the accelerated nuclear programme: the first Chinese atomic device was exploded in 1964 and the first hydrogen bomb in 1968.[75] Yet these projects were so inefficient with economic resources that not only was the PLA left unmodernised, as Mao and Lin Biao intended since its role was primarily political, but economic damage, still being felt in the late 1980s, was inflicted.

VIETNAM AND SINO-US *RAPPROCHEMENT*, 1968–1972

For the United States, tying Cold War policy to South Vietnam caused that policy to become inverted. From July 1965 global policy became a means of victory in Vietnam, rather than Vietnam being a means of pursuing a global policy. By late 1967 key figures in the American establishment had begun seriously to question the deformation of American policy by Vietnam. A group of former senior officials and cabinet members was convened in November 1967 and drew such a conclusion. Clark Clifford, who replaced McNamara as Secretary of Defense in March 1968, recalled:

> I was conscious of our obligations and involvements elsewhere in the world. There were certain hopeful signs in our relations with the Soviet Union, but both nations were hampered in moving toward vitally important talks on the limitation of strategic

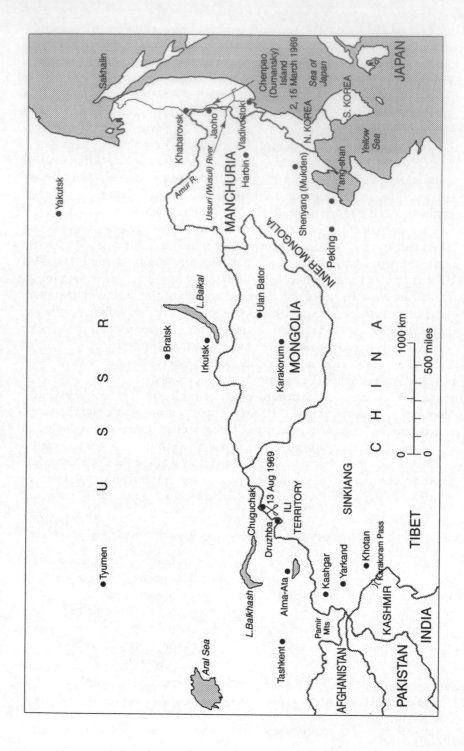

Map 7 Sino-Soviet border clashes

weapons so long as the United States was committed to a military solution in Viet Nam. We could not afford to disregard our interests in the Middle East, South Asia, Africa, Western Europe and elsewhere. Even accepting the validity of our objective in Viet Nam, that objective had to be viewed in the context of our overall national interest, and could not sensibly be pursued at a price so high as to impair our ability to achieve other, and perhaps more important foreign policy objectives.[76]

Clifford and his group, men 'present at the creation', were champions of global containment and also believed that the United States was still in the middle of the 'long haul'.

This was a view shared by Richard Nixon, who won the November 1968 presidential election. Nixon was also more interested in abandoning sinophobic policies and enlisting the PRC as a counter-balance to the Soviet Union rather than the Soviet Union as a counter-balance to China, which had been Kennedy's view in 1963. In April 1967 Ambassador Chester Bowles reported that the 'one somewhat offbeat concept which seemed to be on [Nixon's] mind involved our relationships with the Soviet Union and China. In his opinion we should "stop falling all over ourselves" to improve our relationships with Russia since this would "make better relationships with China impossible". On several occasions he almost suggested that good relations with China were more important than good relations with Russia.'[77] In October 1967 Nixon published an important article in which he argued that although 'Red China [threatens the independence of the Asian nations] ... and its threat is clear, present and repeatedly and insistently expressed',[78] in 'the long view, we cannot afford to leave China forever outside the family of nations'.[79] Nixon said that what he feared most was 'that the Soviets might reach nuclear parity with the United States' at the same time as 'China ... will have a significant deliverable nuclear capability [and might] scatter its weapons among "liberation" forces anywhere in the world'.[80] In Nixon's analysis: 'The world cannot be safe until China changes. Thus our aim, to the extent that we can influence events, should be to induce change. The way to do this is to persuade China that it must change: that it cannot satisfy its imperial ambitions, and that its own national interest requires a turning away from foreign adventuring and a turning inward toward the solution of its own domestic problems.'[81] He rejected an 'anti-Chinese alliance with European powers, even including the Soviet Union' because 'such a course would inevitably carry connotations of Europe vs. Asia, white vs. non-white, which could have catastrophic repercussions throughout the rest of the non-white world in general and Asia in particular'.[82]

In his attitude to China, Nixon was clearly in opposition to the majority foreign-policy élite consensus. He and his National Security Adviser Henry Kissinger were, however, as convinced of the critical importance of credibility as their predecessors in the Kennedy and Johnson administrations. In 1968 Kissinger wrote:

However fashionable it is to ridicule the terms credibility or 'prestige', they are not empty phrases; other nations can gear their actions to ours only if they can count on our steadfastness. The collapse of the American effort in Viet Nam would not mollify many critics; most would simply add the charge of unreliability to the accusation of bad judgement. Those whose safety or national goals depend upon American commitments could only be dismayed. In many parts of the world ... stability depends on a confidence in American promises. Unilateral withdrawal, or a settlement which unintentionally amounts to the same thing, could therefore lead to the erosion of restraints and to an even more dangerous international situation. No American policymaker can simply dismiss these dangers.[83]

Nixon agreed with this assessment. In March 1968 he commented: 'There's no way to win this war. But we can't say that, of course. In fact, we have to say just the opposite, just to keep some degree of bargaining leverage.'

The way out of Vietnam was found in the policy of 'Vietnamisation': US ground troops would be withdrawn and the war turned over to the ARVN. The USA would maintain its credibility by using its air power to stave off total defeat for South Vietnam. Some attempt was made to dress this policy up as a major new departure in America's global strategy: at Guam in July 1969, Nixon explained that, in future, the USA intended to support its allies with *matériel* rather than manpower. Yet the so-called Nixon doctrine moved little beyond Vietnam. Kissinger hoped that Vietnamisation would be a controlled process. In June 1969 he warned that, 'if ... we withdraw at a rate that gives Hanoi the feeling that we are really looking for an excuse to get out, then it will thwart negotiations, because they will just sit there and wait ... [it will be no more than] an elegant bugout'.[84]

Despite their success in engaging both Chinese and Soviet participation in the war, the DRV leadership had come to realise that becoming the cockpit of great-power struggle placed them in an unenviable position. As the Americans escalated the struggle into the 'big war' both on the ground in the south and in the air over the north the divergent aims of the communist participants were laid bare. The Chinese and the Soviets continued to abuse each other; if Vietnam had been first priority for either they might have compromised. Instead they fought for the soul of the Vietnamese struggle. Despite its open declaration of support for the DRV the Soviet Union remained cautious. The Chinese, on the other hand, seemed willing to fight to the last Vietnamese. According to General Nguyen Van Vinh, addressing a COSVN conference in April 1966, some allies were pusillanimous whilst others were too belligerent.[85] To fight selflessly for the communist cause buoyed only by the ambiguous promise of invasion by an historical enemy held little attraction for the North Vietnamese. Nevertheless, the prevailing opinion in the leadership seems to have been relatively optimistic until the military failure of the Tet offensive and its aftermath in early 1968. In April 1968 the DRV government offered to open peace talks with the United States, an offer which was accepted by the Johnson administration. In August 1969 the Nixon administration initiated secret negotiations with the North Vietnamese leadership. In the same month Kissinger persuaded Nixon to postpone troop withdrawals after a Vietnamese attack on the American base at Cam Ranh Bay. Kissinger told the President: 'We have to impress Hanoi with our staying power or we won't have flexibility. It is important that Hanoi understands – and the American people understand – that the three criteria [reductions in enemy military activity; progress in negotiations; and improvement in SVN capability] do apply and we are not just engaged in a mechanical exercise.' Within a fortnight, however, Nixon insisted that over 40 000 US troops should be withdrawn. He decreed that withdrawals would never again be affected by either the state of the war or negotiations with North Vietnam and other powers.[86]

The attempt to link the American withdrawal from Vietnam to wider considerations was abandoned very early in the Nixon presidency. Nixon and Kissinger substituted a desire for 'savage, punishing blow[s]' to demonstrate US will. In 1969–70 these included the bombing of Cambodia and its subsequent invasion in May 1970, on which Nixon reportedly commented to a Pentagon audience, 'I want to take out all of those [North Vietnamese] sanctuaries [in Cambodia]. Knock them all out. You have to electrify people with bold decisions. Bold decisions make history, like Teddy Roosevelt charging up San Juan Hill [in the Spanish-American War of 1898], a small event but dramatic, and people took notice. Let's blow the hell out of them.' The pattern was repeated in 1972 with the mining of Haiphong in May and the 'Christmas bombing' of North Vietnam in December. Nothing, however, was allowed to interfere with the American withdrawal which was effectively completed in August 1972.[87] An agreement to end the war was finally signed by the Americans and the North Vietnamese in January 1973. It provided for the withdrawal of all American troops from Vietnam within 60 days but made no provision for the withdrawal of North Vietnamese forces.

The 1968 Tet offensive and its aftermath had made the North Vietnamese even more dependent on material support from both the PRC and the USSR. China continued to revel in the idea of a protracted and bloody war. In Zhou Enlai's words the war 'had reached a new and higher level of development . . . the US aggressors . . . will no doubt put up an even more frenzied last ditch fight'. The Soviet leadership had lost whatever enthusiasm it had once had for the war. A Soviet commentary on Brezhnev's meeting with an NLF delegation in Moscow in mid-1969 commented that: 'China's ruling group is doing everything in its power to protract the Vietnam war. . . . It regards the war as a factor in its Great Power political game without caring in the least about the interests of the Vietnamese people, [or] the socialist camp . . . the Peking leaders hope to use the Vietnam war to bring the Soviet Union and the USA on a collision course to provoke a military conflict, while they themselves keep well away from it.'[88]

Chinese policy was, however, in the process of change.[89] The final outburst of Cultural Revolution foreign policy had important ramifications for the Cold War. The Cultural Revolution had placed China in the position of introducing uncertainty and violence into the Cold War: mobs lashed out using extreme violence, propaganda was poisonous, an indirect war was being fought with the United States in Vietnam and there was direct military conflict with the Soviet Union in Sinkiang. Red Guards staged or encouraged violence in Burma, Cambodia, Hong Kong and, of all places, Moscow. Mobs attacked Soviet and British diplomats in Peking and other Chinese cities. In May 1967 they attacked their own Foreign Ministry and evicted the Foreign Minister, Chen Yi, a close associate of Zhou Enlai. Sino–Soviet relations deteriorated steadily through the late 1960s until they reached crisis point in 1969. In 1966 China broke off formal relations with the CPSU. Between 1965 and 1969 the main aspect of this quarrel in international affairs was competition within the communist world. In 1967 the Romanian Foreign Minister made a secret visit to Peking. In 1968 the Chinese bitterly criticised the Soviet intervention in Czechoslovakia, and Soviet attempts to 'excommunicate' the CCP were thwarted by Rumania and Yugoslavia in the course of 1969. This competition took on a much more threatening aspect when Chinese troops engaged Russian forces on their common border. Military tension had been building in the area for years. Soviet forces in the Far East had been enlarged from 12 divisions in 1961 to 25 by the time of the conflict. Military confrontation was, however, much more worrying. According to the defector Arkadiy Shevchenko, 'the event . . . had the effect of an electric shock in Moscow. The Politburo was terrified that the Chinese might make a large scale intrusion into Soviet territory. . . . A nightmare vision of invasion by millions of Chinese made the Soviet leaders almost frantic. Despite our overwhelming superiority in weaponry, it would not be easy for the USSR to cope with an assault of such magnitude.' In August and September 1969 the Soviets sounded out the Americans about their reaction to an attack on Chinese nuclear facilities. Seeming Chinese willingness to combine diplomacy with military force opened up a worrying vista. 'The new dangerous provocation of the Maoists', a report to the GDR leadership read, 'reveals Beijing's intention to activate the opportunistic political flirtation with the imperialist countries – above all with the USA and West Germany.'[90]

When PLA forces attacked the Red Army on the borders of Manchuria in March 1969, however, it militarised the conflict with 'revisionism' and thus either remobilised or redirected the Cultural Revolution. In its aftermath the rationalists reasserted control. The external threat could be portrayed as greater than at any time since the end of the Civil War. Mao's attitude changed in about 1968. Red Guards were being mobilised in his name but not necessarily by him; he feared that Lin Biao was planning to overthrow or even kill him. He needed rationalists such as Zhou or Deng (Liu died in prison, from the effects of torture exacerbated by starvation and lack of medical attention, in November 1969) to redress the balance.[91]

In March 1969 Zhou convened a meeting of China's marshals, then excluded from power by Lin Biao, and Foreign Ministry officials. The gathering could only have convened at Mao's express request. It considered two major issues. The first was the possibility of a Soviet military strike against China and the USSR's capability if such a strike was launched. The prognosis was not favourable. In August 1968 the Soviet Union had used military force to crush the Prague Spring, its forces had routed the PLA on the border and in the summer of 1969 nuclear-capable bombers were redeployed from the European theatre to the Far East. The other issue addressed was the possibility that the Soviet Union and the United States might collude to undermine China. Chen Yi argued that the relationship between the superpowers was still primarily marked by conflict, therefore any such collusion was unlikely: the very views Liu Shaoqi had expressed six years previously and for which he was paying the ultimate price as Chen spoke. The forum, however, accepted Chen's view and recommended to Mao that the PRC could avert the Soviet threat by engineering an opening to the United States.

The threat of immediate conflict with the Soviet Union was damped down when Andrey Kosygin met Zhou Enlai in Peking in August 1969, but the Soviet account of the meeting noted, 'it is still too early to make conclusions about the results which this meeting will bring. ... Time will tell whether Peking's intention to move along the path of normalisation will be serious or if this is only a tactical move dictated by the circumstances of the aggravated political struggle within the PRC'. A further assessment of relations in February 1971 concluded that although the 'situation of the border [was] somewhat mitigated' there had been no other area of improvement in relations. Even the border was still a major problem, requiring a major military build-up: 45 divisions were deployed by 1973 and their conventional and nuclear armament was rapidly upgraded. Internationally, the Soviets believed that, 'anti-Sovietism was and continues to be the main ingredient in the anti-Marxist nationalistic line of the present Chinese leadership'. This was expressed in intra-Communist conflict. 'Chinese propaganda never ceases its provocative statements on the Czechoslovak question. Peking has acted similarly with respect to the recent events in Poland.' China was, 'once again ... counting on its ability to either attract individual communist parties to its side, or at least achieve their refusal to publicly criticise the ideology and policy of the CPC leadership'. In July 1970 the Romanian Defence Minister had visited Peking and this presaged a state visit by President Ceauşescu in June 1971.

The Soviets also detected that: 'The imperialist powers, the USA in particular, are playing a sly game in their approach to China. On the one hand they would like to use the anti-Sovietism of the Maoists against the USSR, but, on the other hand, they would like to strengthen their own position in the PRC,

in the vast Chinese market.' In January 1970 the United States made a key
concession to China when it stated at an ambassadorial meeting in Warsaw that
it intended to reduce American military commitments to Taiwan. This strand
was constant in the May 1971 proposal for Kissinger to meet Zhou Enlai and
his secret trip to China in July 1971. Nixon arrived in China for a groundbreak-
ing visit at the beginning of 1972.

The new Zhou–Mao line was based once more on an understanding that the
PRC faced both threats and opportunities from the international environment.
The Mao–Lin Biao line had significantly weakened China. As a retrospective
commentary put it in 1980: 'One of the most important strategies ... in the
struggle against the enemy is: rally all forces that can be rallied, organise the
broadest international united front, and concentrate the main strength to hit the
most important enemy ... The theory of "hitting out in all directions" [attrib-
uted to Lin but actually insisted on by Mao since the early 1960s] trampled down
on many important Marxist-Leninist tactics ... *The consequence was enemies
everywhere, bringing us to the brink of isolation.*' Zhou also saw that there was an
opportunity to recoup this situation. He argued in December 1971, three months
after Lin Biao died, fleeing after an abortive coup attempt, and two months before
Nixon arrived in China: 'The visit of the head of US imperialism renders
bankrupt the China policy of the US. When the US got stuck in Vietnam, the
Soviet revisionists used the opportunity to extend vigorously their sphere of
influence ... the US imperialists have no choice but to improve their relations
with China in order to counter the Soviet revisionists ... [Nixon] has to bring
something along in his pocket; otherwise he will find it hard to give explanations when he returns to the US.' As in the 1950s, it was once again Taiwan
which was the objective and Vietnam which was to be the tool. 'Nixon can't
come unless he wants to talk about Taiwan', Mao said. According to Vietnamese sources: 'on 13 July 1971, a high-ranking Chinese delegation [led by Zhou]
said: Indochina is the most important problem in our meeting with Kissinger
... the US let it be known that US troops could be pulled out of Taiwan only
after US forces were withdrawn from Indochina. To China the withdrawal of
US troops from South Vietnam is more important than the question of China
being admitted to the UN.' The Chinese told the North Vietnamese 'to avail
itself of every opportunity to first solve the question of US troop withdrawal ...
the overthrow of the Saigon puppet administration will take time'. This was the
same formula as that used in 1954. Mao is reputed to have said: 'his broom was
not long enough to sweep Taiwan clean [the same analogy he had used when
speaking to Mikoyan in February 1949] and [North Vietnam's] was not long
enough to get the Americans out of South Vietnam. He wanted to halt
reunification ... and to recognise the puppet regime in the South.'

The Sino-American Shanghai communiqué of February 1972, issued to
mark Nixon's remarkable visit, reflected China's new view of the international
situation: the opportunities open to it and the practical limitation which

existed. China and the United States agreed that 'neither should seek hegemony in the Asia–Pacific region and each is opposed to efforts by any other country or group of countries to establish such hegemony'. In other words, China and the US agreed to create an anti-Soviet balance of power in Asia. They also pledged to reject 'any country colluding with another against other countries, or for any major country to divide up the world into spheres of influence' so China no longer had to worry that the United States and the Soviet Union would ally against it. The PRC thus achieved its defensive criteria. It also went a long way towards the positive goal of reunification. The UN voted to replace Taiwan with the PRC as the representative of China in October 1971. In February 1972 the American government not only acknowledged that 'all Chinese either side of the Taiwan strait maintain there is one China and Taiwan is part of China' but that 'the United States does not challenge that position'. Nixon affirmed 'the ultimate objective of the withdrawal of all US forces and military installations from Taiwan'. The PRC could have Taiwan as long as it did not move against the Americans in the region and could contrive a method short of military invasion to bring about reunification.[92]

THE UNITED STATES AND *DETENTE*

If Nixon differed from the foreign-policy consensus in his Chinese policies, his appointee as National Security Adviser, Henry Kissinger, was even more heretical in his view of US–Soviet relations. Kissinger argued that the world had been transformed in the 1960s. McNamara's acknowledgement of strategic parity with the Soviet Union could no longer be combined with Eisenhower's long-term theory of victory. A new, and semi-permanent, structure of international relations was emerging which had to be carefully managed It would yield victory for neither the United States nor the Soviet Union. In 1968 Kissinger wrote:

> The greatest need of the contemporary system is an agreed concept of order. In its absence, the awesome power is unrestrained by any consensus as to legitimacy; ideology and nationalism, in their different ways, deepen international schisms. ... A new concept of international order is essential; its stability will prove elusive. The problem is particularly serious for the United States. Whatever our intentions or policies, the fact that the United States disposes of the greatest single aggregate of material power is inescapable. A new international order is inconceivable without a significant American contribution. But the nature of this contribution has altered. For the two decades after 1945, our international activities were based on the assumption that technology plus managerial skill gave us the ability to shape the international system and bring about domestic transformations in the 'emerging countries'. This direct 'operational' concept of international order has proved too simple. Political multipolarity makes it impossible to impose an American design. Our deepest challenge will be to evoke the creativity of a pluralistic world, to base order on multipolarity even though overwhelming military strength will remain with the two superpowers.[93]

The foreign-policy élite agreed that America had to leave Vietnam whilst negotiating with the Soviet Union both on that departure and on other issues. Some, such as Clifford, did not call for a fundamental recasting of Cold War strategy, merely a more sensible choice of important and defensible areas. Kissinger, and to a lesser extent Nixon, saw the need for a completely new international order, which would involve close and direct cooperation with the Soviet Union.

Within the new Republican administration, however, there were extremely important differences of emphasis. Nixon's victory had, to a large extent, rested upon his promise to extricate the United States from Vietnam. He was quite willing to contemplate cooperation with the Soviet Union to facilitate the achievement of this goal. Nixon wanted to publicly link the improvement of American–Soviet relations to the Soviet attitude to Vietnam and other areas of tension such as the Middle East. Although he also accepted the reality of strategic sufficiency, he was not interested in the detail of SALT negotiations.[94] Kissinger had a much more developed sense of the need for Soviet–American partnership. He believed that it was the Soviet Union with whom the United States would remain engaged on a global basis; it was the Soviet Union which would remain the only other military superpower; and it was the Soviet Union which presented the main threat to the stable world order he desired.[95]

In July 1963 the United States, the Soviet Union and Britain had signed a test ban treaty, a limited measure which outlawed the atmospheric testing of nuclear weapons.[96] It had the advantage to the Americans of encouraging ever more hostile relations between China and the Soviet Union. Yet it did little to meet the Soviet strategic arms challenge which the American government was sure would come. On television, Kennedy could tell the American people that the partial test ban (PTB) was 'a shaft of light into the darkness' created by 'a vicious circle of conflicting ideology and interest [in which] each increase of tension has produced an increase in arms; each increase of arms has produced an increase of tension'.[97] His Secretary of Defense, Robert McNamara, believed however that the strategic logic of offensive arms would produce a stable balance within which the United States would need to operate. As McNamara and his advisers in the Pentagon understood the situation,

> once each side [had] enough nuclear forces to eliminate the other side's urban society in a second strike the utility of extra nuclear forces is dubious at best. In this context notions of nuclear 'superiority' are devoid of significant meaning ... since the Soviet Union has assured-destruction capability against the United States, 'superior' US nuclear forces are extremely difficult to convert into real political power. The blunt, unavoidable fact is that the Soviet Union could effectively destroy the United States even after absorbing the full weight of a US first strike, and vice versa. Nor do we believe this is likely to change in the future.[98]

McNamara understood that there were two main variables in this new strategic landscape: the size and shape of US strategic forces and projections of the likely size of the Soviet strategic force. The second task proved more difficult to undertake than the first. As McNamara explained in March 1964: 'we must ... project our estimates of the enemy's forces ... long range projections of enemy capabilities must necessarily be highly uncertain, particularly since they deal with a time period beyond the production and deployment lead-times of enemy weapon systems. We are estimating capabilities and attempting to anticipate deployment decisions which our opponents, themselves, may not yet have made.' Nevertheless, on the basis of such tenuous estimates McNamara announced, in February 1963, that the Soviet Union would have 200 ICBMs in fully hardened silos in service by mid-1968. In April 1965, he commented that the Soviet Union would equal US ICBM numbers in 1970, although he discounted the risk of a quantitative arms race.[99]

By 1965 the Secretary of Defense was becoming convinced that the United States should unilaterally cap its own nuclear forces. The rationale for this cap was threefold. First, the overriding objective of the US nuclear force should be 'to deter a deliberate nuclear attack upon the United States or its allies by maintaining at all times a clear and unmistakable ability to inflict an acceptable degree of damage upon an aggressor, or combination of aggressors – even after absorbing a surprise first strike'. Second, that without a cap the US was 'getting ... the worst of both worlds, ... paying for a first strike posture, but settling for a minimum-deterrent capability'. Third, overbuilding of US strategic forces caused unnecessary arms racing: 'we would expect [the Soviets] in their planning, to view our strategic offensive forces as a potential first-strike threat (just as we do theirs) and provide for a second-strike capability. ... Each step by either side, however sensible or precautionary, would elicit a precautionary response from the other side. This 'action-reaction' phenomenon is central to all strategic force planning issues'. By the end of 1966 McNamara's staff had concluded that the United States needed an assured second-strike force capable of destroying 20–25 per cent of the Soviet population and 50 per cent of its industrial capacity. The necessary force would amount to 1000 Minuteman ICBMs, 41 SSBNs carrying Polaris SLBMs and 500 strategic bombers.[100]

McNamara believed that the emerging US–Soviet balance would be stable. He discounted the possibility that the growth of missile forces or the development of ballistic missile defences could upset it. The tendency of McNamara and his advisers to discount worries about the size of Soviet strategic forces or defensive developments proved to be their Achilles heel in domestic political debate. In February 1964 McNamara revealed that US intelligence believed that 'the Soviets are deploying an antiballistic missile system around Leningrad [and] may be starting to deploy one around Moscow'. He argued, however, that although 'this system probably would be effective against single missiles' it would 'not be effective against ballistic missiles equipped with even elementary penetration aids'. Some CIA and DIA intelligence analysts maintained, however, that the Soviets could gain a temporary advantage over US forces, depending on the relative pace of development of offensive and defensive technologies. In addition the 1965 NIE identified a 'greater than expected threat' from a projected force of Soviet SS-9 ICBMs carrying MIRVs. McNamara accordingly advised President Johnson to approve the introduction of a new generation of MIRVed ICBMs and SLBMs.

The Joint Chiefs of Staff, who had lost power to the Secretary of Defense in the early 1960s, now re-emerged as an important force in strategic debates. They lobbied for the deployment of an American BMD system as well as upgraded offensive forces. Earle Wheeler, the JCS chairman, testified before the Senate that if 'the Soviets come to believe that their ballistic missile defence, coupled with a nuclear attack on the United States, would limit damage to the Soviet Union to a level acceptable to them, whatever that level is, our forces would no longer deter, and the first principle of our security policy is gone.'[101] The JCS also used the 'China card', which had so exercised Kennedy, to mobilise congressional support. They pointed out that during the course of 1966 the PRC had successfully tested both a fusion device and a ballistic missile. President Johnson was not willing to let the Republicans make 'lack of defence an election issue'. McNamara was, therefore, forced to find a compromise. His preferred way forward was to call upon the Soviets to begin arms control talks in order to obviate the need to deploy an ABM system. Johnson met the Soviet President, Andrey Kosygin, at Glassboro, New Jersey on 23 June 1967. At this meeting McNamara put it to Kosygin that 'if you proceed with anti-ballistic missile deployment our response will not, should not, be to deploy a similar system ... our response will be to expand our offensive weapons'. Kosygin harshly rejected this approach. Thwarted in this attempt to derail BMD, McNamara announced, in September 1967, that 'there are marginal grounds for concluding that a light deployment of US ABMs against the possibility [of a Chinese missile attack] is prudent'. He later recalled that: the 'only reason this was in there was ... to recognise the political pressure and the fact that the Congress had authorised such a system, appropriated funds for it, and was pushing unmercifully to deploy not the thin system [covering 15 cities] but a thick system [covering 25 cities].'

McNamara's acceptance of the emerging strategic balance was being increasingly challenged.[102] In the same month, as McNamara announced his grudging acceptance of an ABM system, a group of retired military officers and defence officials published a paper claiming that a version of the SS-9 with ten MIRVs could be deployed within 18 months. Soon afterwards McNamara was eased out of office because of his growing opposition to American military policy in Vietnam. In November 1968 when Richard Nixon won the presidency, his appointee as Secretary of Defense, Melvin Laird, sided with McNamara's critics. He accepted that 'the situation caused by the continuing rapid expansion of Soviet strategic offensive forces is a matter of serious concern. For some time, the Soviet forces which became operational in a given year often exceeded the previous intelligence projections for that year.' His deputy, David Packard, commented that 'if you look at the present level of SS-9 missiles and their continuing build-up of these missiles, the survival of our Minuteman force could be endangered'. Packard recommended an ABM system to protect 12 major ICBM bases, a recommendation accepted by Nixon and the Senate.[103] Yet Nixon accepted McNamara's strategic reasoning. In January 1969 he said: 'Our objective is to be sure that the United States has sufficient military power to defend our interests ... I think "sufficiency" is a better term, actually, than either "superiority" or "parity" [because parity would] not necessarily assure that a war may not occur [since either side might win].[104]

The Nixon administration pursued arms control negotiations much more energetically than had its predecessor. Although Johnson had favoured an attempt to stabilise both strategic and diplomatic relations with the Soviets, direct Soviet-American relations became an issue of secondary importance for him, lagging far behind Vietnam and his domestic programmes. Johnson's rhetoric tended to be emollient, however. At the Glassboro summit he told Kosygin: 'there is a ... special responsibility placed upon our own countries because of our strength and our resources. This demands that the relations between our two countries be as reasonable and constructive as we know how to make them.' Dean Rusk judged that whilst 'peaceful coexistence' had been forced on the Soviet Union by American military strength it was unlikely to 'produce a militant and convincing communism ... that is going to transform the rest of the world into Communists'. The administration was not confrontational at times of crisis. The 'hotline' teleprinter between the White House and the Kremlin, set up after the Cuban missile crisis, was used for the first time during the Arab–Israeli Six-Day War in 1967. Even when Soviet forces intervened in Czechoslovakia in August 1968, the only substantive response was to cancel arms control negotiations, due to start in October, with the caveat that the US government would 'strive to make this set-back a very temporary one' since arms control was an 'urgent and overriding interest'. These negotiations with the Soviets were spurred on by four considerations. First, the Johnson presidency had undermined the assumptions which had been accepted under Truman, Eisenhower and Kennedy. It was not possible to return to the *status quo ante*. Second, both Nixon and Kissinger accepted the logic of the nuclear balance; arms control was a way of stabilising that balance. Third, Kissinger went further and argued that the strategic balance required a restructuring of the international system. Fourth, a new type of negotiation with the Soviets allowed the White House to circumvent normal bureaucratic procedures, centralising power and opening the way for the political exploitation of any breakthroughs.

Although the USA had a number of strategic systems with which it had to deal – ABMs, ICBMs, SLBMs and MIRVs – at times it was the fact rather than the details of negotiation which mattered. At a meeting of the NSC in April

1970 a number of options were canvassed. Kissinger favoured a high ceiling on offensive missiles, so that the US would not have to make any cuts, no limits on MIRVs, which the US was developing more rapidly than the Soviet Union, and a very limited number of ABMs, preferably only one site defending the capital. In negotiation he effectively decoupled the ABM issue, on which the Soviets were anxious to agree, from offensive systems. Thus a draft ABM treaty was in existence by March 1971 but it took a further year to negotiate a SALT treaty. Nixon was most exercised by the politics of the issue. He travelled to Moscow in May 1972 to sign both treaties, aware that along with the disengagement from Vietnam, their negotiation would be the centrepiece of his drive for re-election in November 1972.[105] In Moscow he signed the ABM treaty which banned the deployment of ABM systems except as specified; what was later specified was a maximum of two ABM sites, one protecting the capital, the other an ICBM site. The two sides also signed an Interim Offensive Agreement. This was to last for five years. It froze the mix of ICBMs and SLBMs at existing numbers and banned major modernisation of existing ICBM sites.[106]

Nixon also signed two less concrete agreements with the USSR. In May 1972 it was a document on basic principles of relations. It had three main provisions. First a 'common determination that in the nuclear age there is no alternative to conducting ... mutual relations on the basis of peaceful coexistence [and] ... on the principles of sovereignty, equality, non-interference in internal affairs and mutual advantage'. Second, both countries recognised, 'the major importance of preventing the development of situations capable of causing a dangerous exacerbation of their relations. Therefore they will do their utmost to avoid military confrontations and settle differences by peaceful means ... both sides recognise that efforts to obtain unilateral advantage at the expense of the other, directly or indirectly, are inconsistent with these objectives.' Third, they accepted a 'special responsibility to do everything in their power so that conflicts or situations will not arise which would serve to increase international tensions'. In June 1973 the basic principles were supplemented by an agreement on the Prevention of Nuclear War under which 'each Party will refrain from the threat or use of force against the other party, against allies of the other party and against other countries, in circumstances which may endanger international peace and security'. These agreements were dismissed by many in the US government as window-dressing. They reflected not only the preferred Soviet view of international relations but Kissinger's attempt to abandon the Cold War for a new international structure. He defended the basic principles as 'a road map. Now that the map has been laid out, it is up to each country to follow it. ... They can provide a solid framework for the future development of better American–Soviet relations.'[107]

THE SOVIET UNION AND *DETENTE*

Soviet foreign policy under Khrushchev had been dealt two severe blows. Despite a four-year Soviet effort, the status quo in Germany remained unchanged. Attempts to recover prestige lost in Germany with a spectacular *coup de théâtre* in Cuba had gone awry. In the second phase of the Cuban missile crisis Khrushchev had appealed to Kennedy to help create something approaching a Soviet–US condominium in Europe. Whilst Kennedy was willing to take steps to reduce the risks of an inadvertent nuclear war he was unwilling to discard the political advantages the Cuban and German crises had brought to the USA. Within the Soviet leadership foreign policy seems to have played a role in encouraging leadership change. Khrushchev was not ousted in October 1964 because of his foreign-policy failures but he had certainly failed to achieve the successes which would have made him indispensable.[108] The emergence of a new leadership under Brezhnev seemed to presage a general hardening of attitudes. As head of state from 1960 Brezhnev had made a number of trips overseas. His main appeal as a leader in both foreign and domestic affairs, however, was his caution. Soviet commentaries on international affairs during the Brezhnev period stressed Soviet policy based on an adversary which had altered its methods but not its basic hostility.[109] The emergence of 'realism' within American ruling circles came with the changing correlation of forces but 'realists' were not friends; they were merely interested in tactical modifications to the line of monopoly capitalism.

It was the changing 'correlation of forces' which gave the Brezhnev Politburo the greatest grounds for optimism in the 1960s. The strategic weapons programmes which Khrushchev had initiated and boasted about came to fruition under his successors. By 1965 the Soviet Union had deployed over 200 second-generation ICBMs and about 700 IRBMs. Ten years later Soviet land-based strategic missile forces had grown at a spectacular rate. By 1974 there were over 1300 third-generation ICBMs, capable of launch-on-warning, deployed in hardened underground silos. In 1971 the first MRVs were added and in 1974–5 the first MIRVs came into service. At sea progress was equally encouraging. In 1968 the Yankee-class SSBN entered service. A fleet of 34 such boats had been deployed by 1974. Their utility was limited since they still had to approach the American seaboard to launch an attack, but this problem was rectified in 1973 when the Delta-class submarine armed with SLBMs with a range of 4200 km entered service.[110] This build-up of strategic forces was matched by a change of military strategy in Europe. France's defection from NATO and the alliance's subsequent shift to a strategy of 'flexible response' seemed to open up the prospect of a two-phase war in Europe. The United States would be unwilling to use its strategic forces against the Soviet Union if the USSR had a proven second strike capability: a massive land/air offensive into Western Europe could defeat NATO and allow the Soviet Union to beat off an American counter-offensive. Thus at the same time as the Soviet Union was expanding its strategic nuclear forces it was enhancing the size and effectiveness of its forces in Europe: starting in 1968 forces in central Europe went from 26 to 31 divisions. By the early 1970s there were nearly 520 000 troops in the region, including 395 000 in the GDR. Political and military strategy were meshed together: a Soviet war-fighting posture was bound to make the Western Europeans fearful of their own security and the reliability of the United States as an ally.

The rewards of military power made the leadership determined to have more of it. In 1966 Kosygin and Nikolay Podgorny had argued that there should be only a limited increase in defence spending so that the Soviet populace would not suffer 'material restrictions' because of the military build-up. Other leaders, including Brezhnev, preferred to keep the standard of living low so that funds could be given to the military. In part, these disagreements revolved around power and patronage, just as they had since Stalin's death. By 1969 a consensus had emerged around higher military spending and the defence budget was increased accordingly. This debate foreshadowed a cloud on the horizon: how were the different aspects of the correlation of forces to be tied together? In 1966 Kosygin warned his colleagues that the Soviet Union was insufficiently advanced in certain areas of technological innovation.[111] A *samizdat* copy of a book written by Andrey Sakharov, circulated in 1967, claimed: 'We are now catching up with the United States only in some of the old, traditional industries, which are no longer as important as they used to be for the United States (for example, coal and steel). In some of the newer fields, for example, automation, computers, petrochemicals, and especially in industrial research and development, we are not only lagging behind but growing more slowly'.[112] Conservatives in the Politburo dismissed these claims. In March 1968 Brezhnev commented: 'Some colleagues evidently underestimate the accomplishments of scientific thought both here and in other countries of socialism. But at the same time, these people are prone to overestimate the achievements of science and technology in the capitalist world.' Worries were, however, not stilled. At the end of 1969 major criticisms of Soviet economic performance were made at a secret Central Committee plenum. In 1970 Brezhnev publicly acknowledged that although the USSR was 'catching up and surpassing' the USA this was not the case in labour productivity.

At the beginning of 1969 the Vietnam War provided a window of opportunity for direct Soviet engagement with the United States. Through this the Soviets hoped to stabilise the changed correlation of forces, avoiding an American backlash against the Soviet gains of the previous five years. In April 1969 Kissinger had told Anatoliy Dobrynin that US–Soviet relations were 'at a cross-roads' and that 'the Vietnam war was a major obstacle' to improvement. The Soviet Union was willing to cooperate with America over Vietnam. Bringing the war to a conclusion was a minor concession for the Soviets to make. In 1965 the decision to provide massive military backing to North Vietnam had been a major shift in policy from the Khrushchev line. By the beginning of 1968 the Soviet Union had sent 1.8 billion roubles' worth of assistance, well over half in the form of military supplies. The investment had seemed worthwhile: the war offered an opportunity to wreck the Americans' containment strategy and if escalation should occur it would be China, not the Soviet Union, which would be the target. The Vietnamese had, however, proved difficult allies and were of limited utility in the struggle with the Chinese. As the embassy in Hanoi noted in a 1970 report: 'The WPV realise full well that China is situated quite close to Vietnam, whereas the Soviet Union is far away. Vietnam would be hard put to do without Chinese assistance in its struggle and in future peaceful construction. So it would be premature to ask the Vietnamese now to state their clear cut position with respect to USSR and China.' In addition, the war was expensive. In 1968 the Soviets provided 524 million roubles' worth of aid to the DRV; the same amount was allocated for 1969, but peace moves allowed this to be scaled down to 370 million.[113] Dobrynin came away from further talks with Kissinger in June 1969 and reported:

> From the talk as a whole a strong impression was formed that for Nixon the number one problem in foreign policy remains how to withdraw from the Vietnam war on conditions acceptable to him which would assure his re-election as president. Judging by all indications his attempts to convince the USSR to help in settling the conflict will continue in the future, and that will evidently to some degree make itself felt in the course of our negotiations with this administration on other international issues, if not directly, at least in the form of well known delays in the tempo of such negotiations or in decisions on other matters.[114]

Vietnam provided the opportunity for *détente* but its roots lay much deeper. This new-found interest in the status quo meant that the Soviet leadership was willing to engage in the give and take of genuine negotiation. Brezhnev was convinced of the advantages of signing arms control agreements with the United States, although many in the party leadership and military remained sceptical. The Soviet leadership was aware that the United States would drive a hard bargain, but it would accept a genuine bargain. KGB Chairman Yuriy Andropov reported that the Nixon administration, 'will use all means to strive for the consolidation of the quantitative balance of strategic weapons between the USA and the USSR at the present-day level, trying to preserve definite advantages in the most important kinds of strategic weapons'. Marshal Grechko, the Minister of Defence, tried to derail the negotiations on the grounds that the US would not discuss tactical nuclear weapons based in Europe, but Andropov recognised that the Soviet Union would have to sacrifice maximal goals since the USA would not disrupt NATO: 'NSC . . . strongly opposed the inclusion of American means of forward basing . . . motivated in its position by the fact that otherwise the whole structure of

NATO would have to be changed, and the USA would lose an important military advantage, as a result of which the general strategic balance would be changed to the advantage of the USSR.'[115] On the eve of his meeting with Nixon in May 1972, Brezhnev told a Central Committee plenum that there were three main reasons for striking a deal with the Americans. First, although the USA remained 'the main force of imperialism' there was a need to regulate relations. Worsening relations would push up defence expenditure even further, whereas, with a lessening of tension, it might even be decreased. Second, 'the more stable and normal our relations with the United States, the less the threat of world nuclear war'. Third: 'There is an old saying: when you sit to dine with the devil take a long spoon. In other words, you must rely on sufficiently strong positions. ... The correlation of forces between the Soviet Union and the United States both in terms of international influence and prestige, and in the military sphere is now more favourable to us than ever before.'

Brezhnev faced criticism that the SALT I treaty negotiation was a betrayal of international communism, or at least the Soviet Union's world influence, especially after the Americans bombed Haiphong harbour in May 1972. According to Georgiy Arbatov, Nikolay Podgorny and his *protégé*, the Ukrainian leader Petro Shelest, argued that, 'if we agreed to go through with the summit we would be politically humiliated and would lose our authority in the eyes of the world, particularly the Communist world, and with liberation movements'. Brezhnev retorted: 'In taking the decision to go ahead with the meeting the CC of the CPSU proceeded above all from the interests of the Soviet people, of the Soviet State. Our whole policy is subordinated to defence of those interests. This is a class line, because the interests of our country are indistinguishable from the interests of world socialism, the national-liberation and revolutionary movement, the course of peace in the whole world.' This need for the leadership to justify itself within the CPSU and to other communist leaderships suggests how controversial the policy of engagement was. Arbatov recalls the fear that, 'an insufficiently firm class attitude might cause opposition to coalesce within the Party and provide a pretext for an attack against the leadership'. One sop to critics within the leadership was that military effort was not downgraded. In Arbatov's view: 'From his first days in office, Brezhnev treated the military as a very important power base. For him that alone was enough to give the military everything it asked for.' The Chief of the General Staff declared that the leadership would continue, 'to display constant concern for increasing the defence capability of the Soviet Union. The Soviet armed forces have at their disposal everything necessary to reliably defend the state interests of our Motherland.' The acting Foreign Minister, Vasiliy Kuznetsov, chimed in: 'The understanding reached with the United States in the field of strategic arms limitation does not in any degree weaken the defence capability of the Soviet Union and the Warsaw Pact as a whole.' Post-treaty evaluations continued to stress the limitations on the *détente* process and its place within an overall strategy of victory. Communist cadres were told that, 'in preparing for the meeting with President Nixon we had no illusions that as a result of the talks with him it would be possible to resolve all important international problems, that American imperialism would, as it were, abandon its anticommunist strategy in the world arena.' A July 1973 CC evaluation of the process, produced after Brezhnev had strengthened his control of the Politburo by ousting critics of *détente* such as Shelest, read:

> peaceful coexistence is a form of the class struggle directed at strengthening world socialism, the international communist workers' and national liberation movement, the whole anti-imperialist front . . . beginning a turn from 'cold war' to *détente* . . . creates more favourable conditions for strengthening our ideological offensive against imperialism. . . . [the] result of the influence of the economic, political and defence might of world socialism, in the first place of the USSR . . . at a time strategically advantageous to us . . . under the conditions of the further deepening general crisis of capitalism.[116]

THE FRENCH DEFECTION

By 1953 Europe had been effectively stabilised as a Cold War environment. During the 1960s this stability endured. It was, however, challenged by France and Germany. Gaullist foreign policy was the most important challenge to West European stability in the course of the Cold War, yet, despite its potential implications, it remained a remarkably tame challenge. As such it provides important negative evidence about the strength of the anti-Soviet coalition. France had played a pivotal role in shaping this Western alliance but in the 1950s was diverted from a prominent role in Cold War diplomacy by colonial problems. In 1954 an insurrection broke out in Algeria. The pressure of the war in Algeria on the French polity brought about its collapse and, in May 1958, Charles de Gaulle, cleverly playing on the fear of military insurrection, was drafted in to reconstruct the republic. The war in Algeria and its domestic consequences remained at the top of the French political agenda until 1962. De Gaulle, who had written the new constitution to ensure presidential dominance, controlled the foreign policy of the new republic. His idea of France constituted a major break with the structure of the Western alliance. Whereas the FRG's *Ostpolitik* was carried out under the guise of constant recommitment to the West, it was central to De Gaulle's project that France should be clearly differentiated from all other West European countries and from the Western alliance. In the Cold War context, de Gaulle's foreign policy had three important strands: first, the development of France as an independent nuclear power; second, the withdrawal of French forces from NATO; third, an independent diplomacy aimed at the Soviet Union and Eastern Europe.

Even before de Gaulle came to power many of the tensions of the early 1950s had been exacerbated by the manner in which France's political élite believed she had been treated on the world stage. As the influential socialist politician Christian Pineau subsequently remarked, 'the main victim of the [Suez] affair was the Atlantic alliance ... if our allies have abandoned us in difficult, even dramatic, circumstances, they would be capable of doing so again if Europe in its turn found itself in danger'.[117] Although de Gaulle was constrained by France's own fragility in the early years of his rule he moved quickly to make clear France's lack of reliance on the NATO structure as it existed in 1958. In September 1958, still an unelected leader, he suggested to Eisenhower that the United States, France and Britain should form a tripartite directorate within NATO, charged with jointly formulating a global strategy for the West.[118] He also broached the subject of joint planning and control of nuclear weapons. Disappointed but unsurprised by the tepid reaction to his overtures in Washington and London, de Gaulle moved to begin disengaging France from NATO. In March 1959 the Mediterranean fleet was withdrawn from NATO command. Although de Gaulle took a hard line against Soviet moves in Berlin after November 1958, he reacted angrily to the actions of General Lauris Norstad, NATO's SACEUR and commander of American forces in Europe, in beginning the construction of nuclear storage facilities in northern France. In June 1959 the French government announced that no NATO or American nuclear weapons would be allowed on French soil unless French demands for the sharing of nuclear technology were met. In an important address to military officers at the Ecole Militaire in November 1959, de Gaulle commented:

> The view of war and even of a battle in which France would no longer act on her own behalf, and in accordance with her own wishes, such a view is unacceptable. The system that has been called 'integration' has had its day. The consequence is that we must obviously be able to provide ourselves, over the coming years, with a force capable of acting on our behalf, what is commonly called a 'strike force' capable of being deployed at any time and in any place. It goes without saying that the basis for such a force would be atomic weapons – whether we made them ourselves or bought them – but, in either case, they must belong to us. And since it is possible to destroy France from any point in the world, our force must be so made that it can act anywhere in the world. In the domain of defence, this will be our great work over the years ahead.[119]

De Gaulle was clear what he wanted but the next stage of his policy could only be put into place once two developments had taken place. One of the last decisions of the government of the Fourth Republic had been to build and test an atomic device. That test took place on 13 February 1960. During the course of the same year, de Gaulle came to accept that the self-determination for Algeria he had announced in 1959 meant negotiations with the FLN and eventual independence. These negotiations culminated in Algerian independence in July 1962. In May 1962 de Gaulle announced that France's circumstances had changed:

> a French atomic deterrent force is coming into existence and is going to grow continuously. It is a relatively modest force, it is true, but one which is changing and

will completely change the conditions of our own defence, those of our intervention in faraway lands and those of the contribution that we would be able to make to safeguard our allies. Furthermore, a gradual return of our military forces from Algeria is enabling us to acquire a modernised army; one which is not, I dare say, destined to play a separate or isolated role, but one which can play a role that would be France's own. Finally it is absolutely necessary, morally and politically, for us to make our army [parts of which were in seditious revolt against the Algerian settlement] a more integral part of the nation. Therefore, it is necessary for us to restation it, for the most part, on our own soil; for us to give it once again a direct responsibility in the external security of our country; in short for our defence to become once again national defence.

It was true that the Kennedy administration in the United States was both publicly and privately opposed to any nuclear sharing with France. The French Foreign Minister, Maurice Couve de Murville, has suggested that French disenchantment with the Atlantic link grew because of the Vietnam War: 'It was during Johnson's presidency that the United States began gradually, but overtly, to show less direct influence in European affairs. Vietnam became Johnson's almost exclusive preoccupation. What he wanted from Europe was not to have to think about it, so that he could concentrate on what was becoming more and more the most important thing.' De Gaulle was certainly influenced by intra-European relations as well. In January 1963 he effectively closed off close relations with Britain by vetoing its entry into the EEC. In the same month, however, he had signed a treaty of alliance with the FRG. Whatever de Gaulle's hopes for this alliance, they had been dashed by the mid-1960s. The Federal Republic wished to ensure that its relationship with the USA remained of primary importance. Yet France's disengagement from NATO rested on the ideas the general had adumbrated in the late 1950s. As the diplomat François de Rose has commented, 'pulling out of NATO was the decision he wanted and the rest was pretext'.[120] It seems clear that de Gaulle had been set on his course since the Eisenhower administration. In private talks he commented: 'You, Eisenhower, would wage nuclear war for Europe, because you know the interests that are at stake. But as the Soviet Union develops its capacity to strike the cities of North America, one of your successors will agree to wage nuclear war only ... against this continent. When that time comes, I or my successor will have to possess the necessary means to change into nuclear war what the Soviets would have liked to remain a classic war.' In 1964 the forces brought back from Algeria were assigned tactical air units and formed into a formation with no links to NATO. In 1965 all French tactical air forces were placed fully under national command and in 1966 the Mirage IV nuclear bomber came into service, creating de Gaulle's long-planned *force de frappe*. It was announced that all French forces would be withdrawn from NATO command in February 1966 and in the next month all NATO forces were ordered from French territory.[121]

Once the disengagement of French forces from the military command structure of NATO was set in train, de Gaulle could activate the next strand of his foreign policy and develop France's role as a bridge to the East. In December 1963 he declared:

> [France] because she can, because everything invites her to do so, because she is France, must carry out in the world policies that are on a world scale ... without ceding to the illusions in which the weak indulge, but without losing the hope that men's freedom and dignity will everywhere win the day, we must envisage a time when, perhaps, in Warsaw, Prague, Budapest, Bucharest, Sofia, Belgrade, Tirana and Moscow, the communist totalitarian regime, which still manages to imprison peoples, might gradually come to a development reconcilable with our own transformation. Then, prospects matching her resources and capacities would be open to the whole of Europe.

These were not just pious hopes. De Gaulle showed an interest in Eastern Europe which was entirely lacking in America, or even the FRG, where the capitals of Eastern Europe were merely seen as the portals to Berlin. Yet de Gaulle faced the paradox of such activism; reaching East could only result in a dialogue with the Soviet Union. As Nixon and Kissinger were to find eight years later, dealing with the Soviet Union tended to offer succour to its ruling regime. In early 1964 de Gaulle received the Soviet leader Nikolay Podgorny in Paris. France and the USSR signed a commercial agreement in October. Commenting on the treaty, de Gaulle said, 'that, despite accidents of history, our two nations are profoundly bound together in lasting friendship, by the conviction of possessing a common heritage and by mutual cordial interests'. In June 1966 de Gaulle cemented cordial relations by making a full state visit to Moscow.

Although these actions were important for France they had remarkably little impact on the Cold War. The Soviets seem to have regarded de Gaulle's policies with cautious approval. Brezhnev remarked: 'De Gaulle is our enemy. He is very cunning, but his policies are causing a weakening of American positions in Europe.'[122] Yet both in public and private American policy-makers were sanguine both on the issue of NATO and *détente* with the Soviet Union. To American observers it seemed that de Gaulle was unlikely to make a significant impact with his diplomacy and that the immediate damage to NATO could be quickly repaired. According to a CIA analysis, 'the Soviets would not be likely to look with equanimity upon a total disintegration of NATO and an end to the American role in Europe. They may hope that American disenchantment with European entanglements may make attractive to Washington a *modus vivendi* more in keeping with Soviet interests.' American analysts saw de Gaulle's diplomacy increasing the chances of the Soviet–US diarchy he so feared. More than that, however, they identified Germany, rather than France, as vital to the balance of power in Europe:

> *Rapprochement* with de Gaulle quickly could become counterproductive for Moscow if Bonn benefits from France's growing isolation in the West. Both Russia and France

wish to keep the genie of German nationalism in the bottle, and both wish somehow to contain West Germany. Moscow may conclude that NATO was moribund anyway, that de Gaulle has already played his best cards, and that if he tries to go further he may so isolate France that he will lose the ability to exert influence on Germany and in the Western alliance. In that event it would be Germany and not France that gained room to manoeuvre. Furthermore the breakdown of NATO military integration brought about by de Gaulle may open the door to a further build-up of West Germany, including the increased nuclear role Russia fears most of all.[123]

The limits of Soviet strategic, as opposed to tactical, interest in de Gaulle were revealed by his reception in the Eastern European capitals his *rapprochement* with Russia were supposed to open to French influence. During a September 1967 visit to Poland, de Gaulle told leaders of the Polish Communist Party that, 'France always wanted an independent Polish state, while others have not always wanted it. For us you are a popular, secure, respectable and powerful reality, in a world that must be one of balance and independence.' The Polish leader Gomulka's blunt reply was: 'Renascent Poland has drawn all the conclusions stemming from her historical experiences. The alliance with the Soviet Union, combined with the socialist states of Eastern Europe, is the cornerstone of the policy of the People's Republic of Poland.' De Gaulle's policy seemed even more tattered after the 'Prague Spring' was terminated in August 1968. As Etienne Burin des Roziers observed, 'it was a very hard blow for him. His view of the future of Europe involved the re-establishment of our traditional relations with our friends in the East. He considered that *détente* provided the best hope of emancipation on offer. Obviously the Prague affair smashed that hope.'[124]

The period between 1966 and August 1968 saw the most ambitious rhetoric about French nuclear independence from de Gaulle and his nuclear commanders. In a speech in January 1967, de Gaulle suggested that French nuclear weapons would not, necessarily, be targeted against the Soviet Union but against potential threats to French security from all directions.[125] Yet at the same time active behind-the-scenes negotiations were repairing splits within NATO. In August 1967 France's senior military officer, the outspoken Gaullist, Charles Ailleret, concluded an agreement with General Lyman Lemnitzer, NATO's supreme commander. The Ailleret–Lemnitzer agreement provided a framework for Franco-NATO military planning to continue. Although it made clear that the commitment of French forces to a war in Europe was at the discretion of the French government, it also implied that French forces in Germany would form an integrated military force with NATO's Central Army Group. This initial agreement was strengthened after de Gaulle's resignation in 1969 by further agreements covering air forces, in 1970, and the integration of planning between all French forces and NATO forces in central Europe, in 1974.[126] With the 'grand design' stymied by events in Prague, de Gaulle turned once more to the United States. He received a much more sympathetic hearing from the newly elected Richard Nixon. The General preferred Nixon to the grandstanding Kennedy, and the new administration was more willing to accept de Gaulle's insistence on a negotiated settlement to the Vietnam War involving both North Vietnam and the PRC, which France had recognised in 1964.[127] The new relationship was cemented by de Gaulle's successors, most notably in the nuclear field. The Nixon administration was willing to engage in nuclear sharing with France. In 1972 the USA seems to have started the supply of equipment to assist the French nuclear programme. In December 1972 France decided to build a MIRVed SLBM, a project predicated on such assistance.[128]

THE GERMAN QUESTION

The major practical, as opposed to rhetorical, challenge to Western unity occurred in Germany. In the aftermath of the Berlin crisis intra-German instability had been somewhat lessened. In this new context both the East and West German governments were freer to pursue a line which was more at odds with the preferences of their respective superpower backers. Both states had problems of *de jure* legitimacy: exclusion from the United Nations, the legal presence of occupation powers and their armed forces. *De facto*, however, the FRG was rapidly emerging as a powerful state in its own right: an economic success, a power within the European Economic Community and a signatory, in January 1963, of a formal cooperation treaty with the old enemy, France. The GDR, on the other hand, remained almost wholly dependent on its relationship with the Soviet Union.

Bonn had the option of pursuing a 'Warsaw first' policy: seeking political and economic ties with Eastern European countries as a means of isolating the GDR and of opening a conduit to the Soviet Union. Alternatively, it could pursue a 'Berlin first' policy: *sub rosa* dealings with the GDR in an attempt to ameliorate the lot of German individuals and families living either side of the Berlin Wall. Most ambitiously it could seek a 'Moscow first' approach: dealing directly with the Kremlin to reach an accommodation concerning the political structures of central Europe. Negotiations with Moscow could have a number of possible outcomes. On the one hand, they could lead to a solidification of boundaries in and around Germany, guaranteeing the stability of the FRG and its ability to develop as an independent sovereign state, unmolested by the constant threat of Soviet interference in its internal politics. On the other hand, however, the Moscow option might lead to a much more revolutionary settlement – a new 'European security order' which rendered central European politics fluid once more.

Between 1963 and 1966 the FRG effectively had two foreign policies under development. The official policy emanated from the CDU-dominated govern-ment of Chancellor Ludwig Erhard. The unofficial policy was being shaped by the circle around Willy Brandt, the leader of an SPD–FDP government in Berlin. Brandt was an important figure in the short term because of the huge symbolic importance of Berlin to the Cold War and in the slightly longer term because he became Foreign Minister in 1966 and Chancellor in 1969. For all practical purposes the *leitmotiv* of Konrad Adenauer's long chancellorship, lasting from 1949 to 1963, had been the integration of the FRG into the West in general and a very close, even subservient, relationship with the United States in particular. For all the seeming simplicity of Adenauer's policy, he in fact left an ambiguous legacy to his successors. In his last year in office he stressed much more forcefully the 'German mission' of the FRG. This theme had never actually been absent from his rhetoric but it took on a more emotive tinge. In December 1961 Adenauer told the Soviet ambassador in Bonn that 'for the rest of his life he considers the most important [thing] that he still wants to do is bring our relationship with Russia into tolerable order'; in October 1962 he made clear that the 'Federal government is ready to discuss many things' with the Soviet Union in order to ensure that 'our brothers in the Zone [i.e. the population of East Germany] can arrange their lives as they wish. Here considerations of humanity play a larger part for us even than national considerations.'[129] In June 1962 he had proposed a ten-year 'truce' on the German question.

One of the most obvious means by which a route to Moscow could be opened up was through trade. Trade between the FRG and the Soviet Union rose steadily in the early 1960s, more than doubling in value between 1959 and 1962. Indeed the Soviets encouraged the Germans to increase the quantity and variety of exchanges. The United States, however, looked askance at high technology transfers to the Soviet Union. In particular, the Kennedy administration was concerned with the export of large-diameter steel pipes for use in the oil industry, which had been shipped in bulk to the USSR by FRG firms since 1959. The Soviet Union was building a pipeline from the oilfields around Baku in Azerbaijan to its Warsaw Pact allies, including East Germany. In November 1962 the Americans managed to persuade NATO to put an embargo on such exports. The Americans saw this action as a fairly straightforward piece of Cold War geo-politics. 'The major issues of our trade policy are political – not strategic, economic or commercial', wrote Walt Rostow in July 1963. 'They serve as a symbol of US unwillingness to grant the USSR full respectability . . . a symbol that the US dares to discriminate against the USSR under contemporary conditions.' When the Kennedy administration chose to make a symbolic gesture, the government of the FRG was forced to fall into line. It did so, however, extremely reluctantly.[130] In 1963 no senior government leader dared to suggest that the real tension did not lie between the economy and foreign policy but between two different approaches to foreign policy.

Within the FRG's right-wing foreign-policy establishment divergent views over the nature of Germany's relationship with the West did exist. In 1965 the

FRG ambassador in London could write, 'NATO is much more than a purely technical military alliance. NATO is for us the guarantee that member states – above all, the United States – lend the Federal Republic the political support which it needs so urgently in the contest over reunification.' In the same year the FRG ambassador to NATO told the foreign minister, Gerhard Schröder: '[the] integration [of NATO] is without doubt an effective hegemonial instrument of the most powerful in the alliance . . . the US has used NATO to assure its participation in European diplomacy, to contain traditional European rivalries and to preserve a powerful influence over the direction of West German policies.'[131] The Erhard government attempted to ameliorate these tensions by taking the Eastern European route. This had the advantage of displaying active diplomacy on the German problem whilst not alienating those who believed in conforming closely to the United States. Schröder's practical response to the German problem was to pursue a 'policy of movement': an attempt to bring about the ostracism of the GDR through diplomatic–trade links with Eastern Europe. The opening of trade missions with Romania, Hungary and Bulgaria was indeed agreed in 1963 and 1964 but such links were too modest to put any real pressure on the Soviet Union or even the GDR.[132]

In 1963–4 the German problem had remained at the centre of Khrushchev's attention. Although chastened, he still believed that the situation could be manipulated to Soviet advantage. He remained opposed to German reunification on Western terms and the development of West German military power. Yet some of his advisers suggested a flexible Soviet response to Western Europe in order to exploit contradictions undermining Western unity. Their interest was quickened when Ludwig Erhard replaced Konrad Adenauer as West German Chancellor in October 1963. Soon after taking office Erhard allowed the shipment of 300 000 tons of wheat to the Soviet Union previously blocked by Adenauer. In February 1963 a major essay in *Kommunist*, the leading CPSU theoretical journal, argued that Erhard was moving away from Adenauer's policies whilst the SPD favoured an accommodation with Moscow and Berlin. In June 1964, when Ulbricht visited Russia, his argument that FRG–GDR talks were a condition not only of inter-German normalisation but also of 'peaceful coexistence itself' was decisively rejected by Khrushchev.[133] During the Berlin crisis Khrushchev had experienced the sensation that the Soviet dog was being wagged by the East German tail. The variegated richness of West German foreign-policy options was matched by the poverty of choices available to the East German élite. Their grip on power was a direct function of their reliance on Moscow. They had to persuade the Soviet leadership to pursue aggressive diplomacy, as Khrushchev had done between 1958 and 1961, leading to *de facto* recognition of the East German state by the West. The lever they used to pursue this goal was the diplomacy of weakness: the implicit threat that if the Soviet Union did not throw its full weight behind the GDR the regime might collapse, producing both the temptation and the opportunity for German revanchism whether under a NATO umbrella or as the birth of a 'third force'. Such a gambit could only be successful in conditions in which the Soviet leadership actually believed that a powerful GDR was the best guarantee against German revanchism. It would be ineffective if the Soviets came to believe that the 'road to Bonn' was a safer route than the 'road to Berlin'. The SED leadership under Ulbricht had little choice other than to create the impression of their own indispensability to the Soviet Union. East Germany traded extensively with West Germany but the East German government attempted to limit the growth in this trade. At the same time it tried to please its Soviet masters by adopting their policies. East Germany was the first Soviet bloc country to endorse Khrushchev's industrial reforms in 1963. In February 1964 Ulbricht announced a Khrushchevite expansion in chemical production in the GDR, in the face of contrary advice from his economic functionaries.

In April 1964 Khrushchev assailed Erhard for refusing to renounce the FRG's territorial claims and attempting to gain access to nuclear weapons through the NATO multilateral force. The editor of the journal *International Affairs* derided Erhard and claimed to see no difference between German political parties. Arguments about the virtues of flexibility and the hard line rumbled on throughout 1964. In many ways, however, Khrushchev's ouster in October 1964 favoured Ulbricht. In the aftermath of the coup the tendency was, at least initially, to fall back on traditional policies whilst the new regime consolidated itself. On 18 October 1964, in the immediate aftermath of the coup, a CPSU statement called for friendship and cooperation with the US, Great Britain, France and Italy but for German workers to combat revanchism and militarism in the FRG. Andrey Kosygin refused to visit Bonn and the Russian media stepped up propaganda against Germany. This pattern of trying to disrupt NATO by sowing dissension between the Western European countries and the United States, and by continuing to insist on the isolation of Germany, persisted at least until 1968. At the 23rd Party Congress in March 1966 Brezhnev pointed towards contradictions between the USA and Western Europe, symbolised by Franco-American disputes in NATO. He characterised Germany as absolutely revanchist. Although Gromyko suggested that, 'there are forces that come out for a resolute departure from the militaristic past', others such as Malinovsky and Shelest were entirely negative about the FRG. A hard-line communiqué declared that the 'exacerbation of its contradictions is driving imperialism to greater adventurism'. Again, at the beginning of 1967, Brezhnev claimed that 'the goals of West German imperialism remain unchanged'.[134]

An alternative foreign policy was, however, under development in West Germany. Willy Brandt regarded American conduct during the Berlin crisis as tantamount to betrayal. Adenauer had made the FRG the 'good ally' but in Germany's hour of need Kennedy had merely played geo-political games with German interests. As Brandt recalled in 1976: 'in August 1961 a curtain was drawn aside to reveal an empty stage. To put it more bluntly, we lost certain illusions that had outlived the hopes underlying them ... Ulbricht had been allowed to take a swipe at the Western superpower and the United States merely winced with annoyance. My political deliberations in the years that followed were substantially influenced by this day's experience'. At the time he was more succinct. 'Gentlemen,' he told the allied military commanders in Berlin, 'last night you let Ulbricht kick you in the arse.' Brandt's initial reaction was to call for economic sanctions against both the Soviet Union and the 'so-called "GDR" '. By 1963, however, Brandt and his closest adviser, Egon Bahr, had reached the conclusion that the FRG needed to travel both the 'Berlin route' and much more importantly the 'Moscow route'.[135]

In December 1963, in line with what Adenauer had labelled 'considerations of humanity', the West Berlin government signed a 'permit' agreement with an East German official acting 'on the instructions of the deputy chairman of the Council of Ministers of the GDR' to allow West Berliners holiday visits to relatives in East Berlin. In the summer of 1963 Bahr had used the opportunity of Kennedy's American University speech to lay out his and Brandt's 'common thoughts' for a new German foreign policy: 'the application of the strategy of peace to Germany'. Brandt and Bahr argued that the first aim of German policy should be to overcome the division of Germany rather than to fight in the front line of the Cold War on America's behalf. They had to convince the Soviet leadership that change could take place in Germany which would not weaken, and might even strengthen, the Soviet Union's global position: in Bahr's phrase, 'overcoming the status quo by first not changing the status quo'. In order to bring such a change about the FRG would have to deal directly with the Soviet Union in the pursuit of German rather than more general Western interests. Moscow could be used to bring the recalcitrant SED leadership into line. Bahr told his audience at Tutzing, 'The Zone must be transformed with the agreement of the Soviets ... the German question can only be solved with the Soviet Union not against it ... the preconditions for reunification are only to be created with the Soviet Union. They are not to be had in East Berlin, not against the Soviet Union, not without it.' One prong of the Brandt–Bahr strategy was to deal with the Soviet Union on central security issues. The other was to slowly destabilise the regime in the East by trading, but only to the limited extent which would bring evolution rather revolution. Increased tension only strengthened the hard-line Ulbricht. The FRG could attempt to raise the standard of living of the GDR to bring 'relief to its people' but should never attempt to encourage those people to rise up against the SED and thus bring upon themselves 'Soviet intervention out of Soviet interests'. The Wall was 'a sign of the communist regime's fear and urge for self-preservation'. The FRG had to 'diminish the regime's quite justified fears, so that the loosening up of the frontiers and the Wall will be bearable'.[136]

This programme became of central importance when the CDU and the SPD formed a coalition government in December 1966 with Kurt-Georg Kiesinger as Chancellor and Brandt as Foreign Minister. Of course in terms of practical politics the clear course Bahr had laid out in 1963 had to be muddied. The anti-Americanism which played an important part in the Brandt programme, and which was shared by some non-SPD members of the foreign-policy establishment, never became part of declaratory policy. Kiesinger accepted most of the Brandt programme but attempted to portray it in more conciliatory terms. He called for a new 'European peace order', including reconciliation with Czechoslovakia and Poland 'whose desire at last to live in a state area with secure frontiers we now understand better than in earlier times, given the present fate of our own partitioned nation'. He declared that: 'we all know that the overcoming of the division of our people can indeed only be achieved by an arrangement with Moscow, unless we want to wait for one of the scurrilous and dangerous whims of history ... sowing discontent in the East and stirring up countries there against Moscow.' In terms of practical policy Kiesinger was cautious, wishing 'first to seek ground which we can tread together, initially putting to one side the great issues of dispute'. Indeed the main 'achievement' of the 1966 to 1969 government was the initiation of diplomatic relations with Ceauşescu's maverick communist regime in Romania in January 1967, essentially a continuation of Schröder's earlier policy. For Kiesinger a peaceful settlement in Germany was part of a peaceful settlement in Europe: 'one can only see the growing together of the separate parts of Germany bedded into the process of overcoming East–West conflict in Europe'. Yet it was by no means obvious that Germany's allies saw a German settlement as particularly conducive to an improvement in Western relations with the Soviet Union. As Kiesinger himself admitted: 'Germany, a reunited Germany has a critical size. It is too big to play no role in the balance of forces and too small to keep the forces around it in balance by itself. It is therefore hard to imagine that, while the present political structure in Europe continues, the whole of Germany could simply join one or the other side.'

It was Brandt and Bahr who once more drove energetically down the 'Moscow route'. Neither was deflected by Soviet military intervention against Czechoslovak reform communists in the summer of 1968. Indeed Bahr claimed, in an analysis he presented to Brandt in his role as head of the Foreign Ministry's planning staff in September 1969, and which was subsequently used in Brandt's coalition negotiations with the FDP, that Soviet actions of the type seen in Czechoslovakia and 12 years before in Hungary were probably endemic. According to Bahr the Soviet leadership was continually torn by its desire to preserve power and to encourage economic efficiency: a dialectic which led to alternate loosening and tightening of its grip on Eastern Europe. Bahr argued that the need for action by the FRG was becoming more pressing. The United States was in no position to oppose German moves towards the Soviet Union because it needed to make similar overtures as a means of finding a way out of

Vietnam. He feared that the division of Germany was becoming deeper as each year slipped by. The FRG needed to create a 'transitional framework' in order to maintain links with the East until unification was possible and to rid itself of the residual occupation rights which were the 'last relics of the post-war period'. In order to create this framework the FRG could use Soviet proposals for a European security conference and conventional force reductions 'as an instrument for the realisation of our own interests'. In another paper written in June 1968, Bahr outlined the nature of this 'transitional framework' erected in Germany's 'own interests'. It would consist of an entirely new European security system replacing both the Warsaw Pact and NATO. The headquarters of the new organisation set up to oversee this system would be established in Berlin. At the centre of the system would be a nuclear-free zone consisting of the FRG, the GDR, the Benelux nations, Poland and Czechoslovakia. No foreign troops would be allowed in this zone. Its security would be guaranteed by both the Soviet Union and the United States. Bahr described his plan as the 'best option'. In the foreseeable future the West German government would work towards it by encouraging the closest possible diplomatic relations with the Soviet Union and a significant reduction of conventional forces in Europe. Yet only the 'interim solution' really commanded support in the SPD and FDP leadership. The FDP leader and Foreign Minister Walter Scheel and the influential SPD Defence Minister Helmut Schmidt believed that the NATO connection was simply non-negotiable, anchoring Germany in the West, providing nuclear protection and giving Germany the security and support necessary to negotiate with the Soviet Union. Thus the West German negotiating position, as outlined by Brandt in the SPD negotiations with the FDP, was based on a Soviet–German renunciation-of-force agreement; recognition of the Oder–Neisse line, that is, the westward shift of the Polish–German border agreed upon by the Soviet Union, America and Britain at Yalta to compensate Poland for the westward shift of the Polish–Soviet border; and West German adherence to the 1968 nuclear non-proliferation treaty. In other words, the aim of the Brandt government was to regularise relations with the Soviet Union as a way of coercing the government of the GDR rather than to tackle the issue of German reunification directly.[137]

During 1968–9 there was an obvious shift in Soviet policy. It engaged with West Germany, effectively signing a peace treaty and paving the way for the normalisation of FRG–GDR relations. The proximate cause in this change of direction seems to have been two crises: one which came to a head in Czechoslovakia in August 1968; the other the direct military confrontation with China between March and September 1969. In Czechoslovakia a reformist communist movement, led by Alexander Dubcek, seemed to be threatening the cohesion of the Soviet bloc. Czechoslovakia was centrally important to the Soviets in a way that Romania, which had first expressed dissatisfaction with the Warsaw Pact in April 1964, Yugoslavia and Albania, the other schismatic

European communist regimes, were not. Since indigenous communists had had a major presence in Czechoslovakia at the end the Second World War and had successfully seized power in February 1948, no Soviet forces had been stationed on Czech soil. Pre-Dubcek leaders had consistently refused requests for Soviet forces to be deployed in the country. Any form of Czech independence became even more worrying as tactical nuclear weapons were introduced into the Warsaw Pact. Czechoslovakia had an even more important role if a limited war strategy was being contemplated. In December 1965 a Soviet–Czech agreement provided for nuclear warheads to be stored, under Soviet control, at three sites in the country. These sites had not been finished by the time the reformists came to power. Reformist Czech officials and officers displaced pro-Soviets in the Ministry of Defence and pledged to do away with the 'Stalinist security system'. The Soviet military was thus in favour of intervention.[138]

Czechoslovakia had an advanced and active political culture capable of exerting a pull on other central European nations. The leaders of Poland and East Germany, Gomulka and Ulbricht, thus colluded with hard-liners in the Czech Communist Party, led by Vasil Bilak, in demanding Soviet military intervention to snuff out the reformers. Serious negotiations between the Soviet Union and the FRG and the politico-economic penetration of other Eastern European countries were regarded as grave threats to their own existence by the SED leadership between 1966 and 1969. In their view West Germany was pursuing its own 'Locarno' policy whilst still acting as the cat's paw for the United States. The most important development was therefore the reform movement in Czechoslovakia. The Czechoslovak communists were both a threat, falling as they were into the West German trap, and a lever – a means by which the Soviet Union could be persuaded to take a much harder line and initiate real integration with Warsaw Pact countries. The SED leadership criticised the Dubcek government earlier and more harshly than the Soviets. In January 1968 Walter Ulbricht went to Prague and warned against West German attempts to create 'economic dependencies' in Eastern Europe. More ominously the East Germans also lauded Soviet–East German military cooperation as the embodiment of 'our common responsibility for the security of Europe'. The East Germans did all they could to convince the Soviet leadership that what was happening in Prague was German- and American-sponsored 'counter-revolution'. This view eventually found favour with the Brezhnev leadership. Enthusiasm in Prague for Tito and Ceauşescu held out the possibility that Eastern Europe might be disrupted from within. There was even a fear amongst some Politburo members, most notably Shelest, that the reformist spirit might affect the Ukraine and thus spread into the Soviet Union itself. Soviet forces did indeed invade Czechoslovakia on 20 August 1968. Subsequently, 75 000 Soviet troops remained permanently stationed there.

Ulbricht had much more ambitious designs than simply turning on the

Czechs to demonstrate to the Soviets that the GDR was the indispensable
military policeman of Eastern Europe. As he had in 1964 with Khrushchev, he
attempted to convince Khrushchev's ousters that the GDR was indispensable to
any economic reform in the Soviet Union. Ulbricht insisted on the linkage
between the political conflict between capitalist and socialist states and East–
West economic relations. He detected a 'European variant' of the West's 'global
strategy' aimed at 'hollowing out' the economies of Eastern Europe and
relegating them to the importation of third-rate Western technology. The
Warsaw Pact nations should give up 'speculation that socialism can be built with
the help of imperialists'. Neither should they wait for the Soviet Union to bail
them out. 'First our own strength must be mobilised. In the scientific, technical,
and economic cooperation of the socialist countries there exist large reserves that
are not yet exhausted, not by a long shot.' Ulbricht was entirely self-serving in
these declarations. He was attempting to distract the Soviet leadership from the
siren voices emanating from the FRG. Yet there is evidence to suggest that he
genuinely believed his tactics would be successful. He took the remarkable step
of trying to rewrite the definition of socialism, calling it a 'relatively independent
socio-economic formation' which constituted a more protracted historical phase
than had previously been thought, distinct from communism and with its own
laws of development, and referred to East Germany's position within it as a
'developed societal system of socialism'. He also continually stressed his
credentials as an old revolutionary who had been a comrade of Lenin. Most
significantly, Ulbricht did attempt to restructure the East German economy
'precisely for political reasons'. In 1968 the SED revised the goals for the
1966–70 five-year plan which had only been set 12 months previously. Ulbricht
launched the concept of 'dynamic proportioning' by which certain sectors of
industry would be rapidly expanded.[139]

Ulbricht's gambit was unsuccessful since the Soviet leadership wanted little
more than a partnership of convenience with the GDR in 1968. Even within the
SED Ulbricht's economic nostrums were criticised as disastrous. The Politburo agonised over the decision to invade Czechoslovakia. In some sense at least
it seemed undesirable to retain Europe as a completely frozen front. The Soviet
leadership was unwilling to pass up the opportunity of having the post-war
settlement in Europe legitimised and their own dominance of Eastern Europe
recognised. The Soviets wanted to achieve a self-regulating system: communist
élites which could sustain themselves, whilst remaining completely loyal to
Moscow; capable of dealing with Western Europe without being subverted by
it. As a means of achieving this the Soviets offered to negotiate a treaty with the
FRG in September 1969. In the negotiations for the 1970 Moscow treaty, West
Germany promised to sign the nuclear non-proliferation treaty; backed the idea
of a European security conference; and offered to expand economic and
technological ties. The treaty itself recognised 'the existing real situation' in
Europe including the inviolability of 'the Oder–Neisse line, which forms the

western frontier of the People's Republic of Poland, and the frontier between the Federal Republic of Germany and the German Democratic Republic'. In order to facilitate the formalisation of relations between the FRG and the GDR the Soviets engineered the removal of Walter Ulbricht. As Brezhnev put it to Erich Honecker in July 1970: 'it will not be possible for him to rule without us ... After all, we have troops in your country.'

In negotiation with Gromyko in February 1970 Bahr described the 'common interest' of the Soviet Union and the FRG in ensuring that 'the process we were now beginning would remain under full control the whole time'. He pointed out that: 'the Federal government had been attacked in the Bundestag with the argument that the policy of the Federal government would lead to a recognition of the special role – or "predominance", as it was put there – of the Soviet Union among the socialist states. The Federal Chancellor ... would carry out our policy irrespective of these attacks'. Brandt himself gave this approach a more elegant formulation after the Moscow treaty: 'Twenty-five years after the capitulation of the German Reich destroyed by Hitler, the time has come to found our relationship with the East anew – that is, on unconditional mutual renunciation of force, on the basis of the political situation as it exists in Europe ... with this treaty nothing is lost that had not long since been gambled away.' For Brandt and Bahr the settlement with the Soviet Union was rooted in the past and valid long into the future. It was a German solution to primarily German problems. Brandt summed up the future direction of German foreign policy as 'Mitteleuropa. DDR. Berlin'.

Brandt was successful because the Soviet leadership and the new Honecker regime in the GDR, which signed a series of agreements with the FRG, culminating in the FRG–GDR mutual recognition treaty in December 1972, believed it could control such an independent German foreign policy. As Brezhnev told Honecker, 'the conclusion of this treaty will be a success for us, for the Soviet Union, the socialist countries'. The frontiers of the GDR 'will be confirmed for all the world to see'. This would allow the SED to consolidate its rule within the country. Brandt hoped to achieve 'socialdemocratization [of the] GDR' but accepted 'the all sided strengthening of the GDR'. In the 1960s a specifically German view of the international system, based on German problems and European solutions developed. It certainly did so in the context of changing American foreign policy but *détente* and *Ostpolitik* had quite different roots in different perceived national interests. The true radicalism of Brandt's foreign policy was masked to a certain extent by rhetoric and the failure of his second chancellorship which was brought to an end by the exposure of one of his closest aides as an East German spy. Bahr certainly believed that the next item on the agenda should be significant troop reductions in central Europe. Despite this the Brandt government had demonstrated that the whole structure of the Cold War could be altered by independent interaction with one of the superpowers.[140]

NOTES

1 Walt Rostow to Secretary of State, 24 April 1961, *Cuban Missile Crisis*, Doc. 3
2 Operations Co-ordinating Board: Operations Plan for Viet-Nam, 4 June 1958, *FRUS* 1958–60, I, pp. 40–54.
3 Peter Macdonald, *Giap: The Victor in Vietnam* (London, Warner, 1994), pp. 18–22.
4 Douglas Pike, 'Origins of Leadership Change in the Socialist Republic of Vietnam', in Raymond Taras, *Leadership Change in Communist States* (London, Unwin Hyman, 1989), pp. 107–28.
5 Letter by Ho Chi Minh from abroad, 6 June 1941, Gareth Porter, *Vietnam: A History in Documents* (New York, New American Library, 1981), Doc. 1.
6 Phillip Davidson, *Vietnam at War: The History, 1946–1975* (London, Sidgwick and Jackson, 1988), p. 16.
7 Douglas Pike, *Viet Cong: The Organization and Techniques of the National Liberation Front of South Vietnam* (Cambridge, MA, MIT Press, 1968), p. 44.
8 Ken Post, *Revolution, Socialism and Nationalism in Viet Nam* (5 vols., Aldershot, Dartmouth, 1989), I, pp. 118–20 and 150.
9 Pike, *Viet Cong*, p. 44.
10 Study Document of the Secretary-General of the ICP, Truong Chinh, 23–24 September 1941, in Porter, *Vietnam*, Doc. 2.
11 Douglas Pike, *PAVN: People's Army of Vietnam* (Novato, Presidio Press, 1986), pp. 24–35.
12 Speech by Vo Nguyen Giap at founding of Vietnam Liberation Armed Propaganda Brigade, 22 December 1944; Instructions of the Standing Bureau of the ICP, 12 March 1945; Resolutions of the Revolutionary Military Conference of North Vietnam, 20 April 1945; General Uprising Order by Vo Nguyen Giap, 12 August 1945; and Declaration of Independence of Democratic Republic of Vietnam, 2 September 1945: Porter, *Vietnam*, Docs. 5, 6, 9, 16 and 17.
13 Post, *Vietnam*, I, p. 117.
14 Pike, *Viet Cong*, p. 28.
15 Speech by Giap, 2 September 1945 and Ho Chi Minh to President Truman, 17 October 1945, in Porter, *Vietnam*, Docs. 18 and 26.
16 Soutou, 'France'; Ultimatum of French commander of Haiphong, 22 November 1946 and Exchange of Letters between General Morlière and Giap, 28–30 November 1946, in Porter, *Vietnam*, Docs. 35 and 36.
17 A. L. Moffatt to State Department, December 1946, DRV Account of Ho–Paul Mus Meeting 12 May, 1947 and Study on the Vietnamese Resistance by Truong Chinh, September 1947, in Porter, *Vietnam*, Docs. 38, 43 and 48.
18 Davidson, *Vietnam at War*, pp. 57–72.
19 Chen Jian, 'China and the First Indochina War, 1950–54', *China Quarterly*, 133 (1993), pp. 85–110.
20 Goncharov *et al.*, *Uncertain Partners*, pp. 107–8.
21 Khrushchev, *Glasnost Tapes*, pp. 154–6.
22 Article by Truong Chinh on the diplomatic recognition of the DRV, 18 February 1950, in Porter, *Vietnam*, Doc. 59.
23 Khrushchev, *Glasnost Tapes*, pp. 154–6.
24 Pamphlet by Giap on Shifting to the general counteroffensive, February 1950, in Porter, *Vietnam*, Doc. 58.
25 Chen Jian, 'Indochina War'.

26 Porter, *Vietnam*, Doc. 59

27 Pierre Guillen, 'France and Defence of Western Europe: From the Brussels Pact to the Pleven Plan', in Wiggershaus, *Western Security Community*, pp. 140–2.

28 JCS 1992/11, 29 March 1950.

29 JCS 1992/29, 7 October 1950.

30 Wall, *Postwar France*, pp. 233–62.

31 Eisenhower to Churchill, 4 April 1954, in Boyle, ed., *The Churchill–Eisenhower Correspondence*, p. 136.

32 Churchill to Eisenhower, 21 June 1954, in Boyle, *Correspondence*, p. 147.

33 Le Général Ely, Commissaire Général de France en Indochine, à M. Guy Le Chambre, Ministre des Etats Associés, 12 and 16 November, *Documents Diplomatique Français*, 1954 (Paris, Imprimerie Nationale, 1987), Docs. 337 and 357.

34 Churchill to Eisenhower, 21 June 1954, in Boyle, *Correspondence*, p. 147.

35 Richard Barnet, *Allies: America, Europe and Japan since the War* (London, Jonathan Cape, 1984), pp. 186–8.

36 Zhai Qiang, 'China and the Geneva Conference of 1954', *China Quarterly*, 129 (1992), pp. 103–22.

37 Chen Jian, 'Indochina War'; Qiang, 'Geneva Conference' and Kuo-kang Shao, 'Zhou Enlai's Diplomacy and the Neutralization of Indochina, 1954–55', *China Quarterly*, 109 (1986), pp. 483–504.

38 Shao, 'Neutralization'.

39 Qiang, 'Geneva Conference'.

40 Shao, 'Neutralization'.

41 Qiang, 'Geneva Conference'.

42 Report by Ho Chi Minh to the 6th plenum of the Party Central Committee, 15 July 1954, in Porter, *Vietnam*, Doc. 103.

43 R. B. Smith, *An International History of the Vietnam War* (4 vols., London, Macmillan, 1983–), I, p. 62.

44 Smith, *International History*, I, pp. 121–43.

45 Smith, *International History*, I, pp. 127–8.

46 Article by Tran Van Giau on Hanoi radio, 23 November 1957 and Lao Dong directive for the south, 'Situation and Tasks for 1959', 1958, in Porter, *Vietnam*, Docs. 123 and 125.

47 Pike, *PAVN*, pp. 46–7.

48 Smith, *International History*, I, pp. 162–80.

49 Article in Lao Dong Internal Party Journal in the South, February 1960, in Porter, *Vietnam*, Doc. 126.

50 Davidson, *Vietnam at War*, p. 290.

51 Pike, *Viet Cong*, pp. 74–84.

52 NIE 63–59, 26 May 1959, *FRUS* 1958–60, I, p. 201.

53 Despatch from ambassador in Vietnam to Department of State, 7 March 1960, *FRUS* 1958–60, I, pp. 300–3.

54 Ambassador in Vietnam to Department of State, 27 June 1960, *FRUS* 1958–60, I, pp. 509–12.

55 Draft Notes on the First Meeting of the Presidential Task Force on Vietnam, 24 April 1961, *FRUS* 1961–63, I, pp. 77–80.

56 Chester Bowles to Secretary of State and Paper Prepared by the Ambassador to India, *FRUS* 1961–63, I, p. 322 (Bowles) and p. 474 (Galbraith).

57 The Taylor Report, 3 November 1961, *FRUS* 1961–63, I, pp. 477–566.

58 Resolution of an Enlarged Conference of the Central Office for South Viet-Nam (COSVN), October 1961, in Porter, *Vietnam*, Doc. 138.
59 Smith, *International History*, II, p. 112.
60 Post, *Revolution*, IV, pp. 343–4.
61 Smith, *International History*, I, pp. 239–40.
62 Porter, *Vietnam*, Doc. 138.
63 Article by Lao Dong Party Political Bureau Member Nguyen Chi Thanh, July 1963, and Resolution of the Ninth Conference of the Lao Dong Party Central Committee, December 1963, in Porter, *Vietnam*, Docs. 151 and 164.
64 Leslie Gelb and Richard Betts, *The Irony of Vietnam: The System Worked* (Washington, Brookings, 1979), p. 107.
65 Chang, *Friends and Enemies*, p. 262.
66 Smith, *International History*, II, p. 197.
67 Clark Clifford to the President, 17 May 1965, in Gelb and Betts, *Irony*, Appendix 1.
68 Larry Berman, 'Coming to Grips with Lyndon Johnson's War', *Diplomatic History*, 17 (1993), p. 528.
69 Joint Statement Premier Kosygin and Pham Van Dong, 10 February 1965, in Porter, *Vietnam*, Doc. 191.
70 Lao Dong Study Document for Political Reorientation, 5 March 1965, in Porter, *Vietnam*, Doc. 194.
71 Smith, *International History*, III, p. 77.
72 Qiang Zhai, 'Beijing and the Vietnam Conflict, 1964–65: New Chinese Evidence', *CWIHPB*, 6–7 (1995–96), pp. 233–50.
73 Yahuda, *China's Role*, p. 185.
74 Naughton, 'Third Front'.
75 John Wilson Lewis and Xue Litai, 'Strategic Weapons and Chinese Power: The Formative Years', *China Quarterly*, 112 (1987), pp. 541–54.
76 Clark M. Clifford, 'A Viet Nam Reappraisal: The Personal History of One Man's View and How It Evolved', *Foreign Affairs*, 47 (1969), p. 612.
77 Chang, *Friends and Enemies*, p. 283.
78 Richard M. Nixon, 'Asia After Viet Nam', *Foreign Affairs*, 46 (1967), p. 113.
79 Nixon, 'Asia After Viet Nam', p. 121.
80 Nixon, 'Asia After Viet Nam', p. 122.
81 Nixon, 'Asia After Viet Nam', p. 121.
82 Nixon, 'Asia After Viet Nam', p. 122.
83 Robert Litwak, *Détente and the Nixon Doctrine: American Foreign Policy and the Pursuit of Stability, 1969–1976* (Cambridge, Cambridge University Press, 1984) p. 85.
84 Walter Isaacson, *Kissinger* (London, Faber and Faber, 1992), pp. 234–55.
85 Summary of a speech by Chairman of the Lao Dong Party Reunification Department, General Nguyen Van Vinh, at a COSVN Conference, April 1966, in Porter, *Vietnam*, Doc. 209.
86 Isaacson, *Kissinger*, pp. 234–55.
87 Isaacson, *Kissinger*, p. 269.
88 Post, *Revolution*, V, p. 144.
89 Chen Jian, 'China's Involvement in the Vietnam War, 1964–69', *China Quarterly*, 142 (1995), pp. 356–87.
90 Soviet Report to GDR leadership on 2 March 1969 Sino-Soviet Border Clashes, 8 March 1969, *CWIHPB*, 6–7 (1995–96).

91 Thomas Robinson, 'China Confronts the Soviet Union: Warfare and Diplomacy on China's Inner Asian Frontiers', *The Cambridge History of China*, XV, pp. 218–304.

92 Jonathan Pollack, 'The Opening to America', *The Cambridge History of China*, XV, pp. 402–74.

93 Litwak, *Nixon Doctrine* p. 80.

94 Isaacson, *Kissinger*, pp. 316–22.

95 Litwak, *Nixon Doctrine* p. 89.

96 Glenn Seaborg, *Kennedy, Khrushchev and the Test Ban* (Berkeley, University of California Press, 1981).

97 Beschloss, *Crisis Years*, pp. 603–40.

98 Alan Enthoven and Wayne Smith, *How Much is Enough? Shaping the Defense Programme, 1961–1969* (New York, Harper and Row, 1971), pp. 165–96.

99 John Prados, *The Soviet Estimate: US Intelligence Analysis and Soviet Strategic Forces* (Princeton, Princeton University Press, 1986), pp. 183–99.

100 Enthoven and Smith, *How Much is Enough?* pp. 177–84.

101 Prados, *Soviet Estimate*, pp. 151–71.

102 Donald R. Baucom, *The Origins of SDI, 1944–1983* (Kansas, University Press of Kansas, 1992), pp. 33–9.

103 Prados, *Soviet Estimate*, p. 210.

104 Deborah Larson, 'Learning in US–Soviet Relations: The Nixon–Kissinger Structure of Peace', in George Breslauer and Philip Tetlock, eds. *Learning in US and Soviet Foreign Policy* (Boulder, Westview, 1991), pp. 350–99.

105 Stephen Ambrose, *Nixon: The Triumph of a Politician, 1962–1972* (New York, Simon and Schuster, 1989), p. 526.

106 Raymond Garthoff, *Détente and Confrontation: American–Soviet Relations from Nixon to Reagan*, rev. edn (Washington, The Brookings Institution, 1994), pp. 213–16.

107 Garthoff, *Détente and Confrontation*, pp. 325–35.

108 William Tompson, 'The Fall of Nikita Khrushchev', *Soviet Studies*, 43 (1991), pp. 1101–21.

109 Franklyn Griffiths, 'The Sources of American Conduct: Soviet Perspectives and Their Policy Implications', in Sean Lynn-Jones, Stephen Van Evera and Steven Miller, eds., *Soviet Military Policy* (Cambridge, MA, MIT Press, 1989), pp. 23–66.

110 *Nuclear Weapons Data Book*, IV, pp. 139–40.

111 Parrott, *Technology and Innovation*, pp. 182–7.

112 Robin Edmonds, *Soviet Foreign Policy: The Brezhnev Years* (Oxford, Oxford University Press, 1983), pp. 80–1.

113 Ilya Gaiduk, 'The Vietnam War and Soviet–American Relations, 1964–1973: New Russian Evidence', *CWIHPB*, 6–7 (1995–96), pp. 232–58.

114 Garthoff, *Détente and Confrontation*, pp. 281–7.

115 Andropov to Ustinov, 19 April 1971, *CWIHPB*, 4 (1994), pp. 68–70.

116 Garthoff, *Détente and Confrontation*, pp. 387–400.

117 Samuel Wells, 'Charles de Gaulle and the French Withdrawal from NATO's Integrated Command', in Lawrence Kaplan, ed., *American Historians and the Atlantic Alliance* (Kent, Kent State University Press, 1991), pp. 81–94.

118 *Mémorandum du général de Gaulle au Président des Etats-Unis d'Amerique et au Premier Ministre du Royaume-Uni*, 17 September 1958. Annex 4 in Frédéric Bozo, *La France et l'OTAN: De la guerre froide au nouvel ordre européen* (Paris, Masson, 1991).

119 Jean Lacouture, *De Gaulle the Ruler: 1945–1970* (London, Harvill, English abridgement and translation, 1991), p. 416.

120 Wells, 'Charles de Gaulle'.

121 *Aide-Mémoire adressé par le gouvernement français aux quatorze autres pays membres de l'OTAN*. Annex 6 in Bozo, *La France et l'OTAN*.

122 Lacouture, *De Gaulle the Ruler*, pp. 396–7.

123 CIA Directorate of Intelligence, Intelligence Memorandum (prepared by Office of Current Intelligence), *France, the USSR, and European Security*, 20 May 1966.

124 Lacouture, *De Gaulle the Ruler*, p. 473.

125 Lacouture, *De Gaulle the Ruler*, p. 428.

126 Bozo, *La France et l'OTAN*, pp. 109–115.

127 Michel Debré, *Gouverner autrement, 1962–1970* (Paris, Albin Michel, 1993), pp. 250–6.

128 Robert Norris, Andrew Burrows and Richard Fieldhouse. *Nuclear Weapons Data Book*, vol. V: *British, French, and Chinese Nuclear Weapons* (Boulder, Westview, 1994), pp. 189–92.

129 Timothy Garton Ash, *In Europe's Name: Germany and the Divided Continent* (London, Jonathan Cape, 1993), p. 52.

130 Stent, *From Embargo to Ostpolitik* p. 94.

131 Wolfram Hanrieder, *Germany, America, Europe: Forty Years of German Foreign Policy* (New Haven, Yale University Press, 1989) pp. 48 and 174.

132 Stent, *From Embargo to Ostpolitik* p. 97.

133 Michael Sodaro, *Moscow, Germany and the West from Khrushchev to Gorbachev* (London, I. B. Tauris, 1991), pp. 43–71.

134 Sodaro, *Moscow*, pp. 72–107.

135 Garton Ash, *Europe's Name*, p. 60.

136 Garton Ash, *Europe's Name*, pp. 65–6.

137 Garton Ash, *Europe's Name*, p. 67–83.

138 Mark Kramer, 'The Prague Spring and the Soviet Invasion of Czechoslovakia: New Interpretations', *CWIHPB*, 3 (1993), pp. 2–13.

139 Sodaro, *Moscow*, pp. 108–34.

140 Garton Ash, *Europe's Name*, pp. 67–83.

5

A System Under Stress, 1973–1984

THE AMERICAN WORLD VIEW IN THE 1970S

American *détente* had been the product of two factors. The first was the need to find a way of mitigating the global impact of defeat in, and withdrawal from, Vietnam. The second was the emergence of an approximate technical and numerical parity in American and Soviet strategic nuclear forces and, indeed, in military power more generally. These two factors complemented each other; but the most important was the relatively short-term Vietnam problem. This problem was definitively 'solved' by the 1973 Paris accords or, at the very latest, by the North Vietnamese conquest of South Vietnam in 1975. Richard Nixon's belief that the key to winning and holding the presidency was disentanglement from Vietnam, offset by new international political arrangements which isolated the disaster, thus proved more prescient than Henry Kissinger's contention that strategic parity was the foundation stone of a new international order. Once Vietnam had fallen, powerful voices in both the Republican and Democratic parties began to suggest that American interests would be much better served by seeking preponderance within the strategic relationship with the Soviet Union than by managing parity.

These voices were of the greatest importance since failure in Vietnam had had a transforming effect on the American polity. Congress and its supporting penumbra of non-governmental policy entrepreneurs were no longer content to be marshalled by the executive. Instead they were able to exploit a wider lack of faith in government competence to second guess and, on occasion, micromanage, Cold War policy. For the first time since 1950–2 executive foreign policy was challenged from the right. Unlike McCarthyism, however, anti-*détente* critics had real and powerfully argued policy prescriptions.

At the end of the Nixon era and in the first year of the Ford administration Henry Kissinger, combining the offices of Secretary of State and National Security Adviser, was the dominant force in American Cold War policy. By 1976, however, the Reagan challenge within the Republican Party and powerful Congressional figures such as Senator Henry Jackson were undermining his policies. The new Democratic administration of Jimmy Carter, despite its rhetorical commitment to *détente* with morals (as opposed to Kissinger's repeatedly stressed belief in *détente* based upon a global balance of power), was a battleground between Secretary of State Cyrus Vance and National Security Adviser Zbigniew Brzezinski for Carter's foreign-policy soul and between the executive and its hawkish critics in Congress. The first Reagan administration operated with an even more tortuous policy process. Due to the President's inability to grasp details, policy was made through bitter bureaucratic battles leading to a presidential pronouncement or speech, followed by more bitter bureaucratic battles to define what the President had actually meant. All this took place with attention firmly focused on the need for Congressional management. Between them the two administrations produced a return to policies more redolent of the late 1950s and early 1960s: limited dialogue with the Soviet Union; selective containment of Soviet power in the face of sceptical members of Congress who had to be convinced of the efficacy of American intervention; and the search for a sustainable military advantage. These policies reinstituted the briefly abandoned search for victory and accepted that such victory would still be a 'long haul'.

Henry Kissinger had been appointed Secretary of State in September 1973 whilst retaining his role as Nixon's National Security Adviser. Nixon himself was increasingly preoccupied with the progress of the Watergate scandal which was to bring about his downfall in August 1974. In his enhanced position Kissinger continued to argue and act on the assumption that a new structure of international relations was emerging. This structure would rest upon an enduring balance of power.[1] Kissinger's policy of accepting and manipulating this new structure was not shaken by crises. Neither the October 1973 Yom Kippur War nor the fall of Saigon to North Vietnamese forces in April 1975 caused him to rethink his basic posture.[2]

Kissinger believed it was vital for the United States and the Soviet Union to push on with arms control negotiations. In July 1974 he pointed out that 'if we have not reached a [SALT II] agreement well before 1977 [when the SALT I Interim Agreement expired], then I believe you will see an explosion of technology and an explosion of numbers [of strategic nuclear weapons]'. To allow such a development would be against American national interests since 'it will be impossible to describe what strategic superiority means'. He went on to say: 'one of the questions we have to ask ourselves in this country is: what in the name of God is strategic superiority? What is the significance of it, politically, militarily, operationally, at these level of numbers [*sic*]. What do you do with it?' Others in the government disagreed. In January 1974 the Secretary of Defense, James Schlesinger, had publicly argued that the United States' main concern should be the possibility that the Soviet Union would 'marry together the technologies that are now emerging in their R&D programme to throw weight and numbers that they have been allowed under the Interim Agreement, [and] that they would develop a capability that was preponderant to that of the

United States'. By preponderance Schlesinger meant that 'at some point around 1980 or beyond, they would be in a position in which they had a major counterforce option against the United States [i.e. weapons systems capable of destroying American nuclear forces] and we would lack a similar option'. He argued that such a situation would emerge if 'the Soviets were able to develop ... improved technologies presently available to the United States in the form of guidance, MIRVs, warhead technology' and if the United States failed to pursue such technologies because it had used them as bargaining chips to organise a stable diplomatic relationship with the Soviet Union. 'We must have a symmetrical balancing of strategic forces on both sides', he claimed. 'We cannot be in a position in which a major option is open to the Soviet Union which we through a self-denying ordinance have precluded for the United States.'[3] The guidelines for American nuclear planning Schlesinger set in place in the same month were based on the assumption that the United States would strive for and succeed in keeping the technical and numerical edge in strategic nuclear weapons. They called for the maintenance of extended deterrence, 'to deter nuclear attacks against US allies and those other nations whose security is deemed important to US interests' so as to inhibit their nuclear coercion. The guidelines insisted that the United States must maintain the ability 'for limited employment options which enable [it] to conduct selected nuclear operations [against Soviet nuclear forces]' as a means of showing 'determination to resist aggression [coupled with] desire to exercise restraint'. At all times the President should be given the ability to control 'the timing and pace of attack execution, in order to provide the enemy opportunities to reconsider actions'.[4]

Although the United States' government was still firmly committed to seeking a SALT II agreement this commitment hid deep disagreements over what its purposes should be. Whereas Kissinger believed that '*both* sides have to convince their military establishments of the benefits [of arms control] restraint ... not a thought that comes naturally to military people on either side', Schlesinger countered: 'Henry is always tough with everybody but the Russians.' Kissinger believed that arms control negotiations should seek 'offsetting asymmetries': not only could nuclear forces be unequal, but compromises in arms control negotiations could be a way of dealing with non-nuclear issues. He was thus relaxed about the fate of ALCMs and Soviet Backfire bombers and could even comment, in October 1975, that 'in fairness one has to point out that most significant concessions over the last 18 months in the negotiations have been made by the Soviet Union'. The OSD and the JCS on the other hand insisted that if the United States was to negotiate it should seek superiority: pegging ICBM numbers, in which the Soviets were superior, whilst allowing full development of MIRVs and ALCMs where it was believed US technology would prevail.[5] Once Gerald Ford became President in August 1974 this latter view began to gain ground, largely due to pressures from outside the administration.

Kissinger's policy was attacked on three levels. First, criticism was levelled at the whole idea of creating a long-term balance of power in which the Soviet Union's role as a superpower was not only acknowledged but legitimised. Second, the specifics of arms control as part of this process were fiercely debated. Third, Kissinger's critics charged that he gave too much attention to posturing on the periphery rather than strengthening American power. The most public attack on Kissinger's new system came from Henry Jackson, a Democratic senator with presidential ambitions. In 1972 the United States had agreed, as part of the normalisation of relations, to grant the Soviet Union the status of an equal trading partner. In August 1972, however, the Soviet government had imposed what amounted to an exit tax on Jews wishing to leave the Soviet Union. Jackson believed, in the words of his aide Richard Perle, that 'the whole ... trade agreement was bullshit. You can't have a truly reciprocal trade agreement with a nonmarket economy.'[6] He used the Jewish emigration issue, a potential vote winner in the United States, as a lever against the trade agreement by amending the bill going through Congress so that the measure would only come into force once restrictions on Jewish emigration were lifted. The Jackson–Vanik amendment flew in the face of all Kissinger believed about Soviet–American relations. In September 1974 he described it as an 'ex post facto form of linkage [which] ... casts doubts on our reliability as a negotiating partner' and asked incredulously, 'are we ready to face the crises and increased defence budgets that a return to cold war conditions would spawn?' Despite this, Kissinger was forced to negotiate with the Soviet Union on Jewish emigration to buy off Jackson and his supporters. As a result, although the trade bill passed Congress in December 1974 it was renounced by the Soviet Union in January 1975. Kissinger's comment was that 'no country could allow its domestic regulations to be dictated as we were pushing the Soviets to do'.[7]

On the issue of strategic weapons a number of high-profile commentators subjected American policy to scathing criticism. In a series of articles published in 1974 Albert Wohlstetter charged that ever since the 'missile gap', with which John Kennedy chastised Richard Nixon during the 1960 presidential election, had proved to be illusory, American intelligence had consistently under-estimated the rate of growth and the advances made in missile technology by the Soviets. He also dismissed any notion that America was contributing to an arms race that could be obviated by arms control. 'Gross changes in American, and the simultaneous quite different changes in Soviet strategic spending', he argued, 'cannot be understood in terms of a closed cycle of tightly coupled interactions between US and Soviet processes of decision to acquire weapons – as is assumed in the usual action–reaction theory.' In early 1975 Paul Nitze joined the attack.[8] Nitze and Wohlstetter were highly respected commentators but the importance of their opinions was greatly magnified by the fact that they were taken up by the team hoping to replace Gerald Ford with Ronald Reagan as the Republican presidential candidate. Recognising a powerful force within his own party, Ford instructed Kissinger and Schlesinger to develop much more hard-line SALT proposals. In January 1976 Kissinger's opponents within the government – Donald Rumsfeld, who had replaced Schlesinger as Secretary of Defense, and the JCS – thwarted Kissinger's attempt to sign a SALT II agreement before the November presidential elections.[9] More extraordinarily, in June 1976 the director of the CIA, George Bush, set up an *ad hoc* body known as Team B, which included Nitze, to challenge his own organisation's assessments. The team reported after Ford had lost the election but, nevertheless, had a major impact.[10] According to the team leader, Richard Pipes, they concluded that the United States and the Soviet Union had not only divergent but fundamentally incompatible political systems. In particular, the Soviet system produced leaders who viewed 'conflict and violence as natural regulators of all human affairs' and believed that 'thermonuclear war is not suicidal [but] . . . can be fought and won, and thus resort to it must not be ruled out'. They would, therefore, always be willing to use nuclear weapons as 'compellants' in peace and their nuclear forces in an early decisive form in war to pave the way to eventual victory. In their valedictory statements Donald Rumsfeld and Gerald Ford endorsed these views: Rumsfeld commented that Russian military capabilities 'indicate a tendency toward war fighting . . . rather than for more modish Western modes of deterrence through mutual vulnerability'.[11] Ford was even more direct: 'the United States can never tolerate a shift in strategic balance against us, or even a situation where the American people or our allies believe the balance is shifting against us. The United States would risk the most serious political consequences if the world came to believe that our adversaries had a decisive margin of superiority.'[12]

A different balance of political forces combined to thwart Kissinger's vision of a stable balance of power in non-bilateral relations. The main battleground for this dispute was Angola. In 1974–5 a new regime in Portugal decided to relinquish the last, desperately failing, European colonial empire. Kissinger believed that the United States had to act vigorously in Angola to avoid a regime which was friendly to the Soviet Union and Cuba. In July 1975 he secured approval for a CIA plan to channel $31.7 million in military aid to two supposedly anti-Soviet groups involved in the Angolan civil war. Kissinger saw Angola as a test of the United States' post-Vietnam resolve and as a means of showing the Soviets that there was a global balance of power. The United States, he said, 'cannot be indifferent while an outside power embarks upon an interventionist policy – so distant from its homeland and so removed from traditional Russian interests'. He despaired of his conservative critics who were unwilling to seek compromise with the Soviet Union on arms control but were equally unwilling to use force to oppose Soviet adventurism around the globe.[13] Kissinger's critics on Angola, who came from all points of the political spectrum, simply did not accept the logic of American intervention in a country in which, he himself admitted, 'the US has no national interest'.[14] Despite the introduction of Cuban combat units into the country in November 1975 there was little support for US intervention. In December the Senate voted by 43 to 22 to cut off funding for the prosecution of the war in Angola.[15]

There was remarkably little support for Kissinger's concept of a balance of power within the American political system. Even those who had some sympathy with his ideas had been alienated by the furtive, and often vindictive, manner in which he and Nixon had sought to shape foreign policy. Kissinger had been tolerated when he seemed to offer some amelioration of the substantive and psychological crisis brought about by defeat in Vietnam. In the post-Vietnam period notions of American exceptionalism, preponderance and a commitment to a modified, more cautious, form of containment reasserted themselves. It is perhaps ironic that they should do so under the rhetorically innovative presidency of Jimmy Carter. Carter publicly declared: 'We are now free of that inordinate fear of communism which once led the United States to embrace any dictator in that fear.' He also believed that the United States and the Soviet Union had committed themselves to an unsustainable arms race and that each side actually needed very few nuclear weapons, as few as 200, to maintain a stable strategic balance.[16] He was thus an enthusiastic advocate of arms control negotiations and willing to be flexible in addressing legitimate Soviet concerns. Thus he announced the intention to conclude a quick arms control agreement. Some of his advisers, however, accepted the call for American preponderance enunciated by Ford in January 1976. Zbigniew Brzezinski clearly stated:

> I don't consider nuclear superiority to be politically meaningless. I can fully acknowledge the fact that at a certain level strategic weaponry ceases to exercise military significance in terms of marginal differences and consequences, if used. However, the perception by others or by oneself of someone else having – quote unquote – strategic superiority can influence political behaviour. It can induce some countries to act in a fashion that sometimes can be described as 'Finlandization'. And it can induce self-imposed restraint on the party that feels weaker and, last but not least, it can induce the party that feels it enjoys strategic superiority to act politically in a more assertive fashion. In other words, it has the potential for political exploitation, even if in an actual warfare situation the differences may be at best, or at worst, on the margin.[17]

In part the new American approach reflected ideas that Brzezinski had developed much earlier in his career as an academic, of using *détente* as a system-changing offensive strategy. 'Nothing worse could happen to a totalitarian system', he had written, 'than general pacification, since it would deprive it of its enemies.'[18] Carter's arms control proposals were both more sweeping and less negotiable than anything Kissinger had envisaged. Thus Secretary of State Cyrus Vance travelled to Moscow in March 1977 with a proposal to drastically reduce the ICBM ceilings, MIRVs and Soviet heavy ICBMs whilst banning mobile ICBMs and the development of a new generation of ICBMs. The Soviets rejected this whole package.[19]

Like Ford, Carter was under considerable pressure from outside the government to maintain a hard-line position. Although negotiations towards an arms control agreement continued, culminating in the SALT II treaty signed in Vienna in June 1979, this domestic pressure toughened the US stance. Initially, Carter had been keen to get rid of weapons he considered particularly noxious or destabilising. Thus he cancelled the development of enhanced radiation weapons, the so-called neutron bombs, in April 1978 against the advice of all his major advisers. In his March 1977 arms control *démarche* he had offered to cancel the 10-MIRV MX ICBM which America was developing. He even described the MX as a 'nauseating' weapon. Yet continued development of the MX was the price demanded for support of a SALT treaty by the JCS, who would have to testify on its behalf, and the Senate who would have to vote on it. In 1978 Secretary of Defense Harold Brown ridiculed the idea that the Soviets would risk a 'cosmic throw of the dice' by attempting to destroy US strategic forces. The next year he was arguing that 'the growing vulnerability of our land-based forces could, if not corrected, contribute to a perception of US strategic inferiority that would have severely adverse political – and could have potentially destabilising military – consequences'. On the eve of signing the SALT II treaty Carter endorsed the MX.[20] These statements were backed up by a series of presidential directives affecting nuclear forces: most notably, in June 1980, a revised statement on nuclear doctrine based on the possibility of 'slow motion' limited nuclear war and a margin of American technical and numerical superiority wide enough to ensure 'escalation dominance'. These presidential directives had deliberately ambiguous implications. Harold Brown saw them as a means of creating a credible 'countervailing strategy', based upon a secure second strike capability, which would strengthen mutual deterrence. Brzezinski saw a war-fighting doctrine as a means of cowing the Soviets over the whole range of strategic and foreign-policy issues.[21] Brzezinski successfully pushed for the development of a bigger MX. As the much-reviled head of the Arms Control and Disarmament Administration, Paul Warnke, sarcastically interpreted the policy: 'The bigger, the uglier, the nastier the weapon – the better [because it sent off the message]: Shape up, buster. We've got the ability to do you in. We're probably not going to do it – but it's an act of grace on our part.'[22] At the very least this was the definitive triumph of the Schlesinger line over the Kissinger line.

All this was not enough for Carter's critics. The MX was dogged by disagreement over where and how it was to be deployed. Some of the plans discussed appeared so ridiculous that they induced what Congressman Les Aspin termed the 'snicker factor'. More importantly Henry Jackson and his supporters reviled SALT II *tout court*. In June 1979 Senator Jackson declared:

> To enter a treaty which favours the Soviets as this one does on the ground that we will
> be in a worse position [without it], is appeasement in its purest form ... Against

overwhelming evidence of a continuing Soviet strategic and conventional military build-up, there has been a flow of official administration explanations, extenuation, excuses. It is all ominously reminiscent of Great Britain in the 1930s . . . The failure to face reality today, like the failure to do so then, that is the mark of appeasement.

Thus, the Senate ratification hearings for the treaty held between July and December 1979 provided the opportunity for a vigorous attack on Carter's weakness. Although the Foreign Relations Committee voted nine to six in favour of the treaty, the Armed Services Committee, under Jackson's leadership, denounced it as 'not in the National Security interests of the United States'.[23]

THE SOVIET WORLD VIEW IN THE 1970S

The 1970s should have been a decade of optimism for the Soviet leadership. Just as their power projection capabilities outside Eastern Europe became truly formidable the main adversary's capabilities were weakened. Anxiety about the possibility of domestic crisis remained muted. This bred a dangerous arrogance in the conduct of international affairs. The view of the international system and the USSR's place within it developed and articulated by the Soviet leadership was initially based upon the optimistic prognoses of the early 1970s. The entire system of international relations had been changed; not because imperialism had changed but because it had been weakened. The Soviet Union had forced itself into a position of equality with the United States and would soon be able to surpass it. Andrey Gromyko declared that no important problem in the world could be resolved without the participation of the USSR.[24] The efflorescence of such rhetoric was brief. It was effectively ended by the October 1973 crisis in the Middle East.

Between 1967 and 1973 the Soviets believed they had found a new Vietnam. Egypt seemed to be a country which would challenge American interests and frustrate American power and diplomacy without causing a direct threat to the USSR. The Soviets had been supplying the Nasser regime with weapons since 1955. In 1964 the Soviet Mediterranean fleet was formed. Admiral Gorshkov opened negotiations for bases which were concluded in 1966. Then the humiliation of defeat by Israel in the 1967 Six-Day War opened up the prospect of a festering sore in the Arab world. Soviet naval forces were actually deployed to the area in 1967. In April 1967 Brezhnev told Ulbricht and Gomulka that: the 'party [was] pushing the Americans out of the Near East . . . [by] consistent application of the Leninist principle of seeking temporary allies. Nasser is highly confused on ideological questions but he has proved we can rely on him. If we . . . want to achieve progress, we must accept sacrifices. One sacrifice we must bear is the persecution of Egyptian communists by Nasser. But, during this phase, Nasser is of inestimable value to us.' In 1970 the Soviet Union provided Egypt, which had been defeated by the Israeli use of air power, with a complete air defence system including missiles, fighters and 20 000 advisers. In 1971 a Soviet–Egyptian defence treaty was signed. At the time such a treaty with a non-communist state was an innovation, although they were to become familiar in the 1970s.

Unfortunately for the Soviets, alliances with independent states were not a satisfactory innovation. Lack of Soviet control meant that they did not trust their new allies: indeed, they feared that Egypt would 'defect' and become a US client. The Soviets refused to supply modern offensive systems to Egypt. In 1972 the Soviet Union began to demand cash payment for weapons supplies in an attempt to make Sadat, Nasser's successor, more pliable. Sadat responded by expelling his Soviet advisers, whilst stepping up demands for arms deliveries and extending the grant of naval facilities. In an effort to restore their strategic investment, the Soviets did indeed step up arms supplies. According to one observer, 'Grechko had the mistaken idea that . . . Sadat would surely consult with Soviet military experts and military leaders before the beginning of large military operations against Israel.'

On 6 October 1973, however, Egypt launched a massive, unannounced, assault on Israel. Once again the Soviets backed their investment and began a large-scale airlift of arms to the Egyptians. For some, 'the first successes of Egyptian and Syrian military forces were interpreted as a victory of Soviet weapons. Grechko argued that this advantage must be explored, that Israel with all its American military equipment would be humiliated both politically and militarily and that America's position in the Middle East would be damaged.' Others suspected that Egypt and Syria would be defeated but that the Soviet Union had to back its client to prevent its own indirect humiliation. Indeed, after initial reverses, the Israelis launched successful counter-offensives. Egypt was invaded on 16 October and sued for a cease-fire on the 20th. On 18 October Kissinger had come to Moscow during his attempts to broker such a cease-fire. Yet the Israelis carried on their encirclement of the Egyptian army within Egypt. On 24 October the Soviets called for joint American–Soviet military intervention but threatened to intervene unilaterally if cooperation was not forthcoming. The Americans warned the Soviet Union off, going as far as to upgrade the alert status of their nuclear forces. The Yom Kippur War was a fiasco for the Soviets: their clients were defeated and it was made quite clear that their role in the Middle East was peripheral. Brezhnev told the Politburo: 'Here in Moscow Kissinger fooled us and made a deal when he was in Tel Aviv.' Anatoliy Dobrynin recalled, '[Brezhnev] was very emotional. He felt deceived by Nixon and Kissinger. I was worried about our relations with the United States and worried that Brezhnev's anger . . . would lead him to do something rash.' In fact Brezhnev had too much political prestige invested in *détente* to abandon it. In December 1973 he argued: 'Matters would look quite different were it not for this factor of *détente* in the world, which has emerged in the last two or three years. If the current conflict had flared up in a situation of universal, international tension and aggravation of relations, say between the United States and the Soviet Union, the clash in the Middle East might have become more dangerous, it might have assumed a scope endangering world peace.' Brezhnev's health was, however, declining and other Politburo members, including some of the new intake, were outraged by events in the Middle East. Grechko commented: 'In the past we have never asked anybody if we can send our troops and we can do the same now.' Andropov agreed: 'We should respond to mobilisation with mobilisation.'[25] It seemed that the Soviet Union would have to enhance its efforts to improve the correlation of forces.

As early as 1974 some members of the Soviet foreign-policy establishment were concerned about certain trends in American foreign policy. The Nixon administration, and in particular Henry Kissinger, the Soviets thought, had attempted to create the impression that the Soviets had agreed to inaction in the Third World while the United States was entitled to defend 'capitalist neo-imperialism' in the name of freedom. As the decade progressed there seemed to be an increasingly apparent flaw in previous Soviet thinking: the United States had simply failed to respond to *détente* in the expected way and was becoming increasingly assertive in resisting the historical process. The American political establishment ignored the preferred Soviet interpretation that the status quo was a flow of progressive change and vocally disregarded Soviet injunctions to regard peaceful coexistence as a continuation of the ideological struggle between two systems.

By the end of the 1970s a re-evaluation of sorts was taking place in the Soviet world view. This re-evaluation was far from fundamental. It merely suggested that the capitalist threat to the Soviet Union was as great as some pessimists had always believed and that a change in the correlation of forces would bring not peaceful transition but increased risks. Brezhnev could publicly proclaim that the world was becoming more dangerous because the intra-capitalist contradictions at the root of war had become more acute as the struggle for markets, raw materials and energy intensified,[26] yet at the same time Soviet leaders were perturbed by the seeming resilience and political unity of the capitalist world. As so often in Soviet politics the fear of conspiracy rather than accidental contingency soon became the dominant theme. The fear of a united capitalist world was increased as the Soviet Union's allies in the Third World, in whom a great deal of hope had been placed since the 1960s, began, increasingly, to look like broken reeds. These developments threatened the Soviet leadership on three levels: the retention of power by communist parties outside the Soviet Union was challenged, an uncomfortable position for the CPSU; Soviet independence of international action was increasingly constrained; and the avoidance of war seemed to have become more difficult.[27]

Soviet views of security continued to rest primarily on a belief in the military instrument. In the official formulation 'the military strength of a state is by all means a decisive element of its position in the world'. This concentration on the military aspect of power and the belief that combat power was the ultimate guarantor of the Soviet state bred an arrogance within the Soviet élite. The Soviets demanded 'identical security' but this meant more than simply arithmetical parity: 'the number of our divisions is higher than in the United States and this is quite natural', Marshal Petrov, commander-in-chief of ground forces and Deputy Minister of Defence, blithely observed in 1983.[28] 'The width of the territory, the geographic and strategic position of the USSR is such that it must ensure a balance of forces not only in Europe but also in other regions adjacent to its borders ... in the Far East and the South.' Although the very existence of the USSR's armed forces and their high combat readiness was supposed to thwart aggressive imperialist plans, the Soviet strategic objectives of deterring attack, defeating any state which attacked the USSR and minimising war damage to Soviet society required a very powerful military establishment indeed. Any change in the military balance appeared as a threat to the whole Soviet system rather than merely a temporary setback. Yuriy Andropov's 1983 statement that: 'no-one will ever be able to reverse the course of history ... It is high time everybody ... understood that we shall be able to ensure the security of our country, the security of friends and allies under any circumstances ... our country's defence capability is maintained at such a level that it would not be advisable to anyone to stage a trial of strength' was seemingly a confident reassertion of Soviet power. It also expressed a deep-seated irritation with the failure of the United States and its allies to accept the historical inevitability that this power would continue to be unassailable. This unease was caused by a seeming deterioration in the Soviet Union's military situation.

Military power was an issue of such central importance to the regime that it caused controversy both between civilian and military leaders and between civilian–military coalitions within the party. The party leadership's decision to slow the growth of the military budget in 1974 was opposed by Marshal Grechko. In response to attempts to place some limits on Soviet military spending the military began to challenge the dictum that the danger of war had been lessened. Work published by the Ministry of Defence in mid-1976 argued from the premiss that the influence of 'reactionary circles' in the West persisted and that *détente* was not an irreversible process. New weapons could appear suddenly and lead to a 'rapid achievement of military–technical superiority'. The Defence Ministry argued, as had many officers since the Khrushchev period, that the party leadership should not become fixated by the deterrent possibilities of strategic nuclear weapons. The Soviet Union needed superior military capabilities in all fields.[29] According to Colonel-General Nikolay Chervov, 'even if certain weapons were not required for the needs of the army [Minister of Defence] Ustinov would accept them. Sometimes it happened that newly manufactured weapons were immediately taken to stores where they were quickly forgotten about.'[30]

The success of the 'more is better' school was apparent in the later Brezhnev period. In the late 1970s and early 1980s the Soviet military was planning and training for a diverse range of possibilities in order to provide the leadership with options for nuclear, nuclear and conventional, and conventional warfare. The so-called 'Tula-line' (named after a speech given by Brezhnev in a city at the centre of the defence industry) after 1977 stressed conventional war. Changes in strategy were made to accommodate this.[31] The war aim to seize and occupy NATO territory as an alternative economic base for the reconstruction of Soviet communism was reaffirmed. As *Izvestiya* put it, repeating a statement first issued in 1966: 'it is very important to determine which targets and enemy economic regions should be left intact or rapidly reconstructed and used in the interests of strengthening the economic potential of our own country'.[32] The Russian leadership of the late Brezhnev–Andropov–Chernenko period continued to regard the use of the military instrument with favour.[33]

THE THIRD WORLD AND THE NEW COLD WAR

The Third World had an important part in Soviet military doctrine. A major debate on the use of Soviet armed forces outside the Warsaw Pact had raged between 1969 and mid-1974. Academics such as Yevgeniy Primakov and Vitaliy Zhurkin argued against military intervention because of the fear of escalation into a wider conflict. Marshal Malinovsky seemed willing to accept this view, but Marshal Grechko favoured an extended international role for the armed forces in line with the ideas propounded by Admiral Sergey Gorshkov during his campaign for a 'blue water' Soviet navy. For the first time the Soviet navy acquired aircraft carriers. A helicopter carrier was deployed in 1967 and ships carrying short take-off and landing aircraft entered service in 1975. A class of tank-landing ships was commissioned in 1966 and a dozen were in service by 1974. In 1974 Grechko called for two kinds of extra-European military involvement. At one level the Soviet Union needed to establish the political, physical and operational infrastructure for fighting a world war. At the same time the struggle for world influence, including the Sino-Soviet struggle, and access to raw materials meant that 'the historic function of the Soviet armed forces is not restricted merely to their function in defending our Motherland and other socialist countries'.[34]

In the mid-1970s the Soviet leadership also showed considerable enthusiasm for reconstructing a world communist movement to replace the one effectively destroyed by the Sino-Soviet split of the early 1960s. The splits in the movement still, however, effectively constrained Soviet freedom of action. At the June 1976 European Conference of Communist Parties threats of non-attendance by Yugoslavia demonstrated the weaknesses of the 'International'. The conference failed to agree on the leading role of the CPSU, failed to criticise Maoism and upheld each party's right to pursue its own road to socialism. Fear of the Maoist ideological threat led the Soviet Union to embrace radical movements in the Third World in an attempt to create a restored International, institutionalised by a string of friendship treaties. Soviet emissaries encouraged radical governments to reform themselves as Marxist-Leninist vanguard parties: Mozambique in February 1977, Angola in December 1977, the People's Democratic Republic of Yemen in October 1978 and Ethiopia in September 1984. In some cases this transformation was brought about in the face of opposition from indigenous movements. In Ethiopia, for instance, the formation of the Committee for Organising the Party of the Working People in 1979 was initially resisted by Mengistu Haile Mariam. The Nicaraguan Sandinistas, involved at the time in a bloody struggle with American surrogates, were publicly criticised for not following this path.[35]

By 1984, however, there had been a significant change in the Soviet perception of their ability to manipulate anti-imperialism. The Soviets faced the problem that Third World ideology and interests had little in common with the USSR. Some officials had come to accept that, at least in the short term, there were no separate socialist and capitalist economies but one international economy dominated by capitalism. The realities of the capitalist system had also doomed vanguard parties to failure. In the late 1970s and early 1980s a correspondingly less ideological attitude was taken to aid. The sale of armaments for hard currency to set against the trade deficit was undertaken. Economic relations devoid of ideology, such as grain exports from Argentina and Brazil and credits to Morocco to produce phosphates for the Soviet market, were established. A self-proclaimed 'scientific socialist' regime such as that of Machel in Mozambique was refused economic and security backing.

The full force of this analysis was not, however, immediately applied to the core of Soviet foreign policy. Once again strong emphasis was placed on military power.[36] There was a marked increase in military assistance programmes after 1973. In the 1970s new military force projection capabilities were extensively used. Egypt and Syria were resupplied during the 1973 Middle East crisis, Cuban troops were airlifted to Angola in 1975, the Soviet military ran the Ogaden war on behalf of Ethiopia in 1977 and large-scale logistical support was supplied to Vietnam in 1978–9.[37] There was no drop in this activity in the mid-1980s. In 1983, 105 000 troops were in Afghanistan and there were 25 000 military advisers, mainly stationed in Cuba, Syria and Vietnam.[38] These assets were far from idle. In March 1984 the Soviet Union undertook a major naval deployment to the Caribbean including a Moskva-class carrier. In May 1984 the Soviets started to provide military aid to North Korea, in the form of MiG-23 fighters and SA-3 SAMs, after a ten-year interruption. In 1984–5 military supplies started to flow to the New People's Army in the Philippines. Nicaragua was promised greatly increased military aid when the Sandinista leader, Daniel Ortega, visited Moscow in April 1985. In

December 1985 Libya was supplied with SA-5 SAMs. At the same time the Soviets intervened in support of South Yemen rebels, using Soviet ships to supply ammunition and Soviet and Cuban officers to direct artillery fire.[39]

By far the most striking use of Soviet military power, however, occurred in Afghanistan. In December 1979 a large Soviet military force invaded the country. The crisis began when a military coup overthrew the non-aligned Afghan government in April 1978 and a radical Marxist faction came to power. Muslim-led resistance escalated into a major insurgency in Herat in March 1979. By the end of 1979, 40 000 insurgents were operating from bases in Pakistan. The Afghan civil war coincided with political developments in Iran. In January 1979 the Shah of Iran was forced to flee the country by mass demonstrations in favour of a fundamentalist Islamic state. On 4 November 1979 fundamentalists stormed the American embassy in Teheran and took more than 60 American citizens hostage. The Soviets were not dismayed by the humiliation of the Americans in a state which had been built up as an anti-communist bulwark under the auspices of the Nixon doctrine. They were, however, concerned by instability on their southern frontier. In December 1978 the USSR had signed a friendship treaty with Afghanistan. The Soviet leadership was however, reluctant to countenance direct intervention. Foreign Minister Gromyko argued that if the Red Army entered Afghanistan it would 'be an aggressor ... against the Afghan people'. Gromyko and Andropov suggested to the Politburo that an invasion would do little to help the internal situation in Afghanistan, since the situation was 'not ripe for a [socialist] revolution'. Gromyko warned that: 'all that we have done in recent years with such effort in terms of international tensions, arms reductions and much more – all that would be thrown back. .... this will be a nice gift for China. All the non-aligned countries will be against us. In a word serious consequences are to be expected from such an action.'[40] During 1979 the People's Democratic Party of Afghanistan (PDPA) made repeated requests for Soviet assistance but the Soviet Union was only willing to offer military equipment, military advisers and training.[41] Nevertheless, a Soviet airborne battalion secured the airfield at Bagram in July. In August 1979 a special Politburo committee on Afghanistan was set up. In September 1979, following severe factional strife within the communist movement, Hafizullah Amin emerged as leader of the government in Kabul. The Soviets regarded Amin as a dangerous factionalist. They insisted that it was 'crucial to maintain the unity of the party leadership and member-ship'. Since April 1978 the 'Soviet leadership has many times given recommendations and advice to the leaders of the DRA, and on a very high level. They have pointed to their mistakes and excesses. But the Afghan leaders, displaying their political inflexibility and inexperience, rarely heeded such advice.' Amin's succession made this situation even worse. Events within Afghanistan were taken to be a devil's brew of threats which could spill beyond its borders. Afghanistan might play a 'major role in the counter-revolutionary struggle. The situation in Iran and the spark of religious fanaticism all around the Muslim East was the underlying cause of the activisation of the struggle against the government of Afghanistan.' That government's unwillingness to obey Soviet instructions was actually turning it into a catalyst for, rather than a bulwark against, this threat.

> The reactionary forces had started to change the form of struggle, shifting from covert subversive actions to open armed forms of activity. They were able not only to regroup within the country but also to build wide connections with imperialist and clerical groups abroad, which supply them with active propaganda support as well as money and weapons ... Reactionary forces use slogans of extreme anticommunism and antisovietism ... Western special services, especially American and Chinese agencies, are involved in the organisation of the struggle against the government inside the country. They have taken advantage of the fact that Afghanistan's borders with Pakistan and Iran are practically open.[42]

In December 1979 the Politburo committee decided that the situation had worsened to such an extent that the murder of Amin by Soviet special forces and military intervention by over 50 000 Soviet troops was necessary.[43] Although the Soviets had been reinforcing their power projection capabilities for well over a decade, the decision to invade Afghanistan was also the product of specific circumstances. Indeed intervention in a country with a land border with the Soviet Union and in which Russia had taken a traditional interest, had little in common with activities in countries such as Egypt and Angola.

The American government had watched the situation in Afghanistan since the 1978 coup and increasing Soviet involvement with concern. Yet Brzezinski was still worried that 'the President might be prevailed upon ... to view [the] Afghan problem as isolated'. A number of sputtering crises dogged bilateral relations, especially what Carter called 'the Soviet Union's unwarranted involvement in Africa', in particular Somalia and Ethiopia, and fears, which erupted in 1978 and September 1979, that Soviet combat forces would be deployed in Cuba.[44] The main importance of these frictions, however, was that they provided convincing 'types' or 'patterns of behaviour' for what happened in Afghanistan in December 1979. When combined with the destabilisation and overthrow of America's ally, the Shah of Iran, by an indigenous Islamic revolution, Brzezinski's concept of an 'arc of crisis' running from Africa to South East Asia gained ground within the administration.[45]

The Soviet invasion in December 1979 completely converted Carter to Zbig's view. He dismissed the thought that the Soviets had any legitimate security interests in Afghanistan. According to Carter: 'My opinion of the Russians has changed more drastically in the last week than even the previous two and one half years before that. It is only now dawning upon the world the magnitude of the actions the Soviets undertook in invading Afghanistan.'[46] Afghanistan touched a raw nerve in the American political psyche. It combined fears about America's economy, largely the product of economic competition with other capitalist nations and concerns about oil supplies unrelated to the Cold War, with a direct military threat. Although less dependent on oil imports than other Western nations, the United States had seen its oil import bill rise from $4.3 billion in 1972 to $74 billion in 1980 after the Iranian revolution.[47]

Carter's response to the Afghan crisis combined attempts to assert preponderance not only over the Soviet Union but over America's allies. In January he froze the ratification process for the SALT II treaty, although promising to abide by its terms as long as the Soviets did the same. He placed an embargo on further grain exports to the Soviet Union. This second decision was taken against the advice of many of his advisers who argued that the main victims would be American farmers.[48] He also declared a boycott of the 1980 Moscow Olympics. Finally, Carter militarised the Persian Gulf. In another concept developed by Brzezinski, Carter declared on 23 January 1980 that:

> the region now threatened by Soviet troops in Afghanistan is of great strategic importance: it contains more than two-thirds of the world's exportable oil. The Soviet effort to dominate Afghanistan has brought Soviet military forces to within 300 miles of the Indian Ocean and close to the Straits of Hormuz – a waterway through which much of the free world's oil must flow. The Soviet Union is attempting to consolidate a strategic position that poses a grave threat to the free movement of Middle East oil ... let our position be absolutely clear. Any attempt by any outside force to gain control of the Persian Gulf will be regarded as an assault on the vital interests of the United States. And such an assault will be repelled by the use of any means necessary, including military force.[49]

The American response to the Afghan crisis was an attempt to reassert its leadership of the West. More importantly, however, especially for the President, it was a moment of complete conversion to righteous containment.

THE REAGAN ADMINISTRATION AND STRATEGIC WEAPONS

By the end of the Carter presidency even Brzezinski believed the administration had gone too far: He wanted to 'preserve the framework of East–West accommodation even though in recent months it has been stripped to the bone as a result of the Soviet aggression against Afghanistan'.[50] Reagan administration officials conceived the Cold War as a continuing struggle in which the United States should always seek preponderance and, in the long term, victory. Yet they also acknowledged that a degree of stability in relations with the Soviet Union was important to American national security.

Some sections of the government, especially the Department of Defense under Caspar Weinberger, deliberately sought systemic challenges to Soviet power. Plans were drawn up in March 1982 for the 1984 to 1988 period to develop weapons which would '[be] difficult for the Soviets to counter, impose disproportionate costs, open up new areas of major military competition and obsolesce previous Soviet investment.' Even before the Strategic Defence Initiative (SDI), ballistic missile defence technology was seen as one of 'the kind of smart, highly accurate, hopefully non-nuclear, weapons in which we excel', and by implication the Soviets did not. William Colby, at the CIA, was a strong advocate of limiting technical and trade cooperation with the Soviet regime so as to place it under increasing pressure. It was common currency in Western strategic analysis that the Soviet empire was increasingly fragile. Yet attempts to factor the collapse of the Soviet empire into US national strategy were rejected. In September 1984 Herbert Meyer, the vice-chairman of the CIA's National Intelligence Council, delivered a memorandum in which he argued that the Soviet empire had already 'entered its terminal phase' and the immediate period ahead 'will be the most dangerous we have ever known'. The CIA's professional analysts rejected his views. The official government line, hammered out in the first months of 1983, and enunciated by Secretary of State George Shultz in June, was based on the assumption that the Soviet Union would continue to be the other superpower into the foreseeable future. Thus 'the management of our relations with the Soviet Union is of the utmost importance. That relationship touches virtually every aspect of our inter-national concerns and objectives – political, economic and military – and every part of the world.' *Détente* was dismissed as a blind alley. It would be replaced by a new doctrine of containment since 'Soviet ambitions and capabilities have long since reached beyond the geographic bounds that this doctrine [originally] took for granted ... we [still] have to make clear that we will resist encroach-ments on our vital interests and those of our allies and friends.' Nevertheless, this 'new' post-*détente* version of containment was 'based upon the expectation that, faced with demonstration of the West's renewed determination to strengthen its defences, enhance its political and economic cohesion, and oppose adventurism, the Soviet Union will see restraint as its most attractive, or only, option'. Under these conditions Shultz promised to 'respect legitimate Soviet security interests' and 'to seek to engage the Soviet leaders in a constructive dialogue through which we hope to find political solutions to outstanding issues'.[51]

The specific policies which the administration would follow were a matter of intense debate within its ranks and continued to be dogged, although to a lesser extent, by Congressional challenge. The initial Reagan defence budget request called for an increase of $32.6 billion over Carter's January 1981 request for $200.3 billion, which itself had constituted a $26.4 billion increase on the 1979/80 figure.[52] Within the context of these increased funds there was a marked reluctance to give up any strategic systems and thus a major difficulty in addressing 'outstanding issues' in US–Soviet negotiations. The American military wanted 'a continuance of an adherence regime rather than [to] deal with breakout on the Soviet side'. The chairman of the JCS, General David

Jones, even challenged Caspar Weinberger's assertion that SALT obstructed American weapons development. Yet the preferred weapons systems of civilian officials in the Pentagon and the US military ruled out the cancellation of all weapons which could have been used as bargaining counters. When Pentagon advisers suggested that the US should cancel the MX ICBM in return for the Soviets dismantling their SS-18 heavy ICBMs, Richard Perle, the powerful Assistant Secretary of Defense, replied: 'If we give up the MX we're giving up the right to modernise our ICBM force. We'd be saying that we're content to live with our ICBMs vulnerable to attack [and] it's not just the SS-18 which makes them vulnerable.' The MX issue was complex because domestic pressure led many in Congress to oppose the basing of 'war fighting' ICBMs in the western United States. In December 1982 the House of Representatives voted by 245 to 176 to eliminate funding to begin procurement of a requested 100 MXs. Only 50 missiles were eventually approved.

The deployment of ground-launched cruise missiles was tied up with NATO's 1979 'dual track' decision to emplace new cruise and ballistic missiles in Europe in 1983, whilst negotiating with the Soviet Union to obviate this necessity. Some officials believed this decision to be nonsensical. In March 1981 the National Security Adviser, Richard Allen, declared that only pacifists 'believe we can bargain the reduction of a deployed Soviet weapons system for a promise not to deploy our own offsetting system'. Richard Perle produced a study in August 1981 which showed that as few as 100 triple-MIRVed Soviet SS-20 missiles could destroy NATO's 300 most vital military installations; parity in Europe was of no use, only no Soviet missiles would do. This was the origin of the November 1981 'zero option': the United States would not deploy its missiles if the Soviet Union dismantled all their SS-20, SS-4 and SS-5 missiles. Perle argued that there was no half-way house between 0 and 572: the Soviets either buckled to Western pressure or NATO enhanced its military capability, won a propaganda victory and spat in the eye of 'pacifists' whom the President believed were 'all sponsored by a thing called the World Peace Council, which is bought and sold by the Soviet Union'. There could be no negotiation on SLCMs because Weinberger and Perle believed they were exactly the kind of weapon which would 'obsolesce previous Soviet investment'. The abandonment of air-launched cruise missiles was ruled out because, in Perle's words, 'we wouldn't need cruise missiles on our bombers if we could be confident that the bombers themselves would penetrate Soviet air defences'.

There were those, however, in the administration who believed it was possible to conduct serious arms control negotiations with the Soviet Union. For instance the chief INF negotiator Paul Nitze attempted to broker a deal in July 1982 which would have allowed for 75 SS-20s and 75 American GLCMs to be deployed but would have aborted the arrival of Pershing IIs. He was blocked by Weinberger and Perle. In December 1982 Nitze warned his colleagues that:

> we have a political problem in Europe. A considerable percentage of European public opinion is not satisfied with our zero-zero position and would be satisfied with zero on our side. There's another percentage of the European population that doesn't hold out any hope for zero-zero but might be satisfied if we seem to be exploring an equitable solution above zero. The first thing we've got to do is start exploring those solutions so that it becomes more likely that the requisite percentage will support deployment . . . it is almost certain that the Soviets will not buy finite equal limits on both sides. Nor is it clear that a sufficient portion of European public opinion would be satisfied with an equal limits proposal to permit deployment, other than at a political cost so great as to be potentially very damaging to the alliance. There is no point in deployment at the expense of the solidarity of the alliance.

Once again Nitze was rebuffed only to be backed up in January 1983 by Helmut Kohl and Margaret Thatcher. Yet the response of the administration, in the words of Assistant Secretary of State Richard Burt, was a 'search for a cosmetic solution'. In March 1983 Reagan conceded that 'it would be better to have none than have some, [but] it is better to have few than have many'. Nevertheless, the administration insisted that the missiles were a vital part of its political strategy of forcing the Soviet Union to conform to behaviour patterns of which the United States approved. Reagan's message to European leaders was: 'A delay in our deployments would only encourage the Soviets to believe that NATO's resolve was faltering and that could stretch out negotiations endlessly without addressing our legitimate security concerns'. In Burt's more pithy formulation: 'We don't care if the goddamn things work or not. After all, that doesn't matter unless there's a war. What we care about is getting them in.' The GLCMs and Pershing IIs did indeed arrive, in Britain and the FRG respectively, in November 1983. The Soviet response was to walk out of both the INF and the START negotiations.[53]

The problems encountered by the MX ICBM made officials think seriously about a genuinely negotiable rather than a coercive START position in the summer of 1982. In August a motion in the House of Representatives calling for an immediate freeze on nuclear arsenals was only voted down by 204 to 202. At the time of the November 1982 Congressional elections eight states voted for propositions on the ballot calling for such a freeze. Some administration officials began to fear that the 'politics of deploying ICBMs in the United States was becoming too difficult'. Their response to this problem was not, however, to shift the thrust of American diplomacy but to shift the grounds of debate. Administration officials became increasingly interested in the ideas of a number of ex-military and defence industry lobbyists, who had supported Reagan's

1980 presidential campaign, for a space-based anti-ballistic missile system. A Joint Chiefs of Staff panel appointed by Reagan in 1982 was strongly in favour of the idea since they believed: 'we were reaching the point where we were losing our hat, ass and overcoat at Geneva [arms control negotiations]. We had no bargaining chip, no strength, with which to negotiate. The Soviets could just sit at Geneva and watch us throw away all our chips right here in Washington ... we were heading into a strategic valley of death.'[54] ABM defences seemed to offer the possibility of resolving the MX debate, whilst shifting attention to a form of deterrence which would be more palatable. It also, once again, fulfilled the Weinberger criterion of 'obsolescing existing Soviet investment'. In the early months of 1983 the concept of a 'Strategic Defence Initiative' emerged.[55] Since the plan was conceived as a speech rather than as a strategic programme[56] the nature of this 'formidable technical task' which would develop systems so that 'we could intercept and destroy strategic ballistic missiles' was not clear. A detractor, Paul Nitze, recorded that: 'within the United States government ... there was little understanding of what the SDI programme was to entail. Was it to be a research programme only, was it to provide an impenetrable shield, was it to be accomplished within the terms of the ABM treaty and therefore come about as a result of cooperative transition with the Soviet Union, and, finally, in what time periods were all these things to take place?' The programme was divided into two different components. A Strategic Defence Initiative Organisation was set up and the administration fought hard with a recalcitrant Congress, securing $14.68 billion of a requested $20.05 billion, to have it funded from 1985 for five years.[57] At the same time SDI was part of 'a deception programme aimed at the Soviet Union', designed to convince the Soviet leadership that they did, indeed, face a systemic challenge.[58] President Reagan had a deep personal and emotional commitment to the plan. It was part of the coercive pattern of diplomacy on which the United States was already embarked and it became the central point of tension between the United States and the Soviet Union between 1984 and 1987. At the first summit between Reagan and Mikhail Gorbachev in November 1985 failure was guaranteed when Reagan insisted arms control must be linked to the development of space defence.[59]

THE SOVIET UNION AND SYSTEMIC CHALLENGE

At the end of the Brezhnev era alarmists argued that the risks of nuclear war were increasing and that the Soviet Union's response should be to continue to enhance its military capabilities. The most vocal of these alarmists was Marshal Nikolay Ogarkov, the Chief of the General Staff. In 1981 Ogarkov accused the United States of 'taking matters to the point of keeping the world on the brink of war'. Marshal Ustinov also identified a 'radical change' in US policy and the intention 'to resort to the use or threat of arms, including nuclear weapons'.

The first Soviet article which identified a significant change in NATO war planning was published in August 1983. 'It is planned to establish conventional armed forces that would be capable of directly threatening the Soviet Union's territory', the Defence Ministry's paper reported in 1983. 'This cannot but be seen as an emphasis on preparing for large-scale offensive operations, something that is obviously concerned by the adoption of the strategic concept of "airland" battle.' NATO exercises seemed to show that the success of deep strikes in destroying the second echelon could delay the use of nuclear weapons on the battlefield, extending the conventional-only period from a few days to a few weeks. The Soviet leadership had always been very unhappy with the thought that they might not control the escalatory ladder. The inevitability of escalation was stressed in an orchestrated campaign.[60] The alarmists chose to portray these developments as destabilising. In 1983 Ogarkov warned: 'in the world today there is a growing threat of a new world war just as there was in the 1930s'. At the same time as Ogarkov and his military associates were developing their ideas, however, another strain in Soviet strategic thought was also being articulated. A strand of thinking existed which stressed the impossibility of winning a nuclear war and the importance of deterrence.[61] Brezhnev's 1977 Tula declaration that the Soviet Union was not striving for strategic superiority with the aim of delivering 'first strike', understood 'first strike' in the Western sense of a unilateral damage-limiting attack in all-out nuclear war. In effect the Soviets accepted mutually assured destruction. 'Then as now,' wrote Gennadiy Gerasimov, the most charismatic presenter of late-Soviet ideas to the West, in 1983, 'both sides in the nuclear confrontation possessed an assured capability ... to inflict "unacceptable damage" on the attacking party as long as the situation for "mutually assured destruction" exists.' Higher-level Soviet statements were less eirenic in defining deterrence. They continued to reject mutual deterrence on the grounds that only the West needed to be deterred.

The danger of war was a very politically contentious issue. If conflict was imminent the economy needed to be put on a war footing and intransigent policies adopted to deter and avoid conceding anything to the enemy. If war was not imminent mobilisation would actually increase the risk by raising international tensions and damaging the economy. Such a move might even damage the party's grip on power.[62] Even the military was divided on which approach to take. General Yepishev, Chief of the MPD, and General Zaytsev, commander of Soviet forces in Germany, warned that the threat had increased drastically, whereas General Kulikov, the commander-in-chief of the Warsaw Pact, claimed that the situation 'should not be dramatised'. Marshal Ustinov said that 'the storm clouds of a new war are gathering over the world', whereas Foreign Minister Gromyko merely saw the international situation as 'seriously complicated'. Ogarkov openly clashed with Gromyko in 1983. Gromyko defended *détente*, listed the agreements of the 1970s and claimed that Lenin's policy in the 1920s of differentiating between imperialist powers had been, and by implication would continue to be, successful. Ogarkov pointed out that Lenin's disarmament policies had come to nothing. During his brief tenure as General-Secretary, Yuriy Andropov seemed to stress the problems of miscalculation with modern strategic systems and warned: 'we will be compelled to counter the challenge of the American side by deploying corresponding weapon systems of our own, an analogous missile to counter the MX missile, and our own long-range cruise missile, which we are already testing, to counter the US long-range cruise missile'.[63] The dispute was seemingly resolved in April 1984 when Andropov's successor, Konstantin Chernenko, announced that the danger of war was not serious enough to justify the extension of the five-day week to a six-day working week. Ogarkov was relieved of his post and it was announced that, although additional resources were needed for security, social programmes announced in 1981 would not be curtailed. Ogarkov was forced to recant his views in a November 1984 article which highlighted the possibility of eliminating war as a social phenomenon: 'new circumstances', he wrote (presumably with gritted teeth), were 'objectively already creating conditions and possibilities for eliminating world wars from the life of societies'. While the threat of war remained 'already it could be neutralised' and there was the 'absence of the fatal inevitability of war'.

The resolution of the likelihood-of-war debate certainly did not, however, mean that traditional Soviet ideas about the pre-eminence of military power were abandoned during the Andropov–Chernenko interregnum. In 1981 and 1982 Marshals Ogarkov and Ustinov had pushed the need to increase the combat readiness of armed forces as well as enhanced defence mobilisation. As a result of their advocacy all-arms TVDs were created to increase operational readiness. Ogarkov became commander of the vital new western TVD in 1984.[64]

It is notable that although some aspects of Soviet thought about the role of military power changed in the decade 1974 to 1984, practical policies underwent little change. Soviet analysts could, and did, differentiate between the policies followed by the Nixon, Ford, Carter and Reagan presidencies and were more comfortable with some than others, but this changing 'comfort level' did little to alter fundamentally their views on military security. Reagan's announcement of his Strategic Defence Initiative in March 1983 certainly increased tensions between the United States, Western Europe and the Soviet Union, but the Soviet attitude to SDI was in many ways similar to their thinking on the development and deployment of SS-20 medium-range ballistic missiles.

The decision to develop the SS-20 missile was taken in November 1974, at the height of *détente*, in the same month as the Vladivostok summit meeting between Gerald Ford and Leonid Brezhnev.[65] The decision attracted support both from the Foreign Ministry under Andrey Gromyko and the military who were very unhappy with Brezhnev's decision to withdraw demands for compensation for American 'forward-based systems' in order to sign agreements at Vladivostok. 'Brezhnev had to spill political blood to get the Vladivostok accords', according to Deputy Minister of Foreign Affairs Georgiy Korniyenko. At one level the SS-20 was seen as a bargaining counter to lever American nuclear systems out of Europe and create dissension within NATO but, more fundamentally, it was seen as having a military value in its own right. Soviet actions suggest the hair-trigger on which they operated. Major-General Viktor Starodubov recalled in 1981 that 'within a few years, the Soviet Union would have been facing NATO naked had it not modernised its medium-range nuclear weapons'. Even if the development of the SS-20 was a reaction to possible American developments, as Colonel-General Nikolay Chervov, head of the Disarmament and Security Affairs Department of the General Staff, claimed in 1981, these developments were at an early stage in November 1974: the possible development of Pershing II was only announced in June 1975 and the USAF were given the go-ahead to develop an operational GLCM in January 1977.

This fear of being rendered 'naked' was a recurrent factor in Soviet planning. In 1982, for instance, Konstantin Feoktistov, the leading designer of *Vostok* and *Soyuz* spacecraft, warned that if systemic timidity was not overcome it was possible for the USSR to lose the race to develop new technologies.[66] Thus, even though a special commission under Vitaliy Shabanov, the deputy Minister of Armaments, had rejected the creation of a space-based BMD system being pressed on Brezhnev by the designer Chelomey in the late 1970s, SDI was still seen as a systemic challenge.[67] If the Americans could create a radical new type of technology it would be a major setback for the regime at home and abroad. The possibility of such success undermined claims that the centrally planned economy could equal other military powers with fewer resources. The criticism levelled at SDI in the West was regarded as little consolation, even if the US could not devise a 100 per cent effective BMD.[68] Ogarkov and his allies may have been partially discredited, but 'more is better' was still the Soviet élite's consensus until the mid-1980s.

Even in the early 1970s, when the Soviets were convinced that the correlation of forces was moving in their direction, there had been a clear awareness that a growth strategy based on extensive material inputs was not feasible. The growth of the labour force was slowing whilst easily accessible natural resources in European Russia were rapidly being exhausted. According to Soviet statistics, the USSR's national income had doubled between 1965 and 1980. This contrasted with an overall growth in national income by a factor of 14 between the 1940s and 1980s. Growth rates seemed to be slowing rapidly from 10 per cent in the 1950s, 7 per cent in the 1960s and less than 5 per cent in the 1970s to 3 per cent in the early 1980s. This dramatic slowdown resulted in the gap between the size of the Soviet and the US economies widening. Whereas the Soviet economy had been 54 per cent of the American economy in 1970 and had grown to 58 per cent in 1975, by 1980 it had shrunk to 53 per cent. Performance in the agricultural sector was very poor. Between 1960 and 1982 the growth rate from agriculture was only 1.9 per cent, lower than the overall performance for a total economy which was itself slowing down. Between 1972 and 1982 six harvests – 1972, 1975 and each harvest between 1979 and 1982 – fell short of domestic needs. The productivity of farm workers was falling both in absolute terms and relative to the US. By 1981 whilst one Soviet farm worker could feed eight people, one American farm worker could feed 65. In turn there was a slowdown in living standards. Growth in per capita consumption only rose by 2.4 per cent in 1976–80 and a mere 0.2 per cent in 1981–2.[69] In July 1979 a major government and party decree on planning was promulgated as the first major attempt to grapple with the structural problems of the economy since the mid-1960s. Five-year plans put emphasis on intensive inputs. Under the 11th plan (1981–5), for instance, the increased productivity of labour was supposed to account for 90 per cent of the growth of national income.

Intensive inputs presented a severe problem for the Soviet economy however. The Soviet Union's profile looked like that of a developing country. The US and Japan generated five times the overseas trade per head of population. For a modern state to have a large domestic rather than a large international market was not necessarily economically disastrous. Soviet overseas trade had grown quickly in the Cold War period. In 1981 it was over 13 times the 1950 level but as a proportion of GNP it was small: 5.2 per cent in 1980. Much more damaging was the nature of the Soviet Union's trade. Over half its exports were raw materials, whereas there was a continual need for the import of technology. In 1981 the Soviet Union imported $6.7 billion worth of Western machinery, compared with $106 million in 1950. In some areas Western imports were dominant. Western equipment produced between 66 per cent and 100 per cent of polyethylene, polyester and acrylic, 40 per cent of nitrogenous fertiliser and 65 per cent of complex fertiliser in 1981. In the early 1970s consensus had developed on the need to expand and diversify foreign economic activity. Foreign economic ties were regarded as a stimulus to the economy which, through the benefits of the 'scientific-technological revolution', could change productivity and growth. Initially, the Soviet leadership believed that this process could take place without giving the West economic leverage and making the Soviet economy more technologically dependent. Indeed some Soviet leaders believed that Europe and Japan were vulnerable to Soviet pressure because of their high dependence on energy supplies. Others saw long-term benefits and wanted links isolated from political turmoil. According to this view, since the decisive struggle with the West would be economic, it would be perverse to withdraw the Soviet Union from the world economy and thus lose out on technical advance. Yet there was a major constraint on trade in the 1970s: the inability of the USSR to finance it. Serious and chronic balance of payments deficits were exacerbated by a rising hard currency deficit because of loans from Western banks. From 1976 imports of machinery and equipment began to be sharply reduced. The tenth five-year plan (1976–80) was equivocal about technology transfer. The plan introduced major delays in the projected production of versions of Western European trucks and cars, the development of power-consuming industries in East Siberia, the development of agrobusiness complexes to modernise the feed grain and livestock industries, the development of transmission facilities to bring power from Siberia to European Russia, the development of the Kursk metallurgical project and a computer-assisted national economic reporting system. In addition to these practical limitations to the integration of the Soviet Union into the world economy there was fear of dependence in technology and grain.[70] This fear grew steadily in the 1970s. The tenth five-year plan reflected a debate within the leadership about the priorities of modernisation and links with Europe. Enthusiasm was cooled by failures in cars and computers. By the early 1980s the only high-priority projects tied to Western aid were natural gas pipelines and the Baikal–Amur railway.[71]

Western technology, however, remained critical for Soviet industry, especially the defence industry, and a well-organised programme of legal and illegal means existed to acquire it. Between 1972 and 1982 this programme acquired important technology in computers, radar, inertial guidance, lasers, metallurgy, machine tools, integrated circuits, robotics, superplastics, electronics and silicon. The design and production of the microelectronics industry was entirely Western. Soviet mainframe computers were derived from IBM models produced between 1965 and 1975. The most widely used Soviet microprocessor was a direct copy of an Intel product marketed in the early 1970s. Soviet 'personal computers' were direct copies of Western products.[72] Tighter Western export controls in the early 1980s were matched by 'Programma 100' designed to replace 100 products denied by the embargo. According to the Soviets the programme was a complete success: it took three years to replace the loss, largely through espionage. Yet the need for such a programme merely demonstrated the extent of Soviet dependence. In the early 1980s French intelligence obtained Soviet Military–Industrial Commission documents which showed the importance of illegally obtained technology for weapons production. In 1979–80 the KGB was working on about 3000 acquisition tasks. Many Soviet projects benefited: phased array radar, computerised aircraft weapons control systems, the manufacture of fibreglass air tanks for submarines. The Soviet Union 'saved some five years of development time' on its own fighters by using documentation on the F-18 fighter-bomber: 'moreover, F-18 and F-14 documentation served as the impetus for two long-term research projects to design from scratch a new radar-guided air-to-air missile system'.

Although these activities were no doubt gratifying for the Soviet intelligence services they, in fact, demonstrated the fragility of the Soviet economy and the failure to establish a 'socialist' economy. Expedients such as espionage illustrated the growing problem of the gap between military technology *per se*, which could be produced by crash programmes, and military–industrial technology which allowed the consistent production of advanced weapons and needed systemic backing. There were some attempts to provide these systems. The tenth five-year plan (1976–80) gave priority to computer-aided manufacture and the eleventh plan (1981–5) gave computed-aided design high priority. By 1984, however, Aleksandr Yakovlev, who had recently returned from the embassy in Canada to head the prestigious Institute of World Economy and International Relations (IMEMO), was moved to admit that Soviet global economic power had become gravely deficient in the face of the 'scale and might' of the US, Western Europe and Japan. These three centres of world economic power had 'no analogue in history' and were 'substantial components of world influence, and not only in the system of imperialism but also in international relations as a whole'.[73] At the 26th Congress of the CPSU in 1981 Brezhnev was still trumpeting the view that 'the decisive sector of the competition with capitalism is the economy and economic policy' and the superiority of the command economy over a capitalist society ridden with 'unemployment and inflation, crises and recessions'. Yet there was a growing acknowledgement of serious economic problems.

The Soviet Union's politico-economic problem was brought home to the leadership by a crisis in Poland. In Eastern Europe the Soviets faced a challenge which was much more severe than the Czech crisis of 1968. An economic slump in Poland gave birth to the trade union movement, Solidarity. In August 1980, under the terms of the Gdansk accords, the Polish communist government recognised the union's right to exist. The Soviet leadership was displeased with this recognition but, initially, believed the situation could be contained. The Politburo told the leaders of the Polish Communist Party that the accord, 'exacts a high price for the "regulation" it achieves. ... The agreement in essence, signifies the legalisation of the anti-socialist opposition ... the compromise that has been achieved will be only temporary in nature.' The Soviets ordered the Poles to reorganise 'their party, their trade union organisation and their mass media propaganda to defeat Solidarity'. By April 1981, however, the Politburo concluded: 'Solidarity has been transformed into an organised political force, which is able to paralyse the activity of the party and state organs and take *de facto* power into its own hands. If the opposition has not yet done that, then it is primarily because of its fear that Soviet troops would be introduced and because of its hopes that it can achieve its aims without bloodshed and by means of a creeping counter-revolution.' Although Polish leaders were regarded as weak reeds, 'led to panic-ridden fear of confronting Solidarity and a deep-rooted anxiety that Soviet troops will be sent in', the decision was taken to back a centrist military–party group around General Wojtech Jaruzelski. At the same time, 'as a deterrent to counter-revolution, [the Soviet Union would] maximally exploit the fears of the internal reactionaries and international imperialism that the Soviet Union might send its troops into Poland'. Whilst preparing for military intervention the Soviets encouraged Jaruzelski to declare martial law rather than seek compromise with Solidarity and the church. The Soviet leadership demanded that the Polish communists should sort out their own problems because they feared the economic and political consequences of Soviet intervention.

In a meeting of the Politburo just before martial law was declared in Poland, Yuriy Andropov denounced the economic burden Poland was placing on the USSR. The latest demand was for 350 items, including two million tons of grain, 25 000 tons of meat and 625 000 tons of iron, worth 1.4 billion roubles. In a statement which was endorsed by the rest of the Politburo he said: 'We don't intend to introduce troops into Poland. We can't risk such a step . . . I don't know how things will turn out in Poland, but even if Poland falls under the control of Solidarity that's the way it will be. And if the capitalist countries pounce on the Soviet Union, and you know they have already reached agreement on a variety of economic and political sanctions, that will be very burdensome for us. We must be concerned above all with our own country and the strengthening of the Soviet Union.'[74] After martial law was declared in November 1981 the Politburo recognised that although the 'counter-revolution is crushed . . . the tasks ahead are more complicated. . . . All of us clearly understand that the decisive precondition for the full stabilisation of things in Poland is a revival of the economy. In Czechoslovakia after 1968 political efforts made headway precisely because the counter-revolution had not affected the economic sphere. In Poland just the opposite is true.'

Despite Andropov's call to concentrate on the relationship between the Soviet economy and military power, discussion of the defence burden was rare in Soviet literature before the Gorbachev era. In 1981 Brezhnev commented that 'we do not support the arms race: we oppose it. We could find a totally different use for the funds it swallows up.' In 1980 and 1981 he called for superpower restraint in the development of 'qualitatively new' weapons and demanded that military R&D should make a much greater contribution to the civilian economy. The investment debate came to a head when Brezhnev was present at a plenum of the Central Committee in May 1982. The Politburo agreed on a programme 'to guarantee food products for the population of the country in the shortest possible time'. Brezhnev advisers tried to whip up support by putting the issue in terms of the Soviet Union's dependence on hostile powers for supplies of grain. Defence should be maintained at a 'necessary level' but the 'struggle for international *détente* – both political and military *détente* – [would continue as] we are well aware of something else: the successful fulfilment of our plans for agriculture is an important precondition for strengthening peace'.[75] At the end of the Brezhnev era there was some kind of rhetorical commitment to 'butter before guns'. Yet the practical consequences of this rhetoric were far from clear. Just before his death Brezhnev met with the military leadership and acknowledged a need to accelerate military R&D.

In Yuriy Andropov's first speech as General-Secretary to a plenary meeting of Central Committee on 22 November 1982 he said: 'there are many problems in the economy, and I certainly have no ready recipes to solve them'. Andropov noted that 'the principal indicator of the economy's effectiveness – labour productivity – is growing at a rate which cannot satisfy us'. He restated that 'the party is guided by Lenin's far-sighted injunction that we exercise our main influence on the world revolutionary process through our economic policy' but changed the dictum's meaning. Now 'the improvement of the welfare of the [Soviet] people ... was our internationalist duty'.[76] 'It is easy to see', he noted in January 1983, 'that the greater the successes, the stronger our economy, the better the state of affairs in our national economy, the stronger will be our international position.' Andropov's successor, Konstantin Chernenko, stated baldly in February 1984 that 'the system of economic management, the whole of our economic machinery needs to be seriously restructured'.

Yet the Soviet leadership did not believe that the economic crisis they faced was of such severity that the highly centralised economic planning system should be abandoned. Chernenko acknowledged need for innovative solutions but came forward with no specific proposals for economic reform. Indeed the highest leadership had little real grasp of the economic disaster over which they were presiding. The Brezhnev Politburo had not been aware of the ramifications of the technical gap in such areas as computers.[77] Realisation dawned very slowly. Decades of distorted data were hard to break down. It was only in 1983 that a prominent group of economists in the Siberian branch of the Academy of Sciences leaked a report citing the underlying cause of economic malaise as: 'the outdated nature of the system of industrial organisation and economic management or simply the inability of the system to insure complete and efficient utilisation of the workers and of the intellectual potential of the society'. The aircraft designer Oleg Antonov observed in the same year that: 'an enterprise does not get much from improving the quality of its product ... no bonuses can make an enterprise care about quality if this leads to non-fulfilment of the plan in quantitative terms. Because ... the plan is made up of quantitative indices: tons, metres, units, roubles, etc.'[78]

The End of the Chinese Cold War

By the mid-1970s the Chinese seemed to be committed once more to vigorous action on the international stage. They claimed that the intervention of the Middle Kingdom would have a decisive impact on the Cold War. Despite these lofty rhetorical ambitions, however, foreign policy remained subordinate to domestic factional politics. Indeed foreign policy was often a vehicle for the internecine struggles which marked Mao's last years and which were carried on, after his death in 1976, until the emergence of Deng as supreme leader in the late 1970s. Although Deng was aware of the advantages which accrued to China from cooperation with other powers, particularly in the West, his focus too was domestic. Deng's Cold War policies were flexible since his aim was to reconstruct China as a dominant Asian power which could re-integrate the lost lands of Taiwan and Hong Kong. Even these long-term goals took second place to the realisation that the roots of power were economic and that the economic base must have first priority. In the late 1970s a strange situation emerged in which the other powers treated with China on the basis of its rhetoric and its potential power rather than on its actual actions in the international arena.

By 1974 Mao had decided that an international process of 'great upheaval, great division and great reorganisation' had ended with the formation of a coherent new pattern. China's place within this new system was clear. 'China belongs to the third world', Mao declared in February 1974, 'for China cannot compare with the rich or powerful countries politically, economically, etc. She can only be grouped with the relatively poor countries.' At the Tenth Party Congress held in August 1973 he argued for the need for a gradual *rapproche-ment* with the United States, a power 'on the decline', with whom it was necessary to make 'necessary compromises' against the expansionist Soviet Union. China should be 'fully prepared against any war of aggression that US imperialism may launch' but the main threat was 'surprise attack on our country by Soviet revisionist social imperialism'. In 1975, after the fall of Saigon, the *People's Daily* announced that 'the Soviet social imperialists ... are leaving no stone unturned in their efforts to replace US imperialists at a time when the latter are becoming increasingly vulnerable and strategically passive'. In July 1975 Deng cautioned South East Asian leaders to 'beware of the tiger coming from the back door while pushing out the wolf from the front door' and explicitly warned the Thai premier of Soviet designs on South Vietnam and its bases.

Nevertheless Zhou Enlai had discounted any immediate military danger, as opposed to the long-term danger of Soviet hegemony.[79] Zhou had been opposed, however, at the Party Congress by Hang Hongwen, then party vice-chairman but later a member of the 'Gang of Four'. Hang argued that the threat was the same from the two superpowers and that in order to meet that threat China should seek alliance with revolutionary peoples rather than non-communist states. The 'Gang of Four' were able to mount substantial opposition to Zhou and Deng's policy at the Fourth National People's Congress in January 1975 and at a high-level foreign-affairs conference in March of the same year. Their substantial control of the press enabled them to suppress the ideas of Zhou and his supporters in the public domain.[80]

The 'Gang of Four' and their supporters were not pro-Soviet. They called for more resources to be devoted to defence, increased weapons manufacture and more activity on the border. In 1974 it was Zhou's supporters who were the advocates of flexibility: the Soviet Union should be 'despised strategically' but 'respected tactically' and the best way of deterring aggression, they argued, was limited *détente*. In June 1973 the Soviet government made overtures on border relations. Zhou replied publicly in October 1973 that he and Kosygin had agreed in September 1969 that the two countries would accept existing lines of control, avoid clashes and withdraw their forces from all disputed areas on the border. Zhou's statement was, however, not reported by the Chinese media for a year. It was only in October 1974 that a Chinese message from the Standing Committee of the National People's Congress called for a non-aggression treaty based on the 1969 agreement. Some conciliatory gestures were made: for instance Soviet aircrew captured in March 1974 were released in December 1975. At the end of Mao's life Chinese foreign policy was poised between extreme hostility to both the United States and the Soviet Union or tactical conciliation of both the United States and the Soviet Union with a view to negating a Soviet threat. In the last year of his life Mao veered towards Jiang Qing and her supporters, but upon his death in September 1976 they were overthrown by a coup led by the PLA's senior active marshal, Ye Jianying.

Between September 1976 and November 1978 there was an interregnum whilst Mao's chosen successor, Hua Guofeng, was eased out of power by Deng and his supporters. Once this had been achieved, Deng had the opportunity to return to the consideration of China's foreign-policy orientation. The Chinese leadership under Deng had a much less overtly theoretical view of the world than it had under Mao. Indeed it made a number of quite brutal assumptions about international politics which enabled it to decide on an aggressive regional policy. Deng assumed that both the United States and the USSR operated on a global basis and that there was a global balance of power with inbuilt checks and balances. He identified significant weaknesses in both superpowers which could be exploited by China, especially as China was not in the 'front line' of any potential conflicts. China could act positively on a number of long-standing issues with little fear of retribution. The Vietnamese could be brought to heel by armed force, Taiwan could be emasculated as American support for its defence wavered, and Britain could be bullied over the reversion of Hong Kong.

In December 1978 Sino-American relations were normalised and full diplomatic relations began on 1 January 1979. 'We have', claimed the Chinese side, 'managed to win over the United States and have successfully prevented the backstairs deal between the two superpowers to divide the world between them.' In a secret speech in January 1979 Geng Biao, a Politburo member and the secretary-general of Military Affairs Commission, said that the normalisation of relations had 'completely changed the balance of power in the world'. China had scored a massive diplomatic success matched by trade and technology agreements. These were 'severe blows' to the Russians. Geng expected the Soviets 'to stand in the way and interpose obstacles' and make China the 'immediate target' through Vietnam. Vietnam had attacked the Khymer Rouge government in Cambodia in December 1978, capturing Phnom Penh on 7 January and establishing a client regime. In February 1979 China had attacked Vietnam in return, only to be bloodily repulsed. In June 1979 Vietnam joined the COMECON and in November signed a treaty with the USSR. The immediate Chinese reaction was to identify a 'plot' by the 'Soviet superpower with its own hegemonic aims'.

Geng Biao had identified the United States as the 'secondary enemy'. Since 'American imperialism [was] in essence a paper tiger and not a sheet of iron ... it [was] easy to win [the United States] over to our side'. The Americans lacked a 'magnificent goal of political strategy' but were very rich and 'advanced in science and technology, modern weapons and economic resources'. Geng argued for a 'joining of the two forces together'. Chinese policy was to seek an alliance in all but name with the United States. This alliance had a twofold purpose. The Americans would hold down the Soviet Union so that it could not turn on China. At the same time American resources could be used to build up Chinese power. Three years previously Geng had argued that the Americans should be discarded as soon as they had fulfilled their role. The United States was an ally of convenience to be exploited if its leaders were stupid enough to let it be so.[81]

In the USA there was an increasing tendency to envisage a US–China–Soviet strategic relationship in which the United States and China acted as informal allies against the Soviet Union. This was a departure from the policy enunciated under the Ford administration and adhered to by the State Department under Carter. In April 1976 Winston Lord, the head of the State Department's Policy Planning Staff and a close Kissinger aide, had argued that:

> in a triangular relationship it is undeniably advantageous for us to have better relations with each of the two actors than they have with one another ... Our interests compel us to pursue our well-established policies of seeking improved relations with both the USSR and China. Both courses are essential for maintaining a global equilibrium and shaping a more peaceful and positive international structure ... We will make it clear that we are not colluding with, or accommodating, one at the expense of the other.[82]

Yet even in the mid-1970s there was considerable interest in the government in seeking a much closer relationship, 'colluding' with the Chinese through such measures as selling American arms to the PRC, cooperating in anti-Soviet intelligence-gathering and even offering to deploy American troops on Chinese soil in the event of a Sino-Soviet military conflict.[83] Cyrus Vance and Carter initially backed the existing line that: 'the most significant responsibility we have is to balance our new friendship with the PRC and our continued improvement in relations with the Soviet Union ... As we move toward a most-favoured-nation relationship with the PRC, we must face the need to do the

same thing with the Soviet Union.' Once again, however, Zbigniew Brzezinski
proved an effective advocate for an alternative policy. He visited China in May
1978, promising not only that the United States was willing to abandon
Taiwan, by abrogating the US–Taiwanese defence treaty, withdrawing American troops and breaking off diplomatic relations, but that the PRC would be
given American blessing to buy arms from Europe. Full diplomatic relations
between the United States and China were cemented when Deng Xiaoping
visited Washington in January 1979. During this visit the United States was
informed of, and gave tacit approval to, China's intention of waging war with
Vietnam over the issue of Cambodia.[84] China's action was seen as a strike at the
Soviet Union, since Brzezinski had characterised the existing conflict between
Vietnam and Cambodia as 'very interesting, primarily as the first case of a proxy
war between China and the Soviet Union'.[85] The United States and China also
agreed to share intelligence on the Soviet Union, to the extent of allowing
American intelligence facilities to be established in the PRC.

The momentum these exchanges created did not stop at this level of
cooperation. In May 1979 a Department of Defense report argued that it was in
America's strategic interest to bolster Chinese military strength so that it would
be effective in any war with the Soviet Union. Although senior State Department figures counselled caution, America moved in exactly that direction. In
January 1980 Harold Brown opened discussions on 'actions in the field of
defence as well as diplomacy' and by September 1980 twenty licences had been
issued in the US for the export of military support equipment 'falling under the
general categories of air defence radars, transport helicopters, instrumentation
for testing jet engines, communications systems, computing equipment, and
integrated circuits'. Defense Department research found 'that development of
Sino-US security ties had a profound psychological impact on the Soviet
leadership'. This sense of Soviet uncertainty was welcomed but the CIA also
pointed out that China would not really be a major military power in the 1980s.
There was also a growing awareness that there was no real synergy between
Chinese and American strategic interests: China had achieved its own security
aims and was now free to play off the Soviet Union against the United
States.[86]

The Reagan administration was split between those who wished to maintain
the 'strategic triangle' and those who were concerned about China's threat to
Taiwan. Reagan himself was a visceral Sinophobe. The Sino-Soviet split, he
remarked in 1980, was 'an argument over how best to destroy us ... [not]
because of any apparent difference in their belief in Communism or Communism's mission to conquer the world'.[87] In 1981–2, however, both the
Department of State, under Alexander Haig, and Weinberger's Defense
Department believed that an informal alliance with the PRC could be part of
America's coercive diplomacy. In the summer of 1981 the United States
decided it would sell 'lethal weapons' to China, including ground-to-air

missiles, anti-tank weapons and radar, and assist in Chinese defence research.[88] In 1982 the Department of Defense announced: 'Encouragement and, if possible, logistic support will be provided to Chinese military initiatives that would fix Soviet ground, air and naval forces in the USSR's Far Eastern territories' and China was dropped from nuclear targeting plans.[89] This help continued throughout the 1980s. In 1985, for instance, the United States initiated the 'Peace Pearl' programme to upgrade the PLAAF's new F-8 II interceptor.[90] Yet by the summer of 1982 the new Secretary of State, George Shultz, had downgraded Sino-US relations. He argued that 'when the geo-strategic importance of China became the conceptual prism through which Sino-American relations were viewed, it was almost inevitable that American policy-makers became overly solicitous of Chinese interests, concerns and sensitivities'.[91] Shultz preferred not to view China as a global power – what Weinberger had described as 'a potentially decisive factor in the global balance of power' – but as a regional Asian power second in importance for America to Japan and with whom 'frustrations and problems . . . will arise not only out of differences concerning Taiwan but out of differences between our two sys tems'. Accordingly, the reduction of arms sales to Taiwan was to be slowed down. Nevertheless, in May 1983 America agreed to keep liberalising its technology export regime to the PRC.[92] In addition, the relationship with China remained important in a negative sense: increased tensions with the Soviet Union were not compounded by the virulent Sinophobia central to American policy making between 1949 and 1972.

The inauguration of full diplomatic relations was, however, the peak of Chinese amity towards the United States. Within the year Deng was suggesting that there was no real need to be fearful of the Soviet Union. In November 1979 he argued that although the Soviet-Vietnamese alliance was indeed aimed at China it also had other targets. Soviet foreign policy had to be viewed in its overall Cold War context rather than in terms of bilateral Sino-Soviet relations. The firm belief that the Soviet Union had much wider goals than aggrandise-ment against China freed Chinese hands to act against Vietnam. If China had been the main target of Soviet ambitions and had not been part of a global balance of power, war against Vietnam would have been little more than the springing of a deadly trap. In late 1980 and early 1981 articles in the *People's Daily* and *Red Flag* showed there was a faction, possibly in the PLA, who objected to the political strategy of leaning to the West and the slow pace of military modernisation. It advocated temporary compromises with the Soviet Union in order to move ahead with industrialisation, allow hostility to the United States and prepare to take Taiwan by force.[93] In July the reformist Hu Yaobang asserted that the Soviet Union looked threatening but was 'in reality . . . very feeble'. Yet a highly publicised commentary, published in December 1981, concluded that the Soviet Union was not in decline. According to the commentary Soviet economic and military strength was as great as ever and it was better placed to use it than the United States. The Soviet Union's imperial burden, it was argued, was much less than the United States' had been in Vietnam.[94] In 1981 Peking suggested the resumption of border talks and in April 1982 agreed to recommence border trade. It also stopped using the gratuitously insulting term 'revisionist' to describe the Soviet leadership.

According to Soviet political leaders the international situation was tense and the strategic environment was deteriorating in the early 1980s. NATO Europe, Japan and China were highly suspicious of or actively hostile to the Soviet Union. The correlation of forces was moving against the Soviet Union as the United States sought to build a 'global military coalition' against it. On a global scale the Soviets worried about the threat of Japan, its possible 'integration with the NATO bloc' and the emergence of a US–Japan–Korea military alliance. The Soviet military feared that the US would deploy Pershing II and cruise missiles and nuclear-capable F-16s in Japan which had its own 'militarist tendencies'. The ensuing military programmes backed by Japan's economic strength would be a 'long-term' threat to the Soviet Union. At the same time, fear of a Sino-American military and intelligence relationship had an impact on security thinking. In 1981 Marshal Ogarkov claimed that 'the broadening of military–political links of the USA with China and with Japan which is going in the direction of militarisation creates a long-term military threat to our eastern frontiers'.[95] As a response the Soviets sought to neutralise Chinese participation in an anti-Soviet coalition. In March 1982 a Brezhnev speech in Tashkent identified China as a socialist country for the first time since the early 1960s and indicated a willingness to discuss confidence-building measures on the borders. In September 1982 Hu Yaobang affirmed that improvement was possible. In October talks at deputy-foreign-minister level were initiated and became biannual events. In December 1984 a Soviet deputy prime minister was sent to Peking to negotiate various bilateral agreements, thus reinstating diplomatic relations at a senior level.

The Chinese did not believe that the Americans were capable of rolling back Soviet power. An America in a 'passive position' could be manipulated. A simple joint interest in opposing the Soviet Union was not the basis for amicable relations. In the words of an authoritative article: 'if some people still believe that Sino-US relations can only be based on opposition to other countries' hegemonic acts, then this is a retreat. If they believe that China will agree to this retreat, then this is a dream.' In June 1981 the Chinese Foreign Minister Huang Hua issued an ultimatum to Alexander Haig to halt all American arms sales to Taiwan or face a 'rupture' of relations with China. In August 1982 America agreed to gradually reduce arms sales to Taiwan and not to exceed the existing technological level of arms supplies in return for a Chinese commitment to 'peaceful unification'. During the next year, however, the Chinese came to reassess the nature of the relationship between the United States and the Soviet Union. From the middle of 1983 onwards analysts began to agree that the Reagan administration had 'resolutely taken a number of steps to destroy the nuclear strategic balance' by announcing SDI, getting public commitments from West Germany, Britain and Italy to deploy Pershing II and GLCMs, and securing funding for the MX ICBM and the B-1 bomber. The American economy was booming and the Vietnam/Watergate syndrome was fading. At the same time the Soviet economy was 'deteriorating daily' whilst the entrenchment of conservative power in the bureaucracy impeded Andropov's attempted reforms. The Soviet Union was finding the 'burden of strategic competition and foreign expansion' too heavy and thus needed a 'breathing space' to carry out domestic reconstruction. Chinese analysts believed American resurgence made the role of China as a check on the Soviet Union less important. As a result the United States would no longer see China as part of a global Cold War but as an Asian regional power. China's freedom of action would, therefore, be much more limited as it could no longer set its global importance against its regional awkwardness.[96]

In effect China downgraded the concept of the Cold War in its foreign relations. If the Soviet Union was no longer a direct threat to the ruling élite, or to China as a whole, then there was no need to regard the United States as one pole of a delicately poised triangle. Instead, China could deal with the United States (and indeed Japan) on a bilateral basis as an Asian regional power and the hub of a high-technology trading system. Relations would oscillate as China pursued its own goals but this was no longer necessarily a function of the Cold War. This is not to say that the Deng leadership abandoned the Cold War: it merely lessened its foreign-policy priority. The USSR–PRC–USA Cold War triangle was still, potentially, the most important consideration for the Chinese leadership. It made medium-term calculations: the power of the Soviet Union had been curbed and presented no immediate threat. There was no indication that the Chinese regarded its collapse as imminent. These calculations meant that the PRC played little part in the 'end game' of the Cold War despite its earlier role in shaping its course.

THE GERMAN QUESTION

If the Far East lessened in importance, the situation in Europe remained central. Soviet leaders believed that they could dominate political processes in Western Europe by playing on Europeans' fears about the proximity of Soviet military power and their extreme vulnerability to nuclear strike which 'for the majority of countries in West Europe', Marshal Ustinov warned in 1983, 'could be the last'. In 1980 Boris Ponomarev, the head of the Central Committee International Department, outlined a strategy which required: 'raising the struggle for peace to a new level ... what is needed are not anonymous and abstract condemnations of war and of the arms race but urgent and energetic demands ... It is necessary to turn the growing alarm of hundreds of millions of people into practical deeds, into mass purposeful, agreed action'. In 1977–8 there had been considerable opposition in Western Europe to the Carter administration's proposed deployment of 'neutron bombs' – weapons which were perceived as killing people whilst preserving property. The US government withdrew its proposal to deploy the weapons and this was seen as the model for 'mass action' against future US nuclear deployment. According to Vitaliy Shaposhnikov, the Central Committee official in charge of the World Peace Council, 'in its dimensions, social structure and methods the anti-war movement has gone far beyond its former limits . . . The anti-war movement is becoming an increasingly important factor in international life . . . now this movement is so white-hot that it is increasingly becoming a real obstacle to the attainment of the plans of the North Atlantic bloc'.[97]

The key country in Europe remained Germany. By 1973 Willy Brandt had revolutionised Germany's position as a factor in the Cold War. Brandt had carved out an independent role for the Federal Republic. This independence was a source of strength. The West German government could deal with the Soviet Union and the GDR directly in pursuit of specifically German goals. Although the position of the United States remained a key consideration in these dealings, German diplomacy had a relatively wide latitude for the future. *Ostpolitik* also, however, made Germany more vulnerable. Between the late 1950s and the late 1960s it had so obviously been tied into the Western bloc through NATO and the European Community that it was hard to imagine any circumstances in which the FRG could be isolated or destabilised. If Egon Bahr's radical prescription for the effective demilitarisation of central Europe had ever been implemented, German policy could have completely changed the structure of the Cold War in the 1970s. In May 1974, however, Bahr's patron Brandt fell from power and was replaced by a senior member of his own party, Helmut Schmidt. Although Schmidt had been an important member of the SPD–FDP government formed in 1969, his own conception of international politics differed greatly from that of Brandt. Schmidt saw German foreign policy in both a European and a global context. In both he sought the stabilisation of international politics and the creation of an enduring balance of power.[98] In other words the Soviet Union, the USA, the FRG and the GDR would remain, at least until the end of the century, in their existing equilibrium. In 1978 Brezhnev visited Bonn and exchanged assurances that such long-term stability was desirable for both parties. Brezhnev declared that 'the role of the FRG as a state which pursues a distinct and independent policy had begun when the door had been opened to a *rapprochement* with the Soviet Union and the other socialist states'. Schmidt replied that: 'the General-Secretary was right when he said that the international weight of the Federal Republic had grown since the Moscow Treaty. This weight had been used to further *détente* [with the communist states of Eastern Europe] . . . and naturally German-Soviet relations stood at the centre of *Ostpolitik*. This would be so for the next 30 years.' In order to ensure that such trust endured 'into the third millennium' the two states signed a 25-year economic cooperation agreement.

Although the GDR leadership was less magnanimous in its rhetoric, it too wanted stabilisation. In domestic terms this manifested itself in the policy of 'delimitation': the intensification of internal propaganda to convince the GDR's population that despite the mutual recognition by the two German states there was no possibility that their political systems would converge or that reunification would ever take place.[99] In actual policy terms the Honecker regime sought a steady flow of West German subsidy in return for 'humanitarian' concessions on intra-German relations. In 1975 the SED leader Hermann Axen acknowledged in the party newspaper that 'compromises' on the part of socialist states were a necessary element of peaceful coexistence. In 1974 the Soviet Union informed its COMECON partners that the price of Soviet oil would double in the next year and in future would be priced in line with inflated world market prices. Since the GDR received 90 per cent of its oil from the Soviet Union, its dependence on aid from the FRG was increased. By 1976–7 the GDR had run up a net debt of $3.5 billion with the West, had an annual trade deficit with Western countries of about DM4 billion and had received about DM7.5 billion in payments from the FRG over the previous seven years. By 1979 private gifts of hard currency from FRG to GDR citizens spent in government hard currency stores netted the GDR DM700 million per annum. By the end of the decade 40 000 GDR citizens were allowed to visit the FRG each year.[100]

It seemed that the Federal Government would be able to work within this stable international system both for the benefit of the FRG and, progressively, for the German nation. Schmidt hoped that this task would be made easier by the synergy between German foreign policy and American foreign policy as practised by Henry Kissinger. Yet as Schmidt came to power in Germany, Kissinger's star was waning in the United States. In addition, Germany and the other Western countries had to focus on West–West diplomacy, as they responded to the new international political economy created by the 1973 Middle East War and subsequent 'oil shocks', rather than any grand gestures in West–East diplomacy. By 1977, therefore, it seemed that Schmidt's passivity had lost for Germany the position Brandt had gained. His reassertion of Germany's Cold War role between 1977 and 1981 provoked what proved to be the West's last major Cold War crisis.

Germany operated at two levels in the Cold War system of the 1970s and early 1980s. First, it was concerned with the workings of the German–Soviet–German framework established by the 'treaty work' of the early 1970s. This made it the nexus of political power and influence in central Europe. Second, it was at the centre of the East–West politico-military balance in central Europe. This too made it the nexus of political power and influence in central Europe. Yet both the FRG and the GDR endeavoured to insulate the workings of the former network from the workings of the latter. Indeed the two German states were remarkably successful in this effort at differentiation, although at the cost of a circumscribed world role and to the stability of their own societies.

As early as 1966 Schmidt had floated the idea that Germany could pursue both an active policy to ameliorate tension in East–West relations and an active *Ostpolitik* whilst uncoupling the two policies. Thus *détente* and *Ostpolitik* would not be mutually dependent upon each other. If this separation did not take place each could become mutually destructive because of West Germany's growing power. Eleven years later he was still exercised by these dangers.[101] In a *tour d'horizon* known as the Marbella paper (from the Chancellor's winter holiday destination) he wrote that the FRG had risen to be 'in the eyes of the world *de facto* economically the second power in the West'. This emerging consciousness was 'unwanted and dangerous' since it would revive in the minds of other governments 'including especially the Soviet leadership ... memories not only of Auschwitz and Hitler but also of Wilhelm II and Bismarck'. It was therefore necessary 'so far as at all possible, to operate not nationally and independently but in the framework of the European Community and the Alliance. This attempt to cover our actions multilaterally', he added, 'will only partially succeed because we will ... become a leadership factor in both systems [i.e. East–West and within the capitalist world].'[102] In other words there was nothing more likely to arouse the suspicions of both the Soviet Union or Western allies, for both historical and Cold War reasons, than an independently conceived *Ostpolitik*. That suspicion would be exponentially increased as Germany emerged, as he believed it would, as a dominant economic and diplomatic power within the Western world. Since the FRG wanted to achieve both ends it had to be circumspect in both.

Until the late 1970s, therefore, Schmidt was very cautious in his German policy. Gunther Gaus, head of the FRG Permanent Mission in East Berlin (effectively the embassy) said that Schmidt treated German policy as a '*quantité négligeable*'. Another head of the Permanent Mission, Klaus Bolling, recalled that: 'although the impatience ... with the Bonn "immobility" did not escape Schmidt's notice, he was generally only able in the years of world-wide recession caused by two oil-price increases to concentrate his activities on German-German affairs when conflict occurred between Bonn and East Berlin.' Schmidt himself argued that: 'it is not so much due to the formula of change through *rapprochement* (Bahr's phrase) but rather is far more due to concrete steps actually carried out in the direction of the Warsaw Pact states that the encrustation in Europe and in Germany, which arose during the time of the Cold War [always a phrase used of the past in 1970s' German rhetoric], has been reduced in successive years. It is not a matter of formulae but rather that we really do negotiate and change something.' This policy had been suggested by the head of the Foreign Ministry's planning staff, Guido Brunner, as early as 1973 when he said the FRG hoped to create 'common rules of the game for peaceful cooperation and competition. We intend to establish contacts between people, contacts between professional groups, contacts from society to society, as autonomous factors in the process of *détente*.' Government officials were convinced that this quietist approach was making significant progress. The Schmidt government was also reluctant to enlist the Soviet Union's aid in putting pressure on the GDR leadership 'because it would have encouraged the Soviet Union in the installation of itself as a hegemonial power and the FRG did not want the Soviet Union to use even benevolent influence.'[103]

In the late 1970s both German states became more assertive in attempting to preserve the status quo. Both the FRG and the GDR wished to regard *détente* as divisible. As Schmidt told Gromyko in February 1976: 'in my view the quarrel of both world powers over Angola is not so important that the confidence of other peoples in the durability of *détente* should be allowed to suffer from it'.[104] Increased Cold War tension outside Europe was not to disrupt the German–Soviet–German relationship.[105] The viability of this approach was, however, challenged by three major developments at the turn of the decade: NATO's December 1979 decision to modernise its medium-range nuclear missile capability; the Soviet invasion of Afghanistan in the same month; and the emergence of the oppositionist mass trade union movement Solidarity in Poland in 1979–80. In 1981 Schmidt declared that there had been a reversal in the relationship between intra-German relations and the wider international environment. According to his analysis, 'Many years ago the notion of *rapprochement* between East Berlin and the Bonn government, between both German states, frequently aroused the suspicion of third parties: the German question appeared to disturb the status quo; it appeared to endanger the peace in Europe. Today the reverse is more the case: unrest and fear in the world and in Europe endanger the German–German cooperation that has been achieved.' Honecker agreed. According to Klaus Bolling, 'Schmidt had no illusions that the GDR man could speak to his main ally with the same openness which he himself had done to two American Presidents ... he constantly tried [to get Honecker] to actively use his nevertheless considerable influence to make it clear to the men in the Kremlin that a return to a policy of confrontation would mean first of all a heavy burden for the two German states.'[106]

As far as Poland was concerned Schmidt refused to condemn the imposition of martial law and the suppression of Solidarity in December 1981. Indeed he was meeting with Honecker at the time and simply commented: 'Herr Honecker was as dismayed as I, that this has now proved necessary. I very much hope that the Polish nation will succeed in solving their problems.'[107] Schmidt had virtually declared that General Jaruzelski's regime was justified in putting down civil disorder led by a movement which was idolised in the West. Klaus Bolling noted that: 'in the GDR people not only understood Schmidt's reticence they were also grateful for the fact that he was among the minority in the West who thought ahead. The citizen in the GDR could easily imagine after a bloodbath in Poland a long period of the peace of the graveyard would come in Eastern Europe and the GDR, that we, the Germans in both states might have to wait a whole decade before we could talk to one another again.' Indeed the FRG refused to bow to intense American pressure not to implement its 1978 long-term economic agreement with the Soviet Union, and in particular to freeze huge contracts for German firms to provide equipment for a Soviet natural gas pipeline being built from Siberia to supply Western Europe. The Germans pointed out that although America had imposed sanctions on the sale of American equipment for the natural gas pipeline which included, against the State Department's advice, equipment built by European firms under licence, it had, at the same time, concluded a new grain deal with the Soviet government. Intra-German relations were much more important than any 'Cold War posturing'. An assessment written for the SED Politburo at the end of 1981 noted that: '[Schmidt's attitude] has contributed to the fact that so far there has been no unified front of the USA, Western Europe and Japan towards the P[eople's] R[epublic] of Poland, the USSR and the socialist community; and despite the repeated and intensified efforts of the USA ... [has] given the Military Council of People's Poland a breathing-space which is not to be underestimated.'[108]

The problem for the Germans was that although it seemed possible to insulate the trilateral German–Soviet–German relationship from crises it was not possible to insulate these dealings from a fundamental challenge to the politico-military balance of power in Europe. The balance of nuclear forces in Europe was, therefore, a matter of the utmost sensitivity to the government of the Federal Republic. This sensitivity was made clear by its official response to the changes to American declaratory nuclear strategy known as the Schlesinger doctrine. It noted: 'the risks associated with the NATO strategy are not the same for the European allies as they are for the transatlantic parties. By using strategic nuclear weapons the United States risks having its own territory exposed to similar effects from enemy weapons. By contrast, Western Europe and, above all, the Federal Republic of Germany would be a battlefield in any war, whether conducted with conventional or possibly even tactical nuclear weapons, even prior to the strategic nuclear stage.' Within the German foreign-policy establishment a critique emerged which stressed the potential political and military unreliability of the United States. According to Wilhelm Grewe, a former ambassador to Washington, writing in 1979 of the 1968 Non-Proliferation treaty,

> in drawing a balance sheet one cannot avoid some sobering facts: the equality which the Federal Republic obtained by the Paris Agreement of 1954 and by German rearmament has been lost with the Non-Proliferation treaty ... the sense of solidarity among the Atlantic alliance partners was damaged through the collusion of the leading power of the alliance with Moscow ... In particular, the Soviet Union obtained, without a quid

pro quo, an additional element of the European order of the status quo it favours ... Perhaps the Federal Republic was not strong enough to obviate this development. Without doubt, the position was weaker in the second half of the 1960s than in the mid-1950s, when the West believed it could not do without her defence contribution ... In the meantime, it has become fully clear how naive it was to see in this treaty ... an effective instrument for the prevention of nuclear war. It was and is in the first instance an instrument of the superpowers.

This critique was strengthened by the signature of the US–Soviet agreement on the prevention of nuclear war in 1973. In 1978 the FRG's Defence Minister, Hans Apel, was openly 'concerned that a new build-up [of IRBMs] in Western Europe to match the Soviets would eventually "decouple" the US commitment to defend Europe with long-range strategic weapons if necessary'.[109]

Schmidt repeatedly suggested that the so-called 'Euro-strategic' systems, including American forward-based systems (nuclear-capable land and carrier-based aircraft in Europe) should be included in the SALT process. West German officials felt that 'Carter and Brzezinski [believed] that medium-range nuclear weapons had nothing to do with negotiations between the Soviet Union and the United States and that negotiation between the Soviet Union and the United States had nothing to do with Europe'.[110] On the other hand the Soviet Union began to deploy its nuclear-capable medium-range bomber the Tu-26 Backfire in the western Soviet Union in 1974 and, much more worryingly, its fourth-generation mobile multi-warheaded IRBM, the SS-20 in late 1977.[111] Schmidt 'did not apparently fear a military intervention by the Soviet Union but he did fear that Soviet superiority could expose Europe to Soviet political pressure and blackmail'. Schmidt believed that he had reached a 'security–political basis consensus' with Brezhnev when the latter visited Bonn in May 1978 to preserve the military balance in Europe. According to the official German account of the meeting: 'both sides regarded as important that no-one should strive for military superiority. They proceed on the assumption that approximate balance and parity are sufficient to guarantee defence.' Yet the SS-20 deployment rapidly went ahead. Schmidt believed that either Brezhnev had duped him or that he had been overridden by 'hawks' in the Politburo. In either case his hopes for preserving balance through diplomacy had been rebuffed by both the Soviets and the Americans.

Schmidt had by then already aired his views to an 'informed public' in a speech and after-dinner remarks at the IISS in London on 28 October 1977. In his address Schmidt argued that 'changed strategic conditions confront us with new problems'. SALT had codified the nuclear strategic balance between the Soviet Union and the United States. More than that, however, it had actually neutralised their strategic nuclear capabilities. In such a strategic environment the 'disparities between East and West in nuclear tactical and conventional weapons' would be magnified. 'Strategic arms limitations confined to the United States and the Soviet Union will inevitably impair the security of the

West European members of the alliance *vis-à-vis* Soviet military superiority in Europe if we do not succeed in removing the disparities of military power in Europe parallel to the SALT negotiations.' The Chancellor concluded with the statement: 'we must maintain the balance of the full range of deterrence strategy. The Alliance must, therefore, be ready to make available the means to support its present strategy, which is still the right one.' NATO's Nuclear Planning Group had actually already concluded that NATO should deploy its own sub-strategic nuclear missiles. What emerged within the Federal Government in the spring of 1978 was the concept of the 'dual-track': preparations for the deployment of NATO missiles linked to arms control negotiations which would obviate the need for such deployment. The dual-track was formally adopted as NATO policy in December 1979.[112]

This decision made Germany a focal point for East–West conflict. Not only did the Soviet Union launch a massive propaganda campaign against deployment but the internal politics of the SPD and of the Federal Republic itself raised the possibility that the FRG would break with NATO on the issue. Already in 1977 a minor storm had blown up when the *Washington Post* had disclosed that the United States was planning to deploy enhanced radiation warheads on its nuclear weapons in Europe. Some senior SPD politicians, most notably Egon Bahr, were sharply critical of these American plans. He declared 'humanity is going insane ... [if this] symbol of the perversion of human thought ... was deployed'. Schmidt had just managed to assemble a majority for deployment in the party when Jimmy Carter cancelled the weapon in March 1978. Thus the 'neutron bomb' controversy came to a head just as 'dual-track' was launched in the FRG. Elements of the SPD opposed 'dual-track'. Bahr and another architect of early 1970s *Ostpolitik*, Herbert Wehner, the chairman of the parliamentary party, argued for arms control to be given preference over the deployment of new missiles. Both the defence and foreign affairs spokesmen of the party suggested that, at the very least, there should be many years of arms control negotiation before the NATO weapons were deployed. At the SPD Party conference in December 1979 Schmidt had to manoeuvre feverishly to have 'dual-track' approved. Even then party policy emerged with the caveats that the FRG should insist on a 'zero option' – no missiles on either side – in the INF negotiations and that deployment would not be automatic even if the negotiations failed to produce a solution acceptable to the United States. The conference refused to accept a motion blaming the Soviet Union alone for upsetting military parity in Europe. Opposition to the deployment of Pershing II missiles spread far beyond the ranks of the SPD; a mass peace movement coalesced around the issue. It found its expression in petitions to the government to reject deployment – the so-called Krefeld appeal of November 1980 organised by the DKP attracted two million signatures; and mass public protest – a demonstration held in Bonn on 10 October 1981 attracted 250 000 participants. The issue effectively split the SPD. Bahr, Oskar Lafontaine and, to an extent, Brandt himself adopted the rhetoric of the peace movement and mobilised the grass roots of the party against its own Chancellor. At the April 1982 party conference the automatic linkage between the failure of negotiations and the deployment of Pershing IIs was completely rejected and deployment was made dependent on the ill-defined concept of the 'seriousness of negotiations': the implication was that the Americans would not negotiate in Germany's interest and that the whole 'dual-track' should be overthrown if the SPD found their attitude wanting.[113]

The collapse of support in his own party left Schmidt in an uncomfortable position. He told the Reagan administration's chief INF negotiator, Paul Nitze, that if serious negotiations were not seen to be in progress by the autumn of 1982 West European support for the deployment of cruise and Pershing and even the whole position of the United States within NATO would crumble.[114] According to his personal archivist: 'in order to prevent a reversion into the Cold War, Schmidt saw himself more or less pressed into the role of an ambassador on both sides, trying to create, preserve and interpret understanding between East and West not least in German self-interest. In the crisis between the world powers, the Federal Republic tried to remain a steady factor of calculability, stability and moderation.' The Schmidt view of the consequences of this process was that the Federal Republic 'gained a world-wide importance that she had never achieved before in international politics but she had to pay for this new weight and prestige with "irritations" in the relationship with the USA.' An official who accompanied Schmidt on his visit to Moscow in June 1980 recorded the view that:

Schmidt was in a very pivotal position ... from the time of the NATO double-track decision and the Soviet intervention in Afghanistan up to the superpower decision to resume negotiations [i.e. between December 1979 and the resumption of INF talks in November 1981 following the changeover from the Carter to the Reagan administration in the USA], Schmidt was in a position to have a disproportionate influence, not as a mediator, but as a good lawyer to tell the other side what the situation was ... for example he told the Russians Western deployment of Cruise and Pershing would occur and that the Soviets would get nowhere by using the peace movement and refusing to negotiate. The Soviets believed him on this and they trusted his judgement and knew him as an honest man.

In effect Schmidt was setting himself up as a mediator between the Soviet Union and the United States without seeming to do so. His party favoured an even-handed, even pro-Soviet, position but such a stance left the Federal Republic open to the obvious danger of alienating the United States. Since Adenauer the FRG had firmly anchored itself in the West even as it developed its own independent Cold War policies. If it set itself up as a 'third force' the anchor would slip. Schmidt issued the veiled threat that: 'we have an important role to play in this, in the first instance towards our ... allies in America who cannot play their role in the world without the Europeans, that ... means without the full weight of the Federal Republic on the Western side . . . after all we know a lot more about the situation in Eastern Europe and Moscow.' The FRG would therefore act as a interpreter of the Soviets for the Americans as well as the Americans for the Soviets. He warned, however, that this mediation was a 'subsidiary function'. The 'main function' of German diplomacy was 'to influence the Western negotiating position in such a way that it best corresponds with German influence'.[115] Schmidt was willing to stretch the bounds of the Western alliance but not to step outside it. There was, however, pressure to stretch those boundaries to the limit. A chancellery planning staff paper urged him 'for substantive, electoral and coalition–political reasons [to] . . . set new and controversial accents . . . for a mediator role of Europe/the Federal Republic between the United States and the Soviet Union, even if this could lead to dissonance with the United States'. It argued that there should be 'more autonomy for Europe/the Federal Republic . . . [and] thereby conflicts with the neo-conservative ideology and the Reagan–Thatcher administrations'. The FRG should reject the Americans and the British because 'large groups in the USA and GB are in the process of turning away from the common policy and common values of the West. They endanger the social-political attractiveness of the West in competition from the communists. They endanger *détente*.' Criticism of the Soviet Union would be maintained because 'Soviet bureaucratism' was not 'what socialism looks like' but long-term political and economic cooperation would be stepped up since 'to count on the collapse of the Eastern bloc makes no sense'.[116]

Whether the crisis within the SPD would have become a crisis for NATO remains a moot point since its coalition partners, the FDP, deserted the government in September 1982 and brought into power a new CDU administration under Helmut Kohl. It is worth noting that Schmidt was rapidly marginalised in his own party once he fell from power and the SPD came to espouse the politics of 'equidistance' whilst in opposition in the mid-1980s. Kohl and Hans-Dietrich Genscher, who remained as Foreign Minister, effectively carried on Schmidt's mainstream policies whilst rejecting the SPD's radical alternatives. In this they had broad-based support. In March 1982 public opinion polls suggested that 60 per cent of the German electorate were in favour of deploying American missiles in Germany, and only 39 per cent expressed some sympathy with the aims of the peace movement. In March 1983 the CDU–FDP government clearly won federal elections, although that success was certainly not a simple function of support for their foreign policy. Although the peace movement remained strong, mobilising over 1.5 million protesters to demonstrate against the imminent arrival of Pershing II missiles in October 1983, the government had a comfortable majority in the Bundestag to approve the deployment of missiles in November.[117]

Soviet policy towards the FRG oscillated during the early 1980s. There was uncertainty whether to regard the FRG as responsible for the decline of *détente* or simply as a bystander. This debate revolved around the degree to which Schmidt was the architect of NATO's 'dual-track'. Even when Schmidt was replaced by Kohl, debate continued as to whether the Christian Democrat leader should be regarded as 'revanchist' or as partaking of some of the aims of *Ostpolitik*. Vadim Zagladin, deputy head of the Central Committee's international department, argued that the missiles had been forced upon the Europeans by the Americans. Valentin Falin, the former ambassador in the FRG, believed that the dual-track decision had its roots in US government policy rather than Schmidt's 1977 speech on the issue. Viktor Fyodorov, on the other hand, saw the Schmidt–Genscher government as 'one of the initiators' of the deployment. It thus remained unclear to the Soviets whether to single out the FRG for special sanctions. In 1983 and 1984 they initiated military moves against West Germany, by announcing the deployment of 60 SS 12/22s in the GDR and Czechoslovakia and SS-23s in the western USSR, targeted on Germany, in October 1983. At the same time, however, the Soviet Union accepted three major loans, amounting to $540 million, from West German banks.[118] In the end it was business as normal which prevailed

On entering office Kohl made two central foreign-policy commitments. He would always recognise the central importance of the United States to the FRG; in his phrase, 'the alliance is the core of German *raison d'état*'. As a result the German government would show full commitment to dual-track, including missile deployment. At the same time he reaffirmed his desire 'not only to keep the German question theoretically open, but also to be actively engaged for the German right to unity in freedom'. At the end of 1983 he brought these two themes together in an exchange of letters with Erich Honecker. Once more Germany was to be insulated from the changing politico-military Cold War balance in Europe. Kohl wrote that: 'the two states in Germany stand in their relations with each other in a community of responsibility to Europe and to the German people. Precisely in difficult times in West–East relations, both can make an important contribution to stability and peace in Europe, if they come forward to each other and carry forward what is possible in cooperation.' Honecker replied that he too was interested in maintaining this situation. The Soviets put pressure on Honecker to cancel a visit to the FRG in September 1984 and intensified propaganda against German revanchism in the spring and summer of 1984. Yet Kohl's line was seen as essentially a continuation of past German policy. Although the Chancellor's visit to Moscow in July 1983 demonstrated that his government 'takes a more strongly pro-American position than the Schmidt cabinet, the possibilities of continuing to work with it [the Kohl government] . . . continue to exist'. In particular the Soviet leadership noted Kohl's desire for increased contacts 'between people on both sides of the frontier', and his willingness to guarantee a DM1 billion credit to the GDR in order to signal 'to our compatriots, that we don't want to have any missileatomicweapon-fence [*sic*] between us'. Kohl himself assured Willy

Brandt in August 1984 that he knew that the 'Soviet Union is our most important and most powerful neighbour in Eastern Europe'. 'We know', he continued, 'that all conceivable bilateral possibilities, whether ... with the GDR, whether with Poland, Hungary, with Romania, or with whoever, can ultimately be successful if they are bound into the overall conversation.' Thus in the middle of the 1980s the Kohl government recommitted itself to preserving the status quo in Europe into the foreseeable future.[119]

NOTES

1 Robert Litwak, *Détente and the Nixon Doctrine: American Foreign Policy and the Pursuit of Stability, 1969–1976* (Cambridge, Cambridge University Press, 1984) pp. 151–6.
2 Litwak, *Détente and the Nixon Doctrine* pp. 156–67.
3 Litwak, *Détente and the Nixon Doctrine* pp. 168–9.
4 Raymond Garthoff, *Détente and Confrontation: American-Soviet Relations from Nixon to Reagan*, rev. edn (Washington, The Brookings Institution, 1994), p. 466.
5 Garthoff, *Détente and Confrontation*, pp. 479–80.
6 Isaacson, *Kissinger*, p. 613.
7 Garthoff, *Détente and Confrontation*, p. 512.
8 Baucom, *The Origins of SDI*, pp. 72–87.
9 Garthoff, *Détente and Confrontation*, pp. 596–600.
10 Paul Nitze, *From Hiroshima to Glasnost: At the Centre of Decision – A Memoir* (London, Weidenfeld and Nicolson, 1989), pp. 350–5; NIE-3/8-76 Soviet Forces for Intercontinental Conflict Through the Mid-1980s; Soviet Strategic Objectives: An Alternative Report of Team B; NIE 11–4–77 Soviet Strategic Objectives, in Steury, ed., *Intentions and Capabilities: Estimates on Soviet Strategic Forces, 1950–1983*, Documents 32, 33 and 34.
11 Baucom, *The Origins of SDI*, p. 82.
12 Garthoff, *Détente and Confrontation*, p. 608.
13 Isaacson, *Kissinger*, pp. 673–85.
14 Garthoff, *Détente and Confrontation*, pp. 556–82.
15 Litwak, *Détente and the Nixon Doctrine* pp. 175–90.
16 Gaddis Smith, *Morality, Reason and Power: American Diplomacy in the Carter Years* (New York, Hill and Wang, 1986), pp. 65–74.
17 Richard C. Thornton, *The Carter Years: Toward a New Global Order* (New York, Paragon House, 1991), pp. 8–9.
18 Michael B. Froman, *The Development of the Idea of Détente: Coming to Terms* (Basingstoke, Macmillan, 1991), p. 76.
19 G. M. Korniyenko, 'A "Missed Opportunity": Carter–Brezhnev, SALT II and the Vance Mission to Moscow, November 1976–March 1977', and 'The Path to Disagreement: US–Soviet Communications Leading to Vance's March 1977 Trip to Moscow', *CWIHPB*, 5 (1995), pp. 140–3 and 144–54.
20 Smith, *Morality, Reason and Power*, p. 208.
21 Garthoff, *Détente and Confrontation*, pp. 865–77.
22 Smith, *Morality, Reason and Power*, pp. 83–4.
23 Smith, *Morality, Reason and Power*, p. 213.

24 Stephen Sestanovich, 'The Third World in Soviet Foreign Policy, 1955–1985', in Andrzej Korbonski and Francis Fukuyama, eds., *The Soviet Union and the Third World: The Last Three Decades* (Ithaca, Cornell University Press, 1987), pp. 1–23.

25 Richard Ned Lebow and Janice Gross Stein, *We All Lost the Cold War* (Princeton, Princeton, University Press, 1994), pp. 149–288.

26 Margot Light, *The Soviet Theory of International Relations, 1917–1982* (Brighton, Wheatsheaf, 1988), pp. 249–93.

27 Michael MccGwire, *Perestroika and Soviet National Security* (Washington, Brookings, 1991), pp. 115–73.

28 Paul Dibb, *The Limits of Soviet Power: The Incomplete Superpower* (London, Macmillan/IISS, 1985), p. 177.

29 Bruce Parrott, *The Soviet Union and Ballistic Missile Defense* (Boulder, Westview, 1987), pp. 32–3.

30 Gabriel Partos, *The World That Came in from the Cold: Perspectives from East and West on the Cold War* (London, RIIA/BBC, 1993), pp. 128 9.

31 Mary Fitzgerald, 'Gorbachev's Concept of Reasonable Sufficiency in National Defense', in George Hudson, ed., *Soviet National Security Policy under Gorbachev* (Boston, Unwin Hyman, 1989), pp. 175–96.

32 Dibb, *Incomplete Superpower*, p. 158.

33 MccGwire, *Perestroika*, p. 135.

34 Roger Kanet, 'The Evolution of Soviet Policy Toward the Developing World: From Stalin to Brezhnev', in Edward Kolodziej and Roger Kanet, eds., *The Limits of Soviet Power in the Developing World* (Basingstoke, Macmillan, 1989), pp. 36–64.

35 Francis Fukuyama, 'Soviet Strategy in the Third World', in Korbonski and Fukuyama, *Third World*, pp. 24–45.

36 Sestanovich, 'Third World'; Roger Kanet, 'Reassessing Soviet Doctrine: New Priorities and Perspectives', in Kolodziej and Kanet, *Limits of Soviet Power*, pp. 397 425.

37 Fukuyama, 'Third World'.

38 Dibb, *Incomplete Superpower*, pp. 174–5.

39 MccGwire, *Perestroika*, pp. 141–2.

40 Minutes of the Meeting of the Politburo of the CC of the CPSU, 19 March 1979, *CWIHPB*, 4 (fall 1994), pp. 70–1.

41 Record of Meeting of A. N. Kosygin, A. A. Gromyko, D. F. Ustinov and B. N. Ponomarev with N. M. Taraki, 20 March 1979, *CWIHPB*, 4 (fall 1994), pp. 71–3; Record of Conversation of L. I. Brezhnev with N. M. Taraki, *CWIHPB*, 4 (fall 1994), pp. 73–4; Extract from Secret Protocol No. 150 of the CC CPSU Politburo session, 21 April 1979, *CWIHPB*, 4 (fall 1994), pp. 74–5.

42 Memorandum on Protocol No. 149 of the meeting of the Politburo (CC CPSU), 12 April 1979, 'Our Future Policy in Connection with the Situation in Afghanistan', 1 April 1979, *CWIHPB*, 3 (fall 1993), pp. 67–9.

43 Draft resolution of the CC CPSU, 12 December 1979, *CWIHPB*, 4 (fall 1994), p. 76.

44 Garthoff, *Détente and Confrontation*, pp. 686–757.

45 Smith, *Morality, Reason and Power*, pp. 220–4.

46 Smith, *Morality, Reason and Power*, pp. 223–4.

47 Figures derived from T. B. Millar, *The East–West Strategic Balance* (London, George Allen & Unwin, 1981), pp. 77–84 and Fred Halliday, *The Making of the Second Cold War* 2nd edn (London, Verso, 1983), p. 187.

48 Smith, *Morality, Reason and Power*, pp. 224–5.

49 Millar, *The East–West Strategic Balance*, p. 88.

50 Garthoff, *Détente and Confrontation*, p. 1079.

51 Raymond Garthoff, *The Great Transition: American-Soviet Relations and the End of the Cold War* (Washington, The Brookings Institution, 1994), pp. 33–42 and 163–165.

52 Fred Chernoff, 'Ending the Cold War: The Soviet Retreat and the US Military Buildup', *International Affairs*, 67 (1991), pp. 111–26.

53 Strobe Talbott, *Deadly Gambits: The Reagan Administration and the Stalemate in Nuclear Arms Control* (London, Pan, 1985), pp. 21–208.

54 Baucom, *The Origins of SDI*, pp. 181–2.

55 Baucom, *The Origins of SDI*, p. 184.

56 Caspar Weinberger, *Fighting for Peace: Seven Critical Years at the Pentagon* (London, Michael Joseph, 1990), pp. 204–32.

57 Weinberger, *Fighting for Peace*, p. 218.

58 Garthoff, *The Great Transition*, p. 516.

59 Nitze, *From Hiroshima to Glasnost*, pp. 419–20.

60 MccGwire, *Perestroika*, p. 116.

61 Dibb, *Incomplete Superpower*, p. 111.

62 Christopher Andrew and Oleg Gordievsky, *Instructions from the Centre: Top Secret Files on KGB Foreign Operations 1975–1985* (London, Hodder and Stoughton, 1991), pp. 67–90.

63 Dibb, *Incomplete Superpower*, p. 112.

64 MccGwire, *Perestroika*, pp. 120–1; Fitzgerald, 'Reasonable Sufficiency'.

65 Jonathan Haslam, *The Soviet Union and the Politics of Nuclear Weapons: The Problem of the SS-20* (Basingstoke, Macmillan, 1989); James Cant, 'The Development of the SS-20' (Scottish Centre for War Studies at the University of Glasgow, unpublished paper, 1997).

66 Mikhail Tsypkin, 'New Weapons and Attempts at Technical Change', in Derek Leebaert and Timothy Dickinson, eds., *Soviet Strategy and New Military Thinking* (Cambridge, Cambridge University Press, 1992), p. 197; Matthew Evangelista, *Innovation and the Arms Race: How the US and the Soviet Union Develop New Military Technologies* (Ithaca, Cornell University Press, 1988), pp. 68–82.

67 Jeanette Voas, 'Soviet Attitudes Towards Ballistic Missile Defence and the ABM Treaty' (London, IISS, Adelphi Paper 255), p. 14.

68 Parrott, *Ballistic Missile Defense*, p. 18.

69 Dibb, *Incomplete Superpower*, pp. 67–80.

70 Dibb, *Incomplete Superpower*, pp. 214–56.

71 John Hardt and Kate Tomlinson, 'Soviet Economic Policies in Western Europe', in Herbert Ellison, ed., *Soviet Policy Towards Western Europe: Implications for the Atlantic Alliance* (Seattle, University of Washington Press, 1983), pp. 159–208.

72 Richard Judy, 'Technology and Soviet National Security', in Hudson, *National Security*, pp. 109–29.

73 Dibb, *Incomplete Superpower*, p. 251.

74 Mark Kramer, 'Declassified Soviet Documents on the Polish Crisis', *CWIHPB*, 5 (1995), pp. 116–39.

75 Haslam, *Nuclear Weapons*, p. 121.

76 Sestanovich, 'Third World'.

77 Judy, 'Technology and Soviet National Security'.

78 John Tedstrom, 'The Soviet Economy: Growth, Decay and Reform', in Hudson, *National Security*, pp. 71–90; Vladimir Kontorovich, 'The Long-Run Decline in Soviet R&D Productivity', in Henry Rowen and Charles Wolf, eds., *The Impoverished Superpower: Perestroika and the Soviet Military Burden* (San Francisco, ICS Press, 1990), pp. 256–70; Dmitriy Mikheyev, *The Soviet Perspective on the Strategic Defence Initiative* (New York, Pergamon-Brassey's, 1987), pp. 57–65.

79 Yahuda, *China's Role*, pp. 235–68.

80 Harry Harding, 'The Domestic Politics of China's Global Posture, 1973–78', in Thomas Fingar, ed., *China's Quest for Independence: Policy Evolution in the 1970s* (Boulder, Westview, 1980), pp. 93–145.

81 Michael Yahuda, *Towards the End of Isolationism: Chinese Foreign Policy after Mao* (London, Macmillan, 1983), pp. 167–236.

82 Garthoff, *Détente and Confrontation*, pp. 758–62.

83 Douglas T. Stuart and William T. Tow, 'Chinese Military Modernization: The Western Arms Connection', *China Quarterly*, 90 (1982), p. 254.

84 Garthoff, *Détente and Confrontation*, pp. 787–96.

85 Smith, *Morality, Reason and Power*, p. 97.

86 Stuart and Tow, 'Chinese Military Modernization', p. 254.

87 Garthoff, *The Great Transition*, p. 629.

88 Stuart and Tow, 'Chinese Military Modernization', pp. 256–7.

89 Garthoff, *The Great Transition*, p. 636.

90 Richard Latham and Kenneth Allen, 'Defense Reform in China: The PLA Air Force', *Problems of Communism* (May–June 1991), pp. 30–50.

91 Garthoff, *The Great Transition*, p. 633.

92 Robert Ross, 'China Learns to Compromise: Change in US–China Relations, 1982–1984', *China Quarterly*, 128 (1991), pp. 756–8.

93 Thomas Robinson, 'Chinese Military Modernization in the 1980s', *China Quarterly*, 90 (1982), pp. 244–5.

94 Yahuda, *Chinese Foreign Policy after Mao*, pp. 180–5.

95 Dibb, *Incomplete Superpower*, pp. 118–20.

96 Ross, 'US–China'.

97 Haslam, *Nuclear Weapons*, pp. 115–17.

98 See Helmut Schmidt, *The Balance of Power: Germany's Peace Policy and the Super Powers* (London, Kimber, 1971).

99 Hans-Joachim Spanger, *The GDR in East–West Relations* (London, IISS, 1989), p. 16.

100 Sodaro, *Moscow, Germany and the West*, p. 254.

101 Avril Pittman, *From Ostpolitik to Reunification: West German–Soviet Political Relations since 1974* (Cambridge, Cambridge University Press, 1992), p. 73.

102 Garton Ash, *Europe's Name*, pp. 85–7.

103 Pittman, *From Ostpolitik*, pp. 71–4.

104 Garton Ash, *Europe's Name*, p. 92.

105 Spanger, *GDR*, pp. 39–40.

106 Pittman, *From Ostpolitik*, pp. 64–5.

107 Garton Ash, *Europe's Name*, p. 289.

108 Garton Ash, *Europe's Name*, p. 289.

109 Hanrieder, *Germany, America* p. 419.

110 Pittman, *From Ostpolitik*, p. 109.

111 *Nuclear Weapons Data Book*, V, pp. 209–11.

112 Pittman, *From Ostpolitik*, pp. 108–18.

113 Angelika Volle, 'The Political Debate on Security Policy in the Federal Republic', in Karl Kaiser and John Roper, eds., *British–German Defence Co-operation: Partners within the Alliance* (London, Jane's, 1988), pp. 41–59.

114 Talbott, *Deadly Gambits*, p. 92.

115 Pittman, *From Ostpolitik*, pp. 101–8.

116 Garton Ash, *Europe's Name*, p. 97.

117 Volle, 'Political Debate'.

118 Sodaro, *Moscow, Germany and the West*, pp. 286–316.

119 Garton Ash, *Europe's Name*, pp. 98–104.

6

The End of the Cold War, 1985–1991

The end of the Cold War came with shocking rapidity. It was not intended by any of the three main players: the leadership of the CPSU, the American administration or the government of the FRG. The US government continued to believe in the long haul. The governments of West and East Germany continued to operate the system of coexistence negotiated in the early 1970s. The leadership of the CPSU also believed in the long haul. Yet some members of the Politburo were convinced that the Soviet Union needed to restructure its economy in order to guarantee its survival as a superpower. In March 1985, Mikhail Gorbachev was appointed as General-Secretary to oversee such an overhaul. Gorbachev and some of his advisers had become worried about Soviet economic performance as Brezhnev *apparatchiks*, when they observed the inefficiency and corruption of the system. This alarm had been heightened by a number of secret studies carried out during the short Andropov period. They were also convinced that any reform must take place within the context of a favourable international environment. Gorbachev sought, therefore, to return to the *détente* of the 1970s. Compared to the tenor of the debate in the preceding five years, Gorbachev's initial statements showed a significant shift, but they were well within the continuum of established Soviet Cold War policies. Although the Soviet Union had always given an enormously high priority to military security, its leaders since the death of Stalin had also been acutely aware of the need to maintain an effective military-industrial sector and sufficient consumer production to obviate any serious risk of unrest amongst functional élites. Gorbachev met with senior officers in the summer of 1985 and called for stringent limits on military spending and the institution of measures to channel investment from defence to civilian enterprises.[1]

In July 1985 Gorbachev also appointed Eduard Shevardnadze as his Foreign Minister. Shevardnadze has since recalled that they had a fairly clear idea of the foreign-policy line the Soviet Union should pursue. Soviet–US relations would be put on the level of a 'civilised dialogue'. The future would be based on a balance of interests between the two superpowers. In particular, the strategic nuclear relationship would be stabilised. The threat of pre-emption should be removed and military capabilities reduced to a level of 'reasonable sufficiency'. In order to achieve this, the previously resisted issue of intrusive verification for arms control agreements would have to be tackled. The Soviet Union, for its own reasons, would withdraw its forces from the bloody war in Afghanistan. This withdrawal would, however, provide the opportunity to defuse other regional conflicts such as those which surrounded Nicaragua and Cuba. Relations with China would also be normalised.

Gorbachev and Shevardnadze wanted civilised dialogue in Europe too. They believed that the structure for such a dialogue could be built around the 1975 Helsinki agreement. This was a major shift. Although the process had been initiated by the Soviet Union, until 1985 the CSCE accords signed in Helsinki in 1975 were regarded as a failure. Under the accords all of the major European powers, including the United States, had agreed that the post-war frontiers of Europe were 'inviolable' rather than 'unalterable', as the Soviets had demanded. In addition in 1975, and subsequently, prominence was given by the West to the human rights provisions of the Helsinki final accords. 'In various meetings of senior Foreign Ministry officials during the years I served as Gromyko's adviser', Arkadiy Shevchenko later recalled, 'I heard several colleagues, as well as KGB and Central Committee participants in the discussions, caution against the trend in East–West negotiations to expand beyond Soviet goals [i.e. to secure stability in Europe]. Their warnings went unheeded ... Although few Westerners recognised the success their diplomats scored in the relatively unpublicised talks, the Final Act emerged as a notable advance for their ideas and a setback of sorts for the Soviet Union'.[2]

Gorbachev's world view would have gladdened the heart of Henry Kissinger. Indeed in February 1987 Kissinger visited the USSR and declared that the Soviet leader was impressive and sincere. Within the Reagan administration a Kissingeresque world view was maintained by Secretary of State George Shultz who had previously served as Nixon's Treasury Secretary. Just before the November 1984 presidential elections Shultz made a speech. 'Most of all', in the recollection of the head of the State Department's Soviet desk, 'it stressed we were in for the long haul, that our intention was to put relations with the Soviets on a stable and constructive basis for the long term'. Shultz was deliberately conflating two concepts of the Cold War. The long haul was Eisenhower's strategy of victory, stability Kissinger's strategy of stalemate. Shultz further expounded his views just after Gorbachev became General-Secretary in the spring of 1985. With a 'Soviet system driven by ideology and national ambition ... true friendship and cooperation will remain out of reach'. The United States was gaining the upper hand in the Cold War. Its 'key alliances are more united that ever before. ... The Soviets, in contrast, face profound structural economic difficulties and restless allies; their diplomacy and their clients are on the defensive in many parts of the world.' 'Nevertheless,' Shultz argued, 'history will not do our work for us. Experience suggests that the Soviets will periodically do something . . . that is abhorrent or inimical to our interests, dampening hopes for an improvement in East–West relations.' To deal with long-term prospects Shultz called for a policy of engagement. The United States, 'must seek a sustainable strategy . . . in the light of Soviet behaviour but not just a reaction to it. Such a strategy requires a continuing willingness to solve problems through negotiation where this serves our interests (and presumably mutual interests).'[3] Shultz was just one of the policy barons who surrounded Reagan. His advocacy of engagement was, however, strengthened by the sense that the United States could negotiate from advantage. Whereas Gorbachev 'wished to impart a sense of movement and change, but still without alienating support . . . he did not have Reagan's luxury of simply working on the other superpower's external environment until he was ready to negotiate'.[4] Reagan had plenty of time, Gorbachev did not.

Gorbachev believed that European politics had been poisoned by the issue of the Euromissiles. Soviet plans to disrupt NATO in the early 1980s had clearly failed. The argument for retaining SS-20 missiles thus rested upon the needs of military strategy. The missiles were supposed to ensure escalation dominance. Warsaw Pact war plans defined, 'the principal aim of the first strategic operation' as 'a rapid advance, reaching the frontiers of France by the 13th or 15th day, and thereby: taking the territories of Denmark, the FRG, the Netherlands, and Belgium; forcing the withdrawal of these West European countries from the war'. According to the Warsaw Pact's commander, Marshal Kulikov, in 1983, 'a future war will be carried out relentlessly until the total defeat of the enemy is achieved. This compels us to take into account the entire arsenal of weapons of mass destruction, with the uncontrollable dimensions of strategic actions.' Kulikov foresaw, 'NATO plans to escalate to the use of nuclear weapons with a total of over 5000 nuclear warheads, of which 2800 would be used in the first strike'. Yet throughout the 1980s Warsaw Pact planners noted that, 'NATO's military strategy oriented more strongly towards a selective use of nuclear weapons.'[5] The threat of the SS-20s and shorter-range weapons might deter NATO from using their full nuclear options. Such views were, however, challenged from within the Soviet establishment. Some, such as the civilian analyst, Andrey Kokoshkin, even challenged the need for a reactive development of Soviet military technology. In September 1985 Kokoshkin argued that 'emerging technologies' were both very expensive and had feasibility problems. If war did break out in central Europe it would take place in an environment crowded by enormous stores of hydrocarbons, a highly toxic chemical industry and nuclear power stations. It would be impossible for operational commanders to know whether they were being attacked with nuclear or chemical weapons; increased use of automated command and control could mean the loss of civilian control over the military, lowering the nuclear threshold even further. Technologies would lead to a new round in the arms race, as the Soviet military developed new conventional weapons, causing very costly and destabilising competition.[6] At an early stage Gorbachev himself picked up this theme and argued that arms reduction was needed 'in which, as a first step, the overall balance would be preserved, but at the lowest possible levels'. 'We are convinced of the erroneousness of the concept of equating the stockpiling of weapons with the strengthening of security.' Gorbachev did not believe that the supposed military advantages of INF outweighed their political disadvantages: he was, therefore, willing to trade. In October 1985, as an opening gambit, he announced that the Soviet Union would reduce the number of SS-20s stationed in Europe from 270 to 243, the size of the force in 1984 before it was increased as a response to the deployment of Pershing II and GLCMs.

In these circumstances, Ronald Reagan was attracted by the possibilities of personal diplomacy. The second Reagan administration was willing to negotiate both an INF and a START treaty. The President was, however, unwilling to link these negotiations to any scaling down of the SDI programme. At the first summit between Reagan and Mikhail Gorbachev, in November 1985, the United States arrived with a serious START proposal but Reagan insisted that this must be linked to the development of space defence, which the Soviets were invited to concede was legitimate under the terms of the 1972 ABM Treaty.[7] Both his hawkish and dovish advisers believed that the US negotiating position would only change to help the management of public opinion in both the United States and Western Europe, not in response to Soviet positions. The hawks feared, however, that the dynamic of negotiations would lead to unnecessary concessions.

The Soviets had few illusions about the challenge they faced. A secret proposal put to the Central Committee by moderates within the leadership such as Shevardnadze, Aleksandr Yakovlev and Anatoliy Dobrynin stated that the United States policy was intended, 'not only to stop the further spread and consolidation of positions of socialism around the world but also to "exhaust" the USSR and its allies, to disrupt the policy of acceleration of socialism [the slogan used for reform before "restructuring" came into vogue] both through a general arms race, and wearing it down in conflicts in different regions of the world.'[8] Nevertheless, Gorbachev could not abandon arms control: it was the essential prerequisite for further internal reform. Such reform seemed ever more pressing. On 26 April there was a catastrophic accident at the Chernobyl nuclear power plant in the Ukraine. Chernobyl became a symbol of systemic failure. In June 1986 Gorbachev drew up another arms control proposal. All Soviet and American intermediate-range nuclear forces would be withdrawn from Europe but French and British nuclear forces would be untouched. The size of the Soviet INF in Asia would be frozen. In return the United States would promise not to withdraw from the ABM treaty for 15 years and limit BMD research to the 'laboratory'. When he met Reagan in Reykjavik in

The End of the Cold War, 1985–1991   225

October, Gorbachev went even further. Not only did he offer an INF agreement based on mutual withdrawal he offered to negotiate on the size of the Soviet INF in Asia and he reduced his ABM no-withdrawal proposal to ten years. More startlingly, he also suggested that there should be a 50 per cent cut in ICBMs, SLBMs and heavy bombers: US FBS, Britain and France would be unaffected by this move. There was some interest in Gorbachev's *démarche* in the American delegation. Both the State Department doves and the Defense Department hawks were willing to countenance the complete elimination of ICBMs which were difficult to deploy in the continental United States and could be replaced by alternative offensive systems. Reagan was happy to sign an ABM non-withdrawal clause but only on the basis that BMD could be deployed at the end of that period. The talks stalled on the linkage between START and the ABM agreement.

Reykjavik almost recovered the spirit of the wartime conferences: personal diplomacy carried out by heads of government leading to major agreements. In January 1943 Harold Macmillan had likened the Casablanca conference to a 'meeting of the latter period of the Roman empire', and christened the protagonists, Churchill and Roosevelt, 'the Emperor of the East and the Emperor of West'. Many within the American administration were shaken by this return to the imperial presidency: a detailed arms control proposal produced by the military and civil bureaucracy had been casually thrown away. Despite the lack of a substantive agreement, however, Reagan was positive about the summit. 'Believe me,' he told reporters, 'the significance of that meeting at Reykjavik is not that we didn't sign agreements in the end; the significance is that we got as close as we did. The progress we made would've been inconceivable just a few months ago.' Gorbachev, on the other hand, was shaken by his failure. The Americans noted that his 'negotiating brief . . . certainly had a go-for-broke quality about it'.[9] He was, however, in the words of his interpreter, 'General-Secretary, and not Emperor'. The Soviet view was that Reagan was 'being held captive by this [military–industrial complex] . . . [and was] not free to take such a decision'.

Despite the disappointment of Reykjavik, Gorbachev could not afford to delay any longer. In January 1987 he launched full-blown *perestroika*. He told the party élite, 'At some point the country began to lose momentum, difficulties and unresolved problems began to pile up, and there appeared elements of stagnation . . . [there was] a need for change in the economy and other fields . . . [but] the Central Committee and the leadership of the country failed to see in time and in full the need for change and the danger of intensification of crisis phenomena in society.' In February 1987 he offered to eliminate all INF without linking such elimination to any other issue. The INF treaty signed in Washington in December 1987 resulted in the destruction of 889 LRINF and 677 SRINF missiles by the Soviets but only 677 LRINF and 169 SRINF missiles by the Americans. Another summit in Moscow failed to produce a

START treaty. The Americans insisted on a high ceiling for SLCMs and a loose interpretation of the ABM treaty which would enable them to test BMD systems.[10] Once again, Reagan regarded the summit as a success, Gorbachev as a failure. Responding to the friendly atmosphere engendered by his visit, the President declared: 'quite possibly, we're beginning to take down the barriers of the post-war era; quite possibly, we are entering a new era in history, a time of lasting change in the Soviet Union. We will have to see.' Gorbachev was frustrated by this holding policy. He had proposed that NATO and the Warsaw Pact should each reduce their forces by 500 000 men.[11]

> The Americans did not accept our bold and entirely realistic plan ... directed at ... imbalance in Europe and a decisive transition toward the creation on the continent of a situation of non-offensive structure of arms and armed forces at a considerably reduced level. I believe that a good opportunity has been missed to get things moving, lessening the danger of confrontation between the two most powerful alliances and thus enhancing international security.

By mid-1988, Gorbachev was becoming desperate. He launched another major initiative during a speech to the United Nations in December. Over the next two years, the Soviet Union would unilaterally reduce its forces in Europe by 500 000 men, 10 000 tanks, 8500 artillery pieces and 800 combat aircraft.[12]

GORBACHEV AND THE BUSH ADMINISTRATION

By the time Gorbachev made his speech to the United Nations, the dynamics of the Cold War had been transformed. He had embarked on arms reductions as a means of securing a stable environment within which the Soviet Union could reform itself. In 1988 the reform process was beginning to spin out of control. Many of those who had placed Gorbachev in power in 1985, and supported his reformist agenda as a means of making the Soviet Union a more efficient superpower, turned against him when it became clear that, in all likelihood, under Gorbachev the USSR would cease to be a superpower. Gorbachev, vested with the immense powers the Soviet system accorded the General-Secretary, was able to overcome this opposition. In September 1988 Yegor Ligachev, the leading neo-conservative, Andrey Gromyko and Viktor Chebrikov, the head of the KGB, were removed from their posts. Yet they were not the real problem. In order to negate the opposition, Gorbachev had created new political institutions: the partially elected Congress of People's Deputies met for the first time in May 1989. Yet, by removing the spectre of a Western threat, Gorbachev undermined the whole *raison d'être* of the Soviet system. The only thing it had done well was to amass military power: if this was no longer needed, why continue? The only successes Gorbachev could actually boast of were in the field of foreign policy. After 1988 foreign policy was no longer a means to an end, it was the only legitimising feature of the regime.

In November 1988 George Bush was elected to succeed Ronald Reagan as President. In its first few months the Bush administration was passive as it considered its options. Some of his foreign-policy team, led by the Deputy National Security Adviser, Robert Gates, counselled caution. In February 1988, when he had been deputy director of the CIA, Gates had argued that: 'while changes under way offer opportunities for the United States and for a relaxation of tensions, Gorbachev intends improved Soviet economic performance, greater political vitality at home, and more dynamic diplomacy to make the USSR a more competitive and stronger adversary in the years to come.' In office, he maintained that Gorbachev was an aberration. He would be succeeded by an old-style leader and the United States would need to prepare for a new Cold War. At times he managed to convince his immediate superior, Brent Scowcroft, that Gorbachev's foreign policy was still based on *peredyshka*, i.e., gaining a breathing space to reconstruct Soviet power. As late as February 1990 the national security team were suspicious. Their Soviet specialist, Condoleeza Rice told a meeting: 'We keep telling them to knock it off, but the Soviets are still putting military equipment into the Third World. I think we've got to re-ask ourselves the tough question: what are the tangible differences from the old days ... [is] new thinking ... another cover for power politics. ... It's as much an instrument of hardball foreign policy as old thinking was. ... So why, given all this, should we help them?' In September 1989 this line was articulated by Deputy Secretary of State Lawrence Eagleburger. 'For all its risks and uncertainties, the Cold War was characterised by a remarkably stable and predictable set of relationships among the great powers. ... Already we are hearing it said that we need to take measures to ensure the success of Gorbachev's reforms ... [but it would be better to maintain] the security consensus which has served the West so well over the past forty years until the process of democratic reform in the East has truly become irreversible.'

Theirs was not, however, the dominant view in the administration. In May 1989 the new Secretary of State, and Bush's closest confidant, James Baker, met Eduard Shevardnadze in Moscow: 'In excruciating detail he described the madhouse Soviet economy of 1989: repairmen taking payment in vodka, taxi drivers demanding their fares in foreign cigarettes, subsidised bread so cheap it was fed to pigs, corn rotting in the fields. He acknowledged that Gorbachev and his colleagues had underestimated some of the problems and mishandled others.'[13] The Soviet Union did not look like a superpower ready to make a comeback. Unlike Shultz, four years earlier, Bush believed that history would do the United States' work for it. He was irritated by Gorbachev's popularity in the West and was prepared to wait and see. He told Scowcroft that he was, 'sick and tired of getting beat up day after day for having no vision and letting Gorbachev run the show. This is not just public relations we are involved in. There's real danger in jumping ahead. Can't people see that?'[14]

Apart from the maintenance of the political and military structures of

NATO, Bush had two policy options before him. He could continue to engage
with Gorbachev, bolstering his position within the USSR. A Gorbachev-led
Soviet Union held out the hope of stability in Europe and a series of agreements
which would confirm the United States as the unchallenged world power: this
was the Moscow road. For the first time since 1948, however, an American
president also had another option: to challenge Soviet power in Eastern
Europe. This aim had long been central to American propaganda, but had
always been rejected as a realistic policy. In 1975 Kissinger's aide Helmut
Sonnenfeldt had caused a furore by stating the reality of US policy. During a
briefing to American diplomats in London, he said:

> The Soviets' inability to acquire loyalty in Eastern Europe is an unfortunate historical
> failure, because Eastern Europe is within their scope and area of natural interest. . . . So
> it must be our policy to strive for an evolution that makes the relationship between the
> Eastern Europeans and the Soviet Union an organic one. . . . This has worked in
> Poland. The Poles have been able to overcome their romantic political inclinations
> which led to their disasters in the past.

During a televised debate with Jimmy Carter during the 1976 presidential
election campaign, Gerald Ford attempted to distance himself from the
Sonnenfeldt doctrine. Instead, he made a major gaffe. He told a questioner, 'I
don't believe the Poles consider themselves dominated by the Soviet Union. . . .
And the United States does not concede these countries are under the
domination of the Soviet Union.' Carter eviscerated him with the remark, 'I
would like to see Mr Ford convince the Polish Americans and the Czech
Americans and the Hungarian Americans in this country that those countries
don't live under the domination and supervision of the Soviet Union.'[15] At the
time George Bush had been director of the CIA. When Carter won the election,
Bush asked to be retained in post: Carter dismissed him. Bush and his National
Security Adviser, Brent Scowcroft, who had held the same job under Ford,
were, therefore, extremely wary of the Warsaw road.

The Bush administration chose the Moscow road, an essentially negative
policy. In January 1988 Kissinger had suggested that the United States should
negotiate with the Soviet Union on the basis that if the Soviets eschewed the
use of force in Eastern Europe, the United States would not exploit indigenous
political and economic developments or threaten Soviet security interests there.
In particular, there would be no attempt to entice countries, and especially East
Germany, to leave the Warsaw Pact. Bush allowed Kissinger to expound these
ideas to Gorbachev in January 1989. Although Kissinger was publicly disowned
by Baker, his policy prescription was effectively followed. According to the
Secretary of State:

> We've got to ask ourselves: What happens if Gorbachev loses, if things go to hell in a
> handbasket over there? One thing that might happen is that they would begin to move
> externally again - start looking for a bogeyman to blame all their troubles on and to
> consolidate their position at home. Therefore, the question for us is: How can we help?

For starters, and at a minimum, we've got to proceed in Eastern Europe in a way that makes clear we're not trying to take advantage of the Russians' troubles.

Bush agreed, 'It's tempting to say, "Wouldn't it be great if the Soviet Empire broke up?" But that's not really practical or smart is it?'[16] In July 1989, when Bush visited Poland, he told his audiences that cooperation with the Soviet Union should continue. 'We're not here to make you choose between East and West . . . we're not here to poke a stick in the eye of Mr Gorbachev; just the opposite – to encourage the very kind of reforms that he is championing and more reforms.'[17] As a result of Bush's caution he was overtaken by events in Eastern Europe and muscled aside as the arbiter of the Cold War by Helmut Kohl.

THE GERMAN QUESTION

The last five years of Germany's participation in the Cold War saw the Federal Republic's foreign policy pass through four distinct phases. In 1985 the Kohl government's primary aim continued to be the strengthening of relationships within the Western alliance. This phase lasted until at least the end of 1986. In the New Year, however, fortified by victory in the federal elections, Kohl launched his own version of *Ostpolitik*. The Chancellor's new *Ostpolitik* was, in fact, old *Ostpolitik* revived. It was an attempt to use trilateral state-to-state relations to achieve 'relaxation' in the GDR. As in its earlier incarnations the policy assumed the semi-permanence of the existing dispensations in central Europe. The Soviet Union would remain a superpower, maintain its grip, perhaps modified, on the Warsaw Pact and continue to be the guarantor of the East German state well into the twenty-first century. At this stage the main formal conduit for US–USSR relations was arms control negotiations about nuclear weapons in Europe and the FRG, therefore, had a major role to play in the intra-alliance politics of NATO. The Kohl government was caught between enthusiasm for denuclearisation of central Europe, still a major issue in West German politics, and fear of the complete dissolution of the American nuclear guarantee. The nuclear issue seemed to many in the FRG leadership the area of radical change in the politics of the Cold War: it would have an effect on but not necessarily revolutionise German–Soviet–German relations. This tendency for *Ostpolitik* to stress the status quo was reinforced by the Social Democrat opposition. The party, which had moved sharply to the left in 1982, remained an electoral threat throughout the late 1980s, most noticeably in *Länder* elections and in Berlin. In opposition, however, the SPD went even further and developed not an alternative but a parallel foreign policy, based upon party-to-party contacts with the SED. Whatever the motives behind these links they only served to further legitimise both the East German state and the SED's rule of it. Both the CDU/FDP and the SPD's approaches to *Ostpolitik* proved remarkably tenacious. As reformist communists and even non-communists began to come visibly to power, with Gorbachev's obvious blessing, in Poland and Hungary at the beginning of 1989, the FRG's political leaders remained remarkably cautious about change in Germany. Indeed it could be said that German policy dropped from the hands of the West German government, to say nothing of the East German leadership, between September and December 1989. Between January and November 1990, however, it was Germany which effectively ended the Cold War. In the final phase of his Cold War policy, Helmut Kohl abandoned his caution and seized the historic and electoral opportunity presented to him to 'dash' for reunification. He did so with the acquiescence of the United States government but, most tellingly, the FRG almost literally 'bought off' Soviet opposition, thus marking the end of the Soviet Union as even a military or diplomatic superpower.

Between 1985 and 1987 a division opened up between Helmut Kohl and the CDU politicians he appointed to the Defence Ministry, and Hans-Dietrich Genscher the FDP Foreign Minister, and his advisers, over how the FRG should react to Mikhail Gorbachev. The Kohl team were inclined to be wary of Gorbachev and particularly his attempts to alter the nuclear balance in Europe. Genscher, on the other hand, argued that Gorbachev should be taken at face value and that the FRG should offer his government diplomatic and economic aid since he offered the greatest hope of 'relaxation' in central Europe since the Second World War.

Until the beginning of 1987 the Kohl line was in the ascendant. Although Kohl was keen to reduce tensions in Europe, Germany had little direct influence as long as it stressed its alliance rather than its independent role. As Kohl described German policy to Gorbachev in January 1986 it was essentially passive. Kohl claimed: 'In the course and results of the Geneva meeting [between Reagan and Gorbachev] the Federal Republic sees the confirmation of the rightness of its own policy. For years it has urged a confirmation and intensification of the dialogue between the United States and the Soviet Union at the highest level. It has deliberately worked in this direction in the framework of the North Atlantic Alliance and with the government of the USA.' This was a pale reflection of Schmidt's interpreter role but hardly a claim for the centrality of the German–Soviet relationship. Even when he moved on to deal with the German–Soviet–German relationship Kohl advocated a continuation of gradual improvements. He wrote to the Soviet leader:

I am convinced that life in a common European home [Gorbachev's phrase] with fewer tensions will only be possible when relations between the two German states, too, are constantly stimulated as a stabilising element in the context of the overall process of development between West and East. ... Important subjects ... must be particularly the humanitarian aspects of relations between the two German states and the quantitative reduction in the field of family reunification and the possibilities for Soviet citizens of German nationality to emigrate ... the FRG wishes, and this goes for all political forces, a deepening and widening of relations with the Soviet Union.[18]

Even this tentative exploration of the new Soviet regime's intentions was halted later in the year when Kohl allowed a statement to be published which noted that Gorbachev was 'a modern communist leader who understands public relations. Goebbels, one of those responsible for the crimes of the Hitler era, was an expert in public relations, too.' In peculiarly German language he was endorsing George Bush's view.[19] There followed a year-long freeze in FRG–Soviet diplomatic relations. The Chancellor was effectively rebuked by his own Foreign Minister in February 1987. In a major public speech to an international audience Genscher rhetorically asked: 'Are these only words to lull the West? Is this new foreign policy of Gorbachev's merely a policy presented in a new way and enormously better than before, more flexible and more skilled, but ultimately pursuing the old goal of expanding the Soviet Empire and hegemony over the whole European continent? Or else is Gorbachev merely seeking to gain a breathing space for a few years, to let his economy recover and then continue the policy of expansion?' Genscher answered his own questions: 'it would be a mistake of historic dimensions for the West to let this chance slip just because it cannot rid itself of a way of thinking which when it looks at the Soviet Union can always and only suppose the worst possible case. . . . The proper, urgently necessary policy for the West seems to me today instead to take Gorbachev and his "new politics" at their word, with all the consequences.'

This was a striking call for the abandonment of the Cold War. Yet its policy implications were complex. If the Gorbachev regime offered prospects to German interests then the Federal Government would have an interest in supporting it. In central Europe this support would mean the avoidance, as it had under *Ostpolitik*, of 'destabilisation'. One leg of Germany's Eastern policy would remain in place; what would change would be the increasingly criticised nuclear policies pursued by governments since 1977. This change had to be faced almost immediately because at the end of April 1987 the Soviet government proposed that not only should all nuclear missiles with a range of between 1000 and 5000 kilometres be eliminated from Europe, with both superpowers retaining 100 warheads for such missiles outside the continent, but that all weapons with a range of between 500 and 1000 kilometres should also be withdrawn.[20] In 1987 Germany only had a subsidiary role in the US–Soviet INF negotiations; it could delay their conclusion by refusing to give up its 72 Pershing I missiles. Germany was, however, crucial on the issue of shorter-range missiles. In concrete terms these amounted to 88 Lance missiles stationed in the FRG which were due to be replaced with more advanced weapons in the near future. If the Pershing Is and IIs and the Lances were withdrawn, the central front would be well on its way to becoming a denuclearised zone, politically if not militarily (there would still be plenty of air-launched nuclear weapons available to NATO). Genscher argued for concrete action to back his rhetoric. He was vigorously opposed by the CDU Minister of Defence,

Manfred Wörner, who maintained that the United States should still be able to deploy shorter-range missiles if an INF treaty was concluded. Kohl seems to have been troubled mainly by the domestic political implications of the dispute. He attempted to intervene in May 1987 but did so in such a way that at one stage he seemed to be suggesting that the future of weapons with a range of less than 500 kilometres should be considered. The so-called 'triple zero' (no Pershings, no Lances, no nuclear artillery) would really have meant a denuclearised Germany. Kohl believed that the loss of the CDU's majority in elections for the government of Rhineland-Palatinate was a sign of the unpopularity of its nuclear policies. In the aftermath of the defeat, therefore, it was Genscher's policy which was in the ascendant. In August 1987 the FRG announced that it would not modernise its Pershing Is if the USA and the USSR signed an agreement to withdraw medium-range missiles from Europe and promised it would destroy the missiles once the superpowers had dismantled their arsenals of such missiles.[21]

It proved difficult to prevent such arms control issues from becoming publicly linked to the issue of reunification. Kohl, however, remained convinced that the two issues should remain separate. He called demands from within the CDU to use the missile negotiations as a means of pushing for unification 'sheer nonsense'.[22] Although the strategic calculus in central Europe was changing rapidly in 1987–8 the German government remained convinced that its gradualist drive towards amelioration of intra-German relations was the best way forward. In July 1987 when President Richard von Weizsäcker visited Moscow he, as always, formally raised the question of German unification. Gorbachev's response that 'history would decide what would happen in 100 years' was a less definitive rejection of the concept of reunification than the Soviet leadership had previously adhered to but still held out little hope of short-term progress.[23] An opinion poll taken in the FRG showed that support for unity in the western population had leapt from 66 per cent to 81 per cent in two years but that only 8 per cent of the sample considered it a possibility in the next decade. In the same month the political director of the Foreign Ministry, Hermann von Richthofen, told a well-informed audience in the United States that 'we don't want to change the structures on the other side, just as we would not approve of an Eastern policy that aims to change the structures of our side'.[24] According to the Foreign Ministry the way forward lay in careful economic diplomacy. Trade with the East would lead to the 'long-term building of confidence between the blocs and to the stabilisation and reinforcement of East–West relations altogether'. In the long term the twin goals would be 'to replace the condition of non-war [secured] by deterrence with a peace based on trust and cooperative security systems' and to create 'an irreversible system opening process'. As for the previous two decades the FRG insisted that the overriding priority of *Ostpolitik* was marginal change, on both sides, in a stable environment, rather than major change in the East which risked instability. In 1987–8 the FRG wanted to deal directly with

Gorbachev by arranging a high-profile visit for Kohl and Genscher to Moscow and for Gorbachev himself to come to West Germany. The wheels of the 'system opening' machinery would be oiled by money: in October 1988 just before Kohl left for Moscow a DM3 billion credit from a consortium of German banks to finance German deliveries to modernise the Soviet consumer goods industry was announced. Once Kohl was in Moscow a number of other deals were signed, including one worth about DM1 billion for the West Germans to help build a modern nuclear reactor in the USSR.

In Moscow Kohl declared he was there to overcome the division of his country by peaceful means. When Gorbachev came to Germany in June 1989 Kohl called that division a 'running sore'. Yet despite this rhetoric the stabilisation of central Europe was still at the top of the agenda. The Bonn declaration agreed by both powers at the time of the visit was based on the assumption that the Soviet Union and the Federal Republic would continue to be dominant powers in central Europe. The rhetoric was certainly of diarchy. The two governments described the declaration as 'the first document . . . in which two great European states belonging to different systems . . . attempt to reflect philosophically . . . and together to lay down the goals of their policy'. Each would continue to show 'unlimited respect for the integrity and security of each state' in the region. There would be 'continuing differences in values and in political and social orders'. The Bonn declaration was supposed to 'set the course in the perspective of year 2000'. Horst Teltschik, one of Kohl's key foreign-policy advisers, described it as a set of 'guidelines for the course of European politics in the coming decades'.[25] In fact, it was really the last efflorescence of German gradualism. Gorbachev and his circle had already realised that it would be impossible for the Soviet Union to remain the hegemon of Eastern Europe. As Kohl and Gorbachev were meeting in Bonn, the reality of Eastern Europe and East Germany as a closed bloc was just beginning to disintegrate: a process which would take less than six months to complete.

Gorbachev had sown the seeds of his own demise in the winter of 1986. Since at least 1968, the Soviet leadership had wanted Eastern European regimes, contained within the protective carapace of the Brezhnev doctrine, to be politically and economically viable. During the 1970s the regimes had been allowed to borrow from non-communist countries. The loans had been wasted. Although Western creditors had no means for redress they were unlikely to make further loans. The cost of supporting the failing economies of Eastern Europe thus fell on the Soviet Union. In 1989 Poland owed about $40 billion. In 1980–1 alone the Soviets poured nearly $3 billion of hard currency aid into Poland.[26] It would be pointless to reform the Russian economy if monies were simply diverted to other countries in the bloc. Gorbachev owed little political loyalty to Eastern European leaders. As the US ambassador in Hungary observed in late 1986: 'Gorbachev's vibes with these guys were not right, that he had to pay deference to them because they were older, had more tenure in the communist system than he had, and yet they weren't really any of them willing to do anything radical. They'd talk a little bit about it, but they weren't willing to do it. So I remember thinking that he must be very frustrated with these guys as partners.'[27] Gorbachev was indeed frustrated. According to Wojtech Jaruzelski, the Polish leader who had come to power as recently as 1981, Gorbachev said 'that old men like Zhivkov and Honecker did not understand a thing'.[28]

Many of those around the Soviet leader had had some experience of Czechoslovakia in 1969: they believed that Eastern Europe could be reformed along Prague Spring lines by local communists. In addition, they were misled by the Polish experience of 1981. According to Aleksandr Tsipko, an Eastern Europe specialist on the Central Committee staff, 'It was believed that if Jaruzelski had managed to deal with his problems and unrest and riots without any interference from us, then we shouldn't interfere.' In November 1986 Eastern European leaders gathered in Moscow for a COMECON meeting. Gorbachev told them that they had to restructure their rule and gain legitimacy. They could not expect the Soviet Union to keep them in power. He made this policy public during a visit to Prague in April 1987. 'No-one has the right to claim special status in the socialist world. The independence of every Party, its responsibility to its people in its own country, the right to decide questions of the country's development are unconditional principles for us.'[29] Initially, little happened. Some opportunist second-rank communist leaders saw the possibility of challenging the ruling gerontocracy. In Hungary, for instance, Imre Pozsgay told a meeting of party officials in September 1987 that Gorbachevian reform did not mean a multiparty system but socialism with a new leader (himself) within the Soviet bloc.[30]

The major change came in Poland. The banned trade union, Solidarity, and to a certain extent the church, constituted a real oppositional movement. Although it had been weakened by post-1981 repression, Solidarity had survived, nourished by the disintegration of party and state structures during the 1980s. After a struggle within the leadership of the Polish party, Wojtech Jaruzelski decided to engage with the movement. In February 1989 he began 'round table' talks with Solidarity. His aim was to create a communist-dominated, 'popular front' government with a legalised and sanitised trade union movement. In effect Jaruzelski hoped to return to the tactics of the 1945–7 period. Janusz Onyszkiewicz, the Solidarity spokesman at the round table has recalled:

> They thought they had cooked it and we were worried we might indeed legitimise their power. We saw ourselves putting a foot in at the door, to force it wider afterwards. Controlling the media, they were convinced the election was in their pocket. Their worry was not about winning but about winning too convincingly. On many occasions we could see that they were captives of their own propaganda. They believed that

Solidarity had been highjacked by a group of extremists. Remove the extremists and there would be a bona fide workers' movement which obviously could be a partner. Elections were not due for a couple of years. Consenting to immediate elections was a mistake from which they could not recover.[31]

Some Solidarity leaders have argued that Jaruzelski was not far wrong: the round table laid the basis for a communist comeback. In the short term, however, it was a disaster. The elections were held in June 1989. Solidarity had agreed to the formation of a powerless upper house of the Sejm, for which they would contest seats. The lower house would be filled with unopposed communists. Solidarity won 99 out of 100 seats in the upper house, but most tellingly 33 of the 35 party leaders lost their seats in the lower house, when more voters crossed their names off the ballot than voted for them. The party was split over whether to accept a non-communist Prime Minister at the head of the negotiated coalition government. On 22 August the incumbent Prime Minister, Mieczyslaw Rakowski, telephoned Gorbachev for his advice. Gorbachev seemed to feel that the coalition was a workable compromise. In Rakowski's recollection, Gorbachev said, 'the Soviet Union will not change its policy towards Poland and towards the Party. . . . we grant our full support to both Jaruzelski and yourself. . . . Should the opposition move to attack the Party or its achievements of the socialist system, the Soviet Union will change policy towards Poland – do make it clear to the opposition.'[32] Gorbachev still appeared to believe that the implied threat of action which had existed in 1981 would contain the situation in 1989. Yet as Eduard Shevardnadze pointed out, if the Soviets used force it would be the end of *perestroika* in the Soviet Union. The political and military forces which would have to be mobilised to attack Poland were the very forces which would turn on reformists in the USSR. Two days later Tadeusz Mazowiecki became the first post-war non-communist Prime Minister of Poland. Other party leaders felt abandoned and vulnerable. In Hungary, the speaker of the parliament, Matyas Szuros, felt that, 'Gorbachev and all of them were so fully occupied with internal affairs that events were slipping out of their control.' The Politburo member and party Ideological Secretary, Janos Berecz, recorded: 'The Polish army was the best in the Bloc, and we were glad when Jaruzelski introduced martial law but even he was unable to consolidate.'[33]

The issue which destroyed the carefully thought out modulations of the summer of 1989 was that of emigration from the GDR to the FRG. A major strand in *Ostpolitik* had been the desire to ease movement between the two states and between the two halves of Berlin. By the late 1980s a significant proportion of the East German population were making temporary visits to the West. In 1986 about two million made such a journey. What was notable in these figures was the increasing proportion of those of working age (pensioners having relatively liberal movement rights). In 1985, 66 000 non-pensioners made a temporary crossing; in 1986 the figure jumped to about 500 000 and in

1987 it was well over one million.[34] The East German leadership was aware of the trend. In April 1988 Egon Krenz presented a report to the Politburo which noted that applications for permanent emigration had jumped from 78 000 in the previous year to 112 000 in the first few months of the current year. Of the applicants 87 per cent were under 40. By the beginning of 1989 up to one million had applied for permanent emigration. The East German leadership, and Erich Honecker in particular, believed that visits and emigration were part of the policy of creating sufficient comfort for its population rather than opportunities for heroism. Relatively free movement for the bulk of the population and forced deportation for active dissidents were regarded as safety valves for the regime. To ensure that dissent did not become a major factor, the activities of the secret police were stepped up even further in the mid-1980s. In 1973 there had been 53 000 members of the Stasi, by 1989 there were 85 000. It has been estimated that by 1989 these regulars were augmented by 100 000 to 200 000 informers with long-term agreements and millions of freelancers.[35] Not only would his great secret police mass create enough information about the populace to ensure that nothing could be done in private, but the very bonds of civil society would disintegrate leaving the individual alone, and helpless, before the state. In the summer of 1989 the leadership believed its policies were working. In June 1989 the Minister of State Security Erich Mielke reported to Honecker that 'hostile oppositional or other negative forces' only amounted to a few thousand individuals with about 600 political leaders and only 60 'fanatical . . . unteachable enemies of socialism'. One of Mielke's commanders told him: 'so far as the power situation is concerned we have the thing firmly in hand, it's stable'.[36]

What had changed was the emergence of reform communists, with Gorbachev's approval, in other parts of the bloc, especially Hungary. The new Hungarian leadership wished to establish good political relations with the Federal Republic as a means of facilitating economic investment. It was not by accident that Genscher chose Budapest to declare, in June 1989, the same month as the Bonn declaration, that 'the process of reform demands in both East and West that frequently instabilities must be allowed for to permit change towards a stability of higher value. A new stability, resting on democracy, freedom and justice, on openness and plurality in politics, the economy, culture and society. We do want a destabilisation of our eastern neighbours'. This statement was in stark contrast to rhetoric about the need for stability in the German–Soviet–German relationship. In May 1989 Hungary had partially opened its border with Austria. A trickle of people started to use this as a means of escaping from the GDR to the West. By July about 150 had made their way to the German embassy in Vienna; 600 had been turned back by the Hungarians; about 30 had sought refuge in the Federal Republic's embassy in Budapest. The flow of people out of East Germany by this route increased rapidly. Yet although the West German government gave considerable assistance to the refugees it also tried to stem the flow. In August FRG embassies in Eastern Europe were closed to refugees. Kohl called upon the SED to reform itself in the manner of the Polish and Hungarian communists; only if the economy improved would productive East German citizens be willing to stay. At this late stage, however, the Federal Government, denied any desire to disrupt German–German relations by 'depopulating' the East.[37] On 11 September 1989 the Hungarian communist leadership decided to completely open its border with Austria. They did so without consulting the Soviet Union. In the account of the Minister of Justice, Kalman Kulcsar:

> Why didn't we first ask for financial assistance from West Germany? The answer is that we wanted to show that we meant what we were doing and saying. Poland and Hungary were then the only two countries on the road to reform and it was by no means excluded that others in the Warsaw Pact would try something against us. We were pretty sure if hundreds of thousands of East Germans went to the West, the East German regime would fall, and in that case Czechoslovakia was also out. We were not concerned about Romania, the only danger to us came from the DDR. We took the steps for our own sakes. Very few people guessed that the DDR and Czechoslovakia would then collapse.[38]

The SED Politburo was slow to react. Even though Honecker was ailing physically, and some leaders realised the need to address the emigration problem, the East German leadership had been deliberately atomised over the previous 20 years by his suspicion of cabals. The leadership only formally addressed the emigration crisis in September 1989. By this stage, however, a new phenomenon was emerging: opposition to the regime in the form of protest rather than flight. On 9 October 1989 a 70 000 strong 'We want to stay' demonstration occurred in Leipzig. Local communist officials and functionaries such as the conductor Kurt Masur publicly expressed a desire to cooperate with the demonstrators. On 11 October the Politburo agreed to examine the causes behind the mass exodus but reaffirmed the leading role of the party.[39] The leadership made a last major attempt to save itself by ousting Honecker and replacing him with Egon Krenz. Krenz's first public utterance, however, reaffirmed the leading role of the SED. It was the rather farcical attempts of the new leadership to buoy itself up by offering freedom of travel which led to the mass movement of Berliners on the night of the 9–10 November 1989. Lacking any further means of preventing this movement, border posts on the Wall were simply opened.[40]

The events of October 1989 had fundamentally altered thinking within the West German government: 'small steps' no longer seemed relevant in the face of mass protest and the ever-present threat of a massacre. Thus, once the discredited Krenz had been replaced by the Dresden party boss Hans Modrow on 13 November, Kohl moved very quickly to establish a new agenda for Germany. On 28 November before the Bundestag he publicly unveiled a ten-point programme to overcome the division of Germany. He dismissed the possibility of establishing the 'road to unity in smoke-filled rooms or with a timetable in our hands' but made two key proposals which implied a rapid move to reunification. First, the FRG would offer massive economic aid to the East if 'a radical change in the political and economic system is bindingly decided and irreversibly set in motion'. Second, steps would immediately be taken to create 'confederative structures between the two states in Germany with the object of then creating . . . a national federation in Germany'. Kohl's parliamentary subordinates stressed that the FRG's allies had made promises to support the peaceful unification of Germany since the mid-1950s with little prospect of having to make good their assurances; now they should not stand in the way of a genuine opportunity.[41]

In November 1989 Tadeusz Mazowiecki found Gorbachev, 'an open-minded man, ready for dialogue on all subjects except Germany. On this he spoke in the old style, so I was amazed when he accepted its reunification so quickly.'[42] Of course, Gorbachev could hope to find opposition to a reunited Germany from even a non-communist Polish leader. In fact as early as November 1989 Gorbachev had signalled to Kohl that he would be willing to envisage a united Germany in the 'medium term'. Yet the FRG now saw the medium term as relatively short-lived. An initial plan for German and economic and monetary union envisioned it taking place at the end of 1992. As emigrants continued to flood westwards this timetable was rapidly abandoned. On 7 February 1990 the FRG cabinet decided to push to instigate unification by the end of 1990. The Soviets bitterly criticised the new plan, and the possibility that a unified Germany might remain within NATO as a 'joke' and a 'diktat', but their opinions were rapidly coming to be seen by the Germans as irrelevant.[43] Genscher was willing to examine the idea of giving Gorbachev a breathing space, even if this would delay the creation of a fully sovereign unified Germany, until an 'all-European security system' could be created. Kohl, however, dismissed such a delay as 'fatal'. In March 1990 a CDU-backed coalition won elections in East Germany on an implied ticket of rapid unification.[44] By May 1990 Kohl had decided against conducting a statutory election in the FRG in December 1990; instead he would build on his popularity in the East by simply absorbing the territory of the GDR and then holding all-German elections. In a major round of diplomacy carried out in July 1990, first at a NATO summit in London, and then in direct talks with Gorbachev in Moscow, Kohl had his ideas accepted internationally.[45] The key feature of Kohl's approach was to place limitations on German military power whilst effectively paying the Soviets to leave. Under the Kohl–Gorbachev agreement Soviet troops would leave German territory. Once they had gone the German armed forces, which were to remain fully part of NATO, would replace them. Kohl agreed to place a limit of 370 000 men on the size of new all-German armed forces and not to deploy nuclear weapons in the territory of the GDR. The FRG also agreed to subsidise the withdrawal costs of Soviet armed forces and extend DM5 billion in state-backed credit to the Soviet Union. Although there was genuine negotiation in Moscow – Kohl had wanted a quicker timetable, Gorbachev greater limits on German military power – it was clear that the balance German and Soviet governments had striven to maintain until September 1989 had collapsed completely.[46] On 3 October 1990 Germany was reunited.

German reunification was the death knell of both the Cold War and the Soviet Union. According to their foreign-policy adviser, Sergey Tarasenko, 'Gorbachev and Shevardnadze had a very keen feeling that we had to accomplish a huge manoeuvre without losing time. We felt that the Soviet Union was in free fall, that our superpower status would go up in smoke unless it was reaffirmed by the Americans. With the avalanche of 1989 almost behind us, we wanted to reach some kind of plateau that would give us some time to catch our breath and look around.' There was no time. In December 1990, Shevardnadze resigned, warning of an incipient hard-line dictatorship. In August 1991, the hard-liners did indeed launch a coup. It was swiftly overcome by Boris Yeltsin and his followers in Moscow. Yeltsin publicly humiliated Gorbachev by insisting that power should be transferred from the Soviet to his Russian Federation government. Although Gorbachev lingered on for a few more months, his authority was broken. At the end of December 1991, the Soviet Union ceased to exist.[47]

NOTES

1 Parrott, *Ballistic Missile Defense*, p. 49.
2 Haslam, *Nuclear Weapons*, p. 72.
3 George Shultz, 'Shaping American Foreign Policy', *Foreign Affairs*, 63, No. 4 (spring 1985), pp. 705–21.
4 Thomas W. Simons, *The End of the Cold War?* (London, Macmillan, 1990), pp. 69–70.
5 FRG Defence Ministry, 'Military Planning of the Warsaw Pact in Central Europe: A Study' *CWIHPB*, 2 (fall 1992); Lothar Rühl, 'Offensive Defence in the Warsaw Pact', *Survival*, 33 (1991), pp. 442–50.
6 Kimberly Zisk, *Engaging the Enemy: Organisation Theory and Soviet Military Innovation, 1955–1991* (Princeton, Princeton University Press, 1993), pp. 152–4.
7 Nitze, *From Hiroshima to Glasnost*, pp. 419–20.
8 Garthoff, *The Great Transition*, p. 275.
9 Simons, *The End of the Cold War?* p. 88.
10 Joseph Whelan, *The Moscow Summit, 1988: Reagan and Gorbachev in Negotiation* (Boulder, Westview, 1990), pp. 52–3.
11 Whelan, *The Moscow Summit, 1988*, p. 34.
12 Garthoff, *The Great Transition*, pp. 365–8.
13 Michael Beschloss and Strobe Talbott, *At the Highest Levels: The Inside Story of the End of the Cold War* (London, Little, Brown, 1993), p. 74.
14 Beschloss and Talbott, *At the Highest Levels*, pp. 19–68.
15 Isaacson, *Kissinger*, p. 702.

16 Beschloss and Talbott, *At the Highest Levels*, pp. 98–9 and 109.
17 Beschloss and Talbott, *At the Highest Levels*, pp. 86–9.
18 Garton Ash, *Europe's Name*, p. 106.
19 Garton Ash, *Europe's Name*, p. 107.
20 *The Economist* (2 May 1987), pp. 51–2.
21 *The Economist* (23 May 1987), pp. 61–2.
22 *The Economist* (6 June 1987), pp. 60–1.
23 Garton Ash, *Europe's Name*, pp. 107–8.
24 Garton Ash, *Europe's Name*, p. 273.
25 Garton Ash, *Europe's Name*, p. 117.
26 CPSU CC Report on Economic Aid to Poland (1980–81), 23 September 1982, in *CWIHPB*, 5 (1995), pp. 138–9.
27 Don Oberdorfer, *The Turn: How the Cold War Came to an End: The United States and the Soviet Union 1983–1990* (London, Jonathan Cape, 1992), p. 357.
28 David Pryce-Jones, *The War That Never Was: The Fall of the Soviet Empire, 1985–1991* (London, Weidenfeld and Nicolson, 1995), p. 215.
29 Oberdorfer, *The Turn*, pp. 355–6.
30 Pryce-Jones, *The War That Never Was*, p. 221.
31 Pryce-Jones, *The War That Never Was*, p. 203.
32 Oberdorfer, *The Turn*, pp. 360–1.
33 Pryce-Jones, *The War That Never Was*, p. 228.
34 *The Economist* (11 June 1988), pp. 62–3.
35 Elizabeth Pond, *Beyond the Wall: Germany's Road to Unification* (Washington, Brookings, 1993).
36 Garton Ash, *Europe's Name*, p. 202.
37 *The Economist* (19 August 1989), p. 37.
38 Pryce-Jones, *The War That Never Was*, pp. 224–5.
39 *Radio Liberty/Radio Free Europe*, RAD BR/198, 20 October 1989.
40 *The Economist* (23 October 1989).
41 *The Economist* (13 January 1990), pp. 51–2.
42 Pryce-Jones, *The War That Never Was*, p. 218.
43 *The Economist* (10 February 1990), p. 55.
44 *The Economist* (24 March 1990), pp. 57–8.
45 *The Economist* (7 July 1990), p. 49.
46 *The Economist* (21 July 1990), pp. 45–6.
47 Jonathan Steele, *Eternal Russia* (London, Faber and Faber, 1994).

7

Conclusion

There is little doubt that the Cold War came to an end as the result of Soviet economic failure. This failure led in turn to a failure of nerve amongst the Soviet governing élite. Mikhail Gorbachev believed that the USSR could no longer engage the Western alliance in competition at all levels whilst attempting to restructure its own economy. He attempted to redefine this problem by insisting on the Soviet Union's superpower status on the diplomatic level. Although he won considerable admiration in the West, neither the Reagan nor the Bush administrations in the United States or, in the end, the Kohl government in West Germany, were willing to indulge this fantasy. The collapse of Soviet power in the international arena led rapidly to the delegitimisation of the Communist Party and the subsequent collapse of the Soviet empire. Former communists were forced to acknowledge that their ideology was as bankrupt as their country. No state could set itself outside the capitalist system.

In the immediate post war period the capitalist system had been dominated by the United States. The USA enjoyed a massive competitive advantage. In some ways it approached the autarkic ideal. The USA had a 'large, uniquely affluent home market'. The contribution of both imports and exports to gross domestic product was much lower in the United States than for any other advanced economy. Yet the United States was also highly competitive as an industrial exporter. It was a world leader in some industries even before 1939. The Second World War stimulated major research efforts in fields stretching from electronics to nuclear energy. It also prompted massive investment in industrial infrastructure. The wartime investment in military technology had had no time lapse before its place was taken by the Korean rearmament programme. At the time the relationship between government and industry was highly controversial. The degree of government intervention in the economy exercised the minds of American political leaders, especially President Eisenhower. They feared that too much state interference would destroy rather than underpin American economic competitiveness and might have implications for political liberty.[1] It was Eisenhower who coined the pejorative phrase, 'military–industrial complex' in 1961. The Cold War cost the United States a great deal. It has been estimated that the nuclear weapons programme alone cost at least $4 trillion in 1996 dollars between 1940 and 1995.[2] In the medium term, however, Cold War expenditure was a prop rather than a hindrance to the American economy. Many innovations contributed to sustainable development. In 1948, for instance, research by Bell Laboratories, backed by the government, resulted in the invention of the transistor.[3]

American advantages began to wane in the late 1960s. America's balance in merchandise trade went into deficit for the first time in the whole century in 1971. Real wages began to decline in 1973. The home market which had developed in the 1940s under wartime conditions produced the most sophisticated and affluent consumers in the world. American industrial innovation was consistently better than elsewhere giving it both absolute and relative advantages over other nations. Once this advantage had disappeared, Cold War military industry, still the most advanced in the world, was, arguably, no longer in a mutually reinforcing relationship with the civilian economy. American decline can, however, be overstated. American aircraft comprised a 77.5 per cent share of total world exports of the commodity in 1971; American commercial aircraft and helicopters made up 79.4 per cent of total world exports in 1985.[4] In the late 1950s some presidential advisers had feared that it would be the Soviet Union's state-run industries that would out-produce America with resulting consequences for comparative military power and global importance. They were misled by the Soviet Union's ability to refine technologies already in existence in 1945: nuclear power, ballistic missiles, jet aircraft. Despite the brilliance of many Soviet scientists, the USSR struggled to master the easy production of post-war technologies. As it was, America's competitors were its Cold War allies. They were led by West Germany and Japan but included most of the other countries aligned with America from Italy to South Korea. This changed pattern of economic relations in the 1970s did have political consequences. The US–West German relationship, for instance, was increasingly complex. Quite often, however, political relationships maintained their Cold War pattern. Japan, a military ally since 1960, did relatively little to challenge the security relationship with the United States before 1991.

Economic structures were an important determinant of the Cold War's long-run outcome. Yet, as the the great economist John Maynard Keynes wrote in 1923, '*In the long run* we are all dead.' A great many alternatives could have emerged in over 40 years of international relations. The political, as opposed to the economic, failure of the Soviet Union was not pre-ordained. In particular, the pattern of alliances which emerged during the Cold War could have been different.

Between 1949 and 1963 the Sino-Soviet alliance posed enormous problems for American decision-makers who found it hard to discern its internal workings and configure policy accordingly. Yet even before the public Sino-

Soviet split which emerged after 1958, the alliance had been little more than a shadow. A real Sino-Soviet alliance based on a convergence of political interests would have been truly formidable. Yet even as Mao and Stalin negotiated the formal treaty of alliance in 1950 both sides manifested intense mistrust for each other. In the short term the Chinese were dependent on the Soviets for the security of their revolution and thus had no interest in an accommodation with the United States. Anti-American cooperation proved, however, to be difficult to organise. There is no evidence of a properly coordinated allied strategy during the Korean War. Of course, the close strategic relationship which developed between the United States and Great Britain during the Second World War was the exception. The much looser strategic relationship between the United States and the Soviet Union, based on the principle that my enemy's enemy is my friend, was the norm in international relations. As Winston Churchill once remarked, 'If Hitler invaded Hell, I would be willing to make a favourable reference to the Devil in the House of Commons.' Even by this measure, however, Soviet–Chinese links were tenuous.

Ideology, which some assumed would be a binding force between the two communist regimes, was, in fact, divisive. Both Stalin and Mao set themselves up as prophets. Truth could emanate from only one source. Both men's personal rule was based on their prophetic role. Neither could afford it to be challenged. Stalin's epigones were in an even more vulnerable position. Their authority was less, not least because Khrushchev disassociated them from aspects of the Stalinist regime in 1956. Therefore they could not countenance an alternative, and prior, source of ideological authority. By the time of the second Far Eastern war in Vietnam both China and the Soviet Union supported the same side without any functioning strategic relationship. Indeed their participation was, in part, a means of prosecuting the struggle within the communist world.

The two great anti-American powers needed to cooperate if they were to impose their will on an economically and technologically superior United States. Long-lived political cooperation between powers with clashing interests is always difficult to achieve. The emergence and durability of a Western alliance is therefore all the more remarkable. Between 1947 and 1955 the United States and the powers of Western Europe, most notably France, West Germany and Great Britain, bound themselves together in a true Atlantic alliance. This alliance found its main institutional expression in NATO, although it amounted to more than the formal links of the 1949 North Atlantic Treaty. After 1955 NATO became such a stable feature of the international landscape that it can be taken for granted. Yet it succeeded despite the different, and sometimes antagonistic, goals of its major participants.

The Western alliance *could* have failed. It had to face a number of crises which might have fatally disrupted American–European cooperation. Each of these crises revolved around the fate of Germany. The neutralisation or destabilisation of Germany could have fundamentally altered the balance of power in Europe. Between 1945 and 1960 the Soviet Union made determined efforts to achieve this result. It was only the failure of the communist regime in Eastern Germany which forced the Soviets to become more cautious in their attempts at disruption. The German problem was, however, not simply the product of Soviet pressure. It created deep and genuine fissures both within and between Western governments. As Churchill remarked in 1953: 'The fact that there will always be a "German problem" and a "Prussian danger" must be kept before our eyes.' The 'German problem' was not just the fear of a Russo-German cooperation. Churchill was 'earnestly concerned with the question of the possibility of a reunified and neutralised Germany, in so far as the Germans . . . really wanted it' and believed that 'whatever happens we shall have to face the problem of German unity'.[5] According to Churchill's confidant and first secretary-general of NATO Hastings Ismay, the role of the alliance was to keep the Russians out, the Americans in and the Germans down.

These tensions were periodically exposed by crises. In 1948 the London conference, which, in effect, produced an American–French–British agreement to create a West German state, could have ended in failure. France, the major obstacle to agreement, was, however, vulnerable to Anglo-American pressure to compromise because of its post-war economic weakness. Plans for German rearmament, launched by the Americans with British support in 1950, caused a long-running sore in alliance relations. An armed West Germany was incorporated into NATO relatively painlessly after 1955 as the result of skilful diplomacy and the fear of a dissatisfied German state. Yet the legacy of these struggles resurfaced in the 1960s as both France and West Germany made clear their unhappiness with the status quo. France's ability to disrupt the alliance was relatively slight because its main lever had been the denial of a role for an independent, economically strong and militarily significant West German state. That lever had been progressively sacrificed between 1948 and 1955. After 1950 French governments, of both the Fourth and Fifth Republics, saw more advantage for themselves in cooperating with Germany both bilaterally and in multilateral politico-economic organisations such as the European Coal and Steel Community and the European Economic Community.

German power was, on the other hand, waxing in the 1960s. Yet despite the growth of varieties of *Ostpolitik*, even the Brandt government struck a balance between negotiating with the Soviet Union and maintaining the Western alliance. But just as the settlements of the mid-1950s had induced dissatisfaction with the West in the 1960s, the treaty work of the 1970s caused further convulsions within the German body politic in the early 1980s. Perhaps the most serious threat to the Western alliance came with the Euromissile crisis of 1979–83. The crisis was so severe because the alliance was the victim of its own success. West German sovereignty was secure, the Soviet threat seemed questionable. Nuclear strategy had always been a weak point of the alliance.

Since NATO military strategy was designed to achieve the political objective of political cohesion at acceptable cost, it was always open to challenge on the grounds of military irrationality. European nations had been unhappy with the 'trip-wire' strategy adopted at British insistence in 1956 which assumed that a Soviet attack, however limited, would be met by a nuclear response. They were equally alarmed by the 'flexible response' strategy adopted at American insistence in 1967. Indeed the activities of the Kennedy and Johnson administrations in championing this strategy had been one of the issues on which France had withdrawn from NATO's military command structure in 1966. 'Flexible response' was predicated on deterrence at all levels. Short-range nuclear weapons in the West would deter the use of such weapons by the Warsaw Pact. Its problem was the spectre of 'decoupling': the fear that the Americans would attempt to avoid damage to the United States by limiting any conflict to the Western European battlefield. Nuclear fear, Germany's growing independence and a strain of anti-Americanism combined in the early 1980s to threaten not only the details of declaratory NATO strategy – if Pershing II missiles had not been deployed NATO would have lacked a countervailing deterrent to the Soviet SS-20 but the reliability of the alliance itself. In the end the commitment of the West German governments and their electorate to NATO prevailed. The crisis of the early 1980s did, however, increase the willingness of the Kohl government to disregard its allies in the rush to German unity in 1989. German representatives made it quite clear that Germany had repeatedly sacrificed itself for the greater good and that acquiescence to rapid reunification was the price to be paid. More speculatively, it seems likely that the mid-1980s would have had a very different political complexion if the alliance had faltered on the Euromissile issue. At the very least Gorbachevian diplomacy would have had much more political capital with which to work. Indeed, if the Soviets had had the hope of detaching Germany from NATO it seems likely that the leadership's nerve would have held, despite the economic crisis, and the end of the Cold War could have taken 20 rather than five years, with unpredictable consequences for the international system.

The role of nuclear weapons as a potentially destabilising force, as public opinion in the West questioned the balance of power calculations of its political leaders, also points to an alternative ending to the Cold War feared by many: a nuclear catastrophe. The Cold War was virtually coeval with the development and spread of this new form of military technology. Such weapons of mass destruction were indisputably a new element in relations between states. They also, not coincidentally, produced some of the Cold War's most striking images. Nuclear states developed during the Cold War. Nuclear weapons and fear of nuclear war was not a constant factor but one which changed. The United States built about 70 000 warheads and bombs, more than 6000 strategic missiles and nearly 5000 strategic bombers during the Cold War. Its stockpile of usable weapons peaked at about 30 000 in the early 1960s. The Soviet stockpile did not reach its peak of approximately 45 000 until the mid-1980s.[6] It is notable that the gravest risk of nuclear crisis came in 1961–62 when the disparity in effective nuclear power was at its greatest. Yet studies of the Berlin and Cuban crises have suggested that American and Soviet leaders were extremely cautious once they recognised nuclear conflict was a genuine possibility. Khrushchev was reckless in placing nuclear weapons in Cuba but had repented of his decision even before they arrived on the island. During the Berlin crisis, NATO war plans called for an immediate, and massive, nuclear response to any Soviet military action and the American army in Europe had been reorganised on the assumption that it would take part in a nuclear war. Yet Berlin merely served to reinforce the belief of President Kennedy and his advisers that such planning was unrealistic. Of course, the caution of political leaders did not obviate the risk of reckless subordinates. If Soviet forces on Cuba could shoot down, in the excitement of the moment, an American reconnaissance aeroplane with an advanced surface-to-air missile, there was no guarantee that they might not have been tempted to use the nuclear weapons with which they were equipped. Nevertheless, it would seem that nuclear weapons made nuclear powers tactically cautious whilst increasing the sense of strategic threat.

Despite the advent of nuclear weapons, which made the *risk of war* between any of the great powers less likely whilst greatly increasing the *risk of disastrous consequences*, the Cold War was an abandonment of the pattern of international politics which had begun in 1914. The use of war as a means of securing the total defeat of an enemy was more a rhetorical device, symbolised by Roosevelt's use of the phrase 'unconditional surrender' at a press conference in North Africa on 24 January 1943, than a political reality. Within five years of the end of both the First and Second World wars, defeated Germany was negotiating with its erstwhile enemies as a near equal. Yet the willingness to go to war, to mobilise societies to fight at huge human cost for uncertain advantages, did not re-emerge. Instead a more traditional pattern of alliance formation, diplomatic manoeuvre, proxy wars and limited aims reasserted itself. At times, the sense of limits was lost: some Cold Warriors in all participants sounded and acted more like zealots in a confessional struggle. Such limits were, however, quickly reasserted. The Korean War ended in stalemate. Even the 'big war' phase in Vietnam only lasted for three years before the Americans effectively abandoned the struggle. An alliance led by the United States defeated the Soviet Union. Yet in the end Russia lost territory and reformed its political system. It was neither conquered nor occupied.

Notes

1 Aaron Friedberg, 'Why Didn't the United States Become a Garrison State?' *International Security*, 16/4 (spring 1992), pp. 109–42.

2 'Costing a Bomb', *The Economist* (4 January 1997), p. 44.
3 Michael Porter, *The Competitive Advantage of Nations* (London, Macmillan, 1990), pp. 284–307.
4 Porter, *Competitive Advantage*, Appendix B.
5 Donald Cameron Watt, 'Britain and German Security, 1944–1955', in *Foreign and Commonwealth Office, Occasional Papers* No. 3 (London, FCO, 1989), pp. 48–9.
6 'Costing a Bomb', *The Economist* (4 January 1997), p. 44.

Select Bibliography

A bibliography of the Cold War presents peculiar problems. The rapid emergence of new sources has made many older works obsolescent. Much of the new material has, however, yet to be properly digested. Listed below are works which I found particularly useful and which will, I believe, stand the test of time.

THE SEARCH FOR PREPONDERANCE, 1947–1952

The most detailed treatment of American foreign policy is Melvyn Leffler, *A Preponderance of Power: National Security, the Truman Administration and the Cold War* (Stanford, Stanford University Press, 1992). Many of its conclusions can be checked by reference to readily available collections of US government documents. *Foreign Relations of the United States (FRUS)* is a vast edited collection produced by State Department historians which now covers the period up to the mid-1960s. It is extraordinarily useful but has weaknesses. The most noticeable is its concentration on the activities of the State Department which was not always the most important actor in foreign-policy formation. *FRUS* can, however, be supplemented by other published collections of documents on microfilm. The most useful is *Documents of the National Security Council, 1947–1977* (Washington, University Publications of America, 1980 and supplements 1981, 1983 and 1985). Thomas Etzold and John Lewis Gaddis, eds., *Containment: Documents on American Policy and Strategy, 1945–1950* (New York, Columbia University Press, 1978) remains a good selection. Historians employed by the British Foreign and Commonwealth Office provide another scholarly but less extensive collection in *Documents on British Policy Overseas*. Series I covers aspects of the period 1945–7, Series II, 1950–1. The most extensive counter-blast to standard views of American foreign policy is Bruce Cumings, *The Origins of the Korean War* (2 vols., Princeton, Princeton University Press, 1981–90). Cumings denies that he is a 'revisionist' but the clearest statement of 'economic' revisionism is to be found in the second volume of this work. For a more balanced view of the Korean War see William Stueck, *The Korean War: An International History* (Princeton,

Princeton University Press, 1995). Important work has also been done on the politico-economic nexus of the Marshall plan. Michael Hogan, *The Marshall Plan: America, Britain and the Reconstruction of Western Europe, 1947–1952* (Cambridge, Cambridge University Press, 1987) and Alan Milward, *The Reconstruction of Western Europe, 1945–1951* (London, Methuen, 1984) reach rather different conclusions. Both, however, stress economic motivations. The best book on Stalinist political culture is David Holloway, *Stalin and the Bomb: The Soviet Union and Atomic Energy, 1939–1956* (New Haven, Yale University Press, 1994). Another key work is Sergei Goncharov, John Lewis and Xue Litai, *Uncertain Partners: Stalin, Mao and the Korean War* (Stanford, Stanford University Press, 1993), a collaboration between Russian, Chinese and American scholars. A great deal of new material about the communist powers has been made available by the Cold War International History Project. Established in 1991 at the Woodrow Wilson Center in Washington, DC, the project publishes a yearly bulletin, containing translations of newly discovered documents, and working papers by scholars engaged in archival research. Documents published in the bulletin cover the whole period of the Cold War.

Theories of Victory, 1953–1962

FRUS and the other documentary collections are as useful for the Eisenhower administrations as for the Truman. *FRUS* starts to peter out in the Kennedy years but there are a number of important collections on specific crises. William Burr, ed., *The Berlin Crisis, 1958–1962* (Alexandria, Chadwyck-Healey/ National Security Archive, 1994), is massive. Laurence Chang and Peter Kornbluh, eds., *The Cuban Missile Crisis, 1962* (New York, The New Press, 1992) and Mary McAuliffe, ed., *CIA Documents on the Cuban Missile Crisis 1962* (CIA, Washington, 1992) cover what their titles suggest. The correspondence between John F. Kennedy and Nikita Khrushchev at the time of the crisis is published in *Problems of Communism*, XLI (1992). A series of oral history conferences have complemented the documentary record: see James Blight, Bruce Allyn and David Welch, *Cuba on the Brink: Castro, the Missile Crisis and the Soviet Collapse* (New York, Pantheon Books, 1993). The three volumes of Khrushchev's memoirs, *Khrushchev Remembers*, ed. Strobe Talbott (London, Sphere Books, 1971), *Khrushchev Remembers: The Last Testament*, ed. Strobe Talbott (London, Andre Deutsch, 1974) and *Khrushchev Remembers: The Glasnost Tapes*, ed. Jerrold Schechter (Boston, Little Brown, 1990), retain their interest. They are based on tapes Khrushchev made in the late 1960s which were smuggled to the West. The former Soviet leader is self-serving and inaccurate on detail but spoke from a unique viewpoint. Michael Beschloss, *Kennedy v. Khrushchev: The Crisis Years, 1960–63* (London, Faber and Faber, 1991) provides a clear account of the Soviet–American confrontation. Vladislav

Zubok and Constantine Pleshakov, *Inside the Kremlin's Cold War: From Stalin to Khrushchev* (Cambridge, MA, Harvard University Press, 1996) is notable as the first major scholarly work published in English by Russian scholars. Gordon Chang, *Friends and Enemies: The United States, China and the Soviet Union, 1948–1972* (Stanford, Stanford University Press, 1990) stresses the importance of the trilateral relationship.

THE BALANCE OF POWER, 1963–1972

R. B. Smith, *An International History of the Vietnam War* (4 vols., London, Macmillan, 1983-) is an excellent account of the central conflict of the 1960s. Raymond Garthoff, *Détente and Confrontation: American–Soviet Relations from Nixon to Reagan* rev. edn (Washington, The Brookings Institution, 1994) is the key narrative account. Garthoff was a State Department official from the 1950s to the 1970s. He had access to good sources and an impressive clippings library. His dislike of many American political leaders makes him rather too sympathetic to their Soviet counterparts. Walter Isaacson, *Kissinger* (London, Faber and Faber, 1992) navigates through the murky waters of Kissinger's own memoirs. There is no satisfactory standard account of the Brezhnev era, but Robin Edmonds, *Soviet Foreign Policy: The Brezhnev Years* (Oxford, Oxford University Press, 1983) provides a good starting point.

A SYSTEM UNDER STRESS, 1973–1984

Garthoff remains the best narrative. It can be supplemented by Robert Litwak, *Détente and the Nixon Doctrine: American Foreign Policy and the the Pursuit of Stability, 1969–1976* (Cambridge, Cambridge University Press, 1984), Richard C. Thornton, *The Nixon–Kissinger Years: Reshaping America's Foreign Policy* (New York, Paragon House, 1989), Richard C. Thornton, *The Carter Years: Toward a New Global Order* (New York, Paragon House, 1991) and Gaddis Smith, *Morality, Reason and Power: American Diplomacy in the Carter Years* (New York, Hill and Wang, 1986). These four books rely on public rather than archival sources but each offers interesting interpretations. Thornton's view that there was a conflict in the US government between those who wanted to concentrate on the Cold War and those who believed the most dangerous challenge came from other capitalist countries is overstated but suggestive. Strobe Talbott, *Deadly Gambits: The Reagan Administration and the Stalemate in Nuclear Arms Control* (London, Pan, 1985) is a detailed case study based on interviews with key participants. Paul Dibb, *The Limits of Soviet Power: The Incomplete Superpower* (London, Macmillan/IISS, 1985) was perceptive for its time and retains much value. Richard Ned Lebow and Janice Gross Stein, *We All Lost the Cold War* (Princeton, Princeton University Press, 1994) takes a pessimistic view of the dangers of nuclear crisis and contains a good account of the 1973 Arab–Israeli War based on interviews with Soviet officials. Volumes XIV and XV of the *Cambridge History of China*, ed. Denis Twitchett and John Fairbank (15 vols., Cambridge, Cambridge University Press, 1978–91) are authoritative accounts. Timothy Garton Ash, *In Europe's Name: Germany and the Divided Continent* (London, Jonathan Cape, 1993) is a ground-breaking study of German politics.

THE END OF THE COLD WAR, 1985–1991

Raymond Garthoff, *The Great Transition: American-Soviet Relations and the End of the Cold War* (Washington, The Brookings Institution, 1994) is a continuation of his previous volume. Michael Beschloss and Strobe Talbott, *At the Highest Levels: The Inside Story of the End of the Cold War* (London, Little Brown, 1993) charts the relationship between the Bush administration and Mikhail Gorbachev. It is based on interviews with high level sources. David Pryce-Jones, *The War That Never Was: The Fall of the Soviet Empire, 1985–1991* (London, Weidenfeld and Nicolson, 1995) is essentially a collection of interviews with East European politicians. It is kaleidoscopic but fascinating. For such relatively recent events analysis in contemporary periodicals is especially important. I have drawn particularly heavily on those published in the *The Economist* and the research reports of those venerable Cold War institutions, Radio Liberty and Radio Free Europe.

Index